# CORE STATUT
# CRIMINAL LAW 2020–21

**Mark James**

The *Macmillan Core Statutes* series

| | |
|---|---|
| Core Documents on European and International Human Rights | Rhona Smith |
| Core Documents on International Law | Karen Hulme |
| Core EU Legislation | Paul Drury |
| Core Statutes on Commercial & Consumer Law | Graham Stephenson |
| Core Statutes on Company Law | Cowan Ervine |
| Core Statutes on Conflict of Laws | Emmanuel Maganaris |
| Core Statutes on Contract, Tort & Restitution | Graham Stephenson |
| Core Statutes on Criminal Justice & Sentencing | Martin Wasik |
| Core Statutes on Criminal Law | Mark James |
| Core Statutes on Employment Law | Rachel Horton |
| Core Statutes on Evidence | Jonathan McGahan |
| Core Statutes on Family Law | Frances Burton |
| Core Statutes on Intellectual Property | Margaret Dowie-Whybrow |
| Core Statutes on Property Law | Peter Luther & Alan Moran |
| Core Statutes on Public Law & Civil Liberties | Rhona Smith, Eimear Spain & Richard Glancey |

# Macmillan Core Statutes

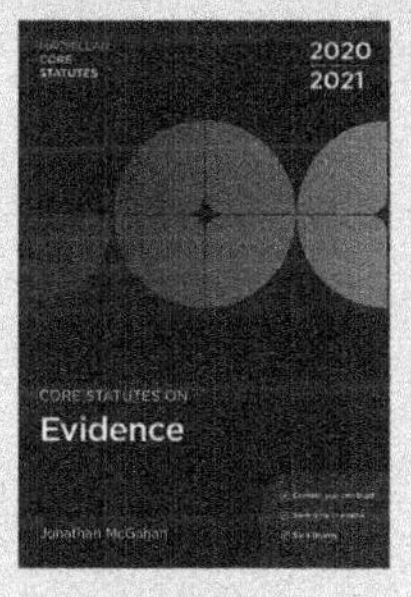

The Macmillan Core Statutes series has been developed to meet the needs of today's law students. Compiled by experienced lecturers, each title contains the essential materials needed at LLB level and, where applicable, on GDL/CPE courses. They are specifically designed to be easy to use under exam conditions and in the lecture hall.

www.macmillanihe.com/corestatutes

This edition published 2020 by
RED GLOBE PRESS

Red Globe Press in the UK is an imprint of Macmillan Education Limited, registered in England, company number 01755588, of 4 Crinan Street, London, N1 9XW.

Red Globe Press® is a registered trademark in the United States, the United Kingdom, Europe and other countries.

ISBN 978-1-352-01044-2

This book is printed on paper suitable for recycling and made from fully managed and sustained forest sources. Logging, pulping and manufacturing processes are expected to conform to the environmental regulations of the country of origin.

A catalogue record for this book is available from the British Library.

A catalog record for this book is available from the Library of Congress.

# CONTENTS

# ALPHABETICAL LIST OF CONTENTS

# PREFACE

Dear Reader,

Thank you for buying the latest version of *Core Statutes on Criminal Law*. For over 20 years, we have developed what we think is a comprehensive study and revision aid that brings together all of the statutes that you are likely to need to refer to in a criminal law unit or module. Each year, the contents are reviewed comprehensively to ensure that the wording is accurate and up to date as well as including new offences that have been created to respond to social, political and technological developments in our world.

The statutes are ordered chronologically, but with two alternative contents lists: one chronological, one alphabetical. This should enable you to navigate your way around the book quickly and easily, especially when in the exam room. This year, amendments to a number of statutes have been made, in particular by the Assaults on Emergency Workers Act 2018, the Offensive Weapons Act 2019 and the Counter-Terrorism and Border Security Act 2019.

I hope that you find this approach a useful aid and wish you the best of luck with your studies.

*Mark James*

# ACCESSORIES AND ABETTORS ACT 1861

## 8. Abettors

Whosoever shall aid, abet, counsel, or procure the commission of any indictable offence, whether the same be an offence at common law or by virtue of any Act passed or to be passed, shall be liable to be tried, indicted, and punished as a principal offender.

# OFFENCES AGAINST THE PERSON ACT 1861

## 4. Conspiring or soliciting to commit murder

Whosoever shall solicit, encourage, persuade, or endeavour to persuade, or shall propose to any person, to murder any other person, whether he be a subject of Her Majesty or not, and whether he be within the Queen's dominions or not, shall be guilty of an offence, and being convicted thereof shall be liable to imprisonment for life.

## 9. Murder or manslaughter abroad

Where any murder or manslaughter shall be committed on land out of the United Kingdom, whether within the Queen's dominions or without, and whether the person killed were a subject of Her Majesty or not, every offence committed by any subject of Her Majesty in respect of any such case, whether the same shall amount to the offence of murder or of manslaughter, ... may be dealt with, inquired of, tried, determined, and punished ... in England or Ireland ...

## 10. Provision for the trial of murder and manslaughter where the death or cause of death only happens in England or Ireland

Where any person being criminally stricken, poisoned, or otherwise hurt upon the sea, or at any place out of England or Ireland, shall die of such stroke, poisoning, or hurt in England or Ireland, or, being criminally stricken, poisoned or otherwise hurt in any place in England or Ireland, shall die of such stroke, poisoning, or hurt upon the sea, or at any place out of England or Ireland, every offence committed in respect of any such case, whether the same shall amount to the offence of murder or of manslaughter, ... may be dealt with, inquired of, tried, determined, and punished ... in England or Ireland ...

## 16. Threats to kill

A person who without lawful excuse makes to another a threat, intending that that other would fear it would be carried out, to kill that other or a third person, shall be guilty of an offence and liable on conviction on indictment to imprisonment for a term not exceeding ten years.

## 17. Impeding a person endeavouring to save himself or another from shipwreck

Whosoever shall unlawfully and maliciously prevent or impede any person, being on board of or having quitted any ship or vessel which shall be in distress, or wrecked, stranded, or cast on shore, in his endeavour to save his life, or shall unlawfully and maliciously prevent or impede any person in his endeavour to save the life of any such person as in this section first aforesaid, shall be guilty of an offence, and being convicted thereof shall be liable ... to imprisonment for life.

## 18. Wounding, or causing grievous bodily harm with intent to do grievous bodily harm, or to resist apprehension

Whosoever shall unlawfully and maliciously by any means whatsoever wound or cause any grievous bodily harm to any person ... with intent ... to do some ... grievous bodily harm to any person, or with intent to resist or prevent the lawful apprehension or detainer of any person, shall be guilty of an offence, and being convicted thereof shall be liable ... to imprisonment for life ...

## 20. Inflicting bodily injury with or without a weapon

Whosoever shall unlawfully and maliciously wound or inflict any grievous bodily harm upon any other person, either with or without any weapon or instrument, shall be guilty of an offence, and being convicted thereof shall be liable … to imprisonment for a term not exceeding seven years.

## 21. Attempting to choke, etc., in order to commit or assist in the committing of any indictable offence

Whosoever shall, by any means whatsoever, attempt to choke, suffocate, or strangle any other person, or shall by any means calculated to choke, suffocate, or strangle, attempt to render any other person insensible, unconscious, or incapable of resistance, with intent in any of such cases thereby to enable himself or any other person to commit, or with intent in any of such cases thereby to assist any other person in committing any indictable offence, shall be guilty of an offence, and being convicted thereof shall be liable … to imprisonment for life …

## 22. Using chloroform, etc., to commit or assist in the committing of any indictable offence

Whosoever shall unlawfully apply or administer to or cause to be taken by, or attempt to apply or administer to or attempt to cause to be administered to or taken by, any person, any chloroform, laudanum, or other stupefying or overpowering drug, matter, or thing, with intent in any of such cases thereby to enable himself or any other person to commit, or with intent in any of such cases thereby to assist any other person in committing any indictable offence, shall be guilty of an offence, and being convicted thereof shall be liable … to imprisonment for life …

## 23. Maliciously administering poison, etc., so as to endanger life or inflict grievous bodily harm

Whosoever shall unlawfully and maliciously administer to or cause to be administered to or taken by any other person any poison or other destructive or noxious thing, so as thereby to endanger the life of such person, or so as thereby to inflict upon such person any grievous bodily harm, shall be guilty of an offence, and being convicted thereof shall be liable … to imprisonment for any term not exceeding ten years …

## 24. Maliciously administering poison, etc., with intent to injure, aggrieve, or annoy any other person

Whosoever shall unlawfully and maliciously administer to or cause to be administered to or taken by any other person any poison or other destructive or noxious thing, with intent to injure, aggrieve, or annoy such person, shall be guilty of an offence, and being … convicted thereof shall be liable to imprisonment for a term not exceeding five years.

## 26. Not providing apprentices or servants with food, etc., or doing bodily harm, whereby life is endangered, or health permanently injured

Whosoever, being legally liable, either as a master or mistress, to provide for any apprentice or servant necessary food, clothing, or lodging, shall wilfully and without lawful excuse refuse or neglect to provide the same, or shall unlawfully and maliciously do or cause to be done any bodily harm to any such apprentice or servant, so that the life of such apprentice or servant shall be endangered, or the health of such apprentice or servant shall be likely to be permanently injured, shall be guilty of an offence, and being convicted thereof shall be liable … to imprisonment for a term not exceeding five years.

## 27. Exposing child, whereby life is endangered, or health permanently injured

Whosoever shall unlawfully abandon or expose any child, being under the age of two years, whereby the life of such child shall be endangered, or the health of such child shall have been or shall be likely to be permanently injured, shall be guilty of an offence, and being convicted thereof shall be liable to imprisonment for a term not exceeding five years.

## 28. Causing bodily injury by gunpowder

Whosoever shall unlawfully and maliciously, by the explosion of gunpowder or other explosive substance, burn, maim, disfigure, disable, or do any grievous bodily harm to any person, shall be guilty of an offence, and being convicted thereof shall be liable, at the discretion of the court, to imprisonment for life.

## 29. Causing gunpowder to explode, or sending to any person an explosive substance, or throwing corrosive fluid on a person, with intent to grievous bodily harm

Whosoever shall unlawfully and maliciously cause any gunpowder or other explosive substance to explode, or send or deliver to or cause to be taken or received by any person any explosive substance or any other dangerous or noxious thing, or put or lay at any place, or cast or throw at or upon or otherwise apply to any person, any corrosive fluid or any destructive or explosive substance, with intent in any of the cases aforesaid to burn, maim, disfigure, or disable any person, or to do some grievous bodily harm to any person, shall, whether any bodily injury be effected or not, be guilty of an offence, and being convicted thereof shall be liable, at the discretion of the court, to imprisonment for life.

## 30. Placing gunpowder near a building etc., with intent to do bodily injury to any person

Whosoever shall unlawfully and maliciously place or throw in, into, upon, against, or near any building, ship, or vessel any gunpowder or other explosive substance, with intent to do any bodily injury to any person, shall, whether or not any explosion take place, and whether or not any bodily injury be effected, be guilty of an offence, and being convicted thereof shall be liable, at the discretion of the court, to imprisonment for any term not exceeding fourteen years.

## 31. Setting or allowing to remain spring guns, etc., with intent to inflict grievous bodily harm

Whosoever shall set or place, or cause to be set or placed, any spring gun, man trap, or other engine calculated to destroy human life or inflict grievous bodily harm, with the intent that the same or whereby the same may destroy or inflict grievous bodily harm upon a trespasser or other person coming in contact therewith, shall be guilty of an offence, and being convicted thereof shall be liable … to imprisonment for a term not exceeding five years; and whosoever shall knowingly and wilfully permit any such spring gun, man trap, or other engine which may have been set or placed in any place then being in or afterwards coming into his possession or occupation by some other person to continue so set or placed, shall be deemed to have set and placed such gun, trap, or engine with such intent as aforesaid: Provided, that nothing in this section contained shall extend to make it illegal to set or place any gun or trap such as may have been or may be usually set or placed with the intent of destroying vermin: Provided also, that nothing in this section shall be deemed to make it unlawful to set or place, or cause to be set or placed, or to be continued set or placed, from sunset to sunrise, any spring gun, man trap, or other engine which shall be set or placed, or caused or continued to be set or placed, in a dwelling-house, for the protection thereof.

## 32. Placing wood, etc., on railway, taking up rails, showing or hiding signals, etc., with intent to endanger passengers

Whosoever shall unlawfully and maliciously put or throw upon or across any railway any wood, stone, or other matter or thing, or shall unlawfully and maliciously take up, remove, or displace any rail, sleeper, or other matter or thing belonging to any railway, or shall unlawfully and maliciously turn, move or divert any points or other machinery belonging to any railway, or shall unlawfully and maliciously make or show, hide or remove, any signal or light upon or near to any railway, or shall unlawfully and maliciously do or cause to be done any other matter or thing, with intent, in any of the cases aforesaid, to endanger the safety of any person travelling or being upon such railway, shall be guilty of an offence, and being convicted thereof shall be liable, at the discretion of the court, to imprisonment for life.

## 33. Casting stone, etc., upon a railway carriage, with intent to endanger the safety of any person therein, or in any part of the same train

Whosoever shall unlawfully and maliciously throw, or cause to fall or strike, at, against, into, or upon any engine, tender, carriage, or truck used upon any railway, any wood, stone, or other matter or thing, with intent to injure or endanger the safety of any person being in or upon such engine, tender, carriage, or truck, or in or upon any other any other engine, tender, carriage, or truck of any train of which such first-mentioned engine, tender, carriage, or truck shall form part, shall be guilty of an offence, and being convicted thereof shall be liable … to imprisonment for life.

### 34. Doing or omitting anything so as to endanger passengers by railway

Whosoever, by any unlawful act, or by any wilful omission or neglect, shall endanger or cause to be endangered the safety of any person conveyed or being in or upon a railway, or shall aid or assist therein, shall be guilty of an offence, and being convicted thereof shall be liable, at the discretion of the court, to be imprisoned for any term not exceeding two years.

### 35. Drivers of carriages injuring persons by furious driving

Whosoever, having the charge of any carriage or vehicle, shall by wanton or furious driving or racing, or other wilful misconduct, or by wilful neglect, do or cause to be done any bodily harm to any person whatsoever, shall be guilty of an offence, and being convicted thereof shall be liable, at the discretion of the court, to be imprisoned for any term not exceeding two years.

### 36. Obstructing or assaulting a clergyman or other minister in the discharge of his duties in place of worship or burial place, or on his way thither

Whosoever shall, by threats or force, obstruct or prevent or endeavour to obstruct or prevent, any clergyman or other minister in or from celebrating divine service or otherwise officiating in any church, chapel, meeting house, or other place of divine worship, or in or from the performance of his duty in the lawful burial of the dead in any churchyard or other burial place, or shall strike or offer any violence to, or shall, upon any civil process, or under the pretence of executing any civil process, arrest any clergyman or other minister who is engaged in, or to the knowledge of the offender is about to engage in, any of the rites or duties in this section aforesaid, or who to the knowledge of the offender shall be going to perform the same or returning from the performance thereof, shall be guilty of an offence, and being convicted thereof shall be liable to a term of imprisonment not exceeding two years.

### 37. Assaulting a magistrate, etc., on account of his preserving wreck

Whosoever shall assault and strike or wound any magistrate, officer, or other person whatsoever lawfully authorized, in or on account of the exercise of his duty in or concerning the preservation of any vessel in distress, or of any vessel, goods, or effects wrecked, stranded, or cast on shore, or lying under water, shall be guilty of an offence, and being convicted thereof shall be liable … to be a term of imprisonment not exceeding seven years …

### 38. Assault with intent to resist arrest

Whosoever … shall assault any person with intent to resist or prevent the lawful apprehension or detainer of himself or of any other person for any offence, shall be guilty of an offence, and being convicted thereof shall be liable, at the discretion of the court, to be imprisoned for any term not exceeding two years.

### 47. Assault occasioning bodily harm

Whosoever shall be convicted upon an indictment of any assault occasioning actual bodily harm shall be liable … to be imprisoned for any term not exceeding five years.

### 57. Bigamy

Whosoever, being married, shall marry any other person during the life of the former husband or wife, whether the second marriage shall have taken place in England or Ireland or elsewhere, shall be guilty of an offence, and being convicted thereof shall be liable to a term of imprisonment not exceeding seven years …:

Provided, that nothing in this section contained shall extend to any second marriage contracted elsewhere than in England and Ireland by any other than a subject of Her Majesty, or to any person marrying a second time whose husband or wife shall have been continually absent from such person for the space of seven years then last past, and shall not have been known by such person to be living within that time, or shall extend to any person who, at the time of such second marriage, shall have been divorced from the bond of the first marriage, or to any person whose former marriage shall have been declared void by the sentence of any court of competent jurisdiction.

### 58. Administering drugs or using instruments to procure abortion

Every woman, being with child, who, with intent to procure her own miscarriage, shall unlawfully administer to herself any poison or other noxious thing, or shall unlawfully use any instrument or other means whatsoever with the like intent, and whosoever, with intent to procure the miscarriage of any woman, whether she be or be not with child, shall unlawfully administer to her or cause to be taken by her any poison or other noxious thing, or shall unlawfully use any instrument or other means whatsoever with the like intent, shall be guilty of an offence, and being convicted thereof shall be liable ... to imprisonment for life ...

### 59. Procuring drugs, etc., to cause abortion

Whosoever shall unlawfully supply or procure any poison or other noxious thing, or any instrument or thing whatsoever, knowing that the same is intended to be unlawfully used or employed with intent to procure the miscarriage of any woman, whether she be or be not with child, shall be guilty of an offence, and being convicted thereof shall be liable ... to a term of imprisonment not exceeding five years ...

### 60. Concealing the birth of a child

If any woman shall be delivered of a child, every person who shall, by any secret disposition of the dead body of the said child, whether such child died before, at, or after its birth, endeavour to conceal the birth thereof, shall be guilty of an offence, and being convicted thereof shall be liable, at the discretion of the court, to be imprisoned for any term not exceeding two years.

### 64. Making or having anything with intent to commit an offence in this Act

Whosoever shall knowingly have in his possession, or make or manufacture, any gunpowder, explosive substance, or any dangerous or noxious thing, or any machine, engine, instrument, or thing, with intent by means thereof to commit, or for the purpose of enabling any other person to commit, any of the offences in this Act mentioned shall be guilty of an offence, and being convicted thereof shall be liable, at the discretion of the court, to be imprisoned for any term not exceeding two years ...

## EXPLOSIVE SUBSTANCES ACT 1883

### 2. Causing explosion likely to endanger life or property

A person who in the United Kingdom or (being a citizen of the United Kingdom and Colonies) in the Republic of Ireland unlawfully and maliciously causes by any explosive substance an explosion of a nature likely to endanger life or to cause serious injury to person or property shall, whether any injury to person or property has been actually caused or not, be guilty of an offence and on conviction on indictment shall be liable to imprisonment for life.

### 3. Attempt to cause explosion, or making or keeping explosive with intent to endanger life or property

A person who in the United Kingdom or a dependency or (being a citizen of the United Kingdom and Colonies) elsewhere unlawfully and maliciously—

(a) does any act with intent to cause, or conspires to cause by an explosive substance, an explosion of a nature likely to endanger life or to cause serious injury to property, whether in the United Kingdom or elsewhere, or

(b) makes or has in his possession or under his control an explosive substance with intent by means thereof to endanger life, or cause serious injury to property whether in the United Kingdom or elsewhere, or to enable any other person so to do,

shall, whether any explosion does or not take place, and whether any injury to person or property has been actually caused or not, be guilty of an offence and on conviction on indictment shall be liable to imprisonment for life, and the explosive substance shall be forfeited.

### 4. Punishment for making or possession of explosive under suspicious circumstances

(1) Any person who makes or knowingly has in his possession or under his control any explosive substance, under such circumstances as to give rise to a reasonable suspicion that he is not making it or does not have it in his possession or under his

control for a lawful object, shall, unless he can show that he made it or had it in his possession or under his control for a lawful object, be guilty of an offence.

### 5. Punishment of accessories

Any person who within or (being a subject of Her Majesty) without Her Majesty's dominions by the supply of or solicitation for money, the providing of premises, the supply of materials, or in any manner whatsoever, procures, counsels, aids, abets, or is accessory to, the commission of any crime under this Act, shall be guilty of an offence, and shall be liable to be tried and punished for that crime, as if he had been guilty as a principal.

### 9. Definitions

(1) In this Act, unless the context otherwise requires—

The expression 'explosive substance' shall be deemed to include any materials for making any explosive substance; also any apparatus, machine, implement, or materials used, or intended to be used, or adapted for causing, or aiding in causing, any explosion in or with any explosive substance; also any part of any such apparatus, machine, or implement.

## TRIAL OF LUNATICS ACT 1883

### 2. Special verdict where accused found guilty, but insane at date of act or omission charged, and orders thereupon

(1) Where in any indictment or information any act or omission is charged against any person as an offence, and it is given in evidence on the trial of such person for that offence that he was insane, so as not to be responsible, according to law, for his actions at the time when the act was done or omission made, then, if it appears to the jury before whom such person is tried that he did the act or made the omission charged, but was insane as aforesaid at the time when he did or made the same, the jury shall return a special verdict that the accused is not guilty by reason of insanity.

## OFFICIAL SECRETS ACT 1911

### 1. Penalties for spying

(1) If any person for any purpose prejudicial to the safety or interests of the State—

(a) approaches, inspects, passes over or is in the neighbourhood of, or enters any prohibited place within the meaning of this Act; or

(b) makes any sketch, plan, model, or note which is calculated to be or might be or is intended to be directly or indirectly useful to an enemy; or

(c) obtains, collects, records, or publishes, or communicates to any other person any secret official code word or pass word, or any sketch, plan, model, article, or note, or other document or information which is directly or indirectly useful to an enemy;

he shall be guilty of an offence ...

(2) On a prosecution under this section, it shall not be necessary to show that the accused person was guilty of any particular act tending to show a purpose prejudicial to the safety or interests of the State, and, notwithstanding that no such act is proved against him, he may be convicted if, from the circumstances of the case, or his conduct, or his known character as proved, it appears that his purpose was a purpose prejudicial to the safety or interests of the State; and if any sketch, plan, model, article, note, document, or information relating to or used in any prohibited place within the meaning of this Act, or anything in such a place or any secret official code word or pass word, is made, obtained, collected, recorded, published, or communicated by any person other than a person acting under lawful authority, it shall be deemed to have been made, obtained, collected, recorded, published or communicated for a purpose prejudicial to the safety or interests of the State unless the contrary is proved.

### 3. Definition of prohibited place

For the purposes of this Act, the expression 'prohibited place' means—

(a) any work of defence, arsenal, naval or air force establishment or station, factory, dockyard, mine, minefield, camp, ship, or aircraft belonging to or occupied by or on behalf of His Majesty, or any telegraph, telephone, wireless or signal station, or office so belonging or occupied, and any place belonging to or occupied by or on behalf of His Majesty and used for the purpose of building, repairing, making or storing any munitions of war, or any sketches, plans, models or documents relating thereto, or for the purpose of getting any metals, oil or minerals of use in time of war;
(b) any place not belonging to His Majesty where any munitions of war, or any sketches, models, plans or documents relating thereto, are being made, repaired, gotten or stored under contract with, or with any person on behalf of, His Majesty, or otherwise on behalf of His Majesty; and
(c) any place belonging to or used for the purposes of His Majesty which is for the time being declared by order of a Secretary of State to be a prohibited place for the purposes of this section on the ground that information with respect thereto, or damage thereto, would be useful to an enemy; and
(d) any railway, road, way, or channel, or other means of communication by land or water (including any works or structures being part thereof or connected therewith), or any place used for gas, water, or electricity works or other works for purposes of a public character, or any place where any munitions of war, or any sketches, models, plans, or documents relating thereto, are being made, repaired, or stored otherwise than on behalf of His Majesty, which is for the time being declared by order of a Secretary of State to be a prohibited place for the purposes of this section, on the ground that information with respect thereto, or the destruction or obstruction thereof, or interference therewith, would be useful to an enemy.

### 7. Penalty for harbouring spies

If any person knowingly harbours any person whom he knows, or has reasonable grounds for supposing, to be a person who is about to commit or who has committed an offence under this Act, or knowingly permits to meet or assemble in any premises in his occupation or under his control any such persons, or if any person having harboured any such person, or permitted to meet or assemble in any premises in his occupation or under his control any such person, wilfully omits or refuses to disclose to a superintendent of police any information which it is in his power to give in relation to any such person he shall be guilty of an offence …

## PERJURY ACT 1911

### 1. Perjury

(1) If any person lawfully sworn as a witness or as an interpreter in a judicial proceeding wilfully makes a statement material in that proceeding, which he knows to be false or does not believe to be true, he shall be guilty of perjury, and shall, on conviction thereof on indictment, be liable to imprisonment for a term not exceeding seven years … or to a fine or to both … imprisonment and a fine.
(2) The expression 'judicial proceeding' includes a proceeding before any court, tribunal, or person having by law power to hear, receive, and examine evidence on oath.
(3) Where a statement made for the purposes of a judicial proceeding is not made before the tribunal itself, but is made on oath before a person authorised by law to administer an oath to the person who makes the statement, and to record or authenticate the statement, it shall, for the purposes of this section, be treated as having been made in a judicial proceeding.
(4) A statement made by a person lawfully sworn in England for the purposes of a judicial proceeding—
    (a) in another part of Her Majesty's dominions; or
    (b) in a British tribunal lawfully constituted in any place by sea or land outside Her Majesty's dominions; or

(c) in a tribunal of any foreign state,

shall, for the purposes of this section, be treated as a statement made in a judicial proceeding in England.

(5) Where for the purposes of a judicial proceeding in England, a person is lawfully sworn under the authority of an Act of Parliament—

(a) in any other part of Her Majesty's dominions; or

(b) before a British tribunal or a British officer in a foreign country, or within the jurisdiction of the Admiralty of England;

a statement made by such person so sworn as aforesaid (unless the Act of Parliament under which it was made otherwise specifically provides) shall be treated for the purposes of this section as having been made in the judicial proceeding in England for the purposes whereof it was made.

(6) The question whether a statement on which perjury is assigned was material is a question of law to be determined by the court of trial.

### 1A. False unsworn statement under Evidence (Proceedings in other Jurisdictions) Act 1975

If any person in giving any testimony (either orally or in writing) otherwise than on oath, where required to do so by an order under section 2 of the Evidence (Proceedings in other Jurisdictions) Act 1975, makes a statement—

(a) which he knows to be false in a material particular, or

(b) which is false in a material particular and which he does not believe to be true, he shall be guilty of an offence and shall be liable on conviction on indictment to imprisonment for a term not exceeding two years or a fine or both.

### 7. Aiders, abettors, suborners, etc.

(1) Every person who aids, abets, counsels, procures, or suborns another person to commit an offence against this Act shall be liable to be proceeded against, indicted, tried and punished as if he were a principal offender.

(2) Every person who incites another person to commit an offence against this Act shall be guilty of an offence, and on conviction thereof on indictment, shall be liable to imprisonment, or to a fine, or to both such imprisonment and fine.

### 15. Interpretation, etc.

(1) For the purposes of this Act, the forms and ceremonies used in administering an oath are immaterial, if the court or person before whom the oath is taken has power to administer an oath for the purpose of verifying the statement in question, and if the oath has been administered in a form and with ceremonies which the person taking the oath has accepted without objection, or has declared to be binding on him.

(2) In this Act—

The expression 'oath' includes 'affirmation' and 'declaration', and the expression 'swear' includes 'affirm' and 'declare'; and

The expression 'statutory declaration' means a declaration made by virtue of the Statutory Declarations Act, 1835, or of any Act, Order in Council, rule or regulation applying or extending the provisions thereof.

## INFANT LIFE (PRESERVATION) ACT 1929

### 1. Punishment for child destruction

(1) Subject as hereinafter in this subsection provided, any person who, with intent to destroy the life of a child capable of being born alive, by any wilful act causes a child to die before it has an existence independent of its mother, shall be guilty of an offence, to wit, of child destruction, and shall be liable on conviction thereof ...to imprisonment for life:

Provided that no person shall be found guilty of an offence under this section unless it is proved that the act which caused the death of the child was not done in good faith for the purpose only of preserving the life of the mother.

(2) For the purposes of this Act, evidence that a woman had at any material time been pregnant for a period of twenty-eight weeks or more shall be a prima facie proof that she was at that time pregnant of a child capable of being born alive.

### 2. Prosecution of offences

(2) Where upon the trial of any person for the murder or manslaughter of any child, or for infanticide, or for an offence under section fifty-eight of the Offences against the Person Act, 1861 (which relates to administering drugs or using instruments to procure abortion), the jury are of opinion that the person charged is not guilty of murder, manslaughter or infanticide, or of an offence under the said section fifty-eight, as the case may be, but that he is shown by the evidence to be guilty of the offence of child destruction, the jury may find him guilty of that offence, and thereupon the person convicted shall be liable to be punished as if he had been convicted upon an indictment for child destruction.

(3) Where upon the trial of any person for the offence of child destruction the jury are of opinion that the person charged is not guilty of any offence, but that he is shown by the evidence to be guilty of an offence under the said section fifty-eight of the Offences against the Person Act, 1861, the jury may find him guilty of that offence, and thereupon the person convicted shall be liable to be punished as if he had been convicted upon an indictment under that section.

## CHILDREN AND YOUNG PERSONS ACT 1933

### 1. Cruelty to persons under sixteen

(1) If any person who has attained the age of sixteen years and has responsibility for any child or young person under that age, wilfully assaults, ill-treats whether physically or otherwise, neglects, abandons, or exposes him, or causes or procures him to be assaulted, ill-treated whether physically or otherwise, neglected, abandoned, or exposed, in a manner likely to cause him unnecessary suffering or injury to health (whether the suffering or injury is of a physical or a psychological nature), that person shall be guilty of an offence ...

(2) For the purposes of this section—

(a) a parent or other person legally liable to maintain a child or young person, or the legal guardian of a child or young person, shall be deemed to have neglected him in a manner likely to cause injury to his health if he has failed to provide adequate food, clothing, medical aid or lodging for him, or if, having been unable otherwise to provide such food, clothing, medical aid or lodging, he has failed to take steps to procure it to be provided under the enactments applicable in that behalf;

(b) where it is proved that the death of an infant under three years of age was caused by suffocation (not being suffocation caused by disease or the presence of any foreign body in the throat or air passages of the infant) while the infant was in bed with some other person who has attained the age of sixteen years, that other person shall, if he was, when he went to bed or at any later time before the suffocation, under the influence of drink or a prohibited drug, be deemed to have neglected the infant in a manner likely to cause injury to its health.

(2A) The reference in subsection (2)(b) to the infant being 'in bed' with another ('the adult') includes a reference to the infant lying next to the adult in or on any kind of furniture or surface being used by the adult for the purpose of sleeping (and the reference to the time when the adult 'went to bed' is to be read accordingly).

(2B) A drug is a prohibited drug for the purposes of subsection (2)(b) in relation to a person if the person's possession of the drug immediately before taking it constituted an offence under section 5(2) of the Misuse of Drugs Act 1971.

(3) A person may be convicted of an offence under this section—

(a) notwithstanding that actual suffering or injury to health, or the likelihood of actual suffering or injury to health, was obviated by the action of another person;

(b) notwithstanding the death of the child or young person in question.

## 3. Allowing persons under sixteen to be in brothels

(1) If any person having responsibility for a child or young person who has attained the age of four years and is under the age of sixteen years, allows that child or young person to reside in or to frequent a brothel, he shall be liable on summary conviction, to a fine not exceeding level 2 on the standard scale, or alternatively ... or in addition thereto, to imprisonment for any term not exceeding six months.

## 5. Giving intoxicating liquor to children under five

If any person gives, or causes to be given, to any child under the age of five years any alcohol (within the meaning given by section 191 of the Licensing Act 2003, but disregarding subsection 1 (f)–(i) of that section), except upon the order of a duly qualified medical practitioner, or in case of sickness, apprehended sickness, or other urgent cause, he shall, on summary conviction, be liable to a fine not exceeding level 1 on the standard scale.

## 7. Sale of tobacco, etc., to persons under eighteen

(1) Any person who sells to a person under the age of eighteen years any tobacco or cigarette papers, whether for his own use or not, shall be liable on summary conviction to a fine not exceeding level 4 on the standard scale:

...

(1A) It shall be a defence for a person charged with an offence under subsection (1) above to prove that he took all reasonable precautions and exercised all due diligence to avoid the commission of the offence.

(5) For the purposes of this section the expression 'tobacco' includes cigarettes, any product containing tobacco and intended for oral or nasal use and smoking mixtures intended as a substitute for tobacco, and the expression 'cigarettes' includes cut tobacco rolled up in papers, tobacco leaf, or other material in such form as to be capable of immediate use for smoking.

## 11. Exposing children under twelve to risk of burning

If any person who has attained the age of sixteen years, having responsibility for any child under the age of twelve years, allows the child to be in any room containing an open fire grate or any heating appliance liable to cause injury to a person by contact therewith not sufficiently protected to guard against the risk of his being burnt or scalded without taking reasonable precautions against that risk, and by reason thereof the child is killed or suffers serious injury, he shall on summary conviction be liable to a fine not exceeding level 1 on the standard scale: Provided that neither this section, nor any proceedings taken thereunder shall affect any liability of any such person to be proceeded against by indictment for any indictable offence.

## 17. Interpretation of Part I

(1) For the purposes of this Part of this Act, the following shall be presumed to have responsibility for a child or young person—
- (a) Any person who—
  - (i) has parental responsibility for him (within the meaning of the Children Act 1989); or
  - (ii) is otherwise legally liable to maintain him; and
- (b) any person who has care of him.

(2) A person who is presumed to be responsible for a child or young person by virtue of subsection (1)(a) shall not be taken to have ceased to be responsible for him by reason only that he does not have care of him.

## 18. Restrictions on employment of children

(1) Subject to the provisions of this section and of any byelaws regulations made thereunder no child shall be employed—
- (a) so long as he is under the age of fourteen years; or
- (aa) to do any work other than light work; or
- (b) before the close of school hours on any day on which he is required to attend school; or
- (c) before seven o'clock in the morning or after seven o'clock in the evening on any day; or

(d) for more than two hours on any day on which he is required to attend school; or
(da) for more than twelve hours in any week in which he is required to attend school; or
(e) for more than two hours on any Sunday; or
(f) ...
(g) for more than eight hours or, if he is under the age of fifteen years, for more than five hours in any day—
   (i) on which he is not required to attend school, and
   (ii) which is not a Sunday; or
(h) for more than thirty-five hours or, if he is under the age of fifteen years, for more than twenty-five hours in any week in which he is not required to attend school; or
(i) for more than four hours in any day without a rest break of one hour; or
(j) at any time in a year unless at that time he has had, or could still have, during a period in the year in which he is not required to attend school, at least two consecutive weeks without employment.

### 23. Prohibition against persons under sixteen taking part in performances endangering life or limb

No person under the age of sixteen years, and no child aged sixteen years, shall take part in any performance to which section 37(2) of the Children and Young Persons Act 1963 applies and in which his life or limbs are endangered and every person who causes or procures such a person or child, or being his parent or guardian allows him, to take part in such a performance, shall be liable on summary conviction to a fine not exceeding level 3 on the standard scale:

Provided that no proceedings shall be taken under this subsection except by or with the authority of a chief officer of police.

### 24. Restrictions on training for performances of a dangerous nature

(1) No child under the age of twelve years shall be trained to take part in performances of a dangerous nature, and no child who has attained that age shall be trained to take part in such performances except under and in accordance with the terms of a licence granted and in force under this section; and every person who causes or procures a person, or being his parent or guardian allows him, to be trained to take part in performances of a dangerous nature in contravention of this section, shall be liable on summary conviction to a fine not exceeding level 3 on the standard scale.
(2) A local authority may grant a licence for a child who has attained the age of twelve years but is under the age of sixteen years to be trained to take part in performances of a dangerous nature.

### 50. Age of criminal responsibility

It shall be conclusively presumed that no child under the age of ten years can be guilty of any offence.

## PUBLIC ORDER ACT 1936

### 1. Prohibition of uniforms in connection with political objects

(1) Subject as hereinafter provided, any person who in any public place or at any public meeting wears uniform signifying his association with any political organisation or with the promotion of any political object shall be guilty of an offence:

Provided that, if the chief officer of police is satisfied that the wearing of any such uniform as aforesaid on any ceremonial, anniversary, or other special occasion will not be likely to involve risk of public disorder, he may, with the consent of a Secretary of State, by order permit the wearing of such uniform on that occasion either absolutely or subject to such conditions as may be specified in the order.
(2) Where any person is charged before any court with an offence under this section, no further proceedings in respect thereof shall be taken against him without the consent of the Attorney-General except such as are authorised by section 6 of the Prosecution

of Offences Act 1979 so, however, that if that person is remanded in custody he shall, after the expiration of a period of eight days from the date on which he was so remanded, be entitled to be released on bail without sureties unless within that period the Attorney- General has consented to such further proceedings as aforesaid.

## 2. Prohibition of quasi-military organisations

(1) If the members or adherents of any association of persons, whether incorporated or not, are—

(a) organised or trained or equipped for the purpose of enabling them to be employed in usurping the functions of the police or of the armed forces of the Crown; or

(b) organised and trained or organised and equipped either for the purpose of enabling them to be employed for the use or display of physical force in promoting any political object, or in such manner as to arouse reasonable apprehension that they are organised and either trained or equipped for that purpose;

then any person who takes part in the control or management of the association, or in so organising or training as aforesaid any members or adherents thereof, shall be guilty of an offence under this section:

Provided that in any proceedings against a person charged with the offence of taking part in the control or management of such an association as aforesaid it shall be a defence to that charge to prove the he neither consented to nor connived at the organisation, training, or equipment of members or adherents of the association in contravention of the provisions of this section.

(2) No prosecution shall be instituted under this section without the consent of the Attorney- General.

(3) If upon application being made by the Attorney-General it appears to the High Court that any association is an association of which members or adherents are organised, trained, or equipped in contravention of the provisions of this section, the Court may make such order as appears necessary to prevent any disposition without the leave of the Court of property held by or for the association and in accordance with rules of court may direct an inquiry and report to be made as to any such property as aforesaid and as to the affairs of the association and make such further orders as appear to the Court to be just and equitable for the application of such property in or towards the discharge of the liabilities of the association lawfully incurred before the date of the application or since that date with the approval of the Court, in or towards the repayment of moneys to persons who became subscribers or contributors to the association in good faith and without knowledge of any such contravention as aforesaid, and in or towards any costs incurred in connection with any such inquiry and report as aforesaid or in winding-up or dissolving the association, and may order that any property which is not directed by the Court to be so applied as aforesaid shall be forfeited to the Crown.

(4) In any criminal or civil proceedings under this section proof of things done or of words written, spoken or published (whether or not in the presence of any party to the proceedings) by any person taking part in the control or management of an association or in organising, training or equipping members or adherents of an association shall be admissible as evidence of the purposes for which, or the manner in which, members or adherents of the association (whether those persons or others) were organised, or trained, or equipped.

(5) If a judge of the High Court is satisfied by information on oath that there is reasonable ground for suspecting that an offence under this section has been committed, and that evidence of the commission thereof is to be found at any premises or place specified in the information, he may, on an application made by an officer of police of a rank not lower than that of inspector, grant a search warrant authorising any such officer as aforesaid named in the warrant and any other officers of police to enter the premises or place at any time within three months from the date of the warrant, if necessary by force, and to search the premises or place and every person found therein, and to seize anything found on the premises or place or on any such person which the officer has reasonable ground for suspecting to be evidence of the commission of such an offence as aforesaid:

Provided that no woman shall, in pursuance of a warrant issued under this subsection, be searched except by a woman.

(6) Nothing in this section shall be construed as prohibiting the employment of a reasonable number or persons as stewards to assist in the preservation of order at any public meeting held upon private premises, or the making of arrangements for that purpose or the instruction of the persons to be so employed in their lawful duties as such stewards, or their being furnished with badges or other distinguishing signs.

## INFANTICIDE ACT 1938

### 1. Offence of infanticide

(1) Where a woman by any wilful act or omission causes the death of her child being a child under the age of twelve months, but at the time of the act or omission the balance of her mind was disturbed by reason of her not having fully recovered from the effect of giving birth to the child or by reason of the effect of lactation consequent upon the birth of the child, then, if the circumstances were such that but for this Act the offence would have amounted to murder or manslaughter, she shall be guilty of an offence, to wit of infanticide, and may for such offence be dealt with and punished as if she had been guilty of the offence of manslaughter of the child.

(2) Where upon the trial of a woman for the murder of her child, being a child under the age of twelve months, the jury are of opinion that she by any wilful act or omission caused its death, but that at the time of the act or omission the balance of her mind was disturbed by reason of her not having fully recovered from the effect of giving birth to the child or by reason of the effect of lactation consequent upon the birth of the child, then the jury may, if the circumstances were such that but for the provisions of this Act they might have returned a verdict of murder or manslaughter, return in lieu thereof a verdict of infanticide.

(3) Nothing in this Act shall affect the power of the jury upon an indictment for the murder of a child to return a verdict of manslaughter, or a verdict of guilty but insane …

## PREVENTION OF CRIME ACT 1953

### 1. Prohibition of the carrying of offensive weapons without lawful authority or reasonable excuse

(1) Any person who without lawful authority or reasonable excuse, the proof whereof shall lie on him, has with him in any public place any offensive weapon shall be guilty of an offence, and shall be liable—
  - (a) on summary conviction, to imprisonment for a term not exceeding six months or a fine not exceeding the prescribed sum or both;
  - (b) on conviction on indictment, to imprisonment for a term not exceeding four years or a fine or both.

(2) Where any person is convicted of an offence under subsection (1) of this section the court may make an order for the forfeiture or disposal of any weapon in respect of which the offence was committed.

(4) In this section 'public place' includes any highway and any other premises or place to which at the material time the public have or are permitted to have access, whether on payment or otherwise; and 'offensive weapon' means any article made or adapted for use for causing injury to the person, or intended by the person having it with him for such use by him or by some other person.

### 1A. Offence of threatening with offensive weapon in public

(1) A person is guilty of an offence if that person—
  - (a) has an offensive weapon with him or her in a public place,
  - (b) unlawfully and intentionally threatens another person with the weapon, and
  - (c) does so in such a way that there is an immediate risk of serious physical harm to that other person.

(2) For the purposes of this section physical harm is serious if it amounts to grievous bodily harm for the purposes of the Offences against the Person Act 1861.

(3) In this section 'public place' and 'offensive weapon' have the same meaning as in section 1. (10) If on a person's trial for an offence under this section (whether on indictment or not) the person is found not guilty of that offence but it is proved that the person committed an offence under section 1, the person may be convicted of the offence under that section.

# SEXUAL OFFENCES ACT 1956

## 33. Keeping a brothel

It is an offence for a person to keep a brothel, or to manage, or act or assist in the management of, a brothel.

## 33A. Keeping a brothel used for prostitution

(1) It is an offence for a person to keep, or to manage, or act or assist in the management of, a brothel to which people resort for practices involving prostitution (whether or not also for other practices).

(2) In this section 'prostitution' has the meaning given by section 51(2) of the Sexual Offences Act 2003.

## 34. Landlord letting premises for use as brothel

It is an offence for the lessor or landlord of any premises or his agent to let the whole or part of the premises with the knowledge that it is to be used, in whole or in part, as a brothel, or, where the whole or part of the premises is used as a brothel, to be wilfully a party to that use continuing.

## 35. Tenant permitting premises to be used as a brothel

(1) It is an offence for the tenant or occupier, or person in charge, of any premises knowingly to permit the whole or part of the premises to be used as a brothel.

(2) Where the tenant or occupier of any premises is convicted of knowingly permitting the whole or part of the premises to be used as a brothel, the First Schedule to this Act shall apply to enlarge the rights of the lessor or landlord with respect to the assignment or determination of the lease or other contract under which the premises are held by the person convicted.

(4) Where the tenant or occupier of any premises is so convicted, and either—

(a) the lessor or landlord, after having the conviction brought to his notice, fails or failed to exercise his statutory rights in relation to the lease or contract under which the premises are or were held by the person convicted; or

(b) the lessor or landlord, after exercising his statutory rights so as to determine that lease or contract, grants or granted a new lease or enters or entered into a new contract of tenancy of the premises to, with or for the benefit of the same person, without having all reasonable provisions to prevent the recurrence of the offence inserted in the new lease or contract;

then, if subsequently an offence under this section is committed in respect of the premises during the subsistence of the lease or contract referred to in paragraph (a) of this subsection or (where paragraph (b) applies) during the subsistence of the new lease or contract, the lessor or landlord shall be deemed to be a party to that offence unless he shows that he took all reasonable steps to prevent the recurrence of the offence.

## 36. Tenant permitting premises to be used for prostitution

It is an offence for the tenant or occupier of any premises knowingly to permit the whole or part of the premises to be used for the purposes of habitual prostitution (whether any prostitute involved is male or female).

# HOMICIDE ACT 1957

## 1. Abolition of 'constructive malice'

(1) Where a person kills another in the course or furtherance of some other offence, the killing shall not amount to murder unless done with the same malice aforethought (express or implied) as is required for a killing to amount to murder when not done in the course or furtherance of another offence.

(2) For the purposes of the foregoing subsection, a killing done in the course or for the purpose of resisting an officer of justice, or of resisting or avoiding or preventing a lawful arrest, or of effecting or assisting an escape or rescue from legal custody, shall be treated as a killing in the course or furtherance of an offence.

## 2. Persons suffering from diminished responsibility

(1) A person ('D') who kills or is a party to the killing of another is not to be convicted of murder if D was suffering from an abnormality of mental functioning which—
- (a) arose from a recognised medical condition,
- (b) substantially impaired D's ability to do one or more of the things mentioned in subsection (1A), and
- (c) provides an explanation for D's acts and omissions in doing or being a party to the killing.

(1A) Those things are—
- (a) to understand the nature of D's conduct;
- (b) to form a rational judgment;
- (c) to exercise self-control.

(1B) For the purposes of subsection (1)(c), an abnormality of mental functioning provides an explanation for D's conduct if it causes, or is a significant contributory factor in causing, D to carry out that conduct.

(2) On a charge of murder, it shall be for the defence to prove that the person charged is by virtue of this section not liable to be convicted of murder.

(3) A person who but for this section would be liable, whether as a principal or as accessory, to be convicted of murder shall be liable instead to be convicted of manslaughter.

(4) The fact that one party to a killing is by virtue of this section not liable to be convicted of murder shall not affect the question whether the killing amounted to murder in the case of any other party to it.

## 4. Suicide pacts

(1) It shall be manslaughter, and shall not be murder, for a person acting in pursuance of a suicide pact between him and another to kill the other or be a party to the other ... being killed by a third person.

(2) Where it is shown that a person charged with the murder of another killed the other or was a party to his ... being killed, it shall be for the defence to prove that the person charged was acting in pursuance of a suicide pact between him and the other.

(3) For the purposes of this section 'suicide pact' means a common agreement between two or more persons having for its object the death of all of them, whether or not each is to take his own life, but nothing done by a person who enters into a suicide pact shall be treated as done by him in pursuance of the pact unless it is done while he has the settled intention of dying in pursuance of the pact.

# OBSCENE PUBLICATIONS ACT 1959

## 1. Test of obscenity

(1) For the purpose of this Act an article shall be deemed to be obscene if its effect or (where the article comprises two or more distinct items) the effect of any one of its items is, if taken as a whole, such as to tend to deprave and corrupt persons who are likely, having regard to all relevant circumstances, to read, see or hear the matter contained or embodied in it.

(2) In this Act 'article' means any description of article containing or embodying matter to be read or looked at or both, and sound record, and any film or other record of a picture or pictures.

(3) For the purposes of this Act a person publishes an article who—

(a) distributes, circulates, sells, lets on hire, gives, or lends it, or who offers it for sale or for letting on hire; or

(b) in the case of an article containing or embodying matter to be looked at or a record, shows, plays or projects it, or, where the matter is data stored electronically, transmits that data.

(4) For the purposes of this Act a person also publishes an article to the extent that any matter recorded on it is included by him in a programme included in a programme service.

(5) Where the inclusion of any matter in a programme so included would, if that matter were recorded matter, constitute the publication of an obscene article for the purposes of this Act by virtue of subsection (4) above, this Act shall have effect in relation to the inclusion of that matter in the programme as if it were recorded matter.

(6) In this section 'programme' and 'programme service' have the same meaning as in the Broadcasting Act 1990.

## 2. Prohibition of publication of obscene matter

(3) A prosecution for an offence against this section shall not be commenced more than two years after the commission of the offence.

(3A) Proceedings for an offence under this section shall not be instituted except by or with the consent of the Director of Public Prosecutions in any case where the article in question is a moving picture film of a width of not less than sixteen millimetres and the relevant publication or the only other publication which followed or could reasonably have been expected to follow from the relevant publication took place or (as the case may be) was to take place in the course of an exhibition of a film; and in this subsection 'the relevant publication' means—

(a) in the case of any proceedings under this section for publishing an obscene article, the publication in respect of which the defendant would be charged if the proceedings were brought; and

(b) in the case of any proceedings under this section for having an obscene article for publication for gain, the publication which, if the proceedings were brought, the defendant would be alleged to have had in contemplation.

(4) A person publishing an article shall not be proceeded against for an offence at common law consisting of the publication of any matter contained or embodied in the article where it is of the essence of the offence that the matter is obscene.

(4A) Without prejudice to subsection (4) above, a person shall not be proceeded against for an offence at common law—

(a) in respect of an exhibition of a film or anything said or done in the course of an exhibition of a film, where it is of the essence of the common law offence that the exhibition or, as the case may be, what was said or done was obscene, indecent, offensive, disgusting or injurious to morality; or

(b) in respect of an agreement to give an exhibition of a film or to cause anything to be said or done in the course of such an exhibition where the common law offence consists of conspiring to corrupt public morals or to do any act contrary to public morals or decency.

(5) A person shall not be convicted of an offence against this section if he proves that he had not examined the article in respect of which he is charged and had no reasonable cause to suspect that it was such that his publication of it would make him liable to be convicted of an offence against this section.

(6) In any proceedings against a person under this section the question whether an article is obscene shall be determined without regard to any publication by another person unless it could reasonably have been expected that the publication by the other person would follow from publication by the person charged.

(7) In this section, 'exhibition of a film' has the meaning given in paragraph 15 of Schedule 1 to the Licensing Act 2003.

## 3. Powers of search and seizure

(1) If a justice of the peace is satisfied by information on oath that there is reasonable ground for suspecting that, in any premises ... or on any stall or vehicle in that area, being premises or a stall or vehicle specified in the information, obscene articles are, or are from time to time kept for publication for gain, the justice may issue a warrant under his hand empowering any constable to enter (if need be by force) and search the premises, or to search the stall or vehicle, and to seize and remove any articles found therein or thereon which the constable has reason to believe to be obscene articles and to be kept for publication for gain.

(2) A warrant under the foregoing subsection shall, if any obscene articles are seized under the warrant, also empower the seizure and removal of any documents found in the premises or, as the case may be, on the stall or vehicle which relate to a trade or business carried on at the premises or from the stall or vehicle.

(3) Subject to subsection (3A) of this section any articles seized under subsection (1) of this section shall be brought before a justice of the peace acting in the local justice area in which the articles were seized, who may thereupon issue a summons to the occupier of the premises or, as the case may be, the user of the stall or vehicle to appear on a day specified in the summons before a magistrates' court acting in that local justice area to show cause why the articles or any of them should not be forfeited; and if the court is satisfied, as respects any of the articles, that at the time when they were seized they were obscene articles kept for publication for gain, the court shall order those articles to be forfeited:

Provided that if the person summoned does not appear, the court shall not make an order unless service of the summons is proved; Provided also that this subsection does not apply in relation to any article seized under subsection (1) of this section which is returned to the occupier of the premises or, as the case may be, to the user of the stall or vehicle in or on which it was found.

(3A) Without prejudice to the duty of a court to make an order for the forfeiture of an article where section 1(4) of the Obscene Publications Act 1964 applies (order made on conviction), in a case where by virtue of subsection (3A) of section 2 of this Act proceedings under the said section 2 for having an article for publication for gain could not be instituted except by or with the consent of the Director of Public Prosecutions; no order for the forfeiture of the article shall be made under this section unless the warrant under which the article was seized was issued on an information laid by or on behalf of the Director of Public Prosecutions.

(4) In addition to the person summoned, any other person being the owner, author or maker of any of the articles brought before the court, or any other person through whose hands they had passed before being seized, shall be entitled to appear before the court on the day specified in the summons to show cause why they should not be forfeited.

(7) For the purposes of this section the question whether an article is obscene shall be determined on the assumption that copies of it would be published in any manner likely having regard to the circumstances in which it was found, but in no other manner.

## 4. Defence of public good

(1) Subject to subsection (1A) of this section a person shall not be convicted of an offence against section two of this Act, and an order for forfeiture shall not be made under the foregoing section, if it is proved that publication of the article in question is justified as being for the public good on the ground that it is in the interests of science, literature, art or learning, or of other objects of general concern.

(1A) Subsection (1) of this section shall not apply where the article in question is a moving picture film or soundtrack, but—

- (a) a person shall not be convicted of an offence against section 2 of this Act in relation to any such film or soundtrack, and
- (b) an order for forfeiture of any such film or soundtrack shall not be made under section 3 of this Act,

if it is proved that publication of the film or soundtrack is justified as being for the public good on the grounds that it is in the interests of drama, opera, ballet or any other art, or of literature or learning.

(2) It is hereby declared that the opinion of experts as to the literary, artistic, scientific or other merits of an article may be admitted in any proceedings under this Act either to establish or to negative the said ground.
(3) In this section 'moving picture soundtrack' means any sound record designed for playing with a moving picture film, whether incorporated with the film or not.

## STREET OFFENCES ACT 1959

### 1. Loitering or soliciting for purposes of prostitution

(1) It shall be an offence for a person aged 18 or over (whether male or female) persistently to loiter or solicit in a street or public place for the purpose of prostitution.
(4) For the purposes of this section—
(a) conduct is persistent if it takes place on two or more occasions in any period of three months;
(b) any reference to a person loitering or soliciting for the purposes of prostitution is a reference to a person loitering or soliciting for the purposes of offering services as a prostitute;
(c) 'street' includes any bridge, road, lane, footway, subway, square, court, alley or passage, whether a thoroughfare or not, which is for the time being open to the public; and the doorways and entrances of premises abutting on a street (as hereinbefore defined), and any ground adjoining and open to a street, shall be treated as forming part of the street.

## SUICIDE ACT 1961

### 1. Suicide to cease to be a crime

The rule of law whereby it is a crime for a person to commit suicide is hereby abrogated.

### 2. Criminal liability for complicity in another's suicide

(1) A person commits an offence if—
(a) D does an act capable of encouraging or assisting the suicide or attempted suicide of another person, and
(b) D's act was intended to encourage or assist an attempt at suicide.
(1A) The person referred to in subsection (1)(a) need not be a specific person (or class of persons) known to, or identified by, D.
(1B) D may commit an offence under this section whether or not a suicide, or an attempt at suicide, occurs.
(2) If on the trial of an indictment for murder or manslaughter of a person it is proved that the deceased person committed suicide, and the accused committed an offence under subsection (1) in relation to that suicide, the jury may find the accused guilty of the offence under subsection (1).
(4) ... no proceedings shall be instituted for an offence under this section except by or with the consent of the Director of Public Prosecutions.

### 2A. Acts capable of encouraging or assisting

(1) If D arranges for a person ('D2') to do an act that is capable of encouraging or assisting the suicide or attempted suicide of another person and D2 does that act, D is also to be treated for the purposes of this Act as having done it.
(2) Where the facts are such that an act is not capable of encouraging or assisting suicide or attempted suicide, for the purposes of this Act it is to be treated as so capable if the act would have been so capable had the facts been as D believed them to be at the time of the act or had subsequent events happened in the manner D believed they would happen (or both).

(3) A reference in this Act to a person ('P') doing an act that is capable of encouraging the suicide or attempted suicide of another person includes a reference to P doing so by threatening another person or otherwise putting pressure on another person to commit or attempt suicide.

### 2B. Course of conduct

A reference in this Act to an act includes a reference to a course of conduct, and a reference to doing an act is to be read accordingly.

## CRIMINAL PROCEDURE (INSANITY) ACT 1964

### 5. Powers to deal with persons not guilty by reason of insanity or unfit to plead etc.

(1) This section applies where—
- (a) a special verdict is returned that the accused is not guilty by reason of insanity; or
- (b) findings have been made that the accused is under a disability and that he did the act or made the omission charged against him.

(2) The court shall make in respect of the accused—
- (a) a hospital order (with or without a restriction order);
- (b) a supervision order; or
- (c) an order for his absolute discharge.

(3) Where—
- (a) the offence to which the special verdict or the findings relate is an offence the sentence for which is fixed by law, and
- (b) the court have power to make a hospital order,

the court shall make a hospital order with a restriction order (whether or not they would have power to make a restriction order apart from this subsection).

(4) In this section—

'hospital order' has the meaning given in section 37 of the Mental Health Act 1983;
'restriction order' has the meaning given to it by section 41 of that Act;
'supervision order' has the meaning given in Part 1 of Schedule 1A to this Act.

### 6. Evidence by prosecution of insanity or diminished responsibility

Where on a trial for murder the accused contends—
- (a) that at the time of the alleged offence he was insane so as not to be responsible according to law for his actions; or
- (b) that at that time he was suffering from such abnormality of mental functioning as is specified in subsection (1) of section 2 of the Homicide Act 1957 (diminished responsibility),

the court shall allow the prosecution to adduce or elicit evidence tending to prove the other of those contentions, and may give directions as to the stage of the proceedings at which the prosecution may adduce such evidence.

## OBSCENE PUBLICATIONS ACT 1964

### 1. Obscene articles intended for publication for gain

(2) For the purpose of any proceedings for an offence against the said section 2 a person shall be deemed to have an article for publication for gain if with a view to such publication he has the article in his ownership, possession or control.

(3) In proceedings brought against a person under the said section 2 for having an obscene article for publication for gain the following provisions shall apply in place of subsections (5) and (6) of that section, that is to say,—
- (a) he shall not be convicted of that offence if he proves that he had not examined the article and had no reasonable cause to suspect that it was such that his

having it would make him liable to be convicted of an offence against that section; and

(b) the question whether the article is obscene shall be determined by reference to such publication for gain of the article as in the circumstances it may reasonably be inferred he had in contemplation and to any further publication that could reasonably be expected to follow from it, but not to any other publication.

(4) Where articles are seized under section 3 of the Obscene Publications Act 1959 (which provides for the seizure and forfeiture of obscene articles kept for publication for gain), and a person is convicted under section 2 of that Act of having them for publication for gain, the court on his conviction shall order the forfeiture of those articles:

Provided that an order made by virtue of this subsection (including an order so made on appeal) shall not take effect until the expiration of the ordinary time within which an appeal in the matter of the proceedings in which the order was made may be instituted or, where such an appeal is duly instituted, until the appeal is finally decided or abandoned; and for this purpose—

(a) an application for a case to be stated or for leave to appeal shall be treated as the institution of an appeal; and

(b) where a decision on appeal is subject to a further appeal, the appeal shall not be deemed to be finally decided until the expiration of the ordinary time within which a further appeal is duly instituted, until the further appeal is finally decided or abandoned.

(5) References in section 3 of the Obscene Publications Act 1959 and this section to publication for gain shall apply to any publication with a view to gain, whether the gain is to accrue by way of consideration for the publication or in any other way.

### 2. Negatives, etc. for production of obscene articles

(1) The Obscene Publications Act 1959 (as amended by this Act) shall apply in relation to anything which is intended to be used, either alone or as one of a set, for the reproduction or manufacture therefrom of articles containing or embodying matter to be read, looked at or listened to, as if it were an article containing or embodying that matter so far as that matter is to be derived from it or from the set.

(2) For the purposes of the Obscene Publications Act 1959 (as so amended) an article shall be deemed to be had or kept for publication if it is had or kept for the reproduction or manufacture therefrom of articles for publication; and the question whether an article so had or kept is obscene shall—

(a) for the purposes of section 2 of the Act be determined in accordance with section 1(3)(b) above as if any reference there to publication of the article were a reference to publication of articles reproduced or manufactured from it; and

(b) for purposes of section 3 of the Act be determined on the assumption that articles reproduced or manufactured from it would be published in any manner likely having regard to the circumstances in which it was found, but in no other manner.

## ABORTION ACT 1967

### 1. Medical termination of pregnancy

(1) Subject to the provisions of this section, a person shall not be guilty of any offence under the law relating to abortion when a pregnancy is terminated by a registered medical practitioner if two medical practitioners are of the opinion, formed in good faith—

(a) that the pregnancy has not exceeded its twenty-fourth week and that the continuance of the pregnancy would involve risk, greater than if the pregnancy were terminated, of injury to the physical or mental health of the pregnant woman or any existing children of her family; or

(b) that the termination is necessary to prevent grave permanent injury to the physical or mental health of the pregnant woman; or

(c) that the continuance of the pregnancy would involve risk to the life of the pregnant woman, greater than if the pregnancy were terminated; or

(d) that there is a substantial risk that if the child were born it would suffer from such physical or mental abnormalities as to be seriously handicapped.

(2) In determining whether the continuance of a pregnancy would involve such risk of injury to health as is mentioned in paragraph (a) or (b) of subsection (1) of this section, account may be taken of the pregnant woman's actual or reasonably foreseeable environment.

(3) Except as provided by subsection (4) of this section, any treatment for the termination of pregnancy must be carried out in a hospital vested in the Secretary of State for the purposes of his functions under the National Health Service Act 2006 or the National Health Service (Scotland) Act 1978 or in a hospital vested in a National Health Service trust, or an NHS foundation trust, or in a place approved for the purposes of this section by the Secretary of State.

(4) Subsection (3) of this section, and so much of subsection (1) as relates to the opinion of two registered medical practitioners, shall not apply to the termination of a pregnancy by a registered practitioner in a case where he is of the opinion, formed in good faith, that the termination is immediately necessary to save the life or to prevent grave permanent injury to the physical or mental health of the pregnant woman.

## 2. Notification

(1) The Minister of Health in respect of England and Wales, and the Secretary of State in respect of Scotland, shall by statutory instrument make regulations to provide—

(a) for requiring any such opinion as is referred to in section 1 of this Act to be certified by the practitioners or practitioner concerned in such form and at such time as may be prescribed by the regulations, and for requiring the preservation and disposal of certificates made for the purposes of the regulations;

(b) for requiring any registered medical practitioner who terminates a pregnancy to give notice of the termination and such other information relating to the termination as may be so prescribed;

(c) for prohibiting the disclosure, except to such persons or for such purposes as may be so prescribed, of notices given or information furnished pursuant to the regulations.

(3) Any person who wilfully contravenes or wilfully fails to comply with the requirements of regulations under subsection (1) of this section shall be liable on summary conviction to a fine not exceeding level 5 on the standard scale.

## 4. Conscientious objection to participation in treatment

(1) Subject to subsection (2) of this section, no person shall be under any duty, whether by contract or by any statutory or other legal requirement, to participate in any treatment authorised by this Act to which he has a conscientious objection:

Provided that in any legal proceedings the burden of proof of conscientious objection shall rest on the person claiming to rely on it.

(2) Nothing in subsection (1) of this section shall affect any duty to participate in treatment which is necessary to save the life or to prevent grave permanent injury to the physical or mental health of a pregnant woman.

## 5. Supplementary provisions

(1) No offence under the Infant Life (Preservation) Act 1929 shall be committed by a registered medical practitioner who terminates a pregnancy in accordance with the provisions of this Act.

(2) For the purposes of the law relating to abortion, anything done with intent to procure a woman's miscarriage (or, in the case of a woman carrying more than one foetus, her miscarriage of any foetus) is unlawfully done unless authorised by section 1 of this Act and, in the case of a woman carrying more than one foetus, anything done with intent to procure her miscarriage of any foetus is authorised by that section if—

(a) the ground for termination of the pregnancy specified in subsection (1)(d) of that section applies in relation to any foetus and the thing is done for the purpose of procuring the miscarriage of that foetus, or

(b) any of the other grounds for termination of the pregnancy specified in that section applies.

### 6. Interpretation

In this Act, the following expressions have meanings hereby assigned to them:—

'the law relating to abortion' means sections 58 and 59 of the Offences against the Person Act 1861, and any rule of law relating to the procurement of abortion.

## CRIMINAL JUSTICE ACT 1967

### 8. Proof of criminal intent

A court or jury, in determining whether a person has committed an offence,—

(a) shall not be bound in law to infer that he intended or foresaw a result of his actions by reason only of its being a natural and probable consequence of those actions; but

(b) shall decide whether he did intend or foresee that result by reference to all the evidence, drawing such inferences from the evidence as appear proper in the circumstances.

## CRIMINAL LAW ACT 1967

### 1. Abolition of distinction between felony and misdemeanour

(1) All distinctions between felony and misdemeanour are hereby abolished.

(2) Subject to the provisions of this Act, on all matters on which a distinction has previously been made between felony and misdemeanour, including mode of trial, the law and practice in relation to all offences cognisable under the law of England and Wales (including piracy) shall be the law and practice applicable at the commencement of this Act in relation to misdemeanour.

### 3. Use of force in making arrest, etc.

(1) A person may use such force as is reasonable in the circumstances in the prevention of crime, or in effecting or assisting in the lawful arrest of offenders or suspected offenders or of persons unlawfully at large.

(2) Subsection (1) above shall replace the rules of the common law on the question when force used for a purpose mentioned in the subsection is justified by that purpose.

### 4. Penalties for assisting offenders

(1) Where a person has committed a relevant offence, any other person who, knowing or believing him to be guilty of the offence or of some other relevant offence, does without lawful authority or reasonable excuse any act with intent to impede his apprehension or prosecution shall be guilty of an offence.

(1A) In this section and section 5 below, 'relevant offence' means—

(a) an offence for which the sentence is fixed by law;

(b) an offence for which a person of 18 years or over (not previously convicted) may be sentenced to imprisonment for a term of five years (or might so be sentenced but for the restrictions imposed by section 33 of the Magistrates' Court Act 1980).

(2) If on the trial of an indictment for a relevant offence the jury are satisfied that the offence charged (or some other offence of which the accused might on that charge be found guilty) was committed, but find the accused not guilty of it, they may find him guilty of any offence under subsection (1) above of which they are satisfied that he is guilty in relation to the offence charged (or that other offence).

(3) A person committing an offence under subsection (1) above with intent to impede another person's apprehension or prosecution shall on conviction on indictment be liable to imprisonment according to the gravity of the other person's offence, as follows:—

(a) if that offence is one for which the sentence is fixed by law, he shall be liable to imprisonment for not more than ten years;

(b) if it is one for which a person (not previously convicted) may be sentenced to imprisonment for a term of fourteen years, he shall be liable to imprisonment for not more than seven years;

(c) if it is not one included above but is one for which a person (not previously convicted) may be sentenced to imprisonment for a term of ten years, he shall be liable to imprisonment for not more than five years;

(d) in any other case, he shall be liable to imprisonment for not more than three years.

(4) No proceedings shall be instituted for an offence under subsection (1) above except by or with the consent of the Director of Public Prosecutions.

## 5. Penalties for concealing offences or giving false information

(1) Where a person has committed a relevant offence, any other person who, knowing or believing that the offence or some other relevant offence has been committed, and that he has information which might be of material assistance in securing the prosecution or conviction of an offender for it, accepts or agrees to accept for not disclosing that information any consideration other than the making good of loss or injury caused by the offence, or the making of reasonable compensation for that loss or injury, shall be liable on conviction on indictment to imprisonment for not more than two years.

(2) Where a person causes any wasteful employment of the police by knowingly making to any person a false report tending to show that an offence has been committed, or to give rise to apprehension for the safety of any persons or property, or tending to show that he has information material to any police inquiry, he shall be liable on summary conviction to imprisonment for not more than six months or to a fine of not more than level 4 on the standard scale or to both.

(3) No proceedings shall be instituted for an offence under this section except by or with the consent of the Director of Public Prosecutions.

(5) The compounding of an offence other than treason shall not be an offence otherwise than under this section.

## 6. Trial of offences

(1) Where a person is arraigned on an indictment—

(a) he shall in all cases be entitled to make a plea of not guilty in addition to any demurrer or special plea;

(b) he may plead not guilty of the offence specifically charged in the indictment but guilty of another offence of which he might be found guilty on that indictment;

(c) if he stands mute of malice or will not answer directly to the indictment, the court may order a plea of not guilty to be entered on his behalf, and he shall then be treated as having pleaded not guilty.

(2) On an indictment for murder a person found not guilty of murder may be found guilty—

(a) of manslaughter, or of causing grievous bodily harm with intent to do so; or

(b) of any offence of which he may be found guilty under an enactment specifically so providing, or under section 4(2) of this Act; or

(c) of any attempt to commit murder, or an attempt to commit any other offence of which he might be found guilty;

but may not be found guilty of any offence not included above.

(3) Where, on a person's trial on indictment for any offence except treason or murder, the jury find him not guilty of the offence specifically charged in the indictment, but the allegations in the indictment amount to or include (expressly or by implication) an allegation of another offence falling within the jurisdiction of the court of trial, the jury may find him guilty of that other offence or of an offence of which he could be found guilty on an indictment specifically charging that other offence.

(4) For purposes of subsection (3) above any allegation of an offence shall be taken as including an allegation of attempting to commit that offence; and where a person is charged on an indictment with attempting to commit an offence or with any assault or other act preliminary to an offence, but not with the completed offence, then (subject to the discretion of the court to discharge the jury or otherwise act with a view to the preferment of an indictment for the completed offence) he may be convicted of the offence charged notwithstanding that he is shown to be guilty of the completed offence.

(5) Where a person arraigned on an indictment pleads not guilty of an offence charged in the indictment but guilty of some other offence of which he might be found guilty on that charge, and he is convicted on that plea of guilty without trial for the offence of which he has pleaded not guilty, then (whether or not the two offences are separately charged in distinct counts) his conviction of the one offence shall be an acquittal of the other.

## SEXUAL OFFENCES ACT 1967

### 6. Premises resorted to for homosexual practices

Premises shall be treated for purposes of sections 33 to 35 of the Act of 1956 as a brothel if people resort to it for the purpose of lewd homosexual practices in circumstances in which resort thereto for lewd heterosexual practices would have led to its being treated as a brothel for the purposes of those sections.

## CRIMINAL APPEAL ACT 1968

### 1. Right of appeal

(1) Subject to subsection (3) below a person convicted of an offence on indictment may appeal to the Court of Appeal against his conviction.

(2) An appeal under this section lies only—

(a) with the leave of the Court of Appeal; or

(b) if, within 28 days from the date of the conviction, the judge of the court of trial grants a certificate that the case if fit for appeal.

### 2. Grounds for allowing an appeal under s 1

(1) Subject to the provisions of this Act, the Court of Appeal—

(a) shall allow an appeal against conviction if they think that the conviction is unsafe; and

(b) shall dismiss such an appeal in any other case.

(2) In the case of an appeal against conviction the Court shall, if they allow the appeal, quash the conviction.

(3) An order of the Court of Appeal quashing a conviction shall, except when under section 7 below the appellant is ordered to be retried, operate as a direction to the court of trial to enter, instead of the record of conviction, a judgment and verdict of acquittal.

### 3. Power to substitute conviction of alternative offence

(1) This section applies on an appeal against conviction, where the appellant has been convicted of an offence to which he did not plead guilty and the jury could on the indictment have found him guilty of some other offence, and on the finding of the jury it appears to the Court of Appeal that the jury must have been satisfied of facts which proved him guilty of the other offence.

(2) The Court may, instead of allowing or dismissing the appeal, substitute for the verdict found by the jury a verdict of guilty of the other offence, and pass such sentence in substitution for the sentence passed at the trial as may be authorised by law for the other offence, not being a sentence of greater severity.

### 3A. Power to substitute conviction of alternative offence after guilty plea

(1) This section applies on an appeal against conviction where—

(a) an appellant has been convicted of an offence to which he pleaded guilty,

(b) if he had not so pleaded, he could on the indictment have pleaded, or been found, guilty of some other offence, and

(c) it appears to the Court of Appeal that the plea of guilty indicates an admission by the appellant of facts which prove him guilty of the other offence.

(2) The Court of Appeal may, instead of allowing or dismissing the appeal, substitute for the appellant's plea of guilty a plea of guilty of the other offence and pass such sentence in substitution for the sentence passed at the trial as may be authorised by law for the other offence, not being a sentence of greater severity.

### 12. Appeal against verdict of not guilty by reason of insanity

A person in whose case there is returned a verdict of not guilty by reason of insanity may appeal to the Court of Appeal against the verdict—
(a) with the leave of the Court of Appeal; or
(b) if, within 28 days from the date of the verdict, the judge of the court of trial grants a certificate that the case if fit for appeal.

### 13. Disposal of appeal under s 12

(1) Subject to the provisions of this section, the Court of Appeal—
(a) shall allow an appeal under section 12 of this Act if they think that the verdict is unsafe; and
(b) shall dismiss such an appeal in any other case.
(2) Where apart from this subsection—
(a) an appeal under section 12 of this Act would fall to be allowed; and
(b) none of the grounds for allowing it relates to the question of the insanity of the accused,
the Court of Appeal may dismiss the appeal if they are of opinion that, but for the insanity of the accused, the proper verdict would have been that he was guilty of an offence other than the offence charged.
(4) Where an appeal under section 12 of this Act is allowed, the following provisions apply—
(a) if the ground, or one of the grounds, for allowing the appeal is that the finding of the jury as to the insanity of the accused ought not to stand and the Court of Appeal are of opinion that the proper verdict would have been that he was guilty of an offence (whether the offence charged or any other offence of which the jury could have found him guilty), the Court—
(i) shall substitute for the verdict of not guilty by reason of insanity a verdict of guilty of that offence; and
(ii) shall, subject to subsection (5) below, have the like powers of punishing or otherwise dealing with the appellant, and other powers, as the court of trial would have had if the jury had come to the substituted verdict; and
(b) in any other case, the Court of Appeal shall substitute for the verdict of the jury a verdict of acquittal.

## FIREARMS ACT 1968

### 1. Requirement of firearm certificate

(1) Subject to any exemption under this Act, it is an offence for a person—
(a) to have in his possession, or to purchase or acquire, a firearm to which this section applies without holding a firearm certificate in force at the time, or otherwise than as authorised by such a certificate;
(b) to have in his possession, or to purchase or acquire, any ammunition to which this section applies without holding a firearm certificate in force at the time, or otherwise than as authorised by such a certificate, or in quantities in excess of those so authorised.
(2) It is an offence for a person to fail to comply with a condition subject to which a firearm certificate is held by him.
(3) This section applies to every firearm except—
(a) a shot gun within the meaning of this Act, that is to say a smooth-bore gun (not being an air gun) which—
(i) has a barrel not less than 24 inches in length and does not have any barrel with a bore exceeding 2 inches in diameter;
(ii) either has no magazine or has a non-detachable magazine incapable of holding more than two cartridges; and
(iii) is not a revolver gun; and
(b) an air weapon (that is to say, an air rifle, air gun or air pistol which does not fall within section 5(1) and which is not of a type declared by rules made by the Secretary of State under section 53 of this Act to be specially dangerous).

(3A) A gun which has been adapted to have such a magazine as is mentioned in subsection (3)(a)(ii) above shall not be regarded as falling within that provision unless the magazine bears a mark approved by the Secretary of State for denoting that fact and that mark has been made, and the adaptation has been certified in writing as having been carried out in a manner approved by him, either by one of the two companies mentioned in section 58(1) of this Act or by such other person as may be approved by him for that purpose.

(4) This section applies to any ammunition for a firearm, except the following articles, namely:—
- (a) cartridges containing five or more shot, none of which exceeds 0.36 inch in diameter;
- (b) ammunition for an air gun, air rifle or air pistol; and
- (c) blank cartridges not more than one inch in diameter measured immediately in front of the rim or cannelure of the base of the cartridge.

## 2. Requirement of certificate for possession of shot guns

(1) Subject to any exemption under this Act, it is an offence for a person to have in his possession, or to purchase or acquire, a shot gun without holding a certificate under this Act authorising him to possess shot guns.

(2) It is an offence for a person to fail to comply with a condition subject to which a shot gun certificate is held by him.

## 3. Business and other transactions with firearms and ammunition

(1) A person commits an offence if, by way of trade or business, he—
- (a) manufactures, sells, transfers, repairs, tests or proves any firearm or ammunition to which section 1 of this Act applies, or a shot gun;
- (b) exposes for sale or transfer, or has in his possession for sale, transfer, repair, test or proof any such firearm or ammunition, or a shot gun; or
- (c) sells or transfers an air weapon, exposes such a weapon for sale or transfer or has such a weapon in his possession for sale or transfer,

without being registered under this Act as a firearms dealer.

(2) It is an offence for a person to sell or transfer to any other person in the United Kingdom, other than a registered firearms dealer, any firearm or ammunition to which section 1 of this Act applies, or a shot gun, unless that other produces a firearm certificate authorising him to purchase or acquire it or as the case may be, his shot gun certificate, or shows that he is by virtue of this Act entitled to purchase or acquire it without holding a certificate.

(3) It is an offence for a person to undertake the repair, tests or proof of a firearm or ammunition to which section 1 of this Act applies, or of a shot gun, for any other person in the United Kingdom other than a registered firearms dealer as such, unless that other produces or causes to be produced a firearm certificate authorising him to have possession of the firearm or ammunition or, as the case may be, his shot gun certificate, or shows that he is by virtue of this Act entitled to have possession of it without holding a certificate.

(4) Subsections (1) and (3) above have effect subject to any exemption under subsequent provisions of this Part of this Act.

(5) A person commits an offence if, with a view to purchasing or acquiring, or procuring the repair, test or proof of, any firearm or ammunition to which section 1 of this Act applies, or a shot gun, he produces a false certificate or a certificate in which any false entry has been made, or personates a person to whom a certificate has been granted, or knowingly or recklessly makes a statement false in any material particular.

(6) It is an offence for a pawnbroker to take in pawn any firearm or ammunition to which section 1 of this Act applies, or a shot gun.

## 4. Conversion of weapons

(1) Subject to this section, it is an offence to shorten the barrel of a shot gun to a length less than 24 inches.

(2) It is not an offence under subsection (1) above for a registered firearms dealer to shorten the barrel of a shot gun for the sole purpose of replacing a defective part of the barrel so as to produce a barrel not less than 24 inches in length.

(3) It is an offence for a person other than a registered firearms dealer to convert into a firearm anything which, though having the appearance of being a firearm, is so constructed as to be incapable of discharging any missile through its barrel.

(4) A person who commits an offence under section 1 of this Act by having in his possession, or purchasing or acquiring, a shotgun which has been shortened contrary to subsection (1) above or a firearm which has been converted contrary to subsection (3) above (whether by a registered firearms dealer or not), without holding a firearm certificate authorising him to have it in his possession, or to purchase or acquire it, shall be treated for the purposes of provisions of this Act relating to the punishment of offences as committing that offence in an aggravated form.

## 4A. Possession of articles for use in connection with conversion

(1) A person, other than a registered firearms dealer, commits an offence if—

(a) the person has in his or her possession or under his or her control an article that is capable of being used (whether by itself or with other articles) to convert an imitation firearm into a firearm, and

(b) the person intends to use the article (whether by itself or with other articles) to convert an imitation firearm into a firearm.

## 5. Weapons subject to general prohibition

(1) A person commits an offence if, without authority, he has in his possession, or purchases or acquires—

(a) any firearm which is so designed or adapted that two or more missiles can be successively discharged without repeated pressure on the trigger;

(ab) any self-loading or pump-action rifled gun other than one which is chambered for .22 rim-fire cartridges;

(aba) any firearm which either has a barrel less than 30 centimetres in length or is less than 60 centimetres in length overall, other than an air weapon, a muzzle-loading gun or a firearm designed as signalling apparatus;

(ac) any self-loading or pump-action smooth-bore gun which is not an air weapon or chambered for .22 rim-fire cartridges and either has a barrel less than 24 inches in length or (excluding any detachable folding, retractable or other movable buttstock) is less than 40 inches in length overall;

(ad) any smooth-bore revolver gun other than one which is chambered for 9mm rim-fire cartridges or a muzzle-loading gun;

(ae) any rocket launcher, or any mortar, for projecting a stabilised missile, other than a launcher or mortar designed for line-throwing or pyrotechnic purposes or as signalling apparatus;

(af) any air rifle, air gun or air pistol which uses, or is designed or adapted for use with, a self-contained gas cartridge system;

(ag) any rifle with a chamber from which empty cartridge cases are extracted using—

(i) energy from propellant gas, or

(ii) energy imparted to a spring or other energy storage device by propellant gas,

other than a rifle which is chambered for .22 rim-fire cartridges;

(b) any weapon of whatever description designed or adapted for the discharge of any noxious liquid, gas or other thing;

(ba) any device (commonly known as a bump stock) which is designed or adapted so that—

(i) it is capable of forming part of or being added to a self-loading lethal barrelled weapon (as defined in section 57(1B) and (2A)), and

(ii) if it forms part of or is added to such a weapon, it increases the rate of fire of the weapon by using the recoil from the weapon to generate repeated pressure on the trigger; and

(c) any cartridge with a bullet designed to explode on or immediately before impact, any ammunition containing or designed or adapted to contain any such noxious thing as is mentioned in paragraph (b) above and, if capable of being used with a firearm of any description, any grenade, bomb (or other like missile), or rocket or shell designed to explode as aforesaid.

(1A) Subject to section 5A of this Act, a person commits an offence if, without authority, he has in his possession, or purchases or acquires—

(a) any firearm which is disguised as another object;
(b) any rocket or ammunition not falling within paragraph (c) of subsection (1) of this section which consists in or incorporates a missile designed to explode on or immediately before impact and is for military use;
(c) any launcher or other projecting apparatus not falling within paragraph (ae) of that subsection which is designed to be used with any rocket or ammunition falling within paragraph (b) above or with ammunition which would fall within that paragraph but for its being ammunition falling within paragraph (c) of this subsection;
(d) any ammunition for military use which consists in or incorporates a missile designed so that a substance contained in the missile will ignite on or immediately before impact;
(e) any ammunition for military use which consists in or incorporates a missile designed, on account of its having a jacket and hard-core, to penetrate armour plating, armour screening or body armour;
(f) any ammunition which is designed to be used with a pistol and incorporates a missile designed or adapted to expand on impact;
(g) anything which is designed to be projected as a missile from any weapon and is designed to be, or has been, incorporated in—
(i) any ammunition falling within any of the preceding paragraphs; or
(ii) any ammunition which would fall within any of those paragraphs but for its being specified in subsection (1) of this section.

(2) The weapons and ammunition specified in subsections (1) and (1A) of this section (including, in the case of ammunition, any missiles falling within subsection (1A)(g) of this section) are referred to in this Act as 'prohibited weapons' and 'prohibited ammunition' respectively.

(2A) A person commits an offence if without authority—
(a) he manufactures any weapon or ammunition specified in subsection (1) of this section,
(b) he sells or transfers any prohibited weapon or prohibited ammunition,
(c) he has in his possession for sale or transfer any prohibited weapon or prohibited ammunition, or
(d) he purchases or acquires for sale or transfer any prohibited weapon or prohibited ammunition.

(3) In this section 'authority' means an authority given in writing by—
(a) the Secretary of State (in or as regards England and Wales), or
(b) the Scottish Ministers (in or as regards Scotland).

(5) It is an offence for a person to whom an authority is given under this section to fail to comply with any condition of the authority.

(7) For the purposes of this section and section 5A of this Act—
(a) any rocket or ammunition which is designed to be capable of being used with a military weapon shall be taken to be for military use;
(b) references to a missile designed so that a substance contained in the missile will ignite on or immediately before impact include references to any missile containing a substance that ignites on exposure to air; and
(c) references to a missile's expanding on impact include references to its deforming in any predictable manner on or immediately after impact.

(8) For the purposes of subsection (1)(aba) and (ac) above, any detachable, folding, retractable or other movable butt-stock shall be disregarded in measuring the length of any firearm.

(9) Any reference in this section to a muzzle-loading gun is a reference to a gun which is designed to be loaded at the muzzle end of the barrel or chamber with a loose charge and a separate ball (or other missile).

## 5A. Exemptions from requirement of authority under section 5

(1) Subject to subsection (2) below, the authority of the Secretary of State shall not be required by virtue of section 5 of this Act for any person to have in his possession, or to purchase, acquire, sell or transfer, any weapon, ammunition or missile specified in subsection (1A) of that section if he is authorised by a certificate under this Act to possess, purchase or acquire that weapon or ammunition subject to a condition that he does so only for the purpose of its being kept or exhibited as part of a collection.

(2) No sale or transfer may be made under subsection (1) above except to a person who—
  (a) produces the authority of the Secretary of State under section 5 of this Act for his purchase or acquisition; or
  (b) shows that he is, under this section or a licence under the Schedule to the Firearms (Amendment) Act 1988 (museums etc.), entitled to make the purchase or acquisition without the authority of the Secretary of State.

(3) The authority of the Secretary of State shall not be required by virtue of subsection (1A) of section 5 of this Act for any person to have in his possession, or to purchase or acquire, any weapon, ammunition or missile specified in subsection (1A) of that section if his possession, purchase or acquisition is exclusively in connection with the carrying on of activities in respect of which—
  (a) that person; or
  (b) the person on whose behalf he has possession, or makes the purchase or acquisition, is recognised, for the purposes of the law of another member State relating to firearms, as a collector of firearms or a body concerned in the cultural or historical aspects of weapons.

(4) The authority of the Secretary of State shall not be required by virtue of section 5 of this Act for any person to have in his possession, or to purchase or acquire or to sell or transfer, any expanding ammunition or the missile for any such ammunition if—
  (a) he is authorised by a firearm certificate or visitor's firearm permit to possess, or purchase or acquire, any expanding ammunition; and
  (b) the certificate or permit is subject to a condition restricting the use of any expanding ammunition to use in connection with any one or more of the following, namely—
    (i) the lawful shooting of deer;
    (ii) the shooting of vermin or, in the course of carrying on activities in connection with the management of any estate other wildlife;
    (iii) the humane killing of animals;
    (iv) the shooting of animals for the protection of other animals or humans.

(5) The authority of the Secretary of State shall not be required by virtue of section 5 of this Act for any person to have in his possession any expanding ammunition or the missile for any such ammunition if—
  (a) he is entitled, under section 10 of this Act, to have a slaughtering instrument and the ammunition for it in his possession; and
  (b) the ammunition or missile in question is designed to be capable of being used with a slaughtering instrument.

(6) The authority of the Secretary of State shall not be required by virtue of section 5 of this Act for the sale or transfer of any expanding ammunition or the missile for any such ammunition to any person who produces a certificate by virtue of which he is authorised under subsection (4) above to purchase or acquire it without the authority of the Secretary of State.

(7) The authority of the Secretary of State shall not be required by virtue of section 5 of this Act for a person carrying on the business of a firearms dealer, or any servant of his, to have in his possession, or to purchase, acquire, sell or transfer, any expanding ammunition or the missile for any such ammunition in the ordinary course of that business.

(8) In this section—
  (a) references to expanding ammunition are references to any ammunition which is designed to be used with a pistol and incorporates a missile which is designed to expand on impact; and
  (b) references to the missile for any such ammunition are references to anything which, in relation to any such ammunition, falls within section 5(1A)(g) of this Act.

## 7. Police permit

(1) A person who has obtained from the chief officer of police for the area in which he resides a permit for the purpose in the prescribed form may, without holding a certificate under this Act, have in his possession a firearm and ammunition in accordance with the terms of the permit.

(2) It is an offence for a person knowingly or recklessly to make a statement false in any material particular for the purpose of procuring, whether for himself or for another person, the grant of a permit under this section.

## 16. Possession of firearm with intent to injure

It is an offence for a person to have in his possession any firearm or ammunition with intent by means thereof to endanger life ... or to enable another person by means thereof to endanger life ... whether any injury has been caused or not.

## 16A. Possession of firearm with intent to cause fear of violence

It is an offence for a person to have in his possession any firearm or imitation firearm with intent—

(a) by means thereof to cause, or
(b) to enable another person by means thereof to cause,

any person to believe that unlawful violence will be used against him or another person.

## 17. Use of firearm to resist arrest

(1) It is an offence for a person to make or attempt to make any use whatsoever of a firearm or imitation firearm with intent to resist or prevent the lawful arrest or detention of himself or another person.
(2) If a person, at the time of his committing or being arrested for an offence specified in Schedule 1 to this Act, has in his possession a firearm or imitation firearm, he shall be guilty of an offence under this subsection unless he shows that he had it in his possession for a lawful object.
(4) For purposes of this section, the definition of 'firearm' in section 57(1) of this Act shall apply without paragraphs (b) and (c) of that subsection, and 'imitation firearm' shall be construed accordingly.

## 18. Carrying firearm with criminal intent

(1) It is an offence for a person to have with him a firearm or imitation firearm with intent to commit an indictable offence, or to resist arrest or prevent the arrest of another, in either case while he has the firearm or imitation firearm with him.
(2) In proceedings for an offence under this section proof that the accused had a firearm or imitation firearm with him and intended to commit an offence, or to resist or prevent arrest, is evidence that he intended to have it with him while doing so.

## 19. Carrying firearm in a public place

A person commits an offence if, without lawful authority or reasonable excuse (the proof whereof lies on him) he has with him in a public place—

(a) a loaded shot gun,
(b) an air weapon (whether loaded or not),
(c) any other firearm (whether loaded or not) together with ammunition suitable for use in that firearm, or
(d) an imitation firearm.

## 20. Trespassing with firearm

(1) A person commits an offence if, while he has a firearm or imitation firearm with him, he enters or is in any building or part of a building as a trespasser and without reasonable excuse (the proof whereof lies on him).
(2) A person commits an offence if, while he has a firearm or imitation firearm with him, he enters or is on any land as a trespasser and without reasonable excuse (the proof whereof lies on him).
(3) In subsection (2) of this section the expression 'land' includes land covered with water.

## 21A. Firing an air weapon beyond premises

(1) A person commits an offence if—
    (a) he has with him an air weapon on any premises; and
    (b) he uses it for firing a missile beyond those premises.
(2) In proceedings against a person for an offence under this section it shall be a defence for him to show that the only premises into or across which the missile was fired were premises the occupier of which had consented to the firing of the missile (whether specifically or by way of a general consent).

## 22. Acquisition and possession of firearms by minors

(1) It is an offence for a person under the age of eighteen to purchase or hire any firearm or ammunition.

(1A) Where a person under the age of eighteen is entitled, as the holder of a certificate under this Act, to have a firearm in his possession, it is an offence for that person to use that firearm for a purpose not authorised by the European weapons directive.

(2) It is an offence for a person under the age of fourteen to have in his possession any firearm or ammunition to which section 1 of this Act applies, except in circumstances where under section 11 (1), (3) or (4) of this Act or section 15 of the Firearms (Amendment) Act 1988 he is entitled to have possession of it without holding a firearm certificate.

(3) It is an offence for a person under the age of fifteen to have with him an assembled shot gun except while under the supervision of a person of or over the age of twenty-one, or while the shot gun is so covered with a securely fastened gun cover that it cannot be fired.

(4) Subject to section 23 below, it is an offence for a person under the age of eighteen to have with him an air weapon or ammunition for an air weapon.

## 23. Exceptions from s. 22(4)

(1) It is not an offence under section 22(4) of this Act for a person to have with him an air weapon or ammunition while he is under the supervision of a person of or over the age of twenty-one; but where a person has with him an air weapon on any premises in circumstances where he would be prohibited from having it with him but for this subsection, it is an offence for the person under whose supervision he is to allow him to use it for firing any missile beyond those premises.

(1A) In proceedings against a person for an offence under subsection (1) it shall be a defence for him to show that the only premises into or across which the missile was fired were premises the occupier of which had consented to the firing of the missile (whether specifically or by way of a general consent).

(2) It is not an offence under section 22(4) of this Act for a person to have with him an air weapon or ammunition at a time when—

(a) being a member of a rifle club or miniature rifle club for the time being approved by the Secretary of State for the purposes of this section or section 15 of the Firearms (Amendment) Act 1988, he is engaged as such a member in or in connection with target shooting; or

(b) he is using the weapon or ammunition at a shooting gallery where the only firearms used are either air weapons or miniature rifles not exceeding 0.23 inch calibre.

(3) It is not an offence under section 22(4) of this Act for a person of or over the age of fourteen to have with him an air weapon or ammunition on private premises with the consent of the occupier.

## 24. Supplying firearms to minors

(1) It is an offence to sell or let on hire any firearm or ammunition to a person under the age of eighteen.

(2) It is an offence—

(a) to make a gift of or lend any firearm or ammunition to which section 1 of this Act applies to a person under the age of fourteen; or

(b) to part with the possession of any such firearm or ammunition to a person under that age, except in circumstances where that person is entitled under section 11(1), (3) or (4) of this Act or section 15 of the Firearms (Amendment) Act 1988 to have possession thereof without holding a firearm certificate.

(3) It is an offence to make a gift of a shot gun or ammunition for a shot gun to a person under the age of fifteen.

(4) It is an offence—

(a) to make a gift of an air weapon or ammunition for an air weapon to a person under the age of eighteen; or

(b) to part with the possession of an air weapon or ammunition for an air weapon to a person under the age of eighteen except where by virtue of section 23 of this Act the person is not prohibited from having it with him.

(5) In proceedings for an offence under any provision of this section it is a defence to prove that the person charged with the offence believed the other person to be of or over the age mentioned in that provision and had reasonable ground for the belief.

## 24ZA. Failing to prevent minors from having air weapons

(1) It is an offence for a person in possession of an air weapon to fail to take reasonable precautions to prevent any person under the age of eighteen from having the weapon with him.

(2) Subsection (1) does not apply where by virtue of section 23 of this Act the person under the age of eighteen is not prohibited from having the weapon with him.

(3) In proceedings for an offence under subsection (1) it is a defence to show that the person charged with the offence—
  (a) believed the other person to be aged eighteen or over; and
  (b) had reasonable ground for that belief.

(4) For the purposes of this section a person shall be taken to have shown the matters specified in subsection (3) if—
  (a) sufficient evidence of those matters is adduced to raise an issue with respect to them; and
  (b) the contrary is not proved beyond a reasonable doubt.

## 24A. Supplying imitation firearms to minors

(1) It is an offence for a person under the age of eighteen to purchase an imitation firearm.

(2) It is an offence to sell an imitation firearm to a person under the age of eighteen.

(3) In proceedings for an offence under subsection (2) it is a defence to show that the person charged with the offence—
  (a) believed the other person to be aged eighteen or over; and
  (b) had reasonable ground for that belief.

(4) For the purposes of this section a person shall be taken to have shown the matters specified in subsection (3) if—
  (a) sufficient evidence of those matters is adduced to raise an issue with respect to them; and
  (b) the contrary is not proved beyond a reasonable doubt.

## 25. Supplying firearm to person drunk or insane

It is an offence for a person to sell or transfer any firearm or ammunition to, or to repair, prove or test any firearm or ammunition for, another person whom he knows or has reasonable cause for believing to be drunk or of unsound mind.

## 57. Interpretation

(1) In this Act, the expression 'firearm' means—
  (a) a lethal barrelled weapon (see subsection (1B));
  (b) a prohibited weapon;
  (c) a relevant component part in relation to a lethal barrelled weapon or a prohibited weapon (see subsection (1D));
  (d) an accessory to a lethal barrelled weapon or a prohibited weapon where the accessory is designed or adapted to diminish the noise or flash caused by firing the weapon.

(1A) ...

(1B) In subsection (1)(a), 'lethal barrelled weapon' means a barrelled weapon of any description from which a shot, bullet or other missile, with kinetic energy of more than one joule at the muzzle of the weapon, can be discharged.

(1C) Subsection (1) is subject to section 57A (exception for airsoft guns).

(1D) For the purposes of subsection (1)(c), each of the following items is a relevant component part in relation to a lethal barrelled weapon or a prohibited weapon—
  (a) a barrel, chamber or cylinder,
  (b) a frame, body or receiver,
  (c) a breech block, bolt or other mechanism for containing the pressure of discharge at the rear of a chamber,

but only where the item is capable of being used as a part of a lethal barrelled weapon or a prohibited weapon.

(2) In this Act, the expression 'ammunition' means ammunition for any firearm and includes grenades, bombs and other like missiles, whether capable of use with a firearm or not, and also includes prohibited ammunition.

(2A) In this Act 'self-loading' and 'pump-action' in relation to any weapon mean respectively that it is designed or adapted (otherwise than as mentioned in section 5(1)(a)) so that it is automatically re-loaded or that it is so designed or adapted that it is re-loaded by the manual operation of the fore-end or forestock of the weapon.

(2B) In this Act 'revolver', in relation to a smooth-bore gun, means a gun containing a series of chambers which revolve when the gun is fired.

(3) For purposes of sections 45, 46, 50, 51(4) and 52 of this Act, the offences under this Act relating specifically to air weapons are those under sections 22(4), 22(5), 23(1), 24(4) and 24ZA(1).

(4) In this Act—

'acquire' means hire, accept as a gift or borrow and 'acquisition' shall be construed accordingly;

'air weapon' has the meaning assigned to it by section 1(3)(b) of this Act;

'another member State' means a member State other than the United Kingdom, and 'other member States' shall be construed accordingly;

'area' means a police area;

'Article 7 authority' means a document issued by virtue of section 32A(1)(b) or (2) of this Act;

...

'certificate' (except in a context relating to the registration of firearms dealers) and 'certificate under this Act' mean a firearm certificate or a shot gun certificate and—

(a) 'firearm certificate' means a certificate granted by a chief officer of police under this Act in respect of any firearm or ammunition to which section 1 of this Act applies and includes a certificate granted in Northern Ireland under section 1 of the Firearms Act 1920 or under an enactment of the Parliament of Northern Ireland amending or substituted for that section; and

(b) 'shot gun certificate' means a certificate granted by a chief officer of police under this Act and authorising a person to possess shot guns;

'civilian officer' means—

(a) as respects England and Wales—

  (i) a person employed by a chief constable established under section 2 of the Police Reform and Social Responsibility Act 2011;

  (ii) a person employed by the Commissioner of the Metropolitan Police, or

  (iii) a person employed by the Corporation of the City of London who is under the direction and control of the Commissioner of Police for the City of London; ...

(b) ...

'European firearms pass' means a document to which the holder of a certificate under this Act is entitled by virtue of section 32A(1)(a) of this Act;

'European weapons directive' means the directive of the Council of the European Communities No 91/477/EEC (directive on the control of the acquisition and possession of weapons);

'firearms dealer' means a person who, by way of trade or business,

(a) manufactures, sells, transfers, repairs, tests or proves firearms or ammunition to which section 1 of this Act applies or shot guns; or

(b) sells or transfers air weapons;

'imitation firearm' means any thing which has the appearance of being a firearm (other than such a weapon as is mentioned in section 5(1)(b) of this Act) whether or not it is capable of discharging any shot, bullet or other missile;

'premises' includes any land;

'prescribed' means prescribed by rules made by the Secretary of State under section 53 of this Act;

'prohibited weapon' and 'prohibited ammunition' have the meanings assigned to them by section 5(2) of this Act;

'public place' includes any highway and any other premises or place to which at the material time the public have or are permitted to have access, whether on payment or otherwise;

'registered', in relation to a firearms dealer, means registered either—

(a) in Great Britain, under section 33 of this Act, or

(b) in Northern Ireland, under section 8 of the Firearms Act 1920 or any enactment of the Parliament of Northern Ireland amending or substituted for that section,

and references to 'the register', 'registration' and a 'certificate of registration' shall be construed accordingly, except in section 40;

'rifle' includes carbine;

'shot gun' has the meaning assigned to it by section 1(3)(a) of this Act and, in sections 3(1) and 45(2) of this Act and in the definition of 'firearms dealer', includes any component part of a shot gun and any accessory to a shot gun designed or adapted to diminish the noise or flash caused by firing the gun;

'slaughtering instrument' means a firearm which is specially designed or adapted for the instantaneous slaughter of animals or for the instantaneous stunning of animals with a view to slaughtering them; and

'transfer' includes let on hire, give, lend and part with possession, and 'transferee' and 'transferor' shall be construed accordingly.

(4A) For the purposes of any reference in this Act to the use of any firearm or ammunition for a purpose not authorised by the European weapons directive, the directive shall be taken to authorise the use of a firearm or ammunition as or with a slaughtering instrument and the use of a firearm and ammunition—
 (a) for sporting purposes;
 (b) for the shooting of vermin, or, in the course of carrying on activities in connection with the management of any estate, of other wildlife; and
 (c) for competition purposes and target shooting outside competitions.

(5) The definitions in subsections (1) to (3) above apply to the provisions of this Act except where the context otherwise requires.

(6) For purposes of this Act—
 (a) the length of the barrel of a firearm shall be measured from the muzzle to the point at which the charge is exploded on firing; and
 (b) a shot gun or an air weapon shall be deemed to be loaded if there is ammunition in the chamber or barrel or in any magazine or other device which is in such a position that the ammunition can be fed into the chamber or barrel by the manual or automatic operation of some part of the gun or weapon.

## 57A. Exception for airsoft guns

(1) An 'airsoft gun' is not to be regarded as a firearm for the purposes of this Act.

(2) An 'airsoft gun' is a barrelled weapon of any description which—
 (a) is designed to discharge only a small plastic missile (whether or not it is also capable of discharging any other kind of missile), and
 (b) is not capable of discharging a missile (of any kind) with kinetic energy at the muzzle of the weapon that exceeds the permitted level.

(3) 'Small plastic missile' means a missile that—
 (a) is made wholly or partly from plastics,
 (b) is spherical, and
 (c) does not exceed 8 millimetres in diameter.

(4) The permitted kinetic energy level is—
 (a) in the case of a weapon which is capable of discharging two or more missiles successively without repeated pressure on the trigger, 1.3 joules;
 (b) in any other case, 2.5 joules.

## 58. Particular savings

(2) Apart from—
 (a) section 21 and Schedule 3, and
 (b) any other provision of this Act so far as it applies in relation to an offence under section 21,

nothing in this Act relating to firearms shall apply to an antique firearm which is sold, transferred, purchased, acquired or possessed as a curiosity or ornament.

(3) The provisions of this Act relating to ammunition shall be in addition to and not in derogation of any enactment relating to the keeping and sale of explosives.

SCHEDULE 1
OFFENCES TO WHICH SECTION 17(2) APPLIES

1. Offences under section 1 of the Criminal Damage Act 1971
2. Offences under any of the following provisions of the Offences against the Person Act 1861 —
   section 20 to 22 (inflicting bodily injury; garrotting; criminal use of stupefying drugs);
   section 30 (laying explosive to building etc.);
   section 32 (endangering railway passengers by tampering with track);
   section 38 (assault with intent to commit felony or resist arrest);
   section 47 (criminal assaults);
2A. Offences under Part 1 of the Child Abduction Act 1984 (abduction of children).
3. ...
4. Theft, robbery, burglary, blackmail and any offence under section 12(1) (taking of motor vehicle or other conveyance without owner's consent) of the Theft Act 1968.
5. Offences under section 89(1) of the Police Act 1996 (assaulting a constable in the execution of his duty).
5A. An offence under section 90(1) of the Criminal Justice Act 1991 (assaulting prisoner custody officer).
5B. An offence under section 13(1) of the Criminal Justice and Public Order Act 1994 (assaulting secure training centre custody officer).
5C. ...
6. Offences under any of the following provisions of the Sexual Offences Act 2003—
   (a) section 1 (rape);
   (b) section 2 (assault by penetration);
   (c) section 4 (causing a person to engage in sexual activity without consent), where the activity caused involved penetration within subsection (4)(a) to (d) of that section;
   (d) section 5 (rape of a child under 13);
   (e) section 6 (assault of a child under 13 by penetration);
   (f) section 8 (causing or inciting a child under 13 to engage in sexual activity), where an activity involving penetration within subsection (3)(a) to (d) of that section was caused;
   (g) section 30 (sexual activity with a person with a mental disorder impeding choice), where the touching involved penetration within subsection (3)(a) to (d) of that section;
   (h) section 31 (causing or inciting a person, with a mental disorder impeding choice, to engage in sexual activity), where an activity involving penetration within subsection (3)(a) to (d) of that section was caused.
6A. An offence under paragraph 14 or 24 of Schedule 10 to the Criminal Justice and Courts Act 2015 (assaulting secure college custody officer).
8. Aiding or abetting the commission of any offence specified in paragraphs 1 to 6A of this Schedule.
9. Attempting to commit any offence so specified.

# THEFT ACT 1968

## 1. Basic definition of theft

(1) A person is guilty of theft if he dishonestly appropriates property belonging to another with the intention of permanently depriving the other of it; and 'thief' and 'steal' shall be construed accordingly.

(2) It is immaterial whether the appropriation is made with a view to gain, or is made for the thief's own benefit.

(3) The five following sections of this Act shall have effect as regards the interpretation and operation of this section (and, except as otherwise provided by this Act, shall apply only for purposes of this section).

## 2. 'Dishonestly'

(1) A person's appropriation of property belonging to another is not to be regarded as dishonest—

   (a) if he appropriates the property in the belief that he has in law the right to deprive the other of it, on behalf of himself or of a third person; or

(b) if he appropriates the property in the belief that he would have the other's consent if the other knew of the appropriation and the circumstances of it; or
(c) (except where the property came to him as trustee or personal representative) if he appropriates the property in the belief that the person to whom the property belongs cannot be discovered by taking reasonable steps.

(2) A person's appropriation of property belonging to another may be dishonest notwithstanding that he is willing to pay for the property.

## 3. 'Appropriates'

(1) Any assumption by a person of the rights of an owner amounts to an appropriation, and this includes, where he has come by the property (innocently or not) without stealing it, any later assumption of a right to it by keeping or dealing with it as owner.
(2) Where property or a right or interest in property is or purports to be transferred for value to a person acting in good faith, no later assumption by him of rights which he believed himself to be acquiring shall, by reason of any defect in the transferor's title, amount to theft of the property.

## 4. 'Property'

(1) 'Property' includes money and all other property, real or personal, including things in action and other intangible property.
(2) A person cannot steal land, or things forming part of land and severed from it by him or by his directions, except in the following cases, that is to say—
(a) when he is a trustee or personal representative, or is authorised by power of attorney, or as liquidator of a company, or otherwise, to sell or dispose of land belonging to another, and he appropriates the land or anything forming part of it by dealing with it in breach of the confidence reposed in him; or
(b) when he is not in possession of the land and appropriates anything forming part of the land by severing it or causing it to be severed, or after it has been severed; or
(c) when, being in possession of the land under a tenancy, he appropriates the whole or part of any fixture or structure let to be used with the land.

For purposes of this subsection 'land' does not include incorporeal hereditaments; 'tenancy' means a tenancy for years or any less period and includes an agreement for such a tenancy, but a person who after the end of a tenancy remains in possession as statutory tenant or otherwise is to be treated as having possession under the tenancy, and 'let' shall be construed accordingly.

(3) A person who picks mushrooms growing wild on any land, or who picks flowers, fruit or foliage from a plant wild on any land, does not (although not in possession of the land) steal what he picks, unless he does it for reward or for sale or other commercial purpose.

For purposes of this subsection 'mushroom' includes any fungus, and 'plant' includes any shrub or tree.

(4) Wild creatures, tamed or untamed, shall be regarded as property; but a person cannot steal a wild creature not tamed nor ordinarily kept in captivity, or the carcase of any such creature, unless either it has been reduced into possession by or on behalf of another person and possession of it has not since been lost or abandoned, or another person is in course of reducing it into possession.

## 5. 'Belonging to another'

(1) Property shall be regarded as belonging to any person having possession or control of it, or having in it any proprietary right or interest (not being an equitable interest arising only from an agreement to transfer or grant an interest).
(2) Where property is subject to a trust, the persons to whom it belongs shall be regarded as including any person having a right to enforce the trust, and an intention to defeat the trust shall be regarded accordingly as an intention to deprive of the property any person having that right.
(3) Where a person receives property from or on account of another, and is under an obligation to the other to retain and deal with that property or its proceeds in a particular way, the property or proceeds shall be regarded (as against him) as belonging to the other.

(4) Where a person gets property by another's mistake, and is under an obligation to make restoration (in whole or in part) of the property or its proceeds or of the value thereof, then to the extent of that obligation the property or proceeds shall be regarded (as against him) as belonging to the person entitled to restoration, and an intention not to make restoration shall be regarded accordingly as an intention to deprive that person of the property or proceeds.

(5) Property of a corporation sole shall be regarded as belonging to the corporation notwithstanding a vacancy in the corporation.

## 6. 'With the intention of permanently depriving the other of it'

(1) A person appropriating property belonging to another without meaning the other permanently to lose the thing itself is nevertheless to be regarded as having the intention of permanently depriving the other of it if his intention is to treat the thing as his own to dispose of regardless of the other's rights; and a borrowing or lending of it may amount to so treating it if, but only if, the borrowing or lending is for a period and in circumstances making it equivalent to an outright taking or disposal.

(2) Without prejudice to the generality of subsection (1) above, where a person, having possession or control (lawfully or not) of property belonging to another, parts with the property under a condition as to its return which he may not be able to perform, this (if done for purposes of his own and without the other's authority) amounts to treating the property as his own to dispose of regardless of the other's rights.

## 7. Theft

A person guilty of theft shall on conviction on indictment be liable to imprisonment for a term not exceeding seven years.

## 8. Robbery

(1) A person is guilty of robbery if he steals, and immediately before or at the time of doing so, and in order to do so, he uses force on any person or puts or seeks to put any person in fear of being then and there subjected to force.

## 9. Burglary

(1) A person is guilty of burglary if—

(a) he enters any building or part of a building as a trespasser and with intent to commit any such offence as is mentioned in subsection (2) below; or

(b) having entered any building or part of a building as a trespasser he steals or attempts to steal anything in the building or that part of it or inflicts or attempts to inflict on any person therein any grievous bodily harm.

(2) The offences referred to in subsection (1)(a) above are offences of stealing anything in the building or part of a building in question, of inflicting on any person therein any grievous bodily harm therein, and of doing unlawful damage to the building or anything therein.

(4) References in subsections (1) and (2) above to a building, and the reference in subsection (3) above to a building which is a dwelling, shall apply also to an inhabited vehicle or vessel, and shall apply to any such vehicle or vessel at times when the person having a habitation in it is not there as well as at times when he is.

## 10. Aggravated burglary

(1) A person is guilty of aggravated burglary if he commits any burglary and at the time has with him any firearm or imitation firearm, any weapon of offence, or any explosive; and for this purpose—

(a) 'firearm' includes an airgun or air pistol, and 'imitation firearm' means anything which has the appearance of being a firearm, whether capable of being discharged or not; and

(b) 'weapon of offence' means any article made or adapted for use for causing injury to or incapacitating a person, or intended by the person having it with him for such use; and

(c) 'explosive' means any article manufactured for the purpose of producing a practical effect by explosion, or intended by the person having it with him for that purpose.

## 11. Removal of articles from places open to the public

(1) Subject to subsections (2) and (3) below, where the public have access to a building in order to view the building or part of it, or a collection or part of a collection housed in it, any person who without lawful authority removes from the building or its grounds the whole or part of any article displayed or kept for display to the public in the building or that part of it or in its grounds shall be guilty of an offence.

For this purpose 'collection' includes a collection got together for a temporary purpose, but references in this section to a collection do not apply to a collection made or exhibited for the purpose of effecting sales or other commercial dealings.

(2) It is immaterial for purposes of subsection (1) above, that the public's access to a building is limited to a particular period or particular occasion; but where anything removed from a building or its grounds is there otherwise than as forming part of, or being on loan for exhibition with, a collection intended for permanent exhibition to the public, the person removing it does not thereby commit an offence under this section unless he removes it on a day when the public have access to the building as mentioned in subsection (1) above.

(3) A person does not commit an offence under this section if he believes that he has lawful authority for the removal of the thing in question or that he would have it if the person entitled to give it knew of the removal and the circumstances of it.

## 12. Taking motor vehicle or other conveyance without authority

(1) Subject to subsections (5) and (6) below, a person shall be guilty of an offence if, without having the consent of the owner or other lawful authority, he takes any conveyance for his own or another's use or, knowing that any conveyance has been taken without such authority, drives it or allows himself to be carried in or on it.

(2) A person guilty of an offence under subsection (1) above shall be liable on summary conviction to a fine not exceeding level 5 on the standard scale, to imprisonment for a term not exceeding six months, or to both.

(4) If on the trial of an indictment for theft the jury are not satisfied that the accused committed theft, but it is proved that the accused committed an offence under subsection (1) above, the jury may find him guilty of the offence under subsection (1) and if he is found guilty of it, he shall be liable as he would have been liable under subsection (2) above on summary conviction.

(5) Subsection (1) above shall not apply in relation to pedal cycles; but, subject to subsection (6) below, a person who, without having the consent of the owner or other lawful authority, takes a pedal cycle for his own or another's use, or rides a pedal cycle knowing it to have been taken without such authority, shall on summary conviction be liable to a fine not exceeding level 3 on the standard scale.

(6) A person does not commit an offence under this section by anything done in the belief that he has lawful authority to do it or that he would have the owner's consent if the owner knew of his doing it and the circumstances of it.

(7) For purposes of this section—

(a) 'conveyance' means any conveyance constructed or adapted for the carriage of a person or persons whether by land, water or air, except that it does not include a conveyance constructed or adapted for use only under the control of a person not carried in or on it, and 'drive' shall be construed accordingly; and

(b) 'owner', in relation to a conveyance which is the subject of a hiring agreement or hire-purchase agreement, means the person in possession of the conveyance under that agreement.

## 12A. Aggravated vehicle-taking

(1) Subject to subsection (3) below, a person is guilty of aggravated taking of a vehicle if—

(a) he commits an offence under section 12(1) above (in this section referred to as a 'basic offence') in relation to a mechanically propelled vehicle; and

(b) it is proved that, at any time after the vehicle was unlawfully taken (whether by him or another) and before it was recovered, the vehicle was driven, or injury or damage was caused, in one or more of the circumstances set out in paragraphs (a) to (d) of subsection (2) below.

(2) The circumstances referred to in subsection (1)(b) above are—
  (a) that the vehicle was driven dangerously on a road or other public place;
  (b) that, owing to the driving of the vehicle, an accident occurred by which injury was caused to any person;
  (c) that, owing to the driving of the vehicle, an accident occurred by which damage was caused to any property, other than the vehicle;
  (d) that damage was caused to the vehicle.

(3) A person is not guilty of an offence under this section if he proves that, as regards any such proven driving, injury or damage as is referred to in subsection (1)(b) above, either—
  (a) the driving, accident or damage referred to in subsection (2) above occurred before he committed the basic offence; or
  (b) he was neither in nor on nor in the immediate vicinity of the vehicle when that driving, accident or damage occurred.

(4) A person guilty of an offence under this section shall be liable on conviction on indictment to imprisonment for a term not exceeding two years or, if it is proved that, in circumstances falling within subsection (2)(b) above, the accident caused the death of the person concerned, fourteen years.

(5) If a person who is charged with an offence under this section is found not guilty of that offence but it is proved that he committed a basic offence, he may be convicted of the basic offence.

(7) For the purposes of this section a vehicle is driven dangerously if—
  (a) it is driven in a way which falls far below what would be expected of a competent and careful driver; and
  (b) it would be obvious to a competent and careful driver that driving the vehicle in that way would be dangerous.

(8) For the purposes of this section a vehicle is recovered when it is restored to its owner or to other lawful possession or custody; and in this subsection 'owner' has the same meaning as in section 12 above.

## 13. Abstracting of electricity

A person who dishonestly uses without due authority, or dishonestly causes to be wasted or diverted, any electricity shall on conviction on indictment be liable to imprisonment for a term not exceeding five years.

## 17. False accounting

(1) Where a person dishonestly, with a view to gain for himself or another or with intent to cause loss to another,—
  (a) destroys, defaces, conceals or falsifies any account or any record or document made or required for any accounting purpose; or
  (b) in furnishing information for any purpose produces or makes use of any account, or any such record or document as aforesaid, which to his knowledge is or may be misleading, false or deceptive in a material particular;

he shall, on conviction on indictment, be liable to imprisonment for a term not exceeding seven years.

(2) For purposes of this section a person who makes or concurs in making in an account or other document an entry which is or may be misleading, false or deceptive in a material particular, or who omits or concurs in omitting a material particular from an account or other document, is to be treated as falsifying the account or document.

## 18. Liability of company officers for certain offences by company

(1) Where an offence committed by a body corporate under section 17 of this Act is proved to have been committed with the consent or connivance of any director, manager, secretary or other similar officer of the body corporate, or any person who was purporting to act in any such capacity, he as well as the body corporate shall be guilty of that offence, and shall be liable to be proceeded against and punished accordingly.

(2) Where the affairs of a body corporate are managed by its members, this section shall apply in relation to the acts and defaults of a member in connection with his functions of management as if he were a director of the body corporate.

## 19. False statements by company directors, etc.

(1) Where an officer of a body corporate or unincorporated association (or person purporting to act as such), with intent to deceive members or creditors of the body corporate or association about its affairs, publishes or concurs in publishing a written statement or account which to his knowledge is or may be misleading, false or deceptive in a material particular, he shall on conviction on indictment be liable to imprisonment for a term not exceeding seven years.

(2) For purposes of this section a person who has entered into a security for the benefit of a body corporate or association is to be treated as a creditor of it.

(3) Where the affairs of a body corporate or association are managed by its members, this section shall apply to any statement which a member publishes or concurs in publishing in connection with his functions of management as if he were an officer of the body corporate or association.

## 20. Suppression, etc. of documents

(1) A person who dishonestly, with a view to gain for himself or another or with intent to cause loss to another, destroys, defaces or conceals any valuable security, any will or other testamentary document or any original document of or belonging to, or filed or deposited in, any court of justice or any government department shall on conviction on indictment be liable to imprisonment for a term not exceeding seven years.

(3) For purposes of this section 'valuable security' means any document creating, transferring, surrendering or releasing any right to, in or over property, or authorising the payment of money or delivery of any property, or evidencing the creation, transfer, surrender or release of any such right, or the payment of money or delivery of any property, or the satisfaction of any obligation.

## 21. Blackmail

(1) A person is guilty of blackmail if, with a view to gain for himself or another or with intent to cause loss to another, he makes any unwarranted demand with menaces; and for this purpose a demand with menaces is unwarranted unless the person making it does so in the belief—

(a) that he has reasonable grounds for making the demand; and

(b) that the use of the menaces is a proper means of reinforcing the demand.

(2) The nature of the act or omission demanded is immaterial, and it is also immaterial whether the menaces relate to action to be taken by the person making the demand.

## 22. Handling stolen goods

(1) A person handles stolen goods if (otherwise than in the course of the stealing) knowing or believing them to be stolen goods he dishonestly receives the goods, or dishonestly undertakes or assists in their retention, removal, disposal or realisation by or for the benefit of another person, or if he arranges to do so.

## 23. Advertising rewards for return of goods stolen or lost

Where any public advertisement of a reward for the return of any goods which have been stolen or lost uses any words to the effect that no questions will be asked, or that the person producing the goods will be safe from apprehension or inquiry, or that money paid for the purchase of the goods or advanced by way of loan on them will be repaid, the person advertising the reward and any person who prints or publishes the advertisement shall on summary conviction be liable to a fine not exceeding level 3 on the standard scale.

## 24. Scope of offences relating to stolen goods

(1) The provisions of this Act relating to goods which have been stolen shall apply whether the stealing occurred in England or Wales or elsewhere, and whether it occurred before or after the commencement of this Act, provided that the stealing (if not an offence under this Act) amounted to an offence where and at the time when the foods were stolen; and references to stolen goods shall be construed accordingly.

(2) For purposes of those provisions references to stolen goods shall include, in addition to the goods originally stolen and parts of them (whether in their original state or not),—

(a) any other goods which directly or indirectly represent or have at any time represented the stolen goods in the hands of the thief as being the proceeds of any disposal or realisation of the whole or part of the goods stolen or of goods so representing the stolen goods; and

(b) any other goods which directly or indirectly represent or have at any time represented the stolen goods in the hands of a handler of the stolen goods or any part of them as being the proceeds of any disposal or realisation of the whole or part of the stolen goods handled by him or of goods so representing them.

(3) But no goods shall be regarded as having continued to be stolen goods after they have been restored to the person from whom they were stolen or to other lawful possession or custody, or after that person and any other person claiming through him have otherwise ceased as regards those goods to have any right to restitution in respect of the theft.

(4) For purposes of the provisions of this Act relating to goods which have been stolen (including subsections (1) to (3) above) goods obtained in England or Wales or elsewhere either by blackmail or, subject to subsection (5) below, by fraud (within the meaning of the Fraud Act 2006) shall be regarded as stolen; and 'steal', 'theft' and 'thief' shall be construed accordingly.

(5) Subsection (1) above applies in relation to goods obtained by fraud as if—

(a) the reference to the commencement of this Act were a reference to the commencement of the Fraud Act 2006, and

(b) the reference to an offence under this Act were a reference to an offence under section 1 of that Act.

## 24A. Dishonestly retaining a wrongful credit

(1) A person is guilty of an offence if—

(a) a wrongful credit has been made to an account kept by him or in respect of which he has any right or interest;

(b) he knows or believes that the credit is wrongful; and

(c) he dishonestly fails to take such steps as are reasonable in the circumstances to secure that the credit is cancelled.

(2) References to a credit are to a credit of an amount of money.

(5) In determining whether a credit to an account is wrongful, it is immaterial (in particular) whether the account is overdrawn before or after the credit is made.

(6) A person guilty of an offence under this section shall be liable on conviction on indictment to imprisonment for a term not exceeding ten years.

(7) Subsection (8) below applies for purposes of provisions of this Act relating to stolen goods (including subsection (2A) above).

(8) References to stolen goods include money which is dishonestly withdrawn from an account to which a wrongful credit has been made, but only to the extent that the money derives from the credit.

(9) 'Account' means an account kept with—

(a) a bank;

(b) a person carrying on a business which falls within subsection (10) below; or

(c) a person falling within any of paragraphs (a) to (j) of the definition of 'electronic money issuer' in regulation 2(1) of the Electronic Money Regulations 2011.

(10) A business falls within this subsection if—

(a) in the course of the business money received by way of deposit is lent to others; or

(b) any other activity of the business is financed, wholly or to any material extent, out of the capital of or the interest on money received by way of deposit.

(11) References in subsection (10) above to a deposit must be read with—

(a) section 22 of the Financial Services and Markets Act 2000;

(b) any relevant order under that section; and

(c) Schedule 2 to that Act;

but any restriction on the meaning of deposit which arises from the identity of the person making it is to be disregarded.

(12) For the purposes of subsection (10) above—

(a) all the activities which a person carries on by way of business shall be regarded as a single business carried on by him; and

(b) 'money' includes money expressed in a currency other than sterling.

**25. Going equipped for stealing, etc.**

(1) A person shall be guilty of an offence if, when not at his place of abode, he has with him any article for use in the course of or in connection with any burglary or theft.

(2) A person guilty of an offence under this section shall on conviction on indictment be liable to imprisonment for a term not exceeding three years.

(3) Where a person is charged with an offence under this section, proof that he had with him any article made or adapted for use in committing a burglary or theft ... shall be evidence that he had it with him for such use.

(5) For purposes of this section an offence under section 12(1) of this Act of taking a conveyance shall be treated as theft.

**27. Evidence and procedure on charge of theft or handling stolen goods**

(3) Where a person is being proceeded against for handling stolen goods (but not for any offence other than handling stolen goods), then at any stage of the proceedings, if evidence has been given of his having or arranging to have in his possession the goods the subject of the charge, or of his undertaking or assisting in, or arranging to undertake or assist in, their retention, removal, disposal or realisation, the following evidence shall be admissible for the purpose of proving that he knew or believed the goods to be stolen goods:—

(a) evidence that he has had in his possession, or has undertaken or assisted in the retention, removal, disposal or realisation of, stolen goods from any theft taking place not earlier than twelve months before the offence charged; and

(b) (provided that seven days' notice in writing has been given to him of the intention to prove the conviction) evidence that he has within the five years preceding the date of the offence charged been convicted of theft or of handling stolen goods.

**32. Effect on existing law and construction of references to offences**

(1) The following offences are hereby abolished for all purposes not relating to offences committed before the commencement of this Act, that is to say—

(a) any offence at common law of larceny, robbery, burglary, receiving stolen property, obtaining property by threats, extortion by colour of office or franchise, false accounting by public officers, concealment of treasure trove and, except as regards offences relating to the public revenue, cheating.

**34. Interpretation**

(1) Sections 4(1) and 5(1) of this Act shall apply generally for purposes of this Act as they apply for purposes of section 1.

(2) For purposes of this Act—

(a) 'gain' and 'loss' are to be construed as extending only to gain or loss in money or other property, but as extending to any such gain or loss whether temporary or permanent; and—

(i) 'gain' includes a gain by keeping what one has, as well as a gain by getting what one has not; and

(ii) 'loss' includes a loss by not getting what one might get, as well as a loss by parting with what one has;

(b) 'goods', except in so far as the context otherwise requires, includes money and every other description of property except land, and includes things severed from the land by stealing.

## TATTOOING OF MINORS ACT 1969

**1. Prohibition of tattooing of minors**

It shall be an offence to tattoo a person under the age of eighteen except when the tattoo is performed for medical reasons by a duly qualified medical practitioner or by a person working under his direction, but it shall be a defence for a person charged to show that at the time the tattoo was performed he had reasonable cause to believe that the person tattooed was of or over the age of eighteen and did in fact so believe.

### 3. Definition

For the purposes of this Act 'tattoo' shall mean the insertion into the skin of any colouring material designed to leave a permanent mark.

## CRIMINAL DAMAGE ACT 1971

### 1. Destroying or damaging property

(1) A person who without lawful excuse destroys or damages any property belonging to another intending to destroy or damage any such property or being reckless as to whether any such property would be destroyed or damaged shall be guilty of an offence.

(2) A person who without lawful excuse destroys or damages any property, whether belonging to himself or another—
- (a) intending to destroy or damage any property or being reckless as to whether any property would be destroyed or damaged; and
- (b) intending by the destruction or damage to endanger the life of another or being reckless as to whether the life of another would be thereby endangered; shall be guilty of an offence.

(3) An offence committed under this section by destroying or damaging property by fire shall be charged as arson.

### 2. Threats to destroy or damage property

A person who without lawful excuse makes to another a threat, intending that that other would fear it would be carried out,—
- (a) to destroy or damage any property belonging to that other or a third person; or
- (b) to destroy or damage his own property in a way which he knows is likely to endanger the life of that other or a third person;

shall be guilty of an offence.

### 3. Possessing anything with intent to destroy or damage property

A person who has anything in his custody or under his control intending without lawful excuse to use it or cause or permit another to use it—
- (a) to destroy or damage any property belonging to some other person; or
- (b) to destroy or damage his own or the user's property in a way which he knows is likely to endanger the life of some other person;

shall be guilty of an offence.

### 4. Punishment of offences

(1) A person guilty of arson under section 1 above or of an offence under section 1 (2) above (whether arson or not) shall on conviction on indictment be liable to imprisonment for life.

(2) A person guilty of any other offence under this Act shall on conviction on indictment be liable to imprisonment for a term not exceeding ten years.

### 5. 'Without lawful excuse'

(1) This section applies to any offence under section 1(1) above and any offence under section 2 or 3 above other than one involving a threat by the person charged to destroy or damage property in a way which he knows is likely to endanger the life of another or involving an intent by the person charged to use or cause or permit the use of something in his custody or under his control so to destroy or damage property.

(2) A person charged with an offence to which this section applies shall whether or not he would be treated for the purposes of this Act as having a lawful excuse apart from this subsection, be treated for those purposes as having a lawful excuse—
- (a) if at the time of the act or acts alleged to constitute the offence he believed that the person or persons whom he believed to be entitled to consent to the destruction of or damage to the property in question had so consented, or would have so consented to it if he or they had known of the destruction or damage and its circumstances; or

(b) if he destroyed or damaged or threatened to destroy or damage the property in question or, in the case of a charge of an offence under section 3 above, intended to use or cause or permit the use of something to destroy or damage it, in order to protect property belonging to himself or another or a right or interest in property which was or which he believed to be vested in himself or another, and at the time of the act or acts alleged to constitute the offence he believed—
(i) that the property, right or interest was in immediate need of protection; and
(ii) that the means of protection adopted or proposed to be adopted were or would be reasonable having regard to all the circumstances.

(3) For the purposes of this section it is immaterial whether a belief is justified or not if it is honestly held.

(4) For the purposes of subsection (2) above a right or interest in property includes any right or privilege in or over land, whether created by grant, licence or otherwise.

(5) This section shall not be construed as casting doubt on any defence recognised by law as a defence to criminal charges.

### 10. Interpretation

(1) In this Act 'property' means property of a tangible nature, whether real or personal, including money and—
(a) including wild creatures which have been tamed or are ordinarily kept in captivity, and any other wild creatures or their carcasses if, but only if, they have been reduced into possession which has not been lost or abandoned or are in the course of being reduced into possession; but
(b) not including mushrooms growing wild on any land or flowers, fruit or foliage of a plant growing wild on any land.

For the purposes of this subsection 'mushroom' includes any fungus and 'plant' includes any shrub or tree.

(2) Property shall be treated for the purposes of this Act as belonging to any person—
(a) having the custody or control of it;
(b) having in it any proprietary right or interest (not being an equitable interest arising only from an agreement to transfer or grant an interest); or
(c) having a charge on it.

(3) Where property is subject to a trust, the persons to whom it belongs shall be so treated as including any person having a right to enforce the trust.

(4) Property of a corporation sole shall be so treated as belonging to the corporation notwithstanding a vacancy in the corporation.

(5) For the purposes of this Act a modification of the contents of a computer shall not be regarded as damaging any computer or computer storage medium unless its effect on that computer or computer storage medium impairs its physical condition.

## MISUSE OF DRUGS ACT 1971

### 2. Controlled drugs and their classification for purposes of this Act

(1) In this Act—
(a) the expression 'controlled drug' means any substance or product for the time being specified—
(i) in Part I, II or III of Schedule 2, or
(ii) in a temporary class drug order as a drug subject to temporary control (but this is subject to section 2A(6));
(b) the expressions 'Class A drug', 'Class B drug', and 'Class C drug' mean any of the substances and products for the time being specified respectively in Part I, Part II and Part III of that Schedule;
(c) the expression 'temporary class drug' means any substance or product which is for the time being a controlled drug by virtue of a temporary class drug order;

and the provisions of Part IV of that Schedule shall have effect with respect to the meanings of expressions used in that Schedule.

## 2A. Temporary class drug orders

(1) The Secretary of State may make an order (referred to in this Act as a 'temporary class drug order') specifying any substance or product as a drug subject to temporary control if the following two conditions are met.

(2) The first condition is that the substance or product is not a Class A drug, a Class B drug or a Class C drug.

(3) The second condition is that—
- (a) the Secretary of State has consulted in accordance with section 2B and has determined that the order should be made, or
- (b) the Secretary of State has received a recommendation under that section that the order should be made.

(4) The Secretary of State may make the determination mentioned in subsection (3)(a) only if it appears to the Secretary of State that—
- (a) the substance or product is a drug that is being, or is likely to be, misused, and
- (b) that misuse is having, or is capable of having, harmful effects.

(5) A substance or product may be specified in a temporary class drug order by reference to—
- (a) the name of the substance or product, or
- (b) a description of the substance or product (which may take such form as the Secretary of State thinks appropriate for the purposes of the specification).

## 2B. Orders under section 2A: role of Advisory Council etc.

(1) Before making an order under section 2A the Secretary of State—
- (a) must consult as mentioned in subsection (2), or
- (b) must have received a recommendation from the Advisory Council to make the order.

(2) The Secretary of State must consult—
- (a) the Advisory Council, or
- (b) if the order is to be made under section 2A(1) and the urgency condition applies, the person mentioned in subsection (3).

(3) The person referred to in subsection (2)(b) is—
- (a) the person who is for the time being the chairman of the Advisory Council appointed under paragraph 1(3) of Schedule 1, or
- (b) if that person has delegated the function of responding to consultation under subsection (1)(a) to another member of the Advisory Council, that other member.

(4) The 'urgency condition' applies if it appears to the Secretary of State that the misuse of the substance or product to be specified in the order as a drug subject to temporary control, or the likelihood of its misuse, poses an urgent and significant threat to public safety or health.

(5) The duty of the Advisory Council or any other person consulted under subsection (1)(a) is limited to giving to the Secretary of State that person's opinion as to whether the order in question should be made.

(6) A recommendation under subsection (1)(b) that a temporary class drug order should be made may be given by the Advisory Council only if it appears to the Council that—
- (a) the substance or product is a drug that is being, or is likely to be, misused, and
- (b) that misuse is having, or is capable of having, harmful effects.

## 3. Restriction of importation and exportation of controlled drugs

(1) Subject to subsection (2) below—
- (a) the importation of a controlled drug; and
- (b) the exportation of a controlled drug, are hereby prohibited.

(2) Subsection (1) above does not apply—
- (a) to the importation or exportation of a controlled drug which is for the time being excepted from paragraph (a) or, as the case may be, paragraph (b) of subsection (1) above by regulations under section 7 of this Act or by provision made in a temporary class drug order by virtue of section 7A; or
- (b) to the importation or exportation of a controlled drug under and in accordance with the terms of a licence issued by the Secretary of State and in compliance with any conditions attached thereto.

## 4. Restriction of production and supply of controlled drugs

(1) Subject to any regulations under section 7 of this Act, or any provision made in a temporary class drug order by virtue of section 7A, for the time being in force, it shall not be lawful for a person—
- (a) to produce a controlled drug; or
- (b) to supply or offer to supply a controlled drug to another.

(2) Subject to section 28 of this Act, it is an offence for a person—
- (a) to produce a controlled drug in contravention of subsection (1) above; or
- (b) to be concerned in the production of such a drug in contravention of that subsection by another.

(3) Subject to section 28 of this Act, it is an offence for a person—
- (a) to supply or offer to supply a controlled drug to another in contravention of subsection (1) above; or
- (b) to be concerned in the supplying of such a drug to another in contravention of that subsection; or
- (c) to be concerned in the making to another in contravention of that subsection of an offer to supply such a drug.

## 4A. Aggravation of offence of supply of controlled drug

(1) This section applies if—
- (a) a court is considering the seriousness of an offence under section 4(3) of this Act, and
- (b) at the time the offence was committed the offender had attained the age of 18.

(2) If either of the following conditions is met the court—
- (a) must treat the fact that the condition is met as an aggravating factor (that is to say, a factor that increases the seriousness of the offence), and
- (b) must state in open court that the offence is so aggravated.

(3) The first condition is that the offence was committed on or in the vicinity of school premises at a relevant time.

(4) The second condition is that in connection with the commission of the offence the offender used a courier who, at the time the offence was committed, was under the age of 18.

(5) In subsection (3), a relevant time is—
- (a) any time when the school premises are in use by persons under the age of 18;
- (b) one hour before the start and one hour after the end of any such time.

(6) For the purposes of subsection (4), a person uses a courier in connection with an offence under section 4(3) of this Act if he causes or permits another person (the courier)—
- (a) to deliver a controlled drug to a third person, or
- (b) to deliver a drug related consideration to himself or a third person.

(7) For the purposes of subsection (6), a drug related consideration is a consideration of any description which—
- (a) is obtained in connection with the supply of a controlled drug, or
- (b) is intended to be used in connection with obtaining a controlled drug.

(8) In this section—
'school premises' means land used for the purposes of a school excluding any land occupied solely as a dwelling by a person employed at the school; and 'school' has the same meaning—
- (a) in England and Wales, as in section 4 of the Education Act 1996;
- (b) in Scotland, as in section 135(1) of the Education (Scotland) Act 1980;
- (c) in Northern Ireland, as in Article 2(2) of the Education and Libraries (Northern Ireland) Order 1986.

## 5. Restriction of possession of controlled drugs

(1) Subject to any regulations under section 7 of this Act for the time being in force, it shall not be lawful for a person to have a controlled drug in his possession.

(2) Subject to section 28 of this Act and to subsection (4) below, it is an offence for a person to have a controlled drug in his possession in contravention of subsection (1) above.

(2A) Subsections (1) and (2) do not apply in relation to a temporary class drug.

(3) Subject to section 28 of this Act, it is an offence for a person to have a controlled drug in his possession, whether lawfully or not, with intent to supply it to another in contravention of section 4(1) of this Act.

(4) In any proceedings for an offence under subsection (2) above in which it is proved that the accused had a controlled drug in his possession, it shall be a defence for him to prove—

(a) that, knowing or suspecting it to be a controlled drug, he took possession of it for the purpose of preventing another from committing or continuing to commit an offence in connection with that drug and that as soon as possible after taking possession of it he took all such steps as were reasonably open to him to destroy the drug or to deliver it into the custody of a person lawfully entitled to take custody of it; or

(b) that, knowing or suspecting it to be a controlled drug, he took possession of it for the purpose of delivering it into the custody of a person lawfully entitled to take custody of it and that as soon as possible after taking possession of it he took all such steps as were reasonably open to him to deliver it into the custody of such a person.

(6) Nothing in subsection (4) above shall prejudice any defence which is open to a person charged with an offence under this section to raise apart from that subsection.

## 6. Restriction of cultivation of cannabis plants

(1) Subject to any regulations under section 7 of this Act for the time being in force, it shall not be lawful for a person to cultivate any plant of the genus Cannabis.

(2) Subject to section 28 of this Act, it is an offence to cultivate any such plant in contravention of subsection (1) above.

## 7. Authorisation of activities otherwise unlawful under foregoing provisions

(1) The Secretary of State may by regulations—

(a) except from section 3(1)(a) or (b), 4(1)(a) or (b) or 5(1) of this Act such controlled drugs as may be specified in the regulations; and

(b) make such other provision as he thinks fit for the purpose of making it lawful for persons to do things which under any of the following provisions of this Act, that is to say sections 4(1), 5(1) and 6(1), it would otherwise be unlawful for them to do.

(2) Without prejudice to the generality of paragraph (b) of subsection (1) above, regulations under that subsection authorising the doing of any such thing as is mentioned in that paragraph may in particular provide for the doing of that thing to be lawful—

(a) if it is done under and in accordance with the terms of a licence or other authority issued by the Secretary of State and in compliance with any conditions attached thereto; or

(b) if it is done in compliance with such conditions as may be prescribed.

(3) Subject to subsection (4) below, the Secretary of State shall so exercise his power to make regulations under subsection (1) above as to secure—

(a) that it is not unlawful under section 4(1) of this Act for a doctor, dentist, veterinary practitioner or veterinary surgeon, acting in his capacity as such, to prescribe, administer, manufacture, compound or supply a controlled drug, or for a pharmacist or a person lawfully conducting a retail pharmacy business, acting in either case in his capacity as such, to manufacture, compound or supply a controlled drug; and

(b) that it is not unlawful under section 5(1) of this Act for a doctor, dentist, veterinary practitioner, veterinary surgeon, pharmacist or person lawfully conducting a retail pharmacy business to have a controlled drug in his possession for the purpose of acting in his capacity as such.

(4) If in the case of any controlled drug the Secretary of State is of the opinion that it is in the public interest—

(a) for production, supply and possession of that drug to be either wholly unlawful or unlawful except for purposes of research or other special purposes; or

(b) for it to be unlawful for practitioners, pharmacists and persons lawfully conducting retail pharmacy business to do in relation to that drug any of the things mentioned in subsection (3) above except under a licence or other authority issued by the Secretary of State,

he may by order designate that drug as a drug to which this subsection applies; and while there is in force an order under this subsection designating a controlled drug as one to which this subsection applies subsection (3) above shall not apply as regards that drug.

(8) References in this section to a person's 'doing' things include references to his having things in his possession.

## 7A. Temporary class drug orders: power to make further provision

(1) This section applies if a temporary class drug order specifies a substance or product as a drug subject to temporary control.

(2) The order may—

(a) include provision for the exception of the drug from the application of section 3(1)(a) or (b) or 4(1)(a) or (b),

(b) make such other provision as the Secretary of State thinks fit for the purpose of making it lawful for persons to do things in respect of the drug which under section 4(1) it would otherwise be unlawful for them to do,

(c) provide for circumstances in which a person's possession of the drug is to be treated as excepted possession for the purposes of this Act, and

(d) include any provision in relation to the drug of a kind that could be made in regulations under section 10 or 22 if the drug were a Class A drug, a Class B drug or a Class C drug (but ignoring section 31(3)).

(3) Provision under subsection (2) may take the form of applying (with or without modifications) any provision made in regulations under section 7(1), 10 or 22.

(4) Provision under subsection (2)(b) may (in particular) provide for the doing of something to be lawful if it is done—

(a) in circumstances mentioned in section 7(2)(a), or

(b) in compliance with such conditions as may be prescribed by virtue of section 7(2)(b).

(5) Section 7(8) applies for the purposes of this section.

(6) Section 31(1) (general provision as to regulations) applies in relation to a temporary class drug order that contains provision made by virtue of this section as it applies to regulations under this Act.

## 8. Occupiers etc., of premises to be punishable for permitting certain activities to take place there

A person commits an offence if, being the occupier or concerned in the management of any premises, he knowingly permits or suffers any of the following activities to take place on those premises, that is to say—

(a) producing or attempting to produce a controlled drug in contravention of section 4(1) of this Act;

(b) supplying or attempting to supply a controlled drug to another in contravention of section 4(1) of this Act, or offering to supply a controlled drug to another in contravention of section 4(1);

(c) preparing opium for smoking;

(d) smoking cannabis, cannabis resin or prepared opium.

## 9. Prohibition of certain activities etc., relating to opium

Subject to section 28 of this Act, it is an offence for a person—

(a) to smoke or otherwise use prepared opium; or

(b) to frequent a place used for the purpose of opium smoking; or

(c) to have in his possession—

(i) any pipes or other utensils made or adapted for use in connection with the smoking of opium, being pipes or utensils which have been used by him or with his knowledge and permission in that connection or which he intends to use or permit others to use in that connection; or

(ii) any utensils which have been used by him or with his knowledge and permission in connection with the preparation of opium for smoking.

## 9A. Prohibition of supply etc., of articles for administering or preparing controlled drugs

(1) A person who supplies or offers to supply any article which may be used or adapted to be used (whether by itself or in combination with another article or other articles) in the administration by any person of a controlled drug to himself or another, believing that the article (or the article as adapted) is to be so used in circumstances where the administration is unlawful, is guilty of an offence.

(2) It is not an offence under subsection (1) above to supply or offer to supply a hypodermic syringe, or any part of one.

(3) A person who supplies or offers to supply any article which may be used to prepare a controlled drug for administration by any person to himself or another believing that the article is to be so used in circumstances where the administration is unlawful is guilty of an offence.

(4) For the purposes of this section, any administration of a controlled drug is unlawful except—

(a) the administration by any person of a controlled drug to another in circumstances where the administration of the drug is not unlawful under section 4(1) of this Act, or

(b) the administration by any person of a controlled drug to himself in circumstances where having the controlled drug in his possession is not unlawful under section 5(1) of this Act.

(5) In this section, references to administration by any person of a controlled drug to himself include a reference to his administering it to himself with the assistance of another.

## 19. Attempts etc., to commit offences

It is an offence for a person to incite another to commit an offence under any other provision of this Act.

## 20. Assisting in or inducing commission outside United Kingdom of offence punishable under a corresponding law

A person commits an offence if in the United Kingdom he assists in or induces the commission in any place outside the United Kingdom of an offence punishable under the provisions of a corresponding law in force in that place.

## 28. Proof of lack of knowledge etc., to be a defence in proceedings for certain offences

(1) This section applies to offences under any of the following provisions of this Act; that is to say section 4(2) and (3), section 5(2) and (3), section 6(2) and section 9.

(2) Subject to subsection (3) below, in any proceedings for an offence to which this section applies it shall be a defence for the accused to prove that he neither knew of nor suspected nor had reason to suspect the existence of some fact alleged by the prosecution which is necessary for the prosecution to prove if he is to be convicted of the offence charged.

(3) Where in any proceedings for an offence to which this section applies it is necessary, if the accused is to be convicted of the offence charged, for the prosecution to prove that some substance or product involved in the alleged offence was the controlled drug which the prosecution alleges it to have been, and it is proved that the substance or product in question was that controlled drug, the accused—

(a) shall not be acquitted of the offence charged by reason only of proving that he neither knew or suspected nor had reason to suspect that the substance or product in question was the particular controlled drug alleged; but

(b) shall be acquitted thereof—

(i) if he proves that he neither believed nor suspected nor had reason to suspect that the substance or product in question was a controlled drug; or

(ii) if he proves that he believed the substance or product in question to be a controlled drug, or a controlled drug of a description, such that, if it had in fact been that controlled drug or a controlled drug of that description, he would not at the material time have been committing any offence to which this section applies.

(4) Nothing in this section shall prejudice any defence which it is open to a person charged with an offence to which this section applies to raise apart from this section.

### 36. Meaning of 'corresponding law', and evidence of certain matters by certificate

(1) In this Act the expression 'corresponding law' means a law stated in a certificate purporting to be issued by or on behalf of the government of a country outside the United Kingdom to be a law providing for the control and regulation in that country of the production, supply, use, export and import of drugs and other substances in accordance with the provisions of the Single Convention on Narcotic Drugs signed at New York on 30th March 1961 or a law providing for the control and regulation in that country of the production, supply, use, export and import of dangerous or otherwise harmful drugs in pursuance of any treaty, convention or other agreement or arrangement to which the government of that country and Her Majesty's Government in the United Kingdom are for the time being parties.

### 37. Interpretation

(1) In this Act, except in so far as the context otherwise requires, the following expressions have the meanings hereby assigned to them respectively, that is to say:—
'produce', where the reference is to producing a controlled drug, means producing it by manufacture, cultivation or any other method and 'production' has a corresponding meaning;
'supplying' includes distributing ...

(2) References in this Act to misusing a drug are references to misusing it by taking it; and the reference in the foregoing provision to the taking of a drug is a reference to the taking of it by a human being by way of any form of self-administration, whether or not involving assistance by another.

(3) For the purposes of this Act the things which a person has in his possession shall be taken to include anything subject to his control which is in the custody of another.

## CRIMINAL LAW ACT 1977

### 1. The offence of conspiracy

(1) Subject to the following provisions of this Part of this Act, if a person agrees with any other person or persons that a course of conduct shall be pursued which, if the agreement is carried out in accordance with their intentions, either—

(a) will necessarily amount to or involve the commission of any offence or offences by one or more parties to the agreement, or

(b) would do so but for the existence of facts which render the commission of the offence or any offences impossible,

he is guilty of conspiracy to commit the offence or offences in question.

(2) Where liability for any offence may be incurred without knowledge on the part of the person committing it of any particular fact or circumstance necessary for the commission of the offence, a person shall nevertheless not be guilty of conspiracy to commit that offence by virtue of subsection (1) above unless he and at least one other party to the agreement intend or know that that fact or circumstance shall or will exist at the time when the conduct constituting the offence is to take place.

(4) In this Part of this Act 'offence' means an offence triable in England and Wales.

### 1A. Conspiracy to commit offences outside England and Wales

(1) Where each of the following conditions is satisfied in the case of an agreement, this Part of this Act has effect in relation to the agreement as it has effect in relation to an agreement falling within section 1 (1) above.

(2) The first condition is that the pursuit of the agreed course of conduct would at some stage involve—

(a) an act by one or more of the parties, or

(b) the happening of some other event, intended to take place in a country or territory outside England and Wales.

(3) The second condition is that that act or other event constitutes an offence under the law in force in that country or territory.
(4) The third condition is that the agreement would fall within section 1(1) above as an agreement relating to the commission of an offence but for the fact that the offence would not be an offence triable in England and Wales if committed in accordance with the parties' intentions.
(5) The fourth condition is that—
  (a) a party to the agreement, or a party's agent, did anything in England and Wales in relation to the agreement before its formation, or
  (b) a party to the agreement became a party in England and Wales (by joining it either in person or through an agent), or
  (c) a party to the agreement, or a party's agent, did or omitted anything in England and Wales in pursuance of the agreement.
(6) In the application of this Part of this Act to an agreement in the case of which each of the above conditions is satisfied, a reference to an offence is to be read as a reference to what would be the offence in question but for the fact that it is not an offence triable in England and Wales.
(7) Conduct punishable under the law in force in any country or territory is an offence under that law for the purposes of this section, however it is described in that law.
(8) Subject to subsection (9) below, the second condition is to be taken to be satisfied unless, not later than rules of court may provide, the defence serve on the prosecution a notice—
  (a) stating that, on the facts as alleged with respect to the agreed course of conduct, the condition is not in their opinion satisfied.
  (b) showing their grounds for that opinion, and
  (c) requiring the prosecution to show that it is satisfied.
(9) The court may permit the defence to require the prosecution to show that the second condition is satisfied without the prior service of a notice under subsection (8) above.
(10) In the Crown Court the question whether the second condition is satisfied shall be decided by the judge alone, and shall be treated as a question of law for the purposes of—
  (a) section 9(3) of the Criminal Justice Act 1987 (preparatory hearing in fraud cases), and
  (b) section 31(3) of the Criminal Procedure and Investigations Act 1996 (preparatory hearing in other cases).
(11) Any act done by means of a message (however communicated) is to be treated for the purposes of the fourth condition as done in England and Wales if the message is sent or received in England and Wales.
(12) In any proceedings in respect of an offence triable by virtue of this section, it is immaterial to guilt whether or not the accused was a British citizen at the time of any act or other event proof of which is required for conviction of the offence.
(13) References in any enactment, instrument or document (except those in this Part of this Act) to an offence of conspiracy to commit an offence include an offence triable in England and Wales as such a conspiracy by virtue of this section (without prejudice to subsection (6)
(14) Nothing in this section applies to an agreement entered into before 4 September 1998.
(15) In relation to an agreement entered into during the period beginning with that date and ending with the commencement of section 72(1) of the Coroners and Justice Act 2009, this section applies as if in subsection (2) for 'England and Wales' there were substituted 'the United Kingdom'.
(16) Nothing in this section imposes criminal liability on any person acting on behalf of, or holding office under, the Crown.

## 2. Exemptions from liability for conspiracy

(1) A person shall not by virtue of section 1 above be guilty of conspiracy to commit any offence if he is an intended victim of that offence.
(2) A person shall not by virtue of section 1 above be guilty of conspiracy to commit any offence or offences if the only other person or persons with whom he agrees are (both

initially and at all times during the currency of the agreement) persons of any one or more of the following descriptions, that is to say—

(a) his spouse or civil partner;

(b) a person under the age of criminal responsibility; and

(c) an intended victim of that offence or of each of those offences.

(3) A person is under the age of criminal responsibility for the purposes of subsection (2)(b) above so long as it is conclusively presumed, by virtue of section 50 of the Children and Young Persons Act 1933, that he cannot be guilty of any offence.

## 4. Restrictions on the institution of proceedings for conspiracy

(1) Subject to subsection (2) below proceedings under section 1 above for conspiracy to commit any offence shall not be instituted against any person except by or with the consent of the Director of Public Prosecutions if the offence or (as the case may be) each of the offences in question is a summary offence.

(2) In relation to the institution of proceedings under section 1 above for conspiracy to commit—

(a) an offence which is subject to a prohibition by or under any enactment on the institution of proceedings otherwise than by, or on behalf or with the consent of, the Attorney-General, or

(b) two or more offences of which at least one is subject to such a prohibition,

subsection (1) above shall have effect with the substitution of a reference to the Attorney-General for the reference to the Director of Public Prosecutions.

(3) Any prohibition by or under any enactment on the institution of proceedings for any offence which is not a summary offence otherwise than by, or on behalf or with the consent of, the Director of Public Prosecutions or any other person shall apply also in relation to proceedings under section 1 above for conspiracy to commit that offence.

(4) Where—

(a) an offence has been committed in pursuance of any agreement; and

(b) proceedings may not be instituted for that offence because any time limit applicable to the institution of any such proceedings has expired,

proceedings under section 1 above for conspiracy to commit that offence shall not be instituted against any person on the basis of that agreement.

(5) Subject to subsection (6) below, no proceedings for an offence triable by virtue of section 1A above may be instituted except by or with the consent of the Attorney General.

(6) The Secretary of State may by order provide that subsection (5) above shall not apply, or shall not apply to any case of a description specified in the order.

(7) An order under subsection (6) above—

(a) shall be made by statutory instrument, and

(b) shall not be made unless a draft has been laid before, and approved by resolution of, each House of Parliament.

## 5. Abolitions, savings, transitional provisions, consequential amendment and repeals

(1) Subject to the following provisions of this section, the offence of conspiracy at common law is hereby abolished.

(2) Subsection (1) above shall not affect the offence of conspiracy at common law so far as relates to conspiracy to defraud.

(3) Subsection (1) above shall not affect the offence of conspiracy at common law if and in so far as it may be committed by entering into an agreement to engage in conduct which—

(a) tends to corrupt public morals or outrages public decency; but

(b) would not amount to or involve the commission of an offence if carried out by a single person otherwise than in pursuance of an agreement.

(6) The rules laid down by sections 1 and 2 above shall apply for determining whether a person is guilty of an offence of conspiracy under any enactment other than section 1 above, but conduct which is an offence under any such other enactment shall not also be an offence under section 1 above.

(7) ...
(8) The fact that the person or persons who, so far as appears from the indictment on which any person has been convicted of conspiracy, were the only other parties to the agreement on which his conviction was based have been acquitted of conspiracy by reference to that agreement (whether after being tried with the person convicted or separately) shall not be a ground for quashing his conviction unless under all the circumstances of the case his conviction is inconsistent with the acquittal of the other person or persons in question.
(9) Any rule of law or practice inconsistent with the provisions of subsection (8) above is hereby abolished.

## 6. Violence for securing entry

(1) Subject to the following provisions of this section, any person who, without lawful authority, uses or threatens violence for the purpose of securing entry into any premises for himself or for any other person is guilty of an offence, provided that—
   (a) there is someone present on those premises at the time who is opposed to the entry which the violence is intended to secure; and
   (b) the person using or threatening the violence knows that that is the case.
(1A) Subsection (1) above does not apply to a person who is a displaced residential occupier or a protected intending occupier of the premises in question or who is acting on behalf of such an occupier; and if the accused adduces sufficient evidence that he was, or was acting on behalf of, such an occupier he shall be presumed to be, or to be acting on behalf of, such an occupier unless the contrary is proved by the prosecution.
(2) Subject to subsection (1A) above, the fact that a person has any interest in or right to possession or occupation of any premises shall not for the purposes of subsection (1) above constitute lawful authority for the use or threat of violence by him or anyone else for the purpose of securing his entry into those premises.
(4) It is immaterial for the purposes of this section—
   (a) whether the violence in question is directed against the person or against the property; and
   (b) whether the entry which the violence is intended to secure is for the purpose of acquiring possession of the premises in question or for any other purpose.

## 7. Adverse occupation of residential premises

(1) Subject to the following provisions of this section and to section 12A(9) below, any person who is on any premises as a trespasser after having entered as such is guilty of an offence if he fails to leave those premises on being required to do so by or on behalf of—
   (a) a displaced residential occupier of the premises; or
   (b) an individual who is a protected intending occupier of the premises.
(2) In any proceedings for an offence under this section it shall be a defence for the accused to prove that he believed that the person requiring him to leave the premises was not a displaced residential occupier or protected intending occupier of the premises or a person acting on behalf of a displaced residential occupier or protected intending occupier.
(3) In any proceedings for an offence under this section it shall be a defence for the accused to prove—
   (a) that the premises in question are or form part of premises used mainly for nonresidential purposes; and
   (b) that he was not on any part of the premises used wholly or mainly for residential purposes.
(4) Any reference in the preceding provisions of this section to any premises includes a reference to any access to them, whether or not any such access itself constitutes premises, within the meaning of this Part of this Act.
(7) Section 12 below contains provisions which apply for determining when any person is to be regarded for the purposes of this Part of this Act as a displaced residential occupier of any premises or of any access to any premises and section 12A below contains provisions which apply for determining when any person is to be regarded for the purposes of this Part of this Act as a protected intending occupier of any premises or of any access to any premises.

## 8. Trespassing with a weapon of offence

(1) A person who is on any premises as a trespasser, after having entered as such, is guilty of an offence if, without lawful authority or reasonable excuse, he has with him on the premises any weapon of offence.

(2) In subsection (1) above 'weapon of offence' means any article made or adapted for use for causing injury to or incapacitating a person, or intended by the person having it with him for such use.

## 9. Trespassing on premises of foreign missions, etc.

(1) Subject to subsection (3) below, a person who enters or is on any premises to which this section applies as a trespasser is guilty of an offence.

(2) This section applies to any premises which are or form part of—

(a) the premises of a diplomatic mission within the meaning of the definition in Article 1(i) of the Vienna Convention on Diplomatic Relations signed in 1961 as that Article has effect in the United Kingdom by virtue of section 2 of and Schedule 1 to the Diplomatic Privileges Act 1964;

(aa) the premises of a closed diplomatic mission;

(b) consular premises within the meaning of the definition in paragraph 1 (j) of Article 1 of the Vienna Convention on Consular Relations signed in 1963 as that Article has effect in the United Kingdom by virtue of section 1 of and Schedule 1 to the Consular Relations Act 1968;

(bb) the premises of a closed consular post;

(c) any other premises in respect of which any organisation or body is entitled to inviolability by or under any enactment; and

(d) any premises which are the private residence of a diplomatic agent (within the meaning of Article 1(e) of the Convention mentioned in paragraph (a) above) or of any other person who is entitled to inviolability of residence by or under any enactment.

(3) In any proceedings for an offence under this section it shall be a defence for the accused to prove that he believed that the premises in question were not premises to which this section applies.

## 12. Supplementary provisions

(1) In this Part of this Act—

(a) 'premises' means any building, any part of a building under separate occupation, any land ancillary to a building, the site comprising any building or buildings together with any land ancillary thereto, and (for the purposes only of sections 10 and 11 above) any other place; and

(b) 'access' means, in relation to any premises, any part of any site or building within which those premises are situated which constitutes an ordinary means of access to those premises (whether or not that is its sole or primary use).

(2) References in this section to a building shall apply also to any structure other than a movable one, and to any movable structure, vehicle or vessel designed or adapted for use for residential purposes; and for the purposes of subsection (1) above—

(a) part of a building is under separate occupation if anyone is in occupation or entitled to occupation of that part as distinct from the whole; and

(b) land is ancillary to a building if it is adjacent to it and used (or intended for use) in connection with the occupation of that building or any part of it.

(3) Subject to subsection (4) below, any person who was occupying any premises as a residence immediately before being excluded from occupation by anyone who entered those premises, or any access to those premises, as a trespasser is a displaced residential occupier of the premises for the purposes of this Part of this Act so long as he continues to be excluded from occupation of the premises by the original trespasser or by any subsequent trespasser.

(4) A person who was himself occupying the premises in question as a trespasser immediately before being excluded from occupation shall not by virtue of subsection (3) above be a displaced residential occupier of the premises for the purposes of this Part of this Act.

(5) A person who by virtue of subsection (3) above is a displaced residential occupier of any premises shall be regarded for the purposes of this Part of this Act as a displaced residential occupier also of any access to those premises.

## 12A. Protected intending occupiers: supplementary provisions

(1) For the purposes of this Part of this Act an individual is a protected intending occupier of any premises at any time if at that time he falls within subsections (2), (4) or (6) below.

(2) An individual is a protected occupier of any premises if—

- (a) he has in those premises a freehold interest or a leasehold interest with not less than two years still to run;
- (b) he requires the premises for his own occupation as a residence;
- (c) he is excluded from occupation of the premises by a person who entered them, or any access to them, as a trespasser; and
- (d) he or a person acting on his behalf holds a written statement—
  - (i) which specifies his interest in the premises;
  - (ii) which states that he requires the premises for occupation as a residence for himself; and
  - (iii) with respect to which the requirements in subsection (3) below are fulfilled.

(3) The requirements referred to in subsection (2)(d)(iii) above are—

- (a) that the statement is signed by the person whose interest is specified in it in the presence of a justice of the peace or commissioner for oaths; and
- (b) that the justice of the peace or commissioner for oaths has subscribed his name as a witness to the signature.

(4) An individual is also a protected intending occupier of any premises if—

- (a) he has a tenancy of those premises (other than a tenancy falling within subsection (2)(a) above or (6)(a) below) or a licence to occupy those premises granted by a person with a freehold interest or a leasehold interest with not less than two years still to run in the premises;
- (b) he requires the premises for his own occupation as a residence;
- (c) he is excluded from occupation of the premises by a person who entered them, or any access to them, as a trespasser; and
- (d) he or a person acting on his behalf holds a written statement—
  - (i) which states that he has been granted a tenancy of those premises or a licence to occupy those premises;
  - (ii) which specifies the interest in the premises of the person who granted that tenancy or licence to occupy ('the landlord');
  - (iii) which states that he requires the premises for occupation as a residence for himself; and
  - (iv) with respect to which the requirements in subsection (5) below are fulfilled.

(5) The requirements referred to in subsection (4)(d)(iv) above are—

- (a) that the statement is signed by the landlord and by the tenant or licensee in the presence of a justice of the peace or commissioner for oaths;
- (b) that the justice of the peace or commissioner for oaths has subscribed his name as a witness to the signatures.

(6) An individual is also a protected intending occupier of any premises if—

- (a) he has a tenancy of those premises (other than a tenancy falling within subsection (2)(a) or (4)(a) above) or a licence to occupy those premises granted by an authority to which this subsection applies;
- (b) he requires the premises for his own occupation as a residence;
- (c) he is excluded from occupation of the premises by a person who entered the premises, or any access to them, as a trespasser; and
- (d) there has been issued to him by or on behalf of the authority referred to in paragraph (a) above a certificate stating that—
  - (i) he has been granted a tenancy of those premises or a licence to occupy those premises as a residence by the authority; and
  - (ii) the authority which granted that tenancy or licence to occupy is one to which this subsection applies, being of a description specified in the certificate.

(7) Subsection (6) above applies to the following authorities—
  (a) any body mentioned in section 14 of the Rent Act 1977 (landlord's interest belonging to local authority etc.);
  (b) the Regulator of Social Housing;
  (ba) a non-profit registered provider of social housing;
  (bb) a profit-making registered provider of social housing, but only in relation to premises which are social housing within the meaning of Part 2 of the Housing and Regeneration Act 2008;
  (c) ...
  (d) a registered social landlord within the meaning of the Housing Act 1985 (see section 5(4) and (5) of that Act).

(8) A person is guilty of an offence if he makes a statement for the purposes of subsection (2)(d) or (4)(d) above which he knows to be false in a material particular or if he recklessly makes such a statement which is false in a material particular.

(9) In any proceedings for an offence under section 7 of this Act where the accused was requested to leave the premises by a person claiming to be or to act on behalf of a protected intending occupier of the premises—
  (a) it shall be a defence for the accused to prove that, although asked to do so by the accused at the time the accused was requested to leave, that person failed at that time to produce to the accused such a statement as is referred to in subsection (2)(d) or (4)(d) above or such a certificate as is referred to in subsection (6)(d) above; and
  (b) any document purporting to be a certificate under subsection (6)(d) above shall be received in evidence and, unless the contrary is proved, shall be deemed to have been issued by or on behalf of the authority stated in the certificate.

(11) A person who is protected intending occupier of any premises shall be regarded for the purposes of this Part of this Act as a protected intending occupier also of any access to those premises.

## INTERPRETATION ACT 1978

### 5. Definitions

In any Act, unless the contrary intention appears, words and expressions listed in Schedule 1 to this Act are to be construed according to that Schedule.

### 6. Gender and number

In any Act, unless the contrary intention appears,—
(a) words importing the masculine gender include the feminine;
(b) words importing the feminine gender include the masculine;
(c) words in the singular include the plural and words in the plural include the singular.

### 15. Repeal of repeal

Where an Act repeals a repealing enactment, the repeal does not revive any enactment previously repealed unless words are added reviving it.

### 16. General savings

(1) Without prejudice to section 15, where an Act repeals an enactment, the repeal does not, unless the contrary intention appears,—
  (a) revive anything not in force or existing at the time at which the repeal takes effect;
  (b) affect the previous operation of the enactment repealed or anything duly done or suffered under that enactment;
  (c) affect any right, privilege, obligation or liability acquired, accrued, or incurred under that enactment;

(e) affect any investigation, legal proceeding or remedy in respect of any such right, privilege, obligation, liability, penalty, forfeiture or punishment; and any such investigation, legal proceeding or remedy may be instituted, continued or enforced, and any such penalty, forfeiture or punishment may be imposed, as if the repealing Act had not been passed.

(2) This section applies to the expiry of a temporary enactment as if it were repealed by an Act.

### 18. Duplicated offences

Where an act or omission constitutes an offence under two or more Acts, or both under an Act and at common law, the offender shall, unless the contrary intention appears, be liable to be prosecuted and punished under either or any of those Acts or at common law, but shall not be liable to be punished more than once for the same offence.

SCHEDULE 1

'Person' includes a body of persons corporate or unincorporate.

Construction of certain expressions relating to offences
In relation to England and Wales—

(a) 'indictable offence' means an offence which, if committed by an adult, is triable on indictment, whether it is exclusively so triable or triable either way;
(b) 'summary offence' means an offence which, if committed by an adult, is triable only summarily;
(c) 'offence triable either way' means an offence which, if committed by an adult, is triable either on indictment or summarily;

and the terms 'indictable', 'summary' and 'triable either way', in their application to offences, are to be construed accordingly.

In the above definitions references to the way or ways in which an offence is triable are to be construed without regard to the effect, if any, of section 22 of the Magistrates' Courts Act 1980 on the mode of trial in a particular case.

## PROTECTION OF CHILDREN ACT 1978

### 1. Indecent photographs of children

(1) Subject to sections 1A and 1B, it is an offence for a person—
(a) to take, or permit to be taken or to make, any indecent photograph or pseudo-photograph of a child ... ; or
(b) to distribute or show such indecent photographs or pseudo-photographs; or
(c) to have in his possession such indecent photographs or pseudo-photographs, with a view to their being distributed or shown by himself or others; or
(d) to publish or cause to be published any advertisement likely to be understood as conveying that the advertiser distributes or shows such indecent photographs or pseudo-photographs, or intends to do so.

(2) For purposes of this Act, a person is to be regarded as distributing an indecent photograph or pseudo-photograph if he parts with possession of it to, or exposes or offers it for acquisition by, another person.

(4) Where a person is charged with an offence under subsection (1)(b) or (c), it shall be a defence for him to prove—
(a) that he had a legitimate reason for distributing or showing the photographs or pseudo-photographs or (as the case may be) having them in his possession; or
(b) that he had not himself seen the photographs or pseudo-photographs and did not know, nor had any cause to suspect, them to be indecent.

### 1A. Marriage and other relationships

(1) This section applies where, in proceedings for an offence under section 1(1)(a) of taking or making an indecent photograph or pseudo-photograph of a child, or for an offence under section 1(1)(b) or (c) relating to an indecent photograph or pseudo-photograph

of a child, the defendant proves that the photograph or pseudo-photograph was of the child aged 16 or over, and that at the time of the offence charged the child and he—
(a) were married or civil partners of each other, or
(b) lived together as partners in an enduring family relationship.

(2) Subsections (5) and (6) also apply where, in proceedings for an offence under section 1(1)(b) or (c) relating to an indecent photograph or pseudo-photograph of a child, the defendant proves that the photograph or pseudo-photograph was of the child aged 16 or over, and that at the time when he obtained it the child and he—
(a) were married or civil partners of each other, or
(b) lived together as partners in an enduring family relationship.

(3) This section applies whether the photograph or pseudo-photograph showed the child alone or with the defendant, but not if it showed any other person.

(4) In the case of an offence under section 1(1)(a), if sufficient evidence is adduced to raise an issue as to whether the child consented to the photograph or pseudo-photograph being taken or made, or as to whether the defendant reasonably believed that the child so consented, the defendant is not guilty of the offence unless it is proved that the child did not so consent and that the defendant did not reasonably believe that the child so consented.

(5) In the case of an offence under section 1(1)(b), the defendant is not guilty of the offence unless it is proved that the showing or distributing was to a person other than the child.

(6) In the case of an offence under section 1(1)(c), if sufficient evidence is adduced to raise an issue both—
(a) as to whether the child consented to the photograph or pseudo-photograph being in the defendant's possession, or as to whether the defendant reasonably believed that the child so consented, and
(b) as to whether the defendant had the photograph or pseudo-photograph in his possession with a view to its being distributed or shown to anyone other than the child,

the defendant is not guilty of the offence unless it is proved either that the child did not so consent and that the defendant did not reasonably believe that the child so consented, or that the defendant had the photograph or pseudo-photograph in his possession with a view to its being distributed or shown to a person other than the child.

## 1B. Exception for criminal proceedings, investigations etc.

(1) In proceedings for an offence under section 1(1)(a) of making an indecent photograph or pseudo-photograph of a child, the defendant is not guilty of the offence if he proves that—
(a) it was necessary for him to make the photograph or pseudo-photograph for the purposes of the prevention, detection or investigation of crime, or for the purposes of criminal proceedings, in any part of the world,
(b) at the time of the offence charged he was a member of the Security Service, or the Secret Intelligence Service, and it was necessary for him to make the photograph or pseudo-photograph for the exercise of any of the functions of that Service, or
(c) at the time of the offence charged he was a member of GCHQ, and it was necessary for him to make the photograph or pseudo-photograph for the exercise of any of the functions of GCHQ.

(2) In this section 'GCHQ' has the same meaning as in the Intelligence Services Act 1994.

## 2. Evidence

(3) In proceedings under this Act relating to indecent photographs of children a person is to be taken as having been a child at any material time if it appears from the evidence as a whole that he was then under the age of 18.

## 3. Offences by corporations

(1) Where a body corporate is guilty of an offence under this Act and it is proved that the offence occurred with the consent or connivance of, or was attributable to any

neglect on the part of, any director, manager, secretary or other officer of the body, or any person who was purporting to act in any such capacity he, as well as the body corporate, shall be deemed to be guilty of that offence and shall be liable to be proceeded against and punished accordingly.

(2) Where the affairs of a body corporate are managed by its members, subsection (1) shall apply in relation to the acts and defaults of a member in connection with his functions of management as if he were a director of the body corporate.

### 7. Interpretation

(1) The following subsections apply for the interpretation of this Act.

(2) References to an indecent photograph include an indecent film, a copy of an indecent photograph or film, and an indecent photograph comprised in a film.

(3) Photographs (including those comprised in a film) shall, if they show children and are indecent, be treated for all purposes of this Act as indecent photographs of children and so as respects pseudo-photographs.

(4) References to a photograph include—
- (a) the negative as well as the positive version; and
- (b) data stored on a computer disc or by other electronic means which is capable of conversion into a photograph.

(4A) References to a photograph also include—
- (a) a tracing or other image, whether made by electronic or other means (of whatever nature)—
  - (i) which is not itself a photograph or pseudo-photograph, but
  - (ii) which is derived from the whole or part of a photograph or pseudo–photograph (or a combination of both); and
- (b) data stored on a computer disc or by other electronic means which is capable of conversion into an image within paragraph (a);

and subsection (8) applies in relation to such an image as it applies in relation to a pseudo-photograph.

(5) 'Film' includes any form of video-recording.

(6) 'Child', subject to subsection (8), means a person under the age of 18.

(7) 'Pseudo-photograph' means an image, whether made by computer-graphics or otherwise howsoever, which appears to be a photograph.

(8) If the impression conveyed by a pseudo-photograph is that the person shown is a child, the pseudo-photograph shall be treated for all purposes of this Act as showing a child and so shall a pseudo- photograph where the predominant impression conveyed is that the person shown is a child notwithstanding that some of the physical characteristics shown are those of an adult.

(9) References to an indecent pseudo-photograph include—
- (a) a copy of an indecent pseudo-photograph; and
- (b) data stored on a computer disc or by other electronic means which is capable of conversion into an indecent pseudo-photograph.

## THEFT ACT 1978

### 3. Making off without payment

(1) Subject to subsection (3) below, a person who, knowing that payment on the spot for any goods supplied or service done is required or expected from him, dishonestly makes off without having paid as required or expected and with intent to avoid payment of the amount due shall be guilty of an offence.

(2) For purposes of this section 'payment on the spot' includes payment at the time of collecting goods on which work has been done or in respect of which service has been provided.

(3) Subsection (1) above shall not apply where the supply of the goods or the doing of the service is contrary to law, or where the service done is such that payment is not legally enforceable.

# MAGISTRATES' COURTS ACT 1980

## 44. Aiders and abettors

(1) A person who aids, abets, counsels or procures the commission by another person of a summary offence shall be guilty of the like offence and may be tried (whether or not he is charged as a principal) either by a court having jurisdiction to try that other person or by a court having by virtue of his own offence jurisdiction to try him.

(2) Any offence consisting in aiding, abetting, counselling or procuring the commission of an offence triable either way (other than an offence listed in Schedule 1 to this Act) shall by virtue of this subsection be triable either way.

# CRIMINAL ATTEMPTS ACT 1981

## 1. Attempting to commit an offence

(1) If, with intent to commit an offence to which this section applies, a person does an act which is more than merely preparatory to the commission of the offence, he is guilty of attempting to commit the offence.

(1A) Subject to section 8 of the Computer Misuse Act 1990 (relevance of external law), if this subsection applies to an act, what the person doing it had in view shall be treated as an offence to which this section applies.

(1B) Subsection (1A) above applies to an act if—

- (a) it is done in England and Wales; and
- (b) it would fall within subsection (1) above as more than merely preparatory to the commission of an offence under section 3 of the Computer Misuse Act 1990 but for the fact that the offence, if completed, would not be an offence triable in England and Wales.

(2) A person may be guilty of attempting to commit an offence to which this section applies even though the facts are such that the commission of the offence is impossible.

(3) In any case where —

- (a) apart from this subsection a person's intention would not be regarded as having amounted to an intent to commit an offence: but
- (b) if the facts of the case had been as he believed them to be, his intention would be so regarded, then, for the purposes of subsection (1) above, he shall be regarded as having had an intent to commit that offence.

(4) This section applies to any offence which, if it were completed, would be triable in England and Wales as an indictable offence, other than—

- (a) conspiracy (at common law or under section 1 of the Criminal Law Act 1977 or any other enactment);
- (b) aiding, abetting, counselling, procuring or suborning the commission of an offence;
- (ba) an offence under section 2(1) of the Suicide Act 1961 (encouraging or assisting suicide);
- (c) offences under section 4 (1) (assisting offenders) or 5 (1) (accepting or agreeing to accept consideration for not disclosing information about an arrestable offence) of the Criminal Law Act 1967.

(5) This section also applies to low-value shoplifting (which is defined in, and is triable only summarily, by virtue of section 22A of the Magistrates' Courts Act 1980).

## 1A. Extended jurisdiction in relation to certain attempts

(1) If this section applies to an act, what the person doing the act had in view shall be treated as an offence to which section 1 (1) above applies.

(2) This section applies to an act if—

- (a) it is done in England and Wales, and
- (b) it would fall within section 1(1) above as more than merely preparatory to the commission of a Group A offence but for the fact that that offence, if completed, would not be an offence triable in England and Wales.

(3) In this section 'Group A offence' has the same meaning as in Part 1 of the Criminal Justice Act 1993.
(4) Subsection (1) above is subject to the provisions of section 6 of the Act of 1993 (relevance of external law).
(5) Where a person does any act to which this section applies, the offence which he commits shall for all purposes be treated as the offence of attempting to commit the relevant Group A offence.

### 6. Effect on common law

(1) The offence of attempt at common law and any offence at common law of procuring materials for crime are hereby abolished for all purposes not relating to acts done before the commencement of this Act.
(2) Except as regards offences committed before the commencement of this Act, references in any enactment passed before this Act which fall to be construed as references to the offence of attempt at common law shall be construed as references to the offence under section 1 above.

### 9. Interference with vehicles

(1) A person is guilty of the offence of vehicle interference if he interferes with a motor vehicle or trailer or with anything carried in or on a motor vehicle or trailer with the intention that any offence specified in subsection (2) below shall be committed by himself or some other person.
(2) The offences mentioned in subsection (1) above are—
(a) theft of the motor vehicle or trailer or part of it;
(b) theft of anything carried in or on the motor vehicle or trailer; and
(c) an offence under section 12(1) of the Theft Act 1968 (taking and driving away without consent);
and, if it is shown that a person accused of an offence under this section intended that one of those offences should be committed, it is immaterial that it cannot be shown which it was.
(5) In this section 'motor vehicle' and 'trailer' have the meanings assigned to them by section 190(1) of the Road Traffic Act 1972.

## FORGERY AND COUNTERFEITING ACT 1981

PART I
FORGERY AND KINDRED OFFENCES

### 1. The offence of forgery

A person is guilty of forgery if he makes a false instrument, with the intention that he or another shall use it to induce somebody to accept it as genuine, and by reason of so accepting it to do or not to do some act to his own or any other person's prejudice.

### 2. The offence of copying a false instrument

It is an offence for a person to make a copy of an instrument which is, and which he knows or believes to be, a false instrument, with the intention that he or another shall use it to induce somebody to accept it as a copy of a genuine instrument, and by reason of so accepting it to do or not to do some act to his own or any other person's prejudice.

### 3. The offence of using a false instrument

It is an offence for a person to use an instrument which is, and which he knows or believes to be, false, with the intention of inducing somebody to accept it as genuine, and by reason of so accepting it to do or not to do some act to his own or any other person's prejudice.

## 4. The offence of using a copy of a false instrument

It is an offence for a person to use a copy of an instrument which is, and which he knows or believes to be, a false instrument, with the intention of inducing somebody to accept it as a copy of a genuine instrument, and by reason of so accepting it to do or not to do some act to his own or any other person's prejudice.

## 5. Offences relating to money orders, share certificates, passports, etc.

(1) It is an offence for a person to have in his custody or under his control an instrument to which this section applies which is, and which he knows or believes to be, false, with the intention that he or another shall use it to induce somebody to accept it as genuine, and by reason of so accepting it to do or not to do some act to his own or any other person's prejudice.

(2) It is an offence for a person to have in his custody or under his control, without lawful authority or excuse, an instrument to which this section applies which is, and which he knows or believes to be, false.

(3) It is an offence for a person to make or to have in his custody or under his control a machine or implement, or paper or any other material, which to his knowledge is or has been specially designed or adapted for the making of an instrument to which this section applies, with the intention that he or another shall make an instrument to which this section applies which is false and that he or another shall use the instrument to induce somebody to accept it as genuine, and by reason of so accepting it to do or not to do some act to his own or any other person's prejudice.

(4) It is an offence for a person to make or to have in his custody or under his control any such machine, implement, paper or material, without lawful authority or excuse.

(5) The instruments to which this section applies are—

- (a) money orders;
- (b) postal orders;
- (c) United Kingdom postage stamps;
- (d) Inland Revenue stamps;
- (e) share certificates;
- (f) ...
- (fa) ...
- (g) cheques and other bills of exchange;
- (h) travellers' cheques;
- (ha) bankers' drafts;
- (hb) promissory notes;
- (j) cheque cards;
- (ja) debit cards;
- (k) credit cards;
- (l) certified copies relating to an entry in a register of births, adoptions, marriages, civil partnerships, conversions or deaths and issued by the Registrar General, the Registrar General for Northern Ireland, a registration officer or a person lawfully authorised to issue certified copies relating to such entries; and
- (m) certificates relating to entries in such registers.

(6) In subsection (5)(e) above 'share certificate' means an instrument entitling or evidencing the title of a person to a share or interest—

- (a) in any public stock, annuity, fund or debt of any government or state, including a state which forms part of another state; or
- (b) in any stock, fund or debt of a body (whether corporate or unincorporated) established in the United Kingdom or elsewhere.

(6A) In subsection (5)(l) above, 'conversion' means the conversion of a civil partnership into a marriage under section 9 of the Marriage (Same Sex Couples) Act 2013 and regulations made under that section.

(7) An instrument is also an instrument to which this section applies if it is a monetary instrument specified for the purposes of this section by an order made by the Secretary of State.

(8) The power under subsection (7) above is exercisable by statutory instrument subject to annulment in pursuance of a resolution of either House of Parliament.

(9), (10), (11) ...

## 8. Meaning of 'instrument'

(1) Subject to subsection (2) below, in this Part of this Act 'instrument' means—
- (a) any document, whether of a formal or informal character;
- (b) any stamp issued or sold by a postal operator;
- (c) any Inland Revenue stamp; and
- (d) any disc, tape, sound track or other device on or in which information is recorded or stored by mechanical, electronic or other means.

(2) A currency note within the meaning of Part II of this Act is not an instrument for the purposes of this Part of this Act.

(3) A mark denoting payment of postage which a postal operator authorises to be used instead of an adhesive stamp is to be treated for the purposes of this Part of this Act as if it were a stamp issued by the postal operator concerned.

(3A) In this section 'postal operator' has the meaning given by section 27 of the Postal Services Act 2011.

## 9. Meaning of 'false' and 'making'

(1) An instrument is false for the purposes of this Part of this Act—
- (a) if it purports to have been made in the form in which it is made by a person who did not in fact make it in that form; or
- (b) if it purports to have been made in the form in which it is made on the authority of a person who did not in fact authorise its making in that form; or
- (c) if it purports to have been made in the terms in which it is made by a person who did not in fact make it in those terms; or
- (d) if it purports to have been made in the terms in which it is made on the authority of a person who did not in fact authorise its making in those terms; or
- (e) if it purports to have been altered in any respect by a person who did not in fact alter it in that respect; or
- (f) if it purports to have been altered in any respect on the authority of a person who did not in fact authorise the alteration in that respect; or
- (g) if it purports to have been made or altered on a date on which, or at a place at which, or otherwise in circumstances in which, it was not in fact made or altered; or
- (h) if it purports to have been made or altered by an existing person but he did not in fact exist.

(2) A person is to be treated for the purposes of this Part of this Act as making a false instrument if he alters an instrument so as to make it false in any respect (whether or not it is false in some other respect apart from that alteration).

## 10. Meaning of 'prejudice' and 'induce'

(1) Subject to subsections (2) and (4) below, for the purposes of this Part of this Act an act or omission intended to be induced is to a person's prejudice if, and only if, it is one which if it occurs—
- (a) will result—
  - (i) in his temporary or permanent loss of property; or
  - (ii) in his being deprived of an opportunity to earn remuneration or greater remuneration; or
  - (iii) in his being deprived of an opportunity to gain a financial advantage otherwise than by way of remuneration; or
- (b) will result in somebody being given an opportunity—
  - (i) to earn remuneration or greater remuneration from him; or
  - (ii) to gain a financial advantage from him otherwise than by way of remuneration; or
- (c) will be the result of his having accepted a false instrument as genuine, or a copy of a false instrument as a copy of a genuine one, in connection with his performance of any duty.

(2) An act which a person has an enforceable duty to do and an omission to do an act which a person is not entitled to do shall be disregarded for the purposes of this Part of this Act.

(3) In this Part of this Act references to inducing somebody to accept a false instrument as genuine, or a copy of a false instrument as a copy of a genuine one, include references to inducing a machine to respond to the instrument or copy as if it were a genuine instrument or, as the case may be, a copy of a genuine one.

(4) Where subsection (3) above applies, the act or omission intended to be induced by the machine responding to the instrument or copy shall be treated as an act or omission to a person's prejudice.

(5) In this section 'loss' includes not getting what one might get as well as parting with what one has.

## PART II
## COUNTERFEITING AND KINDRED OFFENCES

### 14. Offences of counterfeiting notes and coins

(1) It is an offence for a person to make a counterfeit of a currency note or of a protected coin, intending that he or another shall pass or tender it as genuine.

(2) It is an offence for a person to make a counterfeit of a currency note or of a protected coin without lawful authority or excuse.

### 15. Offences of passing, etc., counterfeit notes and coins

(1) It is an offence for a person—
  (a) to pass or tender as genuine any thing which is, and which he knows or believes to be, a counterfeit of a currency note or of a protected coin; or
  (b) to deliver to another any thing which is, and which he knows or believes to be, such a counterfeit, intending that the person to whom it is delivered or another shall pass or tender it as genuine.

(2) It is an offence for a person to deliver to another, without lawful authority or excuse, any thing which is, and which he knows or believes to be, a counterfeit of a currency note or of a protected coin.

### 16. Offences involving the custody or control of counterfeit notes and coins

(1) It is an offence for a person to have in his custody or under his control any thing which is, and which he knows or believes to be, a counterfeit of a currency note or of a protected coin, intending either to pass or tender it as genuine or to deliver it to another with the intention that he or another shall pass or tender it as genuine.

(2) It is an offence for a person to have in his custody or under his control, without lawful authority or excuse, anything which is, and which he knows or believes to be, a counterfeit of a currency note or of a protected coin.

### 27. Meaning of 'currency note' and 'protected coin'

(1) In this Part of this Act—

'currency note' means—
  (a) any note which—
    (i) has been lawfully issued in England and Wales, Scotland, Northern Ireland, any of the Channel Islands, the Isle of Man or the Republic of Ireland; and
    (ii) is or has been customarily used as money in the country where it was issued; and
    (iii) is payable on demand; or
  (b) any note which—
    (i) has been lawfully issued in some country other than those mentioned in paragraph (a)(i) above; and
    (ii) is customarily used as money in that country; and

'protected coin' means any coin which—

(a) is customarily used as money in any country; or
(b) is specified in an order made by the Treasury for the purposes of this Part of this Act.

(2) The power to make an order conferred on the Treasury by subsection (1) above shall be exercisable by statutory instrument.

(3) A statutory instrument containing such an order shall be laid before Parliament after being made.

## 28. Meaning of 'counterfeit'

(1) For the purposes of this Part of this Act a thing is a counterfeit of a currency note or of a protected coin—
(a) if it is not a currency note or a protected coin but resembles a currency note or protected coin (whether on one side only or on both) to such an extent that it is reasonably capable of passing for a currency note or protected coin of that description; or
(b) if it is currency note or protected coin which has been so altered that it is reasonably capable of passing for a currency note or protected coin of some other description.

(2) For the purposes of this Part of this Act—
(a) a thing consisting of one side only of a currency note, with or without the addition of other material, is a counterfeit of such a note;
(b) a thing consisting—
(i) of parts of two or more currency notes; or
(ii) of parts of a currency note, or of parts of two or more currency notes, with the addition of other material,
is capable of being a counterfeit of a currency note.

(3) References in this Part of this Act to passing or tendering a counterfeit of a currency note or a protected coin are not to be construed as confined to passing or tendering it as legal tender.

# AVIATION SECURITY ACT 1982

## 1. Hijacking

(1) A person on board an aircraft in flight who unlawfully, by the use of force or by threats of any kind, seizes the aircraft or exercises control of it commits the offence of hijacking, whatever his nationality, whatever the State in which the aircraft is registered and whether the aircraft is in the United Kingdom or elsewhere, but subject to subsection (2) below.

(2) If—
(a) the aircraft is used in military, customs or police service, or
(b) both the place of take-off and the place of landing are in the territory of the State in which the aircraft is registered, subsection (1) above shall not apply unless—
(i) the person seizing or exercising control of the aircraft is a United Kingdom national; or
(ii) his act is committed in the United Kingdom; or
(iii) the aircraft is registered in the United Kingdom or is used in the military or customs service of the United Kingdom or in the service of any police force in the United Kingdom.

(3) A person who commits the offence of hijacking shall be liable, on conviction on indictment, to imprisonment for life.

(5) For the purposes of this section the territorial waters of any State shall be treated as part of its territory.

## 2. Destroying, damaging or endangering safety of aircraft

(1) It shall, subject to subsection (4) below, be an offence for any person unlawfully and intentionally—

(a) to destroy an aircraft in service or so to damage such an aircraft as to render it incapable of flight or as to be likely to endanger its safety in flight; or
(b) to commit on board an aircraft in flight any act of violence which is likely to endanger the safety of the aircraft.

(2) It shall also, subject to subsection (4) below, be an offence for any person unlawfully and intentionally to place, or cause to be placed, on an aircraft in service any device or substance which is likely to destroy the aircraft, or is likely so to damage it as to render it incapable of flight or as to be likely to endanger its safety in flight; but nothing in this subsection shall be construed as limiting the circumstances in which the commission of any act—
(a) may constitute an offence under subsection (1) above, or
(b) may constitute attempting or conspiring to commit, or aiding, abetting, counselling or procuring, or being art and part in, the commission of such an offence.

(3) Except as provided by subsection (4) below, subsections (1) and (2) above shall apply whether any such act as is therein mentioned is committed in the United Kingdom or elsewhere, whatever the nationality of the person committing the act and whatever the State in which the aircraft is registered.

(4) Subsections (1) and (2) above shall not apply to any act committed in relation to an aircraft used in military, customs or police service unless—
(a) the act is committed in the United Kingdom, or
(b) where the act is committed outside the United Kingdom, the person committing it is a United Kingdom national.

(5) A person who commits an offence under this section shall be liable, on conviction on indictment, to imprisonment for life.

(6) In this section 'unlawfully'—
(a) in relation to the commission of an act in the United Kingdom, means so as (apart from this Act) to constitute an offence under the law of the part of the United Kingdom in which the act is committed, and
(b) in relation to the commission of an act outside the United Kingdom, means so that the commission of the act would (apart from this Act) have been an offence under the law of England and Wales if it had been committed in England and Wales or of Scotland if it had been committed in Scotland.

(7) In this section 'act of violence' means—
(a) any act done in the United Kingdom which constitutes the offence of murder, attempted murder, manslaughter, culpable homicide or assault or an offence under section 18, 20, 21,22, 23, 24, 28 or 29 of the Offences against the Person Act 1861 or under section 2 of the Explosive Substances Act 1883, and
(b) any act done outside the United Kingdom which, if done in the United Kingdom, would constitute such an offence as is mentioned in paragraph (a) above.

## 3. Other acts endangering or likely to endanger safety of aircraft

(1) It shall, subject to subsections (5) and (6) below, be an offence for any person unlawfully and intentionally to destroy or damage any property to which this subsection applies, or to interfere with the operation of any such property, where the destruction, damage or interference is likely to endanger the safety of aircraft in flight.

(2) Subsection (1) above applies to any property used for the provision of air navigation facilities, including any land, building or ship so used, and including any apparatus or equipment so used, whether it is on board an aircraft or elsewhere.

(3) It shall also, subject to subsections (4) and (5) below, be an offence for any person intentionally to communicate any information which is false, misleading or deceptive in a material particular, where the communication of the information endangers the safety of an aircraft in flight or is likely to endanger the safety of aircraft in flight.

(4) It shall be a defence for a person charged with an offence under subsection (3) above to prove—
(a) that he believed, and had reasonable grounds for believing, that the information was true; or
(b) that, when he communicated the information, he was lawfully employed to perform duties which consisted of or included the communication of information

and that he communicated the information in good faith in the performance of those duties.

(5) Subsections (1) and (3) above shall not apply to the commission of any act unless either the act is committed in the United Kingdom, or, where it is committed outside the United Kingdom—
   (a) the person committing it is a United Kingdom national; or
   (b) the commission of the act endangers or is likely to endanger the safety in flight of a civil aircraft registered in the United Kingdom or chartered by demise to a lessee whose principal place of business, or (if he has no place of business) whose permanent residence, is in the United Kingdom; or
   (c) the act is committed on board a civil aircraft which is so registered or so chartered; or
   (d) the act is committed on board a civil aircraft which lands in the United Kingdom with the person who committed the act still on board.

(6) Subsection (1) above shall also not apply to any act committed outside the United Kingdom and so committed in relation to property which is situated outside the United Kingdom and is not used for the provision of air navigation facilities in connection with international air navigation, unless the person committing the act is a United Kingdom national.

(7) A person who commits an offence under this section shall be liable, on conviction on indictment, to imprisonment for life.

(8) In this section 'civil aircraft' means any aircraft other than an aircraft used in military, customs or police service and 'unlawfully' has the same meaning as in section 2 of this Act.

## 4. Offences in relation to certain dangerous articles

(1) It shall be an offence for any person without lawful authority or reasonable excuse (the proof of which shall lie on him) to have with him—
   (a) in any aircraft registered in the United Kingdom, whether at a time when the aircraft is in the United Kingdom or not, or
   (b) in any other aircraft at a time when it is in, or in flight over, the United Kingdom, or
   (c) in any part of an aerodrome in the United Kingdom, or
   (d) in any air navigation installation in the United Kingdom which does not form part of an aerodrome, any article to which this section applies.

(2) This section applies to the following articles, that is to say—
   (a) any firearm, or any article having the appearance of being a firearm, whether capable of being discharged or not;
   (b) any explosive, any article manufactured or adapted (whether in the form of a bomb, grenade or otherwise) so as to have the appearance of being an explosive, whether it is capable of producing a practical effect by explosion or not, or any article marked or labelled so as to indicate that it is or contains an explosive; and
   (c) any article (not falling within either of the preceding paragraphs) made or adapted for use for causing injury to or incapacitating a person or for destroying or damaging property, or intended by the person having it with him for such use, whether by him or by any other person.

(3) For the purposes of this section a person who is for the time being in an aircraft, or in part of an aerodrome, shall be treated as having with him in the aircraft, or in that part of the aerodrome, as the case may be, an article to which this section applies if—
   (a) where he is in an aircraft, the article, or an article in which it is contained, is in the aircraft and has been caused (whether by him or by any other person) to be brought there as being, or as forming part of, his baggage on a flight in the aircraft or has been caused by him to be brought there as being, or as forming part of, any other property to be carried on such a flight, or
   (b) where he is in part of an aerodrome (otherwise than in an aircraft), the article, or an article in which it is contained, is in that or any other part of the aerodrome and has been caused (whether by him or by any other person) to be brought

into the aerodrome as being, or as forming part of, his baggage on a flight from that aerodrome or has been caused by him to be brought there as being, or as forming part of, any other property to be carried on such a flight on which he is also to be carried, notwithstanding that the circumstances may be such that (apart from this subsection) he would not be regarded as having the article with him in the aircraft or in a part of the aerodrome, as the case may be.

(4) A person guilty of an offence under this section shall be liable—
 (a) on summary conviction, to a fine not exceeding the statutory maximum or to imprisonment for a term not exceeding three months or to both;
 (b) on conviction on indictment, to a fine or to imprisonment for a term not exceeding five years or to both.

(5) Nothing in subsection (3) above shall be construed as limiting the circumstances in which a person would, apart from that subsection, be regarded as having an article with him as mentioned in subsection (1) above.

## 38. Interpretation etc.

(1) In this Act, except in so far as the context otherwise requires—

'aerodrome' means the aggregate of the land, buildings and works comprised in an aerodrome within the meaning of the Civil Aviation Act 1982 and (if and so far as not comprised in an aerodrome as defined in that Act) any land, building or works situated within the boundaries of an area designated, by an order made by the Secretary of State which is for the time being in force, as constituting the area of an aerodrome for the purposes of this Act;

'air navigation installation' means any building, works, apparatus or equipment used wholly or mainly for the purpose of assisting air traffic control or as an aid to air navigation, together with any land contiguous or adjacent to any such building, works, apparatus or equipment and used wholly or mainly for purposes connected therewith;

'aircraft registered or operating in the United Kingdom' means any aircraft which is either—
 (a) an aircraft registered in the United Kingdom, or
 (b) an aircraft not so registered which is for the time being allocated for use on a flight any part of which is in the United Kingdom;

'article' includes any substance, whether in solid or liquid form or in the form of a gas or vapour;

'constable' includes any person having the powers and privileges of a constable;

'explosive' means any article manufactured for the purpose of producing a practical effect by explosion, or intended for that purpose by a person having the article with him; 'firearm' includes an airgun or air pistol;

'manager', in relation to an aerodrome, means the person (whether ... the Civil Aviation Authority, a local authority or any other person) by whom the aerodrome is managed;

'military service' includes naval and air force service;

'measures' (without prejudice to the generality of that expression) includes the construction, execution, alteration, demolition or removal of buildings or other works and also includes the institution or modification, and the supervision and enforcement, of any practice or procedure;

'operator' has the same meaning as in the Civil Aviation Act 1982;

'property' includes any land, buildings or works, any aircraft or vehicle and any baggage, cargo or other article of any description;

'United Kingdom national' means an individual who is—
 (a) a British citizen, a British Overseas Territories citizen, a British National (Overseas) or a British Overseas citizen;
 (b) a person who under the British Nationality Act 1981 is a British subject; or
 (c) a British protected person (within the meaning of that Act).

(2) For the purposes of this Act—
 (a) in the case of an air navigation installation provided by, or used wholly or mainly by, the Civil Aviation Authority, that Authority, and
 (b) in the case of any other air navigation installation, the manager of an aerodrome by whom it is provided, or by whom it is wholly or mainly used,

shall be taken to be the authority responsible for that air navigation installation.

(3) For the purposes of this Act—
  (a) the period during which an aircraft is in flight shall be deemed to include any period from the moment when all its external doors are closed following embarkation until the moment when any such door is opened for disembarkation, and, in the case of a forced landing, any period until the competent authorities take over responsibility for the aircraft and for persons and property on board; and
  (b) an aircraft shall be taken to be in service during the whole of the period which begins with the pre-flight preparation of the aircraft for a flight and ends 24 hours after the aircraft lands having completed that flight, and also at any time (not falling within that period) while, in accordance with the preceding paragraph, the aircraft is in flight, and anything done on board an aircraft while in flight over any part of the United Kingdom shall be treated as done in that part of the United Kingdom.

(4) For the purposes of this Act the territorial waters adjacent to any part of the United Kingdom shall be treated as included in that part of the United Kingdom.

# CHILD ABDUCTION ACT 1984

## 1. Offence of abduction of child by parent, etc.

(1) Subject to subsections (5) and (8) below, a person connected with a child under the age of sixteen commits an offence if he takes or sends the child out of the United Kingdom without the appropriate consent.

(2) A person is connected with a child for the purposes of this section if—
  (a) he is a parent of the child; or
  (b) in the case of a child whose parents were not married to, or civil partners of, each other at the time of his birth, there are reasonable grounds for believing that he is the father of the child; or
  (c) he is a guardian of the child; or
  (ca) he is a special guardian of the child; or
  (d) he is a person named in a child arrangements order as a person with whom the child is to live; or
  (e) he has custody of the child.

(3) In this section 'the appropriate consent' in relation to a child, means—
  (a) the consent of each of the following—
    (i) the child's mother;
    (ii) the child's father, if he has parental responsibility for him;
    (iii) any guardian of the child;
    (iiia) any special guardian of the child;
    (iv) any person named in a child arrangements order as a person with whom the child is to live;
    (v) any person who has custody of the child; or
  (b) the leave of the court granted under or by virtue of any provision of Part II of the Children Act 1989; or
  (c) if any person has custody of the child, the leave of the court which awarded custody to him.

(4) A person does not commit an offence under this section by taking or sending a child out of the United Kingdom without obtaining the appropriate consent if—
  (a) he is a person named in a child arrangements order as a person with whom the child is to live and he takes or sends him out of the United Kingdom for a period of less than one month; or
  (b) he is a special guardian of the child, and he takes or sends the child out of the United Kingdom for a period of less than three months.

(4A) Subsection (4) above does not apply if the person taking or sending the child out of the United Kingdom does so in breach of an order under Part II of the Children Act 1989.

(5) A person does not commit an offence under this section by doing anything without the consent of another person whose consent is required under the foregoing provisions if—
   (a) he does it in the belief that the other person—
      (i) has consented; or
      (ia) who is a special guardian of the child; or
      (ii) would consent if he was aware of all the relevant circumstances; or
   (b) he has taken all reasonable steps to communicate with the other person but has been unable to communicate with him; or
   (c) the other person has unreasonably refused to consent.

(5A) Subsection (5)(c) above does not apply if—
   (a) the person who refused to consent is a person—
      (i) named in a child arrangements order as a person with whom the child is to live; or
      (ii) who has custody of the child; or
   (b) the person taking or sending the child out of the United Kingdom is, by so acting, in breach of an order made by a court in the United Kingdom.

(6) Where, in proceedings for an offence under this section, there is sufficient evidence to raise an issue as to the application of subsection (5) above, it shall be for the prosecution to prove that the subsection does not apply.

(7) For the purposes of this section—
   (a) 'guardian of a child', 'special guardian' 'child arrangements order' and 'parental responsibility' have the same meaning as in the Children Act 1989; and
   (b) a person shall be treated as having custody of a child if there is in force an order of a court in the United Kingdom awarding him (whether solely or jointly with another person) custody, legal custody or care and control of the child.

(8) This section shall have effect subject to the provisions of the Schedule to this Act in relation to a child who is in the care of a local authority detained in a place of safety, remanded otherwise than on bail or the subject of proceedings or an order relating to adoption.

## 2. Offence of abduction of child by other persons

(1) Subject to subsection (3) below, a person, other than one mentioned in subsection (2) below, commits an offence if, without lawful authority or reasonable excuse, he takes or detains a child under the age of sixteen—
   (a) so as to remove him from the lawful control of any person having lawful control of the child; or
   (b) so as to keep him out of the lawful control of any person entitled to lawful control of the child.

(2) The persons are—
   (a) where the father and mother of the child in question were married to each other at the time of his birth, the child's father and mother;
   (b) where the father and mother of the child in question were not married to, or civil partners of, each other at the time of his birth, the child's mother; and
   (c) any other person mentioned in section 1(2)(c) to (e) above.

(3) In proceedings against any person for an offence under this section, it shall be a defence for that person to prove—
   (a) where the father and mother of the child in question were not married to each other at the time of his birth—
      (i) that he is the child's father; or
      (ii) that, at the time of the alleged offence, he believed, on reasonable grounds, that he was the child's father; or
   (b) that, at the time of the alleged offence, he believed that the child had attained the age of sixteen.

## 3. Construction of references to taking, sending and detaining

For the purposes of this Part of this Act—
(a) a person shall be regarded as taking a child if he causes or induces the child to accompany him or any other person or causes the child to be taken;
(b) a person shall be regarded as sending a child if he causes the child to be sent;

(c) a person shall be regarded as detaining a child if he causes the child to be detained or induces the child to remain with him or any other person; and
(d) references to a child's parents and to a child whose parents were (or were not) married to, or civil partners of, each other at the time of his birth shall be construed in accordance with section 1 of the Family Law Reform Act 1987 (which extends their meaning).

# PUBLIC ORDER ACT 1986

PART I

## 1. Riot

(1) Where 12 or more persons who are present together use or threaten unlawful violence for a common purpose and the conduct of them (taken together) is such as would cause a person of reasonable firmness present at the scene to fear for his personal safety, each of the persons using unlawful violence for the common purpose is guilty of riot.
(2) It is immaterial whether or not the 12 or more use or threaten unlawful violence simultaneously.
(3) The common purpose may be inferred from conduct.
(4) No person of reasonable firmness need actually be, or be likely to be, present at the scene.
(5) Riot may be committed in private as well as in public places.
(6) A person guilty of riot is liable on conviction on indictment to imprisonment for a term not exceeding ten years or a fine or both.

## 2. Violent disorder

(1) Where 3 or more persons who are present together use or threaten unlawful violence and the conduct of them (taken together) is such as would cause a person of reasonable firmness present at the scene to fear for his personal safety, each of the persons using or threatening unlawful violence is guilty of violent disorder.
(2) It is immaterial whether or not the 3 or more use or threaten unlawful violence simultaneously.
(3) No person of reasonable firmness need actually be, or be likely to be, present at the scene.
(4) Violent disorder may be committed in private as well as in public places.
(5) A person guilty of violent disorder is liable on conviction on indictment to imprisonment for a term not exceeding 5 years or a fine or both, or on summary conviction to imprisonment for a term not exceeding 6 months or a fine not exceeding the statutory maximum or both.

## 3. Affray

(1) A person is guilty of affray if he uses or threatens unlawful violence towards another and his conduct is such as would cause a person of reasonable firmness present at the scene to fear for his personal safety.
(2) Where 2 or more persons use or threaten the unlawful violence, it is the conduct of them taken together that must be considered for the purposes of subsection (1).
(3) For the purposes of this section a threat cannot be made by the use of words alone.
(4) No person of reasonable firmness need actually be, or be likely to be, present at the scene.
(5) Affray may be committed in private as well as in public places.
(6) A person guilty of affray is liable on conviction on indictment to imprisonment for a term not exceeding 3 years or a fine or both, or on summary conviction to imprisonment for a term not exceeding 6 months or a fine not exceeding the statutory maximum or both.

## 4. Fear or provocation of violence

(1) A person is guilty of an offence if he—
    (a) uses towards another person threatening, abusive or insulting words or behaviour; or

(b) distributes or displays to another person any writing, sign or other visible representation which is threatening, abusive or insulting,

with intent to cause that person to believe that immediate unlawful violence will be used against him or another by any person, or to provoke the immediate use of unlawful violence by that person or another, or whereby that person is likely to believe that such violence will be used or it is likely that such violence will be provoked.

(2) An offence under this section may be committed in a public or a private place, except that no offence is committed where the words or behaviour are used, or the writing, sign or other visible representation is distributed or displayed, by a person inside a dwelling and the other person is also inside that or another dwelling.

(3) A person guilty of an offence under this section is liable on summary conviction to imprisonment for a term not exceeding 6 months or a fine not exceeding level 5 on the standard scale or both.

## 4A. Intentional harassment, alarm or distress

(1) A person is guilty of an offence if, with intent to cause a person harassment, alarm or distress, he—

(a) uses threatening, abusive or insulting words or behaviour, or disorderly behaviour, or

(b) displays any writing, sign or other visible representation which is threatening, abusive or insulting,

thereby causing that or another person harassment, alarm or distress.

(2) An offence under this section may be committed in a public or a private place, except that no offence is committed where the words or behaviour are used, or the writing, sign or other visible representation is displayed, by a person inside a dwelling and the person who is harassed, alarmed or distressed is also inside that or another dwelling.

(3) It is a defence for the accused to prove—

(a) that he was inside a dwelling and had no reason to believe that the words or behaviour used, or the writing, sign or other visible representation displayed would be heard or seen by a person outside that or any other dwelling, or

(b) that his conduct was reasonable.

(5) A person guilty of an offence under this section is liable on summary conviction to imprisonment for a term not exceeding 6 months or a fine not exceeding level 5 on the standard scale or both.

## 5. Harassment, alarm or distress

(1) A person is guilty of an offence if he—

(a) uses threatening, or abusive, words or behaviour, or disorderly behaviour, or

(b) displays any writing, sign or other visible representation which is threatening, or abusive,

within the hearing or sight of a person likely to be caused harassment, alarm or distress thereby.

(2) An offence under this section may be committed in a public or a private place, except that no offence is committed where the words or behaviour are used, or the writing, sign or other visible representation is displayed, by a person inside a dwelling and the other person is also inside that or another dwelling.

(3) It is a defence for the accused to prove—

(a) that he had no reason to believe that there was any person within hearing or sight who was likely to be caused harassment, alarm or distress, or

(b) that he was inside a dwelling and had no reason to believe that the words or behaviour used, or the writing, sign or other visible representation displayed, would be heard or seen by a person outside that or any other dwelling, or

(c) that his conduct was reasonable.

## 6. Mental element: miscellaneous

(1) A person is guilty of riot only if he intends to use violence or is aware that his conduct may be violent.

(2) A person is guilty of violent disorder or affray only if he intends to use or threaten violence or is aware that his conduct may be violent or threaten violence.

(3) A person is guilty of an offence under section 4 only if he intends his words or behaviour, or the writing, sign or other visible representation, to be threatening, abusive or insulting, or is aware that it may be threatening, abusive or insulting.
(4) A person is guilty of an offence under section 5 only if he intends his words or behaviour, or the writing, sign or other visible representation, to be threatening, or abusive, or is aware that it may be threatening, or abusive, or (as the case may be) he intends his behaviour to be or is aware that it may be disorderly.
(5) For the purposes of this section a person whose awareness is impaired by intoxication shall be taken to be aware of that of which he would be aware if not intoxicated, unless he shows either that his intoxication was not self-induced or that it was caused solely by the taking or administration of a substance in the course of medical treatment.
(6) In subsection (5) 'intoxication' means any intoxication, whether caused by drink, drugs or other means, or by a combination of means.
(7) Subsections (1) and (2) do not affect the determination for the purposes of riot or violent disorder of the number of persons who use or threaten violence.

## 8. Interpretation

In this Part—
'dwelling' means any structure or part of a structure occupied as a person's home or as other living accommodation (whether the occupation is separate or shared with others) but does not include any part not so occupied, and for this purpose 'structure' includes a tent, caravan, vehicle, vessel or other temporary or movable structure;
'violence' means any violent conduct, so that—
(a) except in the context of affray, it includes violent conduct towards property as well as violent conduct towards persons, and
(b) it is not restricted to conduct causing or intended to cause injury or damage but includes any other violent conduct (for example, throwing at or towards a person a missile of a kind capable of causing injury which does not hit or falls short).

PART III

## 17. Meaning of 'racial hatred'

In this Part 'racial hatred' means hatred against a group of persons ... defined by reference to colour, race, nationality (including citizenship) or ethnic or national origins.

## 18. Use of words or behaviour or display of written material

(1) A person who uses threatening, abusive or insulting words or behaviour, or displays any written material which is threatening, abusive or insulting, is guilty of an offence if—
    (a) he intends thereby to stir up racial hatred, or
    (b) having regard to all the circumstances racial hatred is likely to be stirred up thereby.
(2) An offence under this section may be committed in a public or a private place, except that no offence is committed where the words or behaviour are used, or the written material is displayed, by a person inside a dwelling and are not heard or seen except by other persons in that or another dwelling.
(4) In proceedings for an offence under this section it is a defence for the accused to prove that he was inside a dwelling and had no reason to believe that the words or behaviour used, or the written material displayed, would be heard or seen by a person outside that or any other dwelling.
(5) A person who is not shown to have intended to stir up racial hatred is not guilty of an offence under this section if he did not intend his words or behaviour, or the written material, to be, and was not aware that it might be, threatening, abusive or insulting.
(6) This section does not apply to words or behaviour used, or written material displayed, solely for the purpose of being included in a programme included in a programme service.

## 19. Publishing or distributing written material

(1) A person who publishes or distributes written material which is threatening, abusive or insulting is guilty of an offence if—
  (a) he intends thereby to stir up racial hatred, or
  (b) having regard to all the circumstances racial hatred is likely to be stirred up thereby.

(2) In proceedings for an offence under this section it is a defence for an accused who is not shown to have intended to stir up racial hatred to prove that he was not aware of the content of the material and did not suspect, and had no reason to suspect, that it was threatening, abusive or insulting.

(3) References in this Part to the publication or distribution of written material are to its publication or distribution to the public or a section of the public.

PART V

## 38. Contamination of or interference with goods with intention of causing public alarm or anxiety, etc.

(1) It is an offence for a person, with the intention—
  (a) of causing public alarm or anxiety, or
  (b) of causing injury to members of the public consuming or using the goods, or
  (c) of causing economic loss to any person by reason of the goods being shunned by members of the public, or
  (d) of causing economic loss to any person by reason of steps taken to avoid any such alarm or anxiety, injury or loss

to contaminate or interfere with goods, or make it appear that goods have been contaminated or interfered with, or to place goods which have been contaminated or interfered with, or which appear to have been contaminated and interfered with, in a place where goods of that description are consumed, used, sold or otherwise supplied.

(2) It is also an offence for a person, with any such intention as is mentioned in paragraph (a), (c) or (d) of subsection (1), to threaten that he or another will do, or claim that he or another has done, any of the acts mentioned in that subsection.

(3) It is an offence for a person to be in possession of any of the following articles with a view to the commission of an offence under subsection (1)—
  (a) materials to be used for contaminating or interfering with goods or making it appear that goods have been contaminated or interfered with, or
  (b) goods which have been contaminated or interfered with, or which appear to have been contaminated or interfered with.

(4) A person guilty of an offence under this section is liable—
  (a) on conviction on indictment to imprisonment for a term not exceeding 10 years or a fine or both, or
  (b) on summary conviction to imprisonment for a term not exceeding six months or a fine not exceeding the statutory maximum or both.

(5) In this section 'goods' includes substances whether natural or manufactured and whether or not incorporated in or mixed with other goods.

(6) The reference in subsection (2) to a person claiming that certain acts have been committed does not include a person who in good faith reports or warns that such acts have been, or appear to have been, committed.

# CRIMINAL JUSTICE ACT 1987

## 12. Charges of and penalty for conspiracy to defraud

(1) If—
  (a) a person agrees with any other person or persons that a course of conduct shall be pursued; and

(b) that course of conduct will necessarily amount to or involve the commission of any offence or offences by one or more of the parties to the agreement if the agreement is carried out in accordance with their intentions,

the fact that it will do so shall not preclude a charge of conspiracy to defraud being brought against any of them in respect of the agreement.

# CRIMINAL JUSTICE ACT 1988

## 39. Common assault and battery to be summary offences

(1) Common assault and battery shall be summary offences and a person guilty of either of them shall be liable to a fine not exceeding level 5 on the standard scale, to imprisonment for a term not exceeding six months, or to both.

(2) Subsection (1) is subject to section 1 of the Assaults on Emergency Workers (Offences) Act 2018 (which makes provision for increased sentencing powers for offences of common assault and battery committed against an emergency worker acting in the exercise of functions as such a worker).

## 134. Torture

(1) A public official or person acting in an official capacity, whatever his nationality, commits the offence of torture if in the United Kingdom or elsewhere he intentionally inflicts severe pain or suffering on another in the performance or purported performance of his official duties.

(2) A person not falling within subsection (1) above commits the offence of torture, whatever his nationality, if—

(a) in the United Kingdom or elsewhere he intentionally inflicts severe pain or suffering on another at the instigation or with the consent or acquiescence—

(i) of a public official; or

(ii) of a person acting in an official capacity; and

(b) the official or other person is performing or purporting to perform his official duties when he instigates the commission of the offence or consents to or acquiesces in it.

(3) It is immaterial whether the pain or suffering is physical or mental and whether it is caused by an act or an omission.

(4) It shall be a defence for a person charged with an offence under this section in respect of any conduct of his to prove that he had lawful authority, justification or excuse for that conduct.

(5) For the purposes of this section 'lawful authority, justification or excuse' means—

(a) in relation to pain or suffering inflicted in the United Kingdom, lawful authority, justification or excuse under the law of the part of the United Kingdom where it was inflicted;

(b) in relation to pain or suffering inflicted outside the United Kingdom—

(i) if it was inflicted by a United Kingdom official acting under the law of the United Kingdom or by a person acting in an official capacity under that law, lawful authority, justification or excuse under that law;

(ii) if it was inflicted by a United Kingdom official acting under the law of any part of the United Kingdom or by a person acting in an official capacity under such law, lawful authority, justification or excuse under the law of the part of the United Kingdom under whose law he was acting; and

(iii) in any other case, lawful authority, justification or excuse under the law of the place where it was inflicted.

(6) A person who commits the offence of torture shall be liable on conviction on indictment to imprisonment for life.

## 139. Having article with blade or point in public place

(1) Subject to subsections (4) and (5) below, any person who has an article to which this section applies with him in a public place shall be guilty of an offence.

(2) Subject to subsection (3) below, this section applies to any article which has a blade or is sharply pointed except a folding pocketknife.

(3) This section applies to a folding pocketknife if the cutting edge of its blade exceeds 3 inches.

(4) It shall be a defence for a person charged with an offence under this section to prove that he had good reason or lawful authority for having the article with him in a public place.

(5) Without prejudice to the generality of subsection (4) above, it shall be a defence for a person charged with an offence under this section to prove that he had the article with him—

(a) for use at work;

(b) for religious reasons; or

(c) as part of any national costume.

(7) In this section 'public place' includes any place to which at the material time the public have or are permitted access, whether on payment or otherwise.

### 139AA. Offence of threatening with article with blade or point or offensive weapon

(1) A person is guilty of an offence if that person—

(a) has an article to which this section applies with him or her in a public place or of school premises,

(b) unlawfully and intentionally threatens another person with the article, and

(c) does so in such a way that there is an immediate risk of serious physical harm to that other person.

(2) In relation to a public place this section applies to an article to which section 139 applies.

(3) In relation to school premises this section applies to each of these—

(a) an article to which section 139 applies;

(b) an offensive weapon within the meaning of section 1 of the Prevention of Crime Act 1953.

(4) For the purposes of this section physical harm is serious if it amounts to grievous bodily harm for the purposes of the Offences against the Person Act 1861.

(5) In this section—

'public place' has the same meaning as in section 139;

'school premises' has the same meaning as in section 139A.

### 139A. Offence of having article with blade or point (or offensive weapon) on school premises

(1) Any person who has an article to which section 139 of this Act applies with him on school premises shall be guilty of an offence.

(2) Any person who has an offensive weapon within the meaning of section 1 of the Prevention of Crime Act 1953 with him on school premises shall be guilty of an offence.

(3) It shall be a defence for a person charged with an offence under subsection (1) or (2) above to prove that he had good reason or lawful authority for having the article or weapon with him on the premises in question.

(4) Without prejudice to the generality of subsection (3) above, it shall be a defence for a person charged with an offence under subsection (1) or (2) above to prove that he had the article or weapon in question with him—

(a) for use at work,

(b) for educational purposes,

(c) for religious reasons, or

(d) as part of any national costume.

### 141. Offensive weapons

(1) Any person who manufactures, sells or hires or offers for sale or hire, exposes or has in his possession for the purpose of sale or hire, or lends or gives to any other person, a weapon to which this section applies shall be guilty of an offence and liable—

(a) on summary conviction, to imprisonment for a term not exceeding 12 months or a fine not exceeding the statutory maximum, or to both;

(b) on conviction on indictment, to imprisonment for a term not exceeding 4 years, or to a fine, or to both.

(2) The Secretary of State may by order made by statutory instrument direct that this section shall apply to any description of weapon specified in the order except—

(a) any weapon subject to the Firearms Act 1968; and
(b) crossbows.

(4) The importation of a weapon to which this section applies is hereby prohibited.

(5) It shall be a defence for any person charged in respect of any conduct of his relating to a weapon to which this section applies—
(a) with an offence under subsection (1) above; or
(b) with an offence under section 50(2) or (3) of the Customs and Excise Management Act 1979 (improper importation),

to show that his conduct was only for the purposes of functions carried out on behalf of the Crown or of a visiting force.

(8) It shall be a defence for any person charged in respect of any conduct of his relating to a weapon to which this section applies—
(a) with an offence under subsection (1) above; or
(b) with an offence under section 50(2) or (3) of the Customs and Excise Management Act 1979,

to show that the conduct in question was only for the purposes of making the weapon available to a museum or gallery to which this subsection applies.

(9) If a person acting on behalf of a museum or gallery to which subsection (8) above applies is charged with hiring or lending a weapon to which this section applies, it shall be a defence for him to show that he had reasonable grounds for believing that the person to whom he lent or hired it would use it only for cultural, artistic or educational purposes.

(10) Subsection (8) above applies to a museum or gallery only if it does not distribute profits.

(11A) It shall be a defence for a person charged in respect of conduct of his relating to a weapon to which this section applies—
(a) with an offence under subsection (1) above, or
(b) with an offence under section 50(2) or (3) of the Customs and Excise Management Act 1979,

to show that his conduct was for the purpose only of making the weapon in question available for one or more of the purposes specified in subsection (11B).

(11B) Those purposes are—
(a) the purposes of theatrical performances and of rehearsals for such performances;
(b) the production of films (within the meaning of Part 1 of the Copyright, Designs and Patents Act 1988 – see section 5B of that Act);
(c) the production of television programmes (within the meaning of the Communications Act 2003 – see section 405(1) of that Act).

(11C) For the purposes of this section a person shall be taken to have shown a matter specified in subsection (5), (8), (9) or (11A) if—
(a) sufficient evidence of that matter is adduced to raise an issue with respect to it; and
(b) the contrary is not proved beyond a reasonable doubt.

(11D) The Secretary of State may by order made by statutory instrument—
(a) provide for exceptions and exemptions from the offence under subsection (1) above or from the prohibition in subsection (4) above; and
(b) provide for it to be a defence in proceedings for such an offence, or for an offence under section 50(2) or (3) of the Customs and Excise Management Act 1979, to show the matters specified or described in the order.

(11E) A statutory instrument containing an order under this section shall not be made unless a draft of the instrument has been laid before Parliament and approved by a resolution of each House.

## 141A. Sale of knives and certain articles with blade or point to persons under eighteen

(1) Any person who sells to a person under the age of eighteen years an article to which this section applies shall be guilty of an offence and liable on summary conviction to imprisonment for a term not exceeding six months, or a fine not exceeding level 5 on the standard scale, or both.

(2) Subject to subsection (3) below, this section applies to—
(a) any knife, knife blade or razor blade,
(b) any axe, and
(c) any other article which has a blade or which is sharply pointed and which is made or adapted for use for causing injury to the person.
(3) This section does not apply to any article described in—
(a) section 1 of the Restriction of Offensive Weapons Act 1959,
(b) an order made under section 141 (2) of this Act, or
(c) an order made by the Secretary of State under this section.
(4) It shall be a defence for a person charged with an offence under subsection (1) above to prove that he took all reasonable precautions and exercised all due diligence to avoid the commission of the offence.

### 160. Possession of indecent photograph of child

(1) Subject to section 160A it is an offence for a person to have any indecent photograph or pseudo-photograph of a child ... in his possession.
(2) Where a person is charged with an offence under subsection (1) above, it shall be a defence for him to prove—
(a) that he had a legitimate reason for having the photograph or pseudo-photograph in his possession; or
(b) that he had not himself seen the photograph or pseudo-photograph and did not know, nor had any cause to suspect, it to be indecent; or
(c) that the photograph or pseudo-photograph was sent to him without any prior request made by him or on his behalf and that he did not keep it for an unreasonable time.
(2A) A person shall be liable on conviction on indictment of an offence under this section to imprisonment for a term not exceeding five years or a fine, or both.
(4) Sections 1(3), 2(3), 3 and 7 of the Protection of Children Act 1978 shall have effect as if any reference in them to that Act included a reference to this section.

### 160A. Marriage and other relationships

(1) This section applies where, in proceedings for an offence under section 160 relating to an indecent photograph of a child, the defendant proves that the photograph was of the child aged 16 or over, and that at the time of the offence charged the child and he—
(a) were married or civil partners of each other, or
(b) lived together as partners in an enduring family relationship.
(2) This section also applies where, in proceedings for an offence under section 160 relating to an indecent photograph of a child, the defendant proves that the photograph was of the child aged 16 or over, and that at the time when he obtained it the child and he—
(a) were married or civil partners of each other, or
(b) lived together as partners in an enduring family relationship.
(3) This section applies whether the photograph showed the child alone or with the defendant, but not if it showed any other person.
(4) If sufficient evidence is adduced to raise an issue as to whether the child consented to the photograph being in the defendant's possession, or as to whether the defendant reasonably believed that the child so consented, the defendant is not guilty of the offence unless it is proved that the child did not so consent and that the defendant did not reasonably believe that the child so consented.

## MALICIOUS COMMUNICATIONS ACT 1988

### 1. Offence of sending letters etc. with intent to cause distress or anxiety

(1) Any person who sends to another person—
(a) a letter, electronic communication or article of any description which conveys—
(i) a message which is indecent or grossly offensive;
(ii) a threat; or
(iii) information which is false and known or believed to be false by the sender;

or

(b) any article or electronic communication which is, in whole or part, of an indecent or grossly offensive nature,

is guilty of an offence if his purpose, or one of his purposes, in sending it is that it should, so far as falling within paragraph (a) or (b) above, cause distress or anxiety to the recipient or to any other person to whom he intends that it or its contents or nature should be communicated.

(2) A person is not guilty of an offence by virtue of subsection (1)(a)(ii) above if he shows—

(a) that the threat was used to reinforce a demand made by him on reasonable grounds; and

(b) that he believed, and had reasonable grounds for believing that the use of the threat was a proper means of reinforcing the demand.

(2A) In this section 'electronic communication' includes—

(a) any oral or other communication by means of an electronic communications network; and

(b) any communication (however sent) that is in electronic form.

(3) In this section references to sending include references to delivering or transmitting and to causing to be sent, delivered or transmitted and 'sender' shall be construed accordingly.

# ROAD TRAFFIC ACT 1988

## 1. Causing death by dangerous driving

A person who causes the death of another person by driving a mechanically propelled vehicle dangerously on a road or other public place is guilty of an offence.

## 1A. Causing serious injury by dangerous driving

(1) A person who causes serious injury to another person by driving a mechanically propelled vehicle dangerously on a road or other public place is guilty of an offence.

(2) In this section 'serious injury' means—

(a) in England and Wales, physical harm which amounts to grievous bodily harm for the purposes of the Offences against the Person Act 1861, ...

## 2. Dangerous driving

A person who drives a mechanically propelled vehicle dangerously on a road or other public place is guilty of an offence.

## 2A. Meaning of dangerous driving

(1) For the purposes of sections 1, 1A and 2 above a person is to be regarded as driving dangerously if (and, subject to subsection (2) below, only if)—

(a) the way he drives falls far below what would be expected of a competent and careful driver, and

(b) it would be obvious to a competent and careful driver that driving in that way would be dangerous.

(2) A person is also to be regarded as driving dangerously for the purposes of sections 1, 1A and 2 above if it would be obvious to a competent and careful driver that driving the vehicle in its current state would be dangerous.

(3) In subsections (1) and (2) above 'dangerous' refers to danger either of injury to any person or of serious damage to property; and in determining for the purposes of those subsections what would be expected of, or obvious to, a competent and careful driver in a particular case, regard shall be had not only to the circumstances of which he could be expected to be aware but also to any circumstances shown to have been within the knowledge of the accused.

(4) In determining for the purposes of subsection (2) above the state of a vehicle, regard may be had to anything attached to or carried on or in it and to the manner in which it is attached or carried.

## 2B. Causing death by careless, or inconsiderate, driving

A person who causes the death of another person by driving a mechanically propelled on a road or other public place without due care and attention, or without reasonable care for other persons using the road or place, is guilty of an offence.

## 3. Careless, and inconsiderate, driving

If a person drives a mechanically propelled vehicle on a road or other public place without due care and attention, or without reasonable consideration for other persons using the road or place, he is guilty of an offence.

## 3ZA. Meaning of careless, or inconsiderate, driving

(1) This section has effect for the purposes of sections 2B and 3 above and section 3A below.
(2) A person is to be regarded as driving without due care and attention if (and only if) the way he drives falls below what would be expected of a competent and careful driver.
(3) In determining for the purposes of subsection (2) above what would be expected of a careful and competent driver in a particular case, regard shall be had not only to the circumstances of which he could be expected to be aware but also to any circumstances shown to have been within the knowledge of the accused.
(4) A person is to be regarded as driving without reasonable consideration for other persons only if those persons are inconvenienced by his driving.

## 3ZB. Causing death by driving: unlicensed or uninsured drivers

A person is guilty of an offence under this section if he causes the death of another person by driving a motor vehicle on a road and, at the time when he is driving, the circumstances are such that he is committing an offence under
(a) section 87(1) of this Act (driving otherwise than in accordance with a licence), or
(c) section 143 of this Act (using a motor vehicle while uninsured).

## 3ZC. Causing death by driving: disqualified drivers

A person is guilty of an offence under this section if he or she—
(a) causes the death of another person by driving a motor vehicle on a road, and
(b) at that time, is committing an offence under section 103(1)(b) of this Act (driving while disqualified).

## 3ZD. Causing serious injury by driving: disqualified drivers

(1) A person is guilty of an offence under this section if he or she—
  (a) causes serious injury to another person by driving a motor vehicle on a road, and
  (b) at that time, is committing an offence under section 103(1)(b) of this Act (driving while disqualified).
(2) In this section 'serious injury' means—
  (a) in England and Wales, physical harm which amounts to grievous bodily harm for the purposes of the Offences against the Person Act 1861.

## 3A. Causing death by careless driving when under influence of drink or drugs

(1) If a person causes the death of another person by driving a mechanically propelled vehicle on a road or other public place without due care and attention, or without reasonable consideration for other persons using the road or place, and—
  (a) he is, at the time when he is driving, unfit to drive through drink or drugs, or
  (b) he has consumed so much alcohol that the proportion of it in his breath, blood or urine at that time exceeds the prescribed limit, or
  (ba) he has in his body a specified controlled drug and the proportion of it in his blood or urine at that time exceeds the specified limit for that drug, or
  (c) he is, within 18 hours after that time, required to provide a specimen in pursuance of section 7 of this Act, but without reasonable excuse fails to provide it, or
  (d) he is required by a constable to give his permission for a laboratory test of a specimen of blood taken from him under section 7A of this Act, but without reasonable excuse fails to do so,

he is guilty of an offence.

(2) For the purposes of this section a person shall be taken to be unfit to drive at any time when his ability to drive properly is impaired.

(3) Subsection (1)(b), (ba), (c) and (d) above shall not apply in relation to a person driving a mechanically propelled vehicle other than a motor vehicle.

## 4. Driving, or being in charge, when under influence of drink or drugs

(1) A person who, when driving or attempting to drive a mechanically propelled vehicle on a road or other public place, is unfit to drive through drink or drugs is guilty of an offence.

(2) Without prejudice to subsection (1) above, a person who, when in charge of a mechanically propelled vehicle which is on a road or other public place, is unfit to drive through drink or drugs is guilty of an offence.

(3) For the purposes of subsection (2) above, a person shall be deemed not to have been in charge of a mechanically propelled vehicle if he proves that at the material time the circumstances were such that there was no likelihood of his driving it so long as he remained unfit to drive through drink or drugs.

(4) The court may, in determining whether there was such a likelihood as is mentioned in subsection (3) above, disregard any injury to him and any damage to the vehicle.

(5) For the purposes of this section, a person shall be taken to be unfit to drive if his ability to drive properly is for the time being impaired.

## 5. Driving or being in charge of a motor vehicle with alcohol concentration above prescribed limit

(1) If a person—

(a) drives or attempts to drive a motor vehicle on a road or other public place, or

(b) is in charge of a motor vehicle on a road or other public place,

after consuming so much alcohol that the proportion of it in his breath, blood or urine exceeds the prescribed limit he is guilty of an offence.

(2) It is a defence for a person charged with an offence under subsection (1)(b) above to prove that at the time he is alleged to have committed the offence the circumstances were such that there was no likelihood of his driving the vehicle whilst the proportion of alcohol in his breath, blood or urine remained likely to exceed the prescribed limit.

(3) The court may, in determining whether there was such a likelihood as is mentioned in subsection (2) above, disregard any injury to him and any damage to the vehicle.

## 5A. Driving or being in charge of a motor vehicle with concentration of specified controlled drug above specified limit

(1) This section applies where a person ('D')—

(a) drives or attempts to drive a motor vehicle on a road or other public place, or

(b) is in charge of a motor vehicle on a road or other public place,

and there is in D's body a specified controlled drug.

(2) D is guilty of an offence if the proportion of the drug in D's blood or urine exceeds the specified limit for that drug.

(3) It is a defence for a person ('D') charged with an offence under this section to show that—

(a) the specified controlled drug had been prescribed or supplied to D for medical or dental purposes,

(b) D took the drug in accordance with any directions given by the person by whom the drug was prescribed or supplied, and with any accompanying instructions (so far as consistent with any such directions) given by the manufacturer or distributor of the drug, and

(c) D's possession of the drug immediately before taking it was not unlawful under section 5(1) of the Misuse of Drugs Act 1971 (restriction of possession of controlled drugs) because of an exemption in regulations made under section 7 of that Act (authorisation of activities otherwise unlawful under foregoing provisions).

(4) The defence in subsection (3) is not available if D's actions were—

(a) contrary to any advice, given by the person by whom the drug was prescribed or supplied, about the amount of time that should elapse between taking the drug and driving a motor vehicle, or

(b) contrary to any accompanying instructions about that matter (so far as consistent with any such advice) given by the manufacturer or distributor of the drug.

(5) If evidence is adduced that is sufficient to raise an issue with respect to the defence in subsection (3), the court must assume that the defence is satisfied unless the prosecution proves beyond reasonable doubt that it is not.

(6) It is a defence for a person ('D') charged with an offence by virtue of subsection (1)(b) to prove that at the time D is alleged to have committed the offence the circumstances were such that there was no likelihood of D driving the vehicle whilst the proportion of the specified controlled drug in D's blood or urine remained likely to exceed the specified limit for that drug.

(7) The court may, in determining whether there was such a likelihood, disregard any injury to D and any damage to the vehicle.

(8) In this section, and in sections 3A, 6C(1), 6D and 10, 'specified' means specified in regulations made—

(a) by the Secretary of State, in relation to driving or attempting to drive, or being in charge of a vehicle, in England and Wales;

(9) A limit specified under subsection (2) may be zero.

## 14. Seat belts: adults

(1) The Secretary of State may make regulations requiring, subject to such exceptions as may be prescribed, persons who are driving or riding in motor vehicles on a road to wear seat belts of such description as may be prescribed.

(2) Regulations under this section—

(a) may make different provision in relation to different classes of vehicles, different descriptions of persons and different circumstances,

(b) shall include exceptions for—

(i) the driver of or a passenger in a motor vehicle constructed or adapted for carrying goods, while on a journey which does not exceed the prescribed distance and which is undertaken for the purpose of delivering or collecting any thing,

(ii) the drivers of vehicles while performing a manoeuvre which includes reversing,

(iii) any person holding a valid certificate signed by a medical practitioner to the effect that it is inadvisable on medical grounds for him to wear a seat belt,

(bb) may include an exception for any person holding a certificate to the like effect as that mentioned in paragraph (b)(iii) above which was issued in a member State and which, under the law of that State, is valid for purposes corresponding to those of this section,

(c) may make any prescribed exceptions subject to such conditions as may be prescribed, and

(d) may prescribe cases in which a fee of a prescribed amount may be charged on an application for any certificate required as a condition of any prescribed exception.

(3) Regulations under this section requiring the wearing of seat belts by persons riding in motor vehicles shall not apply to children under the age of fourteen years.

## 15. Restriction on carrying children not wearing seat belts in motor vehicles

(1) Except as provided by regulations, where a child under the age of fourteen years is in the front of a motor vehicle, a person must not without reasonable excuse drive the vehicle on a road unless the child is wearing a seat belt in conformity with regulations.

(1A) Where—

(a) a child is in the front of a motor vehicle other than a bus,

(b) the child is in a rear-facing child restraining device, and

(c) the passenger seat where the child is placed is protected by a front air bag,

a person must not without reasonable excuse drive the vehicle on a road unless the air bag is deactivated.

(2) It is an offence for a person to drive a motor vehicle in contravention of subsection (1) or (1A) above.

(3) Except as provided by regulations, where—

(a) a child under the age of three years is in the rear of a motor vehicle, or

(b) a child of or over that age but under the age of fourteen years is in the rear of a motor vehicle and any seat belt is fitted in the rear of that vehicle,

a person must not without reasonable excuse drive the vehicle on a road unless the child is wearing a seat belt in conformity with regulations.

(3A) Except as provided by regulations, where—

(a) a child who is under the age of 12 years and less than 150 centimetres in height is in the rear of a passenger car,

(b) no seat belt is fitted in the rear of the passenger car, and

(c) a seat in the front of the passenger car is provided with a seat belt but is not occupied by any person,

a person must not without reasonable excuse drive the passenger car on a road.

(4) It is an offence for a person to drive a motor vehicle in contravention of subsection (3) above.

(9) In this section—

'bus' means a motor vehicle that—

(a) has at least four wheels,

(b) is constructed or adapted for the carriage of passengers,

(c) has more than eight seats in addition to the driver's seat, and

(d) has a maximum design speed exceeding 25 kilometres per hour;

'maximum laden weight' has the meaning given by Part IV of Schedule 6 to the Road Traffic Regulation Act 1984;

'passenger car' means a motor vehicle which—

(a) is constructed or adapted for use for the carriage of passengers and is not a goods vehicle,

(b) has no more than eight seats in addition to the driver's seat,

(c) has four or more wheels,

(d) has a maximum design speed exceeding 25 kilometres per hour, and

(e) has a maximum laden weight not exceeding 3.5 tonnes,

'regulations' means regulations made by the Secretary of State under this section, ...

'seat belt' includes any description of restraining device for a child and any reference to wearing a seat belt is to be construed accordingly.

(9A) The reference in subsection (1) above to the air bag being deactivated includes a reference to the case where the air bag is designed or adapted in such a way that it cannot inflate enough to pose a risk of injury to a child travelling in a rear-facing child restraining device in the seat in question.

## 16. Wearing of protective headgear

(1) The Secretary of State may make regulations requiring, subject to such exceptions as may be specified in the regulations, persons driving or riding (otherwise than in side-cars) on motor cycles of any class specified in the regulations to wear protective headgear of such description as may be so specified.

(2) A requirement imposed by regulations under this section shall not apply to any follower of the Sikh religion while he is wearing a turban.

(4) A person who drives or rides a motor cycle in contravention of regulations under this section is guilty of an offence; but notwithstanding any enactment or rule of law no person other than the person actually committing the contravention is guilty of an offence by reason of the contravention unless the person actually committing the contravention is a child under the age of sixteen years.

## 41D. Breach of requirements as to control of vehicle, mobile telephones etc.

A person who contravenes or fails to comply with a construction and use requirement—

(a) as to not driving a motor vehicle in a position which does not give proper control or a full view of the road and traffic ahead, or not causing or permitting the driving of a motor vehicle by another person in such a position, or

(b) as to not driving or supervising the driving of a motor vehicle while using a hand-held mobile telephone or other hand-held interactive communication device, or not causing or permitting the driving of a motor vehicle by another person using such a telephone or other device,

is guilty of an offence.

# OFFICIAL SECRETS ACT 1989

## 1. Security and intelligence

(1) A person who is or has been—

(a) a member of the security and intelligence services; or

(b) a person notified that he is subject to the provisions of this subsection,

is guilty of an offence if without lawful authority he discloses any information, document or other article relating to security or intelligence which is or has been in his possession by virtue of his position as a member of any of those services or in the course of his work while the notification is or was in force.

(2) The reference in subsection (1) above to disclosing information relating to security or intelligence includes a reference to making any statement which purports to be a disclosure of such information or is intended to be taken by those to whom it is addressed as being such a disclosure.

(3) A person who is or has been a Crown servant or government contractor is guilty of an offence if without lawful authority he makes a damaging disclosure of any information, document or other article relating to security or intelligence which is or has been in his possession by virtue of his position as such but otherwise than as mentioned in subsection (1) above.

(4) For the purposes of subsection (3) above a disclosure is damaging if—

(a) it causes damage to the work of, or of any part of, the security and intelligence services; or

(b) it is of information or a document or other article which is such that its unauthorised disclosure would be likely to cause such damage or which falls within a class or description of information, documents or articles the unauthorised disclosure of which would be likely to have that effect.

(5) It is a defence for a person charged with an offence under this section to prove that at the time of the alleged offence he did not know, and had no reasonable cause to believe, that the information, document or article in question related to security or intelligence or, in the case of an offence under subsection (2), that the disclosure would be damaging within the meaning of that subsection.

(6) Notification that a person is subject to subsection (1) above shall be effected by a notice in writing served on him by a Minister of the Crown; and such a notice may be served if, in the Minister's opinion, the work undertaken by the person in question is or includes work connected with the security and intelligence services and its nature is such that the interests of national security require that he should be subject to the provisions of that subsection.

(7) Subject to subsection (8) below, a notification for the purposes of subsection (1) above shall be in force for the period of five years beginning with the day on which it is served but may be renewed by further notices under subsection (6) above for periods of five years at a time.

(8) A notification for the purposes of subsection (1) above may at any time be revoked by a further notice in writing served by the Minister on the person concerned; and the Minister shall serve such a further notice as soon as, in his opinion, the work undertaken by that person ceases to be such as is mentioned in subsection (6) above.

(9) In this section 'security or intelligence' means the work of, or in support of, the security and intelligence services or any part of them, and references to information relating to security or intelligence include references to information held or transmitted by those services or by persons in support of, or of any part of, them.

## 2. Defence

(1) A person who is or has been a Crown servant or government contractor is guilty of an offence if without lawful authority he makes a damaging disclosure of any information, document or other article relating to defence which is or has been in his possession by virtue of his position as such.

(2) For the purposes of subsection (1) above a disclosure is damaging if—

(a) it damages the capability of, or of any part of, the armed forces of the Crown to carry out their tasks or leads to loss of life or injury to members of those forces or serious damage to the equipment or installations of those forces; or

(b) otherwise than as mentioned in paragraph (a) above, it endangers the interests of the United Kingdom abroad, seriously obstructs the promotion or protection by the United Kingdom of those interests or endangers the safety of British citizens abroad; or

(c) it is of information or of a document or article which is such that its unauthorised disclosure would be likely to have any of those effects.

(3) It is a defence for a person charged with an offence under this section to prove that at the time of the alleged offence he did not know, and had no reasonable cause to believe, that the information, document or article in question related to defence or that its disclosure would be damaging within the meaning of subsection (1) above.

(4) In this section 'defence' means—

(a) the size, shape, organisation, logistics, order of battle, deployment, operations, state of readiness and training of the armed forces of the Crown;

(b) the weapons, stores or other equipment of those forces and the invention, development, production and operation of such equipment and research relating to it;

(c) defence policy and strategy and military planning and intelligence;

(d) plans and measures for the maintenance of essential supplies and services that are or would be needed in time of war.

## 3. International relations

(1) A person who is or has been a Crown servant or government contractor is guilty of an offence if without lawful authority he makes a damaging disclosure of—

(a) any information, document or other article relating to international relations; or

(b) any confidential information, document or other article which was obtained from a State other than the United Kingdom or an international organisation, being information or a document or article which is or has been in his possession by virtue of his position as a Crown servant or government contractor.

(2) For the purposes of subsection (1) above a disclosure is damaging if—

(a) it endangers the interests of the United Kingdom abroad, seriously obstructs the promotion or protection by the United Kingdom of those interests or endangers the safety of British citizens abroad; or

(b) it is of information or of a document or article which is such that its unauthorised disclosure would be likely to have any of those effects.

(3) In the case of information or a document or article within subsection (1)(b) above—

(a) the fact that it is confidential, or

(b) its nature or contents,

may be sufficient to establish for the purposes of subsection (2)(b) above that the information, document or article is such that its unauthorised disclosure would be likely to have any of the effects there mentioned.

(4) It is a defence for a person charged with an offence under this section to prove that at the time of the alleged offence he did not know, and had no reasonable cause to believe, that the information, document or article in question was such as is mentioned in subsection (1) above or that its disclosure would be damaging within the meaning of that subsection.

(5) In this section 'international relations' means the relations between States, between international organisations or between one or more States and one or more such organisations and includes any matter relating to a State other than the United Kingdom or to an international organisation which is capable of affecting the relations of the United Kingdom with another State or with an international organisation.

(6) For the purposes of this section any information, document or article obtained from a State or organisation is confidential at any time while the terms on which it was obtained require it to be held in confidence or while the circumstances in which it was obtained make it reasonable for the State or organisation to expect that it would be so held.

## 4. Crime and special investigation powers

(1) A person who is or has been a Crown servant or government contractor is guilty of an offence if without lawful authority he discloses any information, document or other article to which this section applies and which is or has been in his possession by virtue of his position as such.

(2) This section applies to any information, document or other article—

(a) the disclosure of which—

(i) results in the commission of an offence; or

(ii) facilitates an escape from legal custody or the doing of any other act prejudicial to the safekeeping of persons in legal custody; or

(iii) impedes the prevention or detection of offences or the apprehension or prosecution of suspected offenders; or

(b) which is such that its unauthorised disclosure would be likely to have any of those effects.

(3) This section also applies to—

(a) any information obtained by reason of the interception of any communication in obedience to a warrant issued under section 2 of the Interception of Communications Act 1985, or under the authority of an interception warrant under section 5 of the Regulation of Investigatory Powers Act 2000, any information relating to the obtaining of information by reason of any such interception and any document or other article which is or has been used or held for use in, or has been obtained by reason of, any such interception;

(b) any information obtained by reason of action authorised by a warrant issued under section 3 of the Security Service Act 1989 or under section 5 of the Intelligence Services Act 1994 or by an authorisation given under section 7 of that Act, any information relating to the obtaining of information by reason of any such action and any document or other article which is or has been used or held for use in, or has been obtained by reason of, any such action; and

(c) any information obtained under a warrant under Chapter 1 of Part 2 or Chapter 1 of Part 6 of the Investigatory Powers Act 2016, any information relating to the obtaining of information under such a warrant and any document or other article which is or has been used or held for use in, or has been obtained by reason of, the obtaining of information under such a warrant.

(4) It is a defence for a person charged with an offence under this section in respect of a disclosure falling within subsection (2)(a) above to prove that at the time of the alleged offence he did not know, and had no reasonable cause to believe, that the disclosure would have any of the effects there mentioned.

(5) It is a defence for a person charged with an offence under this section in respect of any other disclosure to prove that at the time of the alleged offence he did not know, and had no reasonable cause to believe, that the information, document or article in question was information or a document or article to which this section applies.

(6) In this section 'legal custody' includes detention in pursuance of any enactment or any instrument made under an enactment.

## 5. Information resulting from unauthorised disclosures or entrusted in confidence

(1) Subsection (2) below applies where—

(a) any information, document or other article protected against disclosure by the foregoing provisions of this Act has come into a person's possession as a result of having been—

(i) disclosed (whether to him or another) by a Crown servant or government contractor without lawful authority; or

(ii) entrusted to him by a Crown servant or government contractor on terms requiring it to be held in confidence or in circumstances in which the

Crown servant or government contractor could reasonably expect that it would be so held; or

(iii) disclosed (whether to him or another) without lawful authority by a person to whom it was entrusted as mentioned in sub-paragraph (ii) above; and

(b) the disclosure without lawful authority of the information, document or article by the person into whose possession it has come is not an offence under any of those provisions.

(2) Subject to subsections (3) and (4) below, the person into whose possession the information, document or article has come is guilty of an offence if he discloses it without lawful authority knowing, or having reasonable cause to believe, that it is protected against disclosure by the foregoing provisions of this Act and that it has come into his possession as mentioned in subsection (1) above.

(3) In the case of information or a document or article protected against disclosure by sections 1 to 3 above, a person does not commit an offence under subsection (2) above unless—

(a) the disclosure by him is damaging; and

(b) he makes it knowing, or having reasonable cause to believe, that it would be damaging;

and the question whether a disclosure is damaging shall be determined for the purposes of this subsection as it would be in relation to a disclosure of that information, document or article by a Crown servant in contravention of section 1(3), 2(1) or 3(1) above.

(4) A person does not commit an offence under subsection (2) above in respect of information or a document or other article which has come into his possession as a result of having been disclosed—

(a) as mentioned in subsection (1)(a)(i) above by a government contractor; or

(b) as mentioned in subsection (1)(a)(iii) above,

unless that disclosure was by a British citizen or took place in the United Kingdom, in any of the Channel Islands or in the Isle of Man or a colony.

(5) For the purposes of this section information or a document or article is protected against disclosure by the foregoing provisions of this Act if—

(a) it relates to security or intelligence, defence or international relations within the meaning of section 1, 2 or 3 above or is such as is mentioned in section 3(1)(b) above; or

(b) it is information or a document or article to which section 4 above applies;

and information or a document or article is protected against disclosure by sections 1 to 3 above if it falls within paragraph (a) above.

(6) A person is guilty of an offence if without lawful authority he discloses any information, document or other article which he knows, or has reasonable cause to believe, to have come into his possession as a result of a contravention of section 1 of the Official Secrets Act 1911.

## 6. Information entrusted in confidence to other States or international organisations

(1) This section applies where—

(a) any information, document or other article which—

(i) relates to security or intelligence, defence or international relations; and

(ii) has been communicated in confidence by or on behalf of the United Kingdom to another State or to an international organisation,

has come into a person's possession as a result of having been disclosed (whether to him or another) without the authority of that State or organisation or, in the case of an organisation, of a member of it; and

(b) the disclosure without lawful authority of the information, document or article by the person into whose possession it has come is not an offence under any of the foregoing provisions of this Act.

(2) Subject to subsection (3) below, the person into whose possession the information, document or article has come is guilty of an offence if he makes a damaging disclosure of it knowing, or having reasonable cause to believe, that it is such as is mentioned in subsection (1) above, that it has come into his possession as there mentioned and that its disclosure would be damaging.

(3) A person does not commit an offence under subsection (2) above if the information, document or article is disclosed by him with lawful authority or has previously been made available to the public with the authority of the State or organisation concerned or, in the case of an organisation, of a member of it.

(4) For the purposes of this section 'security or intelligence', 'defence' and 'international relations' have the same meaning as in sections 1, 2 and 3 above and the question whether a disclosure is damaging shall be determined as it would be in relation to a disclosure of the information, document or article in question by a Crown servant in contravention of sections 1(3), 2(1) and 3(1) above.

(5) For the purposes of this section information or a document or article is communicated in confidence if it is communicated on terms requiring it to be held in confidence or in circumstances in which the person communicating it could reasonably expect that it would be so held.

## 7. Authorised disclosures

(1) For the purposes of this Act a disclosure by—
   (a) a Crown servant; or
   (b) a person, not being a Crown servant or government contractor, in whose case a notification for the purposes of section 1 (1) above is in force,

is made with lawful authority if, and only if, it is made in accordance with his official duty.

(2) For the purposes of this Act a disclosure by a government contractor is made with lawful authority if, and only if, it is made—
   (a) in accordance with an official authorisation; or
   (b) for the purposes of the functions by virtue of which he is a government contractor and without contravening an official restriction.

(3) For the purposes of this Act a disclosure made by any other person is made with lawful authority if, and only if, it is made—
   (a) to a Crown servant for the purposes of his functions as such; or
   (b) in accordance with an official authorisation.

(4) It is a defence for a person charged with an offence under any of the foregoing provisions of this Act to prove that at the time of the alleged offence he believed that he had lawful authority to make the disclosure in question and had no reasonable cause to believe otherwise.

(5) In this section 'official authorisation' and 'official restriction' mean, subject to subsection (6) below, an authorisation or restriction duly given or imposed by a Crown servant or government contractor or by or on behalf of a prescribed body or a body of a prescribed class.

(6) In relation to section 6 above 'official authorisation' includes an authorisation duly given by or on behalf of the State or organisation concerned or, in the case of an organisation, a member of it.

## 8. Safeguarding of information

(1) Where a Crown servant or government contractor, by virtue of his position as such, has in his possession or under his control any document or other article which it would be an offence under any of the foregoing provisions of this Act for him to disclose without lawful authority he is guilty of an offence if—
   (a) being a Crown servant, he retains the document or article contrary to his official duty; or
   (b) being a government contractor, he fails to comply with an official direction for the return or disposal of the document or article,

or if he fails to take such care to prevent the unauthorised disclosure of the document or article as a person in his position may reasonably be expected to take.

(2) It is a defence for a Crown servant charged with an offence under subsection (1)(a) above to prove that at the time of the alleged offence he believed that he was acting in accordance with his official duty and had no reasonable cause to believe otherwise.

(3) In subsections (1) and (2) above references to a Crown servant include any person, not being a Crown servant or government contractor, in whose case a notification for the purposes of section 1(1) above is in force.

(4) Where a person has in his possession or under his control any document or other article which it would be an offence under section 5 above for him to disclose without lawful authority, he is guilty of an offence if—
  (a) he fails to comply with an official direction for its return or disposal; or
  (b) where he obtained it from a Crown servant or government contractor on terms requiring it to be held in confidence or in circumstances in which that servant or contractor could reasonably expect that it would be so held, he fails to take such care to prevent its unauthorised disclosure as a person in his position may reasonably be expected to take.

(5) Where a person has in his possession or under his control any document or other article which it would be an offence under section 6 above for him to disclose without lawful authority, he is guilty of an offence if he fails to comply with an official direction for its return or disposal.

(6) A person is guilty of an offence if he discloses any official information, document or other article which can be used for the purpose of obtaining access to any information, document or other article protected against disclosure by the foregoing provisions of this Act and the circumstances in which it is disclosed are such that it would be reasonable to expect that it might be used for that purpose without authority.

(7) For the purposes of subsection (6) above a person discloses information or a document or article which is official if—
  (a) he has or has had it in his possession by virtue of his position as a Crown servant or government contractor; or
  (b) he knows or has reasonable cause to believe that a Crown servant or government contractor has or has had it in his possession by virtue of his position as such.

(8) Subsection (5) of section 5 above applies for the purposes of subsection (6) above as it applies for the purposes of that section.

(9) In this section 'official direction' means a direction duly given by a Crown servant or government contractor or by or on behalf of a prescribed body or a body of a prescribed class.

## 12. 'Crown servant' and 'government contractor'

(1) In this Act 'Crown servant' means—
  (a) a Minister of the Crown;
  (aa) a member of the Scottish Executive or a junior Scottish Minister;
  (ab) the First Minister for Wales, a Welsh Minister appointed under section 48 of the Government of Wales Act 2006, the Counsel General to the Welsh Government or a Deputy Welsh Minister;
  (c) any person employed in the civil service of the Crown, including Her Majesty's Diplomatic Service, Her Majesty's Overseas Civil Service, the civil service of Northern Ireland and the Northern Ireland Court Service;
  (d) any member of the naval, military or air forces of the Crown, including any person employed by an association established for the purposes of Part XI of the Reserve Forces Act 1996;
  (e) any constable and any other person employed or appointed in or for the purposes of any police force (including the Police Service of Northern Ireland and the Police Service of Northern Ireland Reserve) or of the Serious Organised Crime Agency;
  (f) any person who is a member or employee of a prescribed body or a body of a prescribed class and either is prescribed for the purposes of this paragraph or belongs to a prescribed class of members or employees of any such body;
  (g) any person who is the holder of a prescribed office or who is an employee of such a holder and either is prescribed for the purposes of this paragraph or belongs to a prescribed class of such employees.

(2) In this Act 'government contractor' means, subject to subsection (3) below, any person who is not a Crown servant but who provides, or is employed in the provision of, goods or services—
  (a) for the purposes of any Minister or person mentioned in paragraph (a) or (ab) of subsection (1) above, of any office holder in the Scottish Administration, of any of the services, forces or bodies mentioned in that subsection or of the holder of any office prescribed under that subsection; or

(b) under an agreement or arrangement certified by the Secretary of State as being one to which the government of a State other than the United Kingdom or an international organisation is a party or which is subordinate to, or made for the purposes of implementing, any such agreement or arrangement.

(3) Where an employee or class of employees of any body, or of any holder of an office, is prescribed by an order made for the purposes of subsection (1) above—

(a) any employee of that body, or of the holder of that office, who is not prescribed or is not within the prescribed class; and

(b) any person who does not provide, or is not employed in the provision of, goods or services for the purposes of the performance of those functions of the body or the holder of the office in connection with which the employee or prescribed class of employees is engaged,

shall not be a government contractor for the purposes of this Act.

## 13. Other interpretation provisions

(1) In this Act—

'disclose' and 'disclosure', in relation to a document or other article, include parting with possession of it;

'international organisation' means, subject to subsections (2) and (3) below, an organisation of which only States are members and includes a reference to any organ of such an organisation;

'prescribed' means prescribed by an order made by the Secretary of State;

'State' includes the government of a State and any organ of its government and references to a State other than the United Kingdom include references to any territory outside the United Kingdom.

(2) In section 12(2)(b) above the reference to an international organisation includes a reference to any such organisation whether or not one of which only States are members and includes a commercial organisation.

(3) In determining for the purposes of subsection (1) above whether only States are members of an organisation, any member which is itself an organisation of which only States are members, or which is an organ of such an organisation, shall be treated as a State.

## 15. Acts done abroad

(1) Any act—

(a) done by a British citizen or Crown servant; or

(b) done by any person in any of the Channel Islands or the Isle of Man or any colony,

shall, if it would be an offence by that person under any provision of this Act other than section 8(1), (4) or (5) when done by him in the United Kingdom, be an offence under that provision.

# COMPUTER MISUSE ACT 1990

## 1. Unauthorised access to computer material

(1) A person is guilty of an offence if—

(a) he causes a computer to perform any function with intent to secure access to any program or data held in any computer, or to enable any such access to be secured;

(b) the access he intends to secure, or to enable to be secured, is unauthorised; and

(c) he knows at the time when he causes the computer to perform the function that that is the case.

(2) The intent a person has to have to commit an offence under this section need not be directed at—

(a) any particular program or data;

(b) a program or data of any particular kind; or

(c) a program or data held in any particular computer.

## 2. Unauthorised access with intent to commit or facilitate commission of further offences

(1) A person is guilty of an offence under this section if he commits an offence under section 1 above ('the unauthorised access offence') with intent—
  (a) to commit an offence to which this section applies; or
  (b) to facilitate the commission of such an offence (whether by himself or by any other person);

and the offence he intends to commit or facilitate is referred to below in this section as the further offence.

(2) This section applies to offences—
  (a) for which the sentence is fixed by law; or
  (b) for which a person of twenty-one years of age or over (not previously convicted) may be sentenced to imprisonment for a term of five years (or, in England and Wales, might be so sentenced but for the restrictions imposed by section 33 of the Magistrates' Courts Act 1980).

(3) It is immaterial for the purposes of this section whether the further offence is to be committed on the same occasion as the unauthorised access offence or on any future occasion.

(4) A person may be guilty of an offence under this section even though the facts are such that the commission of the further offence is impossible.

## 3. Unauthorised acts with intent to impair, or with recklessness as to impairing, operation of computer, etc.

(1) A person is guilty of an offence if—
  (a) he does any unauthorised act in relation to a computer;
  (b) at the time when he does the act he knows that it is unauthorised; and
  (c) either subsection (2) or subsection (3) below applies.

(2) This subsection applies if the person intends by doing the act—
  (a) to impair the operation of any computer;
  (b) to prevent or hinder access to any program or data held in any computer; or
  (c) to impair the operation of any such program or the reliability of any such data; ...
  (d) ...

(3) This subsection applies if the person is reckless as to whether the act will do any of the things mentioned in paragraphs (a) to (c) of subsection (2) above.

(4) The intention referred to in subsection (2) above, or the recklessness referred to in subsection (3) above, need not relate to—
  (a) any particular computer;
  (b) any particular program or data; or
  (c) a program or data of any particular kind.

(5) In this section—
  (a) a reference to doing an act includes a reference to causing an act to be done;
  (b) 'act' includes a series of acts;
  (c) a reference to impairing, preventing or hindering something includes a reference to doing so temporarily.

## 3ZA. Unauthorised acts causing, or creating risk of, serious damage

(1) A person is guilty of an offence if—
  (a) the person does any unauthorised act in relation to a computer;
  (b) at the time of doing the act the person knows that it is unauthorised;
  (c) the act causes, or creates a significant risk of, serious damage of a material kind; and
  (d) the person intends by doing the act to cause serious damage of a material kind or is reckless as to whether such damage is caused.

(2) Damage is of a 'material kind' for the purposes of this section if it is—
  (a) damage to human welfare in any place;
  (b) damage to the environment of any place;
  (c) damage to the economy of any country; or
  (d) damage to the national security of any country.

(3) For the purposes of subsection (2)(a) an act causes damage to human welfare only if it causes—
  (a) loss to human life;
  (b) human illness or injury;
  (c) disruption of a supply of money, food, water, energy or fuel;
  (d) disruption of a system of communication;
  (e) disruption of facilities for transport; or
  (f) disruption of services relating to health.

(4) It is immaterial for the purposes of subsection (2) whether or not an act causing damage—
  (a) does so directly;
  (b) is the only or main cause of the damage.

(5) In this section—
  (a) a reference to doing an act includes a reference to causing an act to be done;
  (b) 'act' includes a series of acts;
  (c) a reference to a country includes a reference to a territory, and to any place in, or part or region of, a country or territory.

## 3A. Making, supplying or obtaining articles for use in offence under section 1, 3 or 3ZA

(1) A person is guilty of an offence if he makes, adapts, supplies or offers to supply any article intending it to be used to commit, or to assist in the commission of, an offence under section 1, 3 or 3ZA.

(2) A person is guilty of an offence if he supplies or offers to supply any article believing that it is likely to be used to commit, or to assist in the commission of, an offence under section 1, 3 or 3ZA.

(3) A person is guilty of an offence if he obtains any article—
  (a) intending to use it to commit, or to assist in the commission of, an offence under section 1, 3 or 3ZA, or
  (b) with a view to its being supplied for use to commit, or to assist in the commission of, an offence under section 1, 3 or 3ZA.

(4) In this section 'article' includes any program or data held in electronic form.

## 4. Territorial scope of offences under this Act

(1) Except as provided below in this section, it is immaterial for the purposes of any offence under section 1, 3 or 3ZA above—
  (a) whether any act or other event proof of which is required for conviction of the offence occurred in the home country concerned; or
  (b) whether the accused was in the home country concerned at the time of any such act or event.

(2) Subject to subsection (3) below, in the case of such an offence at least one significant link with domestic jurisdiction must exist in the circumstances of the case for the offence to be committed.

(3) There is no need for any such link to exist for the commission of an offence under section 1 above to be established in proof of an allegation to that effect in proceedings for an offence under section 2 above.

(4) Subject to section 8 below, where—
  (a) any such link does in fact exist in the case of an offence under section 1 above; and
  (b) commission of that offence is alleged in proceedings for an offence under section 2 above;

section 2 above shall apply as if anything the accused intended to do or facilitate in any place outside the home country concerned which would be an offence to which section 2 applies if it took place in the home country concerned were the offence in question.

(4A) It is immaterial for the purposes of an offence under section 3A whether the accused was in the home country concerned at the time of any act or other event proof of which is required for conviction of the offence if there is a significant link with domestic jurisdiction in relation to the offence.

(6) References in this Act to the home country concerned are references—
(a) in application of this Act to England and Wales, to England and Wales;
(b) in the application of this Act to Scotland, to Scotland; and
(c) in the application of this Act to Northern Ireland, to Northern Ireland.

## 5. Significant links with domestic jurisdiction

(1) The following provisions of this section apply for the interpretation of section 4 above.
(1A) In relation to an offence under section 1, 3, 3ZA or 3A, where the accused was in a country outside the United Kingdom at the time of the act constituting the offence there is a significant link with domestic jurisdiction if—
(a) the accused was a United Kingdom national at that time; and
(b) the act constituted an offence under the law of the country in which it occurred.
(2) In relation to an offence under section 1, either of the following is a significant link with domestic jurisdiction—
(a) that the accused was in the home country concerned at the time when he did the act which caused the computer to perform the function; or
(b) that any computer containing any program or data to which the accused by doing that act secured or intended to secure unauthorised access, or enabled or intended to enable unauthorised access to be secured, was in the home country concerned at that time.
(3) In relation to an offence under section 3, either of the following is a significant link with domestic jurisdiction—
(a) that the accused was in the home country concerned at the time when he did the unauthorised act (or caused it to be done); or
(b) that the unauthorised act was done in relation to a computer in the home country concerned.
(3A) In relation to an offence under section 3ZA, any of the following is also a significant link with domestic jurisdiction—
(a) that the accused was in the home country concerned at the time when he did the unauthorised act (or caused it to be done);
(b) that the unauthorised act was done in relation to a computer in the home country concerned;
(c) that the unauthorised act caused, or created a significant risk of, serious damage of a material kind (within the meaning of that section) in the home country concerned.

## 6. Territorial scope of inchoate offences related to offences under this Act

(1) On a charge of conspiracy to commit an offence under this Act the following questions are immaterial to the accused's guilt—
(a) the question where any person became a party to the conspiracy; and
(b) the question whether any act, omission or other event occurred in the home country concerned.
(2) On a charge of attempting to commit an offence under this Act above the following questions are immaterial to the accused's guilt—
(a) the question where the attempt was made; and
(b) the question whether it had an effect in the home country concerned.
(3) ...

## 8. Relevance of external law

(1) A person is guilty of an offence triable by virtue of section 4(4) above only if what he intended to do or facilitate would involve the commission of an offence under the law in force where the whole or any part of it was intended to take place.
(3) A person is guilty of an offence triable by virtue of section 1(1A) of the Criminal Attempts Act 1981 ... only if what he had in view would involve the commission of an offence under the law in force where the whole or any part of it was intended to take place.
(4) Conduct punishable under the law in force in any place is an offence under that law for the purposes of this section, however it is described in that law.

(5) Subject to subsection (7) below, a condition specified in subsection (1) or (3) above shall be taken to be satisfied unless not later than rules of court may provide the defence serve on the prosecution a notice—
  (a) stating that, on the facts as alleged with respect to the relevant conduct, the condition is not in their opinion satisfied;
  (b) showing their grounds for that opinion; and
  (c) requiring the prosecution to show that it is satisfied.

(6) In subsection (5) above 'the relevant conduct' means—
  (a) where the condition in subsection (1) above is in question, what the accused intended to do or facilitate; and
  (c) where the condition in subsection (3) above is in question, what the accused had in view.

(7) The court, if it thinks fit, may permit the defence to require the prosecution to show that the condition is satisfied without the prior service of a notice under subsection (5) above.

(9) In the Crown Court the question whether the condition is satisfied shall be decided by the judge alone.

## 9. British citizenship immaterial

(1) Except as provided by section 5(1A), in any proceedings brought in England and Wales in respect of any offence to which this section applies it is immaterial to guilt whether or not the accused was a British citizen at the time of any act, omission or other event proof of which is required for conviction of the offence.

(2) This section applies to the following offences—
  (a) any offence under this Act;
  (b) ...
  (c) any attempt to commit an offence under this Act; and
  (d) ...

## 17. Interpretation

(1) The following provisions of this section apply for the interpretation of this Act.

(2) A person secures access to any program or data held in a computer if by causing a computer to perform any function he—
  (a) alters or erases the program or data;
  (b) copies or moves it to any storage medium other than that in which it is held or to a different location in the storage medium in which it is held;
  (c) uses it; or
  (d) has it output from the computer in which it is held (whether by having it displayed or in any other manner);

and references to access to a program or data (and to an intent to secure such access or to enable such access to be secured) shall be read accordingly.

(3) For the purposes of subsection (2)(c) above a person uses a program if the function he causes the computer to perform—
  (a) causes the program to be executed; or
  (b) is itself a function of the program.

(4) For the purposes of subsection (2)(d) above—
  (a) a program is output if the instructions of which it consists are output; and
  (b) the form in which any such instructions or any other data is output (and in particular whether or not it represents a form in which, in the case of instructions, they are capable of being executed or, in the case of data, it is capable of being processed by a computer) is immaterial.

(5) Access of any kind by any person to any program or data held in a computer is unauthorised if—
  (a) he is not himself entitled to control access of the kind in question to the program or data; and
  (b) he does not have consent to access by him of the kind in question to the program or data from any person who is so entitled;

but this subsection is subject to section 10.

(6) References to any program or data held in a computer include references to any program or data held in any removable storage medium which is for the time being in the computer; and a computer is to be regarded as containing any program or data held in any such medium.

(7) A modification of the contents of any computer takes place if, by the operation of any function of the computer concerned or any other computer—
   (a) any program or data held in the computer concerned is altered or erased; or
   (b) any program or data is added to its contents; and any act which contributes towards causing such a modification shall be regarded as causing it.

(8) An act done in relation to a computer is unauthorised if the person doing the act (or causing it to be done)—
   (a) is not himself a person who has responsibility for the computer and is entitled to determine whether the act may be done; and
   (b) does not have consent to the act from any such person.

   In this subsection 'act' includes a series of acts.

(9) References to the home country concerned shall be read in accordance with section 4(6) above.

(10) References to a program include references to part of a program.

# CRIMINAL PROCEDURE (INSANITY AND UNFITNESS TO PLEAD) ACT 1991

## 1. Acquittals on grounds of insanity

(1) A jury shall not return a special verdict under section 2 of the Trial of Lunatics Act 1883 (acquittal on ground of insanity) except on the written or oral evidence of two or more registered medical practitioners at least one of whom is duly approved.

## 6. Interpretation etc.

(1) In this Act—

'duly approved', in relation to a registered medical practitioner, means approved for the purposes of section 12 of the Mental Health Act 1983 by the Secretary of State, or by another person by virtue of section 12ZA or 12ZB of that Act, as having special experience in the diagnosis or treatment of mental disorder.

# DANGEROUS DOGS ACT 1991

## 1. Dogs bred for fighting

(1) This section applies to—
   (a) any dog of the type known as the pit bull terrier;
   (b) any dog of the type known as the Japanese tosa; and
   (c) any dog of any type designated for the purposes of this section by an order of the Secretary of State, being a type appearing to him to be bred for fighting or to have the characteristics of a type bred for that purpose.

(2) No person shall—
   (a) breed, or breed from, a dog to which this section applies;
   (b) sell or exchange such a dog or offer, advertise or expose such a dog for sale or exchange;
   (c) make or offer to make a gift of such a dog or advertise or expose such a dog as a gift;
   (d) allow such a dog of which he is the owner or of which he is for the time being in charge to be in a public place without being muzzled and kept on a lead; or
   (e) abandon such a dog of which he is the owner or, being the owner or for the time being in charge of such a dog, allow it to stray.

(3) After such day as the Secretary of State may by order appoint for the purposes of this subsection no person shall have any dog to which this section applies in his possession or custody except—

(a) in pursuance of the power of seizure conferred by the subsequent provisions of this Act; or

(b) in accordance with an order for its destruction made under those provisions;

but the Secretary of State shall by order make a scheme for the payment to the owners of such dogs who arrange for them to be destroyed before that day of sums specified in or determined under the scheme in respect of those dogs and the cost of their destruction.

(4) Subsection (2)(b) and (c) above shall not make unlawful anything done with a view to the dog in question being removed from the United Kingdom before the day appointed under subsection (3) above.

(5) The Secretary of State may by order provide that the prohibition in subsection (3) above shall not apply in such cases and subject to compliance with such conditions as are specified in the order and any such provision may take the form of a scheme of exemption containing such arrangements (including provision for the payment of charges or fees) as he thinks appropriate.

(6) A scheme under subsection (3) or (5) above may provide for specified functions under the scheme to be discharged by such persons or bodies as the Secretary of State thinks appropriate.

(6A) A scheme under subsection (3) or (5) may in particular include provision requiring a court to consider whether a person is a fit and proper person to be in charge of a dog.

## 2. Other specially dangerous dogs

(1) If it appears to the Secretary of State that dogs of any type to which section 1 above does not apply present a serious danger to the public he may by order impose in relation to dogs of that type restrictions corresponding, with such modifications, if any, as he thinks appropriate, to all or any of those in subsection (2)(d) and (e) of that section.

(2) An order under this section may provide for exceptions from any restriction imposed by the order in such cases and subject to compliance with such conditions as are specified in the order.

(3) An order under this section may contain such supplementary or transitional provisions as the Secretary of State thinks necessary or expedient and may create offences punishable on summary conviction with imprisonment for a term not exceeding six months or a fine not exceeding level 5 on the standard scale or both.

(4) In determining whether to make an order under this section in relation to dogs of any type and, if so, what the provisions of the order should be, the Secretary of State shall consult with such persons or bodies as appear to him to have relevant knowledge or experience, including a body concerned with animal welfare, a body concerned with veterinary science and practice and a body concerned with breeds of dogs.

(5) The power to make an order under this section shall be exercisable by statutory instrument and no such order shall be made unless a draft of it has been laid before and approved by a resolution of each House of Parliament.

## 3. Keeping dogs under proper control

(1) If a dog is dangerously out of control in any place in England and Wales (whether or not a public place)—

(a) the owner; and

(b) if different, the person for the time being in charge of the dog,

is guilty of an offence, or, if the dog while so out of control injures any person or assistance dog, an aggravated offence, under this subsection.

(1A) A person ('D') is not guilty of an offence under subsection (1) in a case which is a householder case.

(1B) For the purposes of subsection (1A) 'a householder case' is a case where—

(a) the dog is dangerously out of control while in or partly in a building, or part of a building, that is a dwelling or is forces accommodation (or is both), and

(b) at that time—

(i) the person in relation to whom the dog is dangerously out of control ('V') is in, or is entering, the building or part as a trespasser, or

(ii) D (if present at that time) believed V to be in, or entering, the building or part as a trespasser.

Section 76(8B) to (8F) of the Criminal Justice and Immigration Act 2008 (use of force at place of residence) apply for the purposes of this subsection as they apply for the purposes of subsection (8A) of that section (and for those purposes the reference in section 76(8D) to subsection (8A)(d) is to be read as if it were a reference to paragraph (b)(ii) of this subsection).

(2) In proceedings for an offence under subsection (1) above against a person who is the owner of a dog but was not at the material time in charge of it, it shall be a defence for the accused to prove that the dog was at the material time in the charge of a person whom he reasonably believed to be a fit and proper person to be in charge of it.

(3) ...

## 4. Destruction and disqualification orders

(1) Where a person is convicted of an offence under section 1 or 3(1) above or of an offence under an order made under section 2 above the court—
  (a) may order the destruction of any dog in respect of which the offence was committed and, subject to subsection (1A) below, shall do so in the case of an offence under section 1 or an aggravated offence under section 3(1) above; and
  (b) may order the offender to be disqualified, for such period as the court thinks fit, for having custody of a dog.

(1A) Nothing in subsection (1)(a) above shall require the court to order the destruction of a dog if the court is satisfied—
  (a) that the dog would not constitute a danger to public safety; and
  (b) where the dog was born before 30th November 1991 and is subject to the prohibition in section 1(3) above, that there is a good reason why the dog has not been exempted from that prohibition.

(1B) For the purposes of subsection (1A)(a), when deciding whether a dog would constitute a danger to public safety, the court—
  (a) must consider—
    (i) the temperament of the dog and its past behaviour, and
    (ii) whether the owner of the dog, or the person for the time being in charge of it, is a fit and proper person to be in charge of the dog, and
  (b) may consider any other relevant circumstances.

(2) Where a court makes an order under subsection (1)(a) above for the destruction of a dog owned by a person other than the offender... the owner may appeal to the Crown Court against the order.

(3) A dog shall not be destroyed pursuant to an order under subsection (1)(a) above—
  (a) until the end of the period for giving notice of appeal against the conviction or ..., against the order; and
  (b) if notice of appeal is given within that period, until the appeal is determined or withdrawn,

unless the offender and, in a case to which subsection (2) above applies, the owner of the dog give notice to the court that made the order that there is to be no appeal.

(4) Where a court makes an order under subsection (1)(a) above it may—
  (a) appoint a person to undertake the destruction of the dog and require any person having custody of it to deliver it up for that purpose; and
  (b) order the offender to pay such sum as the court may determine to be the reasonable expenses of destroying the dog and of keeping it pending its destruction.

(5) Any sum ordered to be paid under subsection (4)(b) above shall be treated for the purposes of enforcement as if it were a fine imposed on conviction.

(6) Any person who is disqualified for having custody of a dog by virtue of an order under subsection (1)(b) above may, at any time after the end of the period of one year beginning with the date of the order, apply to the court that made it (or a magistrates' court acting in the same local justice area as that court) for a direction terminating the disqualification.

(7) On an application under subsection (6) above the court may—
  (a) having regard to the applicant's character, his conduct since the disqualification was imposed and any other circumstances of the case, grant or refuse the application; and

(b) order the applicant to pay all or any part of the costs of the application;

and where an application in respect of an order is refused no further application in respect of that order shall be entertained if made before the end of the period of one year beginning with the date of the refusal.

(8) Any person who—

(a) has custody of a dog in contravention of an order under subsection (1)(b) above; or

(b) fails to comply with a requirement imposed on him under subsection (4)(a) above,

is guilty of an offence and liable on summary conviction to a fine not exceeding level 5 on the standard scale.

## 4A. Contingent destruction orders

(1) Where—

(a) a person is convicted of an offence under section 1 above or an aggravated offence under section 3(1) above;

(b) the court does not order the destruction of the dog under section 4(1)(a) above; and

(c) in the case of an offence under section 1 above, the dog is subject to the prohibition in section 1(3) above,

the court shall order that, unless the dog is exempted from that prohibition within the requisite period, the dog shall be destroyed.

(2) Where an order is made under subsection (1) above in respect of a dog, and the dog is not exempted from the prohibition in section 1(3) above within the requisite period, the court may extend that period.

(3) Subject to subsection (2) above, the requisite period for the purposes of such an order is the period of two months beginning with the date of the order.

(4) Where a person is convicted of an offence under section 3(1) above, the court may order that, unless the owner of the dog keeps it under proper control, the dog shall be destroyed.

(5) An order under subsection (4) above—

(a) may specify the measures to be taken for keeping the dog under proper control, whether by muzzling, keeping on a lead, excluding it from specified places or otherwise; and

(b) if it appears to the court that the dog is a male and would be less dangerous if neutered, may require it to be neutered.

(6) Subsections (2) to (4) of section 4 above shall apply in relation to an order under subsection (1) or (4) above as they apply in relation to an order under subsection (1)(a) of that section.

## 4B. Destruction orders otherwise than on a conviction

(1) Where a dog is seized under section 5(1) or (2) below or in exercise of a power of seizure conferred by any other enactment and it appears to a justice of the peace, ... —

(a) that no person has been or is to be prosecuted for an offence under this Act or an order under section 2 above in respect of that dog (whether because the owner cannot be found or for any other reason); or

(b) that the dog cannot be released into the custody or possession of its owner without the owner contravening the prohibition in section 1(3) above,

he may order the destruction of the dog and, subject to subsection (2) below, shall do so if it is one to which section 1 above applies.

(2) Nothing in subsection (1)(b) above shall require the justice ... to order the destruction of a dog if he is satisfied—

(a) that the dog would not constitute a danger to public safety; and

(b) where the dog was born before 30th November 1991 and is subject to the prohibition in section 1(3) above, that there is a good reason why the dog has not been exempted from that prohibition.

(2A) For the purposes of subsection (2)(a), when deciding whether a dog would constitute a danger to public safety, the justice or sheriff—
(a) must consider—
(i) the temperament of the dog and its past behaviour, and
(ii) whether the owner of the dog, or the person for the time being in charge of it, is a fit and proper person to be in charge of the dog, and
(b) may consider any other relevant circumstances.
(3) Where in a case falling within subsection (1)(b) above the justice ... does not order the destruction of the dog, he shall order that, unless the dog is exempted from the prohibition in section 1(3) above within the requisite period, the dog shall be destroyed.
(4) Subsections (2) to (4) of section 4 above shall apply in relation to an order under subsection (1)(b) or (3) above as they apply in relation to an order under subsection (1)(a) of that section.
(5) Subsections (2) and (3) of section 4A above shall apply in relation to an order under subsection (3) above as they apply in relation to an order under subsection (1) of that section, except that the reference to the court in subsection (2) of that section shall be construed as a reference to the justice ...

### 6. Dogs owned by young persons

Where a dog is owned by a person who is less than sixteen years old any reference to its owner in section 1(2)(d) or (e) or 3 above shall include a reference to the head of the household, if any, of which that person is a member ...

### 7. Muzzling and leads

(1) In this Act—
(a) references to a dog being muzzled are to its being securely fitted with a muzzle sufficient to prevent it biting any person; and
(b) references to its being kept on a lead are to its being securely held on a lead by a person who is not less than sixteen years old.

## FOOTBALL (OFFENCES) ACT 1991

### 1. Designated football matches

(1) In this Act a 'designated football match' means an association football match designated, or of a description designated, for the purposes of this Act by order of the Secretary of State.

Any such order shall be made by statutory instrument which shall be subject to annulment in pursuance of a resolution of either House of Parliament.
(2) References in this Act to things done at a designated football match include anything done at the ground—
(a) within the period beginning two hours before the start of the match or (if earlier) two hours before the time at which it is advertised to start and ending one hour after the end of the match; or
(b) where the match is advertised to start at a particular time on a particular day but does not take place on that day, within the period beginning two hours before and ending one hour after the advertised starting time.

### 2. Throwing of missiles

It is an offence for a person at a designated football match to throw anything at or towards—
(a) the playing area, or any area adjacent to the playing area to which spectators are not generally admitted, or
(b) any area in which spectators or other persons are or may be present, without lawful authority or lawful excuse (which shall be for him to prove).

### 3. Indecent or racialist chanting

(1) It is an offence to engage or take part in chanting of an indecent or racialist nature at a designated football match.

(2) For this purpose—
(a) 'chanting' means the repeated uttering of any words or sounds (whether alone or in concert with one or more others); and
(b) 'of a racialist nature' means consisting of or including matter which is threatening, abusive or insulting to a person by reason of his colour, race, nationality (including citizenship) or ethnic or national origins.

### 4. Going onto the playing area

It is an offence for a person at a designated football match to go onto the playing area, or any area adjacent to the playing area to which spectators are not generally admitted, without lawful authority or lawful excuse (which shall be for him to prove).

## PRISON SECURITY ACT 1992

### 1. Offence of prison mutiny

(1) Any prisoner who takes part in a prison mutiny shall be guilty of an offence and liable, on conviction on indictment, to imprisonment for a term not exceeding ten years or to a fine or to both.
(2) For the purposes of this section there is a prison mutiny where two or more prisoners, while on the premises of any prison, engage in conduct which is intended to further a common purpose of overthrowing lawful authority in that prison.
(3) For the purposes of this section the intentions and common purpose of prisoners may be inferred from the form and circumstances of their conduct and it shall be immaterial that conduct falling within subsection (2) above takes a different form in the case of different prisoners.
(4) Where there is a prison mutiny, a prisoner who has or is given a reasonable opportunity of submitting to lawful authority and fails, without reasonable excuse, to do so shall be regarded for the purposes of this section as taking part in the mutiny.
(6) In this section—
'conduct' includes acts and omissions;
'prison' means any prison or young offender institution ... which is under the general superintendence of, or is provided by, the Secretary of State under the Prison Act 1952, including a contracted out prison within the meaning of Part IV of the Criminal Justice Act 1991;
'prisoner' means any person for the time being in a prison as a result of any requirement imposed by a court or otherwise that he be detained in legal custody.

## CRIMINAL JUSTICE ACT 1993

### 1. Offences to which this Part applies

(1) This Part applies to two groups of offences—
(a) any offence mentioned in subsection (2) (a 'Group A offence') and
(b) any offence mentioned in subsection (3) (a 'Group B offence').
(2) The Group A offences are—
(a) an offence under any of the following provisions of the Theft Act 1968—
section 1 (theft);
...
section 17 (false accounting);
section 19 (false statements by company directors, etc.);
section 21 (blackmail);
section 22 (handling stolen goods);
section 24A (retaining credits from dishonest sources, etc.);
(b) ...
(bb) an offence under any of the following provisions of the Fraud Act 2006—

(i) section 1 (fraud);
(ii) section 6 (possession etc. of articles for use in frauds);
(iii) section 7 (making or supplying articles for use in frauds);
(iv) section 9 (participating in fraudulent business carried on by sole trader etc.);
(v) section 11 (obtaining services dishonestly);

(c) an offence under any of the following provisions of the Forgery and Counterfeiting Act 1981 —
section 1 (forgery);
section 2 (copying a false instrument); section 3 (using a false instrument);
section 4 (using a copy of a false instrument);
section 5 (offences which relate to money orders, share certificates, passports, etc.);
section 14 (offences of counterfeiting notes and coins);
section 15 (offences of passing etc. counterfeit notes and coins);
section 16 (offences involving the custody or control of counterfeit notes and coins);
section 17 (offences involving the making or custody or control of counterfeiting materials and implements);
section 20 (prohibition of importation of counterfeit notes and coins);
section 21 (prohibition of exportation of counterfeit notes and coins);

(ca) an offence under any of sections 4 to 6 of the Identity Documents Act 2010;
(d) the common law offence of cheating in relation to the public revenue.

(3) The Group B offences are—
(a) conspiracy to commit a Group A offence;
(b) conspiracy to defraud;
(c) attempting to commit a Group A offence;
(d) incitement to commit a Group A offence.

(4) The Secretary of State may by order amend subsection (2) or (3) by adding or removing any offence.

(5) The power to make such an order shall be exercisable by statutory instrument.

(6) No order shall be made under subsection (4) unless a draft of it has been laid before and approved by a resolution of each House of Parliament.

## 2. Jurisdiction in respect of Group A offences

(1) For the purposes of this Part, 'relevant event', in relation to any Group A offence, means (subject to subsection (1A)) any act or omission or other event (including any result of one or more acts or omissions) proof of which is required for conviction of the offence.

(1A) In relation to an offence under section 1 of the Fraud Act 2006 (fraud), 'relevant event' includes—
(a) if the fraud involved an intention to make a gain and the gain occurred, that occurrence;
(b) if the fraud involved an intention to cause a loss or to expose another to a risk of loss and the loss occurred, that occurrence.

(2) For the purpose of determining whether or not a particular event is a relevant event in relation to a Group A offence, any question as to where it occurred is to be disregarded.

(3) A person may be guilty of a Group A offence if any of the events which are relevant events in relation to the offence occurred in England and Wales.

## 3. Questions immaterial to jurisdiction in the case of certain offences.

(1) A person may be guilty of a Group A or Group B offence whether or not—
(a) he was a British citizen at any material time;
(b) he was in England and Wales at any such time.

(2) On a charge of conspiracy to commit a Group A offence, or on a charge of conspiracy to defraud in England and Wales, the defendant may be guilty of the offence whether or not—
(a) he became a party to the conspiracy in England and Wales;

(b) any act or omission or other event in relation to the conspiracy occurred in England and Wales.

(3) On a charge of attempting to commit a Group A offence, the defendant may be guilty of the offence whether or not—

(a) the attempt was made in England and Wales;

(b) it had an effect in England and Wales.

(4) Subsection (1)(a) does not apply where jurisdiction is given to try the offence in question by an enactment which makes provision by reference to the nationality of the person charged.

(5) Subsection (2) does not apply in relation to any charge under the Criminal Law Act 1977 brought by virtue of section 1A of that Act.

(6) Subsection (3) does not apply in relation to any charge under the Criminal Attempts Act 1981 brought by virtue of section 1A of that Act.

### 4. Rules for determining certain jurisdictional questions relating to the location of events

In relation to a Group A or Group B offence—

(a) there is an obtaining of property in England and Wales if the property is either despatched from or received at a place in England and Wales; and

(b) there is a communication in England and Wales of any information, instruction, request, demand or other matter if it is sent by any means—

(i) from a place in England and Wales to a place elsewhere; or

(ii) from a place elsewhere to a place in England and Wales.

### 5. Conspiracy, attempt and incitement

(3) A person may be guilty of conspiracy to defraud if—

(a) a party to the agreement constituting the conspiracy, or a party's agent, did anything in England and Wales in relation to the agreement before its formation, or

(b) a party to it became a party in England and Wales (by joining it either in person or through an agent), or

(c) a party to it, or a party's agent, did or omitted anything in England and Wales in pursuance of it,

and the conspiracy would be triable in England and Wales but for the fraud which the parties to it had in view not being intended to take place in England and Wales.

### 6. Relevance of external law

(1) A person is guilty of an offence triable by virtue of section 5(3), only if the pursuit of the agreed course of conduct would at some stage involve—

(a) an act or omission by one or more of the parties, or

(b) the happening of some other event,

constituting an offence under the law in force where the act, omission or other event was intended to take place.

(2) A person is guilty of an offence triable by virtue of section 1A of the Criminal Attempts Act 1981, or by virtue of section 5(4), only if what he had in view would involve the commission of an offence under the law in force where the whole or any part of it was intended to take place.

(3) Conduct punishable under the law in force in any place is an offence under that law for the purposes of this section, however it is described in that law.

## SEXUAL OFFENCES ACT 1993

### 1. Abolition of presumption of sexual incapacity

The presumption of criminal law that a boy under the age of fourteen is incapable of sexual intercourse is hereby abolished.

# CRIMINAL JUSTICE AND PUBLIC ORDER ACT 1994

## 63. Powers to remove persons attending or preparing for a rave

(1) This section applies to a gathering on land in the open air of 20 or more persons (whether or not trespassers) at which amplified music is played during the night (with or without intermissions) and is such as, by reason of its loudness and duration and the time at which it is played, is likely to cause serious distress to the inhabitants of the locality; and for this purpose—

- (a) such a gathering continues during intermissions in the music and, where the gathering extends over several days, throughout the period during which amplified music is played at night (with or without intermissions); and
- (b) 'music' includes sounds wholly or predominantly characterised by the emission of a succession of repetitive beats.

(1A) This section also applies to a gathering if—

- (a) it is a gathering on land of 20 or more persons who are trespassing on the land; and
- (b) it would be a gathering of a kind mentioned in subsection (1) above if it took place on land in the open air.

(2) If, as respects any land in the open air, a police officer of at least the rank of superintendent reasonably believes that—

- (a) two or more persons are making preparations for the holding there of a gathering to which this section applies,
- (b) ten or more persons are waiting for such a gathering to begin there, or
- (c) ten or more persons are attending such a gathering which is in progress,

he may give a direction that those persons and any other persons who come to prepare or wait for or to attend the gathering are to leave the land and remove any vehicles or other property which they have with them on the land.

(3) A direction under subsection (2) above, if not communicated to the persons referred to in subsection (2) by the police officer giving the direction, may be communicated to them by any constable at the scene.

(4) Persons shall be treated as having had a direction under subsection (2) above communicated to them if reasonable steps have been taken to bring it to their attention.

(5) A direction under subsection (2) above does not apply to an exempt person.

(6) If a person knowing that a direction has been given which applies to him—

- (a) fails to leave the land as soon as reasonably practicable, or
- (b) having left again enters the land within the period of 7 days beginning with the day on which the direction was given,

he commits an offence ...

(7) In proceedings for an offence under subsection (6) above it is a defence for the accused to show that he had a reasonable excuse for failing to leave the land as soon as reasonably practicable or, as the case may be, for again entering the land.

(7A) A person commits an offence if—

- (a) he knows that a direction under subsection (2) above has been given which applies to him, and
- (b) he makes preparations for or attends a gathering to which this section applies within the period of 24 hours starting when the direction was given.

(10) In this section—

'exempt person', in relation to land (or any gathering on land), means the occupier, any member of his family and any employee or agent of his and any person whose home is situated on the land;

'land in the open air' includes a place partly open to the air;

'occupier', 'trespasser' and 'vehicle' have the same meaning as in section 61.

## 68. Offence of aggravated trespass

(1) A person commits the offence of aggravated trespass if he trespasses on land ... and, in relation to any lawful activity which persons are engaging in or are about to engage in on that or adjoining land ... does there anything which is intended by him to have the effect—

(a) of intimidating those persons or any of them so as to deter them or any of them from engaging in that activity,
(b) of obstructing that activity, or
(c) of disrupting that activity.

(2) Activity on any occasion on the part of a person or persons on land is 'lawful' for the purposes of this section if he or they may engage in the activity on the land on that occasion without committing an offence or trespassing on the land.

(5) In this section 'land' does not include—
(a) the highways and roads excluded from the application of section 61 by paragraph (b) of the definition of 'land' in subsection (9) of that section;

## 69. Powers to remove persons committing or participating in aggravated trespass

(1) If the senior police officer present at the scene reasonably believes—
(a) that a person is committing, has committed or intends to commit the offence of aggravated trespass on land ...; or
(b) that two or more persons are trespassing on land in the open air and are present there with the common purpose of intimidating persons so as to deter them from engaging in a lawful activity or of obstructing or disrupting a lawful activity,
he may direct that person or (as the case may be) those persons (or any of them) to leave the land.

(2) A direction under subsection (1) above, if not communicated to the persons referred to in subsection (1) by the police officer giving the direction, may be communicated to them by any constable at the scene.

(3) If a person knowing that a direction under subsection (1) above has been given which applies to him—
(a) fails to leave the land as soon as practicable, or
(b) having left again enters the land as a trespasser within the period of three months beginning with the day on which the direction was given,
he commits an offence ...

(4) In proceedings for an offence under subsection (3) it is a defence for the accused to show—
(a) that he was not trespassing on the land, or
(b) that he had a reasonable excuse for failing to leave the land as soon as practicable or, as the case may be, for again entering the land as a trespasser.

## 166. Sale of tickets by unauthorised persons

(1) It is an offence for an unauthorised person to—
(a) sell a ticket for a designated football match, or
(b) otherwise to dispose of such a ticket to another person.

(2) For this purpose—
(a) a person is 'unauthorised' unless he is authorised in writing to sell or otherwise dispose of tickets for the match ... by the organisers of the match;
(aa) a reference to selling a ticket includes a reference to—
(i) offering to sell a ticket;
(ii) exposing a ticket for sale;
(ii) making a ticket available for sale by another;
(iv) advertising that a ticket is available for purchase; and
(v) giving a ticket to a person who pays or agrees to pay for some other goods or services or offering to do so;
(b) a 'ticket' means anything which purports to be a ticket; and
(c) a 'designated football match' means a football match of a description, or a particular football match, for the time being designated for the purposes of this section by order made by the Secretary of State.

(2A) An order under subsection (2)(c) may designate descriptions of football matches wherever played or when played at descriptions of ground or in any area specified in the order.

(2B) The power of the Secretary of State to make an order under subsection (2)(c) shall be exercisable by statutory instrument which shall be subject to annulment in pursuance of a resolution of either House of Parliament.

## 166A. Supplementary provision relating to sale and disposal of tickets on internet

(1) Nothing in section 166 makes it an offence for a service provider established outside of the United Kingdom to do anything in the course of providing information society services.

(2) If—

(a) a service provider established in the United Kingdom does anything in an EEA State other than the United Kingdom in the course of providing information society services, and

(b) the action, if done in England and Wales, would constitute an offence falling within section 166(1),

the service provider shall be guilty in England and Wales of an offence under that section.

(3) A service provider is not capable of being guilty of an offence under section 166 in respect of anything done in the course of providing so much of an information society service as consists in—

(a) the transmission in a communication network of information falling within subsection (4), or

(b) the storage of information provided by a recipient of the service, except where subsection (5) applies.

(4) Information falls within this subsection if—

(a) it is provided by a recipient of the service; and

(b) it is the subject of automatic, intermediate and temporary storage which is solely for the purpose of making the onward transmission of the information to other recipients of the service at their request more efficient.

(5) This subsection applies at any time in relation to information if—

(a) the service provider knew when that information was provided that it contained material contravening section 166; or

(b) that information is stored at that time (whether as mentioned in subsection (3)(b) or (4)) in consequence of the service provider's failure expeditiously to remove the information, or to disable access to it, upon obtaining actual knowledge that the information contained material contravening section 166.

(6) In this section—

'the Directive' means Directive 2000/31/EC of the European Parliament and of the Council of 8 June 2000 on certain legal aspects of information society services, in particular electronic commerce, in the Internal Market (Directive on electronic commerce);

'information society services'—

(a) has the meaning set out in Article 2(a) of the Directive (which refers to Article 1(2) of Directive 98/34/EC of the European Parliament and of the Council of 22 June 1998 laying down a procedure for the provision of information in the field of technical standards and regulations, as amended by Directive 98/48/EC of 20 July 1998); and

(b) is summarised in recital 17 of the Directive as covering 'any service normally provided for remuneration, at a distance, by means of electronic equipment for the processing (including digital compression) and storage of data, and at the individual request of a recipient of a service';

'EEA State' means a state which is for the time being a member State, Norway, Iceland or Liechtenstein;

'recipient of the service' means any person who, for professional ends or otherwise, uses an information society service, in particular for the purposes of seeking information or making it accessible;

'service provider' means any person providing an information society service.

# LAW REFORM (YEAR AND A DAY RULE) ACT 1996

## 1. Abolition of 'year and a day rule'

The rule known as the 'year and a day rule' (that is, the rule that, for the purposes of offences involving death and of suicide, an act or omission is conclusively presumed not to have caused a person's death if more than a year and a day elapsed before he died) is abolished for all purposes.

## 2. Restriction on institution of proceedings for a fatal offence

(1) Proceedings to which this section applies may only be instituted by or with the consent of the Attorney General.

(2) This section applies to proceedings against a person for a fatal offence if—

- (a) the injury alleged to have caused the death was sustained more than three years before the death occurred, or
- (b) the person has previously been convicted of an offence committed in circumstances alleged to be connected with the death.

(3) In subsection (2) 'fatal offence' means—

- (a) murder, manslaughter, infanticide or any other offence of which one of the elements is causing a person's death,
- (b) an offence under section 2(1) of the Suicide Act 1961 (offence of encouraging or assisting suicide) in connection with the death of a person, or
- (c) an offence under section 5 of the Domestic Violence, Crime and Victims Act 2004 of causing or allowing the death of a child or vulnerable adult.

## 3. Commencement etc.

(2) Section 1 does not affect the continued application of the rule referred to in that section to a case where the act or omission (or the last of the acts or omissions) which caused the death occurred before the day on which this Act is passed.

# POLICE ACT 1996

## 89. Assaults on constables

(1) Any person who assaults a constable in the execution of his duty, or a person assisting a constable in the execution of his duty, shall be guilty of an offence and liable on summary conviction to imprisonment for a term not exceeding six months or to a fine not exceeding level 5 on the standard scale, or to both.

(2) Any person who resists or wilfully obstructs a constable in the execution of his duty, or a person assisting a constable in the execution of his duty shall be guilty of an offence and liable on summary conviction to imprisonment for a term not exceeding one month or to a fine not exceeding level 3 on the standard scale, or to both.

## 90. Impersonation, etc.

(1) Any person who with intent to deceive impersonates a member of a police force or special constable, or makes any statement or does any act calculated falsely to suggest that he is such a member or constable, shall be guilty of an offence and liable on summary conviction to imprisonment for a term not exceeding six months or to a fine not exceeding level 5 on the standard scale, or to both.

(2) Any person who, not being a constable, wears any article of police uniform in circumstances where it gives him an appearance so nearly resembling that of a member of a police force as to be calculated to deceive shall be guilty of an offence and liable on summary conviction to a fine not exceeding level 3 on the standard scale.

(3) Any person who, not being a member of a police force or special constable, has in his possession any article of police uniform shall, unless he proves that he obtained possession of that article lawfully and has possession of it for a lawful purpose, be guilty of an offence and liable on summary conviction to a fine not exceeding level 1 on the standard scale.

(4) In this section—
 (a) 'article of police uniform' means any article of uniform or any distinctive badge or mark or document of identification usually issued to members of police forces or special constables, or anything having the appearance of such an article, badge, mark or document; and
 (b) 'special constable' means a special constable appointed for a police area.

# SEXUAL OFFENCES (CONSPIRACY AND INCITEMENT) ACT 1996

## 2. Incitement to commit certain sexual acts outside the United Kingdom

(1) This section applies where—
 (a) any act done by a person in England and Wales would amount to the offence of incitement to commit a listed sexual offence but for the fact that what he had in view would not be an offence triable in England and Wales,
 (b) the whole or part of what he had in view was intended to take place in a country or territory outside the United Kingdom, and
 (c) what he had in view would involve the commission of an offence under the law in force in that country or territory.

(2) Where this section applies—
 (a) what he had in view is to be treated as that listed sexual offence for the purposes of any charge of incitement brought in respect of that act, and
 (b) any such charge is accordingly triable in England and Wales.

(3) Any act done by means of a message (however communicated) is to be treated as done in England and Wales if the message is sent or received in England and Wales.

## 3. Sections 1 and 2: supplementary

(1) Conduct punishable under the law in force in any country or territory is an offence under that law for the purposes of section 2, however it is described in that law.

(2) Subject to subsection (3), a condition in section … 2(1)(c) is to be taken to be satisfied unless, not later than rules of court may provide, the defence serve on the prosecution a notice—
 (a) stating that, on the facts as alleged with respect to what the accused had in view, the condition is not in their opinion satisfied,
 (b) showing their grounds for that opinion, and
 (c) requiring the prosecution to show that it is satisfied.

(4) The court, if it thinks fit, may permit the defence to require the prosecution to show that the condition is satisfied without the prior service of a notice under subsection (2).

(5) In the Crown Court the question whether the condition is satisfied is to be decided by the judge alone.

(6) In any proceedings in respect of any offence triable by virtue of section 2, it is immaterial to guilt whether or not the accused was a British citizen at the time of any act or other event proof of which is required for conviction of the offence.

(8) References to an offence of incitement to commit a listed sexual offence include an offence triable in England and Wales as such an incitement by virtue of section 2 (without prejudice to subsection (2) of that section).

(9) Subsection (8) applies to references in any enactment, instrument or document (except those in section 2 of this Act and in Part I of the Criminal Law Act 1977).

## 5. Interpretation

In this Act 'listed sexual offence' has the meaning given by the Schedule.

SCHEDULE
LISTED SEXUAL OFFENCES

1. (1) In relation to England and Wales, the following are listed sexual offences:
 (b) an offence under any of sections 1 to 12, 14 and 15 to 26 of the Sexual Offences Act 2003.

(2) Sub-paragraph (1)(b) does not apply where the victim of the offence has attained the age of sixteen years.

# KNIVES ACT 1997

## 1. Unlawful marketing of knives

(1) A person is guilty of an offence if he markets a knife in a way which—
  (a) indicates, or suggests, that it is suitable for combat; or
  (b) is otherwise likely to stimulate or encourage violent behaviour involving the use of the knife as a weapon.

(2) 'Suitable for combat' and 'violent behaviour' are defined in section 10.

(3) For the purposes of this Act, an indication or suggestion that a knife is suitable for combat may, in particular, be given or made by a name or description—
  (a) applied to the knife;
  (b) on the knife or on any packaging in which it is contained; or
  (c) included in any advertisement which, expressly or by implication, relates to the knife.

(4) For the purposes of this Act, a person markets a knife if—
  (a) he sells or hires it;
  (b) he offers, or exposes, it for sale or hire; or
  (c) he has it in his possession for the purpose of sale or hire.

## 2. Publications

(1) A person is guilty of an offence if he publishes any written, pictorial or other material in connection with the marketing of any knife and that material—
  (a) indicates, or suggests, that the knife is suitable for combat; or
  (b) is otherwise likely to stimulate or encourage violent behaviour involving the use of the knife as a weapon.

(2) A person who is guilty of an offence under this section is liable—
  (a) on summary conviction to imprisonment for a term not exceeding 12 months or to a fine not exceeding the statutory maximum, or to both;
  (b) on conviction on indictment to imprisonment for a term not exceeding 4 years or to a fine, or to both.

## 3. Exempt trades

(1) It is a defence for a person charged with an offence under section 1 to prove that—
  (a) the knife was marketed—
    (i) for use by the armed forces of any country;
    (ii) as an antique or curio; or
    (iii) as falling within such other category (if any) as may be prescribed;
  (b) it was reasonable for the knife to be marketed in that way; and
  (c) there were no reasonable grounds for suspecting that a person into whose possession the knife might come in consequence of the way in which it was marketed would use it for an unlawful purpose.

(2) It is a defence for a person charged with an offence under section 2 to prove that—
  (a) the material was published in connection with marketing a knife—
    (i) for use by the armed forces of any country;
    (ii) as an antique or curio; or
    (iii) as falling within such other category (if any) as may be prescribed.

## 4. Other defences

(1) It is a defence for a person charged with an offence under section 1 to prove that he did not know or suspect, and had no reasonable grounds for suspecting, that the way in which the knife was marketed—
  (a) amounted to an indication or suggestion that the knife was suitable for combat; or
  (b) was likely to stimulate or encourage violent behaviour involving the use of the knife as a weapon.

(2) It is a defence for a person charged with an offence under section 2 to prove that he did not know or suspect, and had no reasonable grounds for suspecting, that the material—

(a) amounted to an indication or suggestion that the knife was suitable for combat; or
(b) was likely to stimulate or encourage violent behaviour involving the use of the knife as a weapon.

(3) It is a defence for a person charged with an offence under section 1 or 2 to prove that he took all reasonable precautions and exercised all due diligence to avoid committing the offence.

### 9. Offences by bodies corporate

(1) If an offence under this Act committed by a body corporate is proved—
(a) to have been committed with the consent or connivance of an officer, or
(b) to be attributable to any neglect on his part,

he as well as the body corporate is guilty of be offence and liable to be proceeded against and punished accordingly.

(2) In subsection (1) 'officer', in relation to a body corporate, means a director, manager, secretary or other similar officer of the body, or a person purporting to act in any such capacity.

(3) If the affairs of a body corporate are managed by its members, subsection (1) applies in relation to the acts and defaults of a member in connection with his functions of management as if he were a director of the body corporate.

### 10. Interpretation

In this Act—

'the court' means—

(a) in relation to England and Wales or Northern Ireland, the Crown Court or a magistrate's court;

'knife' means an instrument which has a blade or is sharply pointed;

'marketing' and related expressions are to be read with section 1(4);

'publication' includes a publication in electronic form and, in the case of a publication which is, or may be, produced from electronic data, any medium on which the data are stored;

'suitable for combat' means suitable for use as a weapon for inflicting injury on a person or causing a person to fear injury:

'violent behaviour' means an unlawful act inflicting injury on a person or causing a person to fear injury.

## PROTECTION FROM HARASSMENT ACT 1997

### 1. Prohibition of harassment

(1) A person must not pursue a course of conduct—
(a) which amounts to harassment of another, and
(b) which he knows or ought to know amounts to harassment of the other.

(1A) A person must not pursue a course of conduct—
(a) which involves harassment of two or more persons, and
(b) which he knows or ought to know involves harassment of those persons, and
(c) by which he intends to persuade any person (whether or not one of those mentioned above)—
(i) not to do something that he is entitled or required to do, or
(ii) to do something that he is not under any obligation to do.

(2) For the purposes of this section or section 2A(2)(c), the person whose course of conduct is in question ought to know that it amounts to or involves harassment of another if a reasonable person in possession of the same information would think the course of conduct amounted to or involved harassment of the other.

(3) Subsection (1) or (1A) does not apply to a course of conduct if the person who pursued it shows—
(a) that it was pursued for the purpose of preventing or detecting crime,
(b) that it was pursued under any enactment or rule of law or to comply with any condition or requirement imposed by any person under any enactment, or
(c) that in the particular circumstances the pursuit of the course of conduct was reasonable.

## 2. Offence of harassment

(1) A person who pursues a course of conduct in breach of section 1(1) or (1A) is guilty of an offence.

## 2A. Offence of stalking

(1) A person is guilty of an offence if—
  (a) the person pursues a course of conduct in breach of section 1(1), and
  (b) the course of conduct amounts to stalking.

(2) For the purposes of subsection (1)(b) (and section 4A(1)(a)) a person's course of conduct amounts to stalking of another person if—
  (a) it amounts to harassment of that person,
  (b) the acts or omissions involved are ones associated with stalking, and
  (c) the person whose course of conduct it is knows or ought to know that the course of conduct amounts to harassment of the other person.

(3) The following are examples of acts or omissions which, in particular circumstances, are ones associated with stalking—
  (a) following a person,
  (b) contacting, or attempting to contact, a person by any means,
  (c) publishing any statement or other material—
    (i) relating or purporting to relate to a person, or
    (ii) purporting to originate from a person,
  (d) monitoring the use by a person of the internet, email or any other form of electronic communication,
  (e) loitering in any place (whether public or private),
  (f) interfering with any property in the possession of a person,
  (g) watching or spying on a person.

(6) This section is without prejudice to the generality of section 2.

## 4. Putting people in fear of violence

(1) A person whose course of conduct causes another to fear, on at least two occasions, that violence will be used against him is guilty of an offence if he knows or ought to know that his course of conduct will cause the other so to fear on each of those occasions.

(2) For the purposes of this section, the person whose course of conduct is in question ought to know that it will cause another to fear that violence will be used against him on any occasion if a reasonable person in possession of the same information would think the course of conduct would cause the other so to fear on that occasion.

(3) It is a defence for a person charged with an offence under this section to show that—
  (a) his course of conduct was pursued for the purpose of preventing or detecting crime,
  (b) his course of conduct was pursued under any enactment or rule of law or to comply with any condition or requirement imposed by any person under any enactment, or
  (c) the pursuit of his course of conduct was reasonable for the protection of himself or another or for the protection of his or another's property.

## 4A. Stalking involving fear of violence or serious alarm or distress

(1) A person ('A') whose course of conduct—
  (a) amounts to stalking, and
  (b) either—
    (i) causes another ('B') to fear, on at least two occasions, that violence will be used against B, or
    (ii) causes B serious alarm or distress which has a substantial adverse effect on B's usual day-to-day activities,

is guilty of an offence if A knows or ought to know that A's course of conduct will cause B so to fear on each of those occasions or (as the case may be) will cause such alarm or distress.

(2) For the purposes of this section A ought to know that A's course of conduct will cause B to fear that violence will be used against B on any occasion if a reasonable person in possession of the same information would think the course of conduct would cause B so to fear on that occasion.

(3) For the purposes of this section A ought to know that A's course of conduct will cause B serious alarm or distress which has a substantial adverse effect on B's usual day-to-day activities if a reasonable person in possession of the same information would think the course of conduct would cause B such alarm or distress.

(4) It is a defence for A to show that—

(a) A's course of conduct was pursued for the purpose of preventing or detecting crime,

(b) A's course of conduct was pursued under any enactment or rule of law or to comply with any condition or requirement imposed by any person under any enactment, or

(c) the pursuit of A's course of conduct was reasonable for the protection of A or another or for the protection of A's or another's property.

## 7. Interpretation of this group of sections

(1) This section applies for the interpretation of sections 1 to 5A.

(2) References to harassing a person include alarming the person or causing the person distress.

(3) A 'course of conduct' must involve—

(a) in the case of conduct in relation to a single person (see section 1 (1)), conduct on at least two occasions in relation to that person, or

(b) in the case of conduct in relation to two or more persons (see section 1(1A)), conduct on at least one occasion in relation to each of those persons.

(3A) A person's conduct on any occasion shall be taken, if aided, abetted, counselled or procured by another—

(a) to be conduct on that occasion of the other (as well as conduct of the person whose conduct it is); and

(b) to be conduct in relation to which the other's knowledge and purpose, and what he ought to have known, are the same as they were in relation to what was contemplated or reasonably foreseeable at the time of the aiding, abetting, counselling or procuring.

(4) 'Conduct' includes speech.

(5) References to a person, in the context of the harassment of a person, are references to a person who is an individual.

# CRIME AND DISORDER ACT 1998

## 28. Meaning of 'racially or religiously aggravated'

(1) An offence is racially or religiously aggravated for the purposes of sections 29 to 32 below if—

(a) at the time of committing the offence, or immediately before or after doing so, the offender demonstrates towards the victim of the offence hostility based on the victim's membership (or presumed membership) of a racial or religious group; or

(b) the offence is motivated (wholly or partly) by hostility towards members of a racial or religious group based on their membership of that group.

(2) In subsection (1)(a) above—

'membership', in relation to a racial or religious group, includes association with members of that group;

'presumed' means presumed by the offender.

(3) It is immaterial for the purposes of paragraph (a) or (b) of subsection (1) above whether or not the offender's hostility is also based, to any extent, on any other factor not mentioned in that paragraph.

(4) In this section 'racial group' means a group of persons defined by reference to race, colour, nationality (including citizenship) or ethnic or national origins.

(5) In this section 'religious group' means a group of persons defined by reference to religious belief or lack of religious belief.

### 29. Racially or religiously aggravated assaults

(1) A person is guilty of an offence under this section if he commits–
- (a) an offence under section 20 of the Offences Against the Person Act 1861 (malicious wounding or grievous bodily harm);
- (b) an offence under section 47 of that Act (actual bodily harm); or
- (c) common assault,

which is racially or religiously aggravated for the purposes of this section.

### 30. Racially or religiously aggravated criminal damage

(1) A person is guilty of an offence under this section if he commits an offence under section 1(1) of the Criminal Damage Act 1971 (destroying or damaging property belonging to another) which is racially or religiously aggravated for the purposes of this section.

(3) For the purposes of this section, section 28(1)(a) above shall have effect as if the person to whom the property belongs or is treated as belonging for the purposes of that Act were the victim of the offence.

### 31. Racially or religiously aggravated public order offences

(1) A person is guilty of an offence under this section if he commits–
- (a) an offence under section 4 of the Public Order Act 1986 (fear or provocation of violence);
- (b) an offence under section 4A of that Act (intentional harassment, alarm or distress); or
- (c) an offence under section 5 of that Act (harassment, alarm or distress),

which is racially or religiously aggravated for the purposes of this section.

(6) If, on the trial on indictment of a person charged with an offence falling within subsection (1)(a) or (b) above, the jury find him not guilty of the offence charged, they may find him guilty of the basic offence mentioned in that provision.

(7) For the purposes of subsection (1)(c) above, section 28(1)(a) above shall have effect as if the person likely to be caused harassment, alarm or distress were the victim of the offence.

### 32. Racially or religiously aggravated harassment etc.

(1) A person is guilty of an offence under this section if he commits–
- (a) an offence under section 2 or 2A of the Protection from Harassment Act 1997 (offences of harassment and stalking); or
- (b) an offence under section 4 or 4A of that Act (putting people in fear of violence and stalking involving fear of violence or serious alarm or distress),

which is racially or religiously aggravated for the purposes of this section.

(5) If, on the trial on indictment of a person charged with an offence falling within subsection (1)(a) above, the jury find him not guilty of the offence charged, they may find him guilty of either basic offence mentioned in that provision.

(6) If, on the trial on indictment of a person charged with an offence falling within subsection (1)(b) above, the jury find him not guilty of the offence charged, they may find him guilty of an offence falling within subsection (1)(a) above.

### 34. Abolition of rebuttable presumption that a child is doli incapax

The rebuttable presumption of criminal law that a child aged 10 or over is incapable of committing an offence is hereby abolished.

## HUMAN RIGHTS ACT 1998

### 1. The Convention Rights

(1) In this Act 'the Convention rights' means the rights and fundamental freedoms set out in–
- (a) Articles 2 to 12 and 14 of the Convention,
- (b) Articles 1 to 3 of the First Protocol, and

(c) Article 1 of the Thirteenth Protocol,

as read with Articles 16 to 18 of the Convention.

(2) Those Articles are to have effect for the purposes of this Act subject to any designated derogation or reservation (as to which see sections 14 and 15).

(3) The Articles are set out in Schedule 1.

## 2. Interpretation of Convention Rights

(1) A court or tribunal determining a question which has arisen in connection with a Convention right must take into account any—

(a) judgment, decision, declaration or advisory opinion of the European Court of Human Rights,

(b) opinion of the Commission given in a report adopted under Article 31 of the Convention,

(c) decision of the Commission in connection with Article 26 or 27(2) of the Convention, or

(d) decision of the Committee of Ministers taken under Article 46 of the Convention,

whenever made or given, so far as, in the opinion of the court or tribunal, it is relevant to the proceedings in which that question has arisen.

(2) Evidence of any judgment, decision, declaration or opinion of which account may have to be taken under this section is to be given in proceedings before any court or tribunal in such manner as may be provided by rules.

## 3. Interpretation of legislation

(1) So far as it is possible to do so, primary legislation and subordinate legislation must be read and given effect in a way which is compatible with the Convention rights.

(2) This section—

(a) applies to primary legislation and subordinate legislation whenever enacted;

(b) does not affect the validity, continuing operation or enforcement of any incompatible primary legislation; and

(c) does not affect the validity, continuing operation or enforcement of any incompatible subordinate legislation if (disregarding any possibility of revocation) primary legislation prevents removal of the incompatibility.

## 4. Declaration of incompatibility

(1) Subsection (2) applies in any proceedings in which a court determines whether a provision of primary legislation is compatible with a Convention right.

(2) If the court is satisfied that the provision is incompatible with a Convention right, it may make a declaration of that incompatibility.

(3) Subsection (4) applies in any proceedings in which a court determines whether a provision of subordinate legislation, made in the exercise of a power conferred by primary legislation, is compatible with a Convention right.

(4) If the court is satisfied—

(a) that the provision is incompatible with a Convention right, and

(b) that (disregarding any possibility of revocation) the primary legislation concerned prevents removal of the incompatibility,

it may make a declaration of that incompatibility.

(5) In this section 'court' means—

(a) the Supreme Court;

(b) the Judicial Committee of the Privy Council;

(c) the Court Martial Appeal Court;

(d) in Scotland, the High Court of Justiciary sitting otherwise than as a trial court or the Court of Session;

(e) in England and Wales or Northern Ireland, the High Court or the Court of Appeal;

(f) the Court of Protection, in any matter being dealt with by the President of the Family Division, the Chancellor of the High Court or a puisne judge of the High Court.

(6) A declaration under this section ('a declaration of incompatibility')—

(a) does not affect the validity, continuing operation or enforcement of the provision in respect of which it is given; and

(b) is not binding on the parties to the proceedings in which it is made.

# SCHEDULE 1
# THE ARTICLES

## PART I
## THE CONVENTION

### RIGHTS AND FREEDOMS

#### *Article 2*
#### *Right to life*

1. Everyone's right to life shall be protected by law. No one shall be deprived of his life intentionally save in the execution of a sentence of a court following his conviction of a crime for which this penalty is provided by law.
2. Deprivation of life shall not be regarded as inflicted in contravention of this Article when it results from the use of force which is no more than absolutely necessary:
   (a) in defence of any person from unlawful violence;
   (b) in order to effect a lawful arrest or to prevent the escape of a person lawfully detained;
   (c) in action lawfully taken for the purpose of quelling a riot or insurrection.

#### *Article 3*
#### *Prohibition of torture*

No one shall be subjected to torture or to inhuman or degrading treatment or punishment.

#### *Article 4*
#### *Prohibition of slavery and forced labour*

1. No one shall be held in slavery or servitude.
2. No one shall be required to perform forced or compulsory labour.
3. For the purpose of this Article the term 'forced or compulsory labour' shall not include:
   (a) any work required to be done in the ordinary course of detention imposed according to the provisions of Article 5 of this Convention or during conditional release from such detention;
   (b) any service of a military character or, in case of conscientious objectors in countries where they are recognised, service exacted instead of compulsory military service;
   (c) any service exacted in case of an emergency or calamity threatening the life or well-being of the community;
   (d) any work or service which forms part of normal civic obligations.

#### *Article 5*
#### *Right to liberty and security*

1. Everyone has the right to liberty and security of person. No one shall be deprived of his liberty save in the following cases and in accordance with a procedure prescribed by law:
   (a) the lawful detention of a person after conviction by a competent court;
   (b) the lawful arrest or detention of a person for non-compliance with the lawful order of a court or in order to secure the fulfilment of any obligation prescribed by law;
   (c) the lawful arrest or detention of a person effected for the purpose of bringing him before the competent legal authority on reasonable suspicion of having committed an offence or when it is reasonably considered necessary to prevent his committing an offence or fleeing after having done so;
   (d) the detention of a minor by lawful order for the purpose of educational supervision or his lawful detention for the purpose of bringing him before the competent legal authority;
   (e) the lawful detention of persons for the prevention of the spreading of infectious diseases, of persons of unsound mind, alcoholics or drug addicts or vagrants;
   (f) the lawful arrest or detention of a person to prevent his effecting an unauthorised entry into the country or of a person against whom action is being taken with a view to deportation or extradition.

*Article 6*
*Right to a fair trial*

1. In the determination of his civil rights and obligations or of any criminal charge against him, everyone is entitled to a fair and public hearing within a reasonable time by an independent and impartial tribunal established by law. Judgment shall be pronounced publicly but the press and public may be excluded from all or part of the trial in the interest of morals, public order or national security in a democratic society, where the interests of juveniles or the protection of the private life of the parties so require, or to the extent strictly necessary in the opinion of the court in special circumstances where publicity would prejudice the interests of justice.
2. Everyone charged with a criminal offence shall be presumed innocent until proved guilty according to law.

*Article 7*
*No punishment without law*

1. No one shall be held guilty of any criminal offence on account of any act or omission which did not constitute a criminal offence under national or international law at the time when it was committed. Nor shall a heavier penalty be imposed than the one that was applicable at the time the criminal offence was committed.
2. This Article shall not prejudice the trial and punishment of any person for any act or omission which, at the time when it was committed, was criminal according to the general principles of law recognised by civilised nations.

*Article 8*
*Right to respect for private and family life*

1. Everyone has the right to respect for his private and family life, his home and his correspondence.
2. There shall be no interference by a public authority with the exercise of this right except such as is in accordance with the law and is necessary in a democratic society in the interests of national security, public safety or the economic well-being of the country, for the prevention of disorder or crime, for the protection of health or morals, or for the protection of the rights and freedoms of others.

*Article 9*
*Freedom of thought, conscience and religion*

1. Everyone has the right to freedom of thought, conscience and religion; this right includes freedom to change his religion or belief and freedom, either alone or in community with others and in public or private, to manifest his religion or belief, in worship, teaching, practice and observance.
2. Freedom to manifest one's religion or beliefs shall he subject only to such limitations as are prescribed by law and are necessary in a democratic society in the interests of public safety, for the protection of public order, health or morals, or for the protection of the rights and freedoms of others.

*Article 10*
*Freedom of expression*

1. Everyone has the right to freedom of expression. This right shall include freedom to hold opinions and to receive and impart information and ideas without interference by public authority and regardless of frontiers. This Article shall not prevent States from requiring the licensing of broadcasting television or cinema enterprises.
2. The exercise of these freedoms, since it carries with it duties and responsibilities, may be subject to such formalities, conditions, restrictions or penalties as are prescribed by law and are necessary in a democratic society, in the interests of national security, territorial integrity or public safety, for the prevention of disorder or crime, for the protection of health or morals, for the protection of the reputation or rights of others, for preventing the disclosure of information received in confidence, or for maintaining the authority and impartiality of the judiciary.

*Article 11*
*Freedom of assembly and association*

1. Everyone has the right to freedom of peaceful assembly and to freedom of association with others, including the right to form and to join trade unions for the protection of his interests.
2. No restrictions shall be placed on the exercise of these rights other than such as are prescribed by law and are necessary in a democratic society in the interests of national security or public safety, for the prevention of disorder or crime, for the protection of health or morals or for the protection of the rights and freedoms of others. This Article shall not prevent the imposition of lawful restrictions on the exercise of these rights by members of the armed forces, of the police or of the administration of the State.

*Article 14*
*Prohibition of discrimination*

The enjoyment of the rights and freedoms set forth in this Convention shall be secured without discrimination on any ground such as sex, race, colour, language, religion, political or other opinion, national or social origin, association with a national minority, property, birth or other status.

*Article 16*
*Restrictions on political activity of aliens*

Nothing in Articles 10, 11 and 14 shall be regarded as preventing the High Contracting Parties from imposing restrictions on the political activity of aliens.

*Article 17*
*Prohibition of abuse of rights*

Nothing in this Convention may be interpreted as implying for any State, group or person any right to engage in any activity or perform any act aimed at the destruction of any of the rights and freedoms set forth herein or at their limitation to a greater extent than is provided for in the Convention.

*Article 18*
*Limitation on use of restrictions on rights*

The restrictions permitted under this Convention to the said rights and freedoms shall not be applied for any purpose other than those for which they have been prescribed.

PART II
THE FIRST PROTOCOL

*Article 1*
*Protection of property*

Every natural or legal person is entitled to the peaceful enjoyment of his possessions. No one shall be deprived of his possessions except in the public interest and subject to the conditions provided for by law and by the general principles of international law.

# TERRORISM ACT 2000

PART I
INTRODUCTORY

## 1. Terrorism: interpretation

(1) In this Act 'terrorism' means the use or threat of action where—
 (a) the action falls within subsection (2),

(b) the use or threat is designed to influence the government or an international governmental organisation or to intimidate the public or a section of the public, and
(c) the use or threat is made for the purpose of advancing a political, religious, racial or ideological cause.

(2) Action falls within this subsection if it—
(a) involves serious violence against a person,
(b) involves serious damage to property,
(c) endangers a person's life, other than that of the person committing the action,
(d) creates a serious risk to the health or safety of the public or a section of the public, or
(e) is designed seriously to interfere with or seriously to disrupt an electronic system.

(3) The use or threat of action falling within subsection (2) which involves the use of firearms or explosives is terrorism whether or not subsection (1)(b) is satisfied.

(4) In this section—
(a) 'action' includes action outside the United Kingdom,
(b) a reference to any person or to property is a reference to any person, or to property, wherever situated,
(c) a reference to the public includes a reference to the public of a country other than the United Kingdom, and
(d) 'the government' means the government of the United Kingdom, of a Part of the United Kingdom or of a country other than the United Kingdom.

(5) In this Act a reference to action taken for the purposes of terrorism includes a reference to action taken for the benefit of a proscribed organisation.

## PART II
## PROSCRIBED ORGANISATIONS

### 3. Proscription

(1) For the purposes of this Act an organisation is proscribed if—
(a) it is listed in Schedule 2, or
(b) it operates under the same name as an organisation listed in that Schedule.

### 11. Membership

(1) A person commits an offence if he belongs or professes to belong to a proscribed organisation.

(2) It is a defence for a person charged with an offence under subsection (1) to prove—
(a) that the organisation was not proscribed on the last (or only) occasion on which he became a member or began to profess to be a member, and
(b) that he has not taken part in the activities of the organisation at any time while it was proscribed.

(4) In subsection (2) 'proscribed' means proscribed for the purposes of any of the following—
(a) this Act;
(b) the Northern Ireland (Emergency Provisions) Act 1996;
(c) the Northern Ireland (Emergency Provisions) Act 1991;
(d) the Prevention of Terrorism (Temporary Provisions) Act 1989;
(e) the Prevention of Terrorism (Temporary Provisions) Act 1984;
(f) the Northern Ireland (Emergency Provisions) Act 1978;
(g) the Prevention of Terrorism (Temporary Provisions) Act 1976;
(h) the Prevention of Terrorism (Temporary Provisions) Act 1974;
(i) the Northern Ireland (Emergency Provisions) Act 1973.

### 12. Support

(1) A person commits an offence if—
(a) he invites support for a proscribed organisation, and
(b) the support is not, or is not restricted to, the provision of money or other property (within the meaning of section 15).

(1A) A person commits an offence if the person—

(a) expresses an opinion or belief that is supportive of a proscribed organisation, and
(b) in doing so is reckless as to whether a person to whom the expression is directed will be encouraged to support a proscribed organisation.

(2) A person commits an offence if he arranges, manages or assists in arranging or managing a meeting which he knows is—
(a) to support a proscribed organisation,
(b) to further the activities of a proscribed organisation, or
(c) to be addressed by a person who belongs or professes to belong to a proscribed organisation.

(3) A person commits an offence if he addresses a meeting and the purpose of his address is to encourage support for a proscribed organisation or to further its activities.

(4) Where a person is charged with an offence under subsection (2)(c) in respect of a private meeting it is a defence for him to prove that he had no reasonable cause to believe that the address mentioned in subsection (2)(c) would support a proscribed organisation or further its activities.

(5) In subsections (2) to (4)—
(a) 'meeting' means a meeting of three or more persons, whether or not the public are admitted, and
(b) a meeting is private if the public are not admitted.

## 13. Uniform and publication of images

(1) A person in a public place commits an offence if he—
(a) wears an item of clothing, or
(b) wears, carries or displays an article,
in such a way or in such circumstances as to arouse reasonable suspicion that he is a member or supporter of a proscribed organisation.

(1A) A person commits an offence if the person publishes an image of—
(a) an item of clothing, or
(b) any other article,
in such a way or in such circumstances as to arouse reasonable suspicion that the person is a member or supporter of a proscribed organisation.

(1B) In subsection (1A) the reference to an image is a reference to a still or moving image (produced by any means).

PART III
TERRORIST PROPERTY

## 14. Terrorist property

(1) In this Act 'terrorist property' means—
(a) money or other property which is likely to be used for the purposes of terrorism (including any resources of a proscribed organisation),
(b) proceeds of the commission of acts of terrorism, and
(c) proceeds of acts carried out for the purposes of terrorism.

(2) In subsection (1)—
(a) a reference to proceeds of an act includes a reference to any property which wholly or partly, and directly or indirectly, represents the proceeds of the act (including payments or other rewards in connection with its commission), and
(b) the reference to an organisation's resources includes a reference to any money or other property which is applied or made available, or is to be applied or made available, for use by the organisation.

## 15. Fund-raising

(1) A person commits an offence if he—
(a) invites another to provide money or other property, and
(b) intends that it should be used, or has reasonable cause to suspect that it may be used, for the purposes of terrorism.

(2) A person commits an offence if he—
   (a) receives money or other property, and
   (b) intends that it should be used, or has reasonable cause to suspect that it may be used, for the purposes of terrorism.
(3) A person commits an offence if he—
   (a) provides money or other property, and
   (b) knows or has reasonable cause to suspect that it will or may be used for the purposes of terrorism.
(4) In this section a reference to the provision of money or other property is a reference to its being given, lent or otherwise made available, whether or not for consideration.

## 16. Use and possession

(1) A person commits an offence if he uses money or other property for the purposes of terrorism.
(2) A person commits an offence if he—
   (a) possesses money or other property, and
   (b) intends that it should be used, or has reasonable cause to suspect that it may be used, for the purposes of terrorism.

## 17. Funding arrangements

A person commits an offence if—
   (a) he enters into or becomes concerned in an arrangement as a result of which money or other property is made available or is to be made available to another, and
   (b) he knows or has reasonable cause to suspect that it will or may be used for the purposes of terrorism.

## 18. Money laundering

(1) A person commits an offence if he enters into or becomes concerned in an arrangement which facilitates the retention or control by or on behalf of another person of terrorist property—
   (a) by concealment,
   (b) by removal from the jurisdiction,
   (c) by transfer to nominees, or
   (d) in any other way.
(2) It is a defence for a person charged with an offence under subsection (1) to prove that he did not know and had no reasonable cause to suspect that the arrangement related to terrorist property.

## 19. Disclosure of information: duty

(1) This section applies where a person—
   (a) believes or suspects that another person has committed an offence under any of sections 15 to 18, and
   (b) bases his belief or suspicion on information which comes to his attention—
      (i) in the course of a trade, profession, business, or
      (ii) in the course of his employment (whether or not in the course of a trade, profession or business).
(1A) But this section does not apply if the information came to the person in the course of a business in the regulated sector.
(2) The person commits an offence if he does not disclose to a constable as soon as is reasonably practicable—
   (a) his belief or suspicion, and
   (b) the information on which it is based.
(3) It is a defence for a person charged with an offence under subsection (2) to prove that he had a reasonable excuse for not making the disclosure.
(4) Where—
   (a) a person is in employment,
   (b) his employer has established a procedure for the making of disclosures of the matters specified in subsection (2), and

(c) he is charged with an offence under that subsection,

it is a defence for him to prove that he disclosed the matters specified in that subsection in accordance with the procedure.

(5) Subsection (2) does not require disclosure by a professional legal adviser of—

(a) information which he obtains in privileged circumstances, or

(b) a belief or suspicion based on information which he obtains in privileged circumstances.

(6) For the purpose of subsection (5) information is obtained by an adviser in privileged circumstances if it comes to him, otherwise than with a view to furthering a criminal purpose—

(a) from a client or a client's representative, in connection with the provision of legal advice by the adviser to the client,

(b) from a person seeking legal advice from the adviser, or from the person's representative, or

(c) from any person, for the purpose of actual or contemplated legal proceedings.

(7) For the purposes of subsection (1)(a) a person shall be treated as having committed an offence under one of sections 15 to 18 if—

(a) he has taken an action or been in possession of a thing, and

(b) he would have committed an offence under one of those sections if he had been in the United Kingdom at the time when he took the action or was in possession of the thing.

(7A) The reference to a business in the regulated sector must be construed in accordance with Schedule 3A.

(7B) The reference to a constable includes a reference to a National Crime Agency officer authorised for the purposes of this section by the Director General of that Agency.

## 21. Cooperation with police

(1) A person does not commit an offence under any of sections 15 to 18 if he is acting with the express consent of a constable.

(2) Subject to subsections (3) and (4), a person does not commit an offence under any of sections 15 to 18 by involvement in a transaction or arrangement relating to money or other property if he discloses to a constable—

(a) his suspicion or belief that the money or other property is terrorist property, and

(b) the information on which his suspicion or belief is based.

(3) Subsection (2) applies only where a person makes a disclosure—

(a) after he becomes concerned in the transaction concerned,

(b) on his own initiative, and

(c) as soon as is reasonably practicable.

(4) Subsection (2) does not apply to a person if—

(a) a constable forbids him to continue his involvement in the transaction or arrangement to which the disclosure relates, and

(b) he continues his involvement.

(5) It is a defence for a person charged with an offence under any of sections 15(2) and (3) and 16 to 18 to prove that—

(a) he intended to make a disclosure of the kind mentioned in subsections (2) and (3), and

(b) there is reasonable excuse for his failure to do so.

(6) Where—

(a) a person is in employment, and

(b) his employer has established a procedure for the making of disclosures of the same kind as may be made to a constable under subsection (2),

this section shall have effect in relation to that person as if any reference to disclosure to a constable included a reference to disclosure in accordance with the procedure.

(7) A reference in this section to a transaction or arrangement relating to money or other property includes a reference to use or possession.

## PART IV
## TERRORIST INVESTIGATIONS

### 39. Disclosure of information, etc.

(1) Subsection (2) applies where a person knows or has reasonable cause to suspect that a constable is conducting or proposes to conduct a terrorist investigation.

(2) The person commits an offence if he—
- (a) discloses to another anything which is likely to prejudice the investigation, or
- (b) interferes with material which is likely to be relevant to the investigation.

(3) Subsection (4) applies where a person knows or has reasonable cause to suspect that a disclosure has been or will be made under any of sections 19 to 21 or 38B.

(4) The person commits an offence if he—
- (a) discloses to another anything which is likely to prejudice an investigation resulting from the disclosure under that section, or
- (b) interferes with material which is likely to be relevant to an investigation resulting from the disclosure under that section.

(5) It is a defence for a person charged with an offence under subsection (2) or (4) to prove—
- (a) that he did not know and had no reasonable cause to suspect that the disclosure or interference was likely to affect a terrorist investigation, or
- (b) that he had a reasonable excuse for the disclosure or interference.

(6) Subsections (2) and (4) do not apply to a disclosure which is made by a professional legal adviser—
- (a) to his client or to his client's representative in connection with the provision of legal advice by the adviser to the client and not with a view to furthering a criminal purpose, or
- (b) to any person for the purpose of actual or contemplated legal proceedings and not with a view to furthering a criminal purpose.

(8) For the purposes of this section—
- (a) a reference to conducting a terrorist investigation includes a reference to taking part in the conduct of, or assisting, a terrorist investigation, and
- (b) a person interferes with material if he falsifies it, conceals it, destroys it or disposes of it, or if he causes or permits another to do any of those things.

## PART V
## COUNTER-TERRORIST POWERS

### 48. Authorisations

(1) An authorisation under this section authorises any constable in uniform to prohibit or restrict the parking of vehicles on a road specified in the authorisation.

(2) An authorisation may be given only if the person giving it considers it expedient for the prevention of acts of terrorism.

(3) An authorisation may be given—
- (a) where the road specified is in England and Wales and is wholly or partly within a police area other than one mentioned in paragraphs (b) or (c), by a police officer for the area who is of at least the rank of assistant chief constable;
- (b) where the road specified is wholly or partly in the metropolitan police district, by a police officer for the district who is of at least the rank of commander of the metropolitan police;
- (c) where the road specified is wholly or partly in the City of London, by a police officer for the City who is of at least the rank of commander in the City of London police force;
- (ca) where the road specified is in Scotland, by a constable of the Police Service of Scotland who is of at least the rank of assistant chief constable;
- (d) where the road specified is in Northern Ireland, by a member of the Police Service of Northern Ireland who is of at least the rank of assistant chief constable.

(4) If an authorisation is given orally, the person giving it shall confirm it in writing as soon as is reasonably practicable.

## 49. Exercise of power

(1) The power conferred by an authorisation under section 48 shall be exercised by placing a traffic sign on the road concerned.

## 51. Offences

(1) A person commits an offence if he parks a vehicle in contravention of a prohibition or restriction imposed by virtue of section 48.

(2) A person commits an offence if—

(a) he is the driver or other person in charge of a vehicle which has been permitted to remain at rest in contravention of any prohibition or restriction imposed by virtue of section 48, and

(b) he fails to move the vehicle when ordered to do so by a constable in uniform.

(3) It is a defence for a person charged with an offence under this section to prove that he had a reasonable excuse for the act or omission in question.

(4) Possession of a current disabled person's badge shall not itself constitute a reasonable excuse for the purposes of subsection (3).

## 52. Interpretation

In sections 48 to 51—

'disabled person's badge' means a badge issued, or having effect as if issued, under any regulations for the time being in force under section 21 of the Chronically Sick and Disabled Persons Act 1970;

'driver' means, in relation to a vehicle which has been left on any road, the person who was driving it when it was left there;

'parking' means leaving a vehicle or permitting it to remain at rest;

'traffic sign' has the meaning given in section 142(1) of the Road Traffic Regulation Act 1984; 'vehicle' has the same meaning as in section 99(5) of the Road Traffic Regulation Act 1984.

# PART VI
# MISCELLANEOUS

## 54. Weapons training

(1) A person commits an offence if he provides instruction or training in the making or use of—

(a) firearms,

(aa) radioactive material or weapons designed or adapted for the discharge of any radioactive material,

(b) explosives, or

(c) chemical, biological or nuclear weapons.

(2) A person commits an offence if he receives instruction or training in the making or use of—

(a) firearms,

(aa) radioactive material or weapons designed or adapted for the discharge of any radioactive material,

(b) explosives, or

(c) chemical, biological or nuclear weapons.

(3) A person commits an offence if he invites another to receive instruction or training and the receipt—

(a) would constitute an offence under subsection (2), or

(b) would constitute an offence under subsection (2) but for the fact that it is to take place outside the United Kingdom.

(4) For the purpose of subsections (1) and (3)—

(a) a reference to the provision of instruction includes a reference to making it available either generally or to one or more specific persons, and

(b) an invitation to receive instruction or training may be either general or addressed to one or more specific persons.

(5) It is a defence for a person charged with an offence under this section in relation to instruction or training to prove that his action or involvement was wholly for a purpose other than assisting, preparing for or participating in terrorism.

## 55. Weapons training: interpretation

In section 54—

'biological weapon' means a biological agent or toxin (within the meaning of the Biological Weapons Act 1974) in a form capable of use for hostile purposes or anything to which section 1(1)(b) of that Act applies,

'chemical weapon' has the meaning given by section 1 of the Chemical Weapons Act 1996, and

'radioactive material' means radioactive material capable of endangering life or causing harm to human health.

## 56. Directing terrorist organisation

(1) A person commits an offence if he directs, at any level, the activities of an organisation which is concerned in the commission of acts of terrorism.

## 57. Possession for terrorist purposes

(1) A person commits an offence if he possesses an article in circumstances which give rise to a reasonable suspicion that his possession is for a purpose connected with the commission, preparation or instigation of an act of terrorism.

(2) It is a defence for a person charged with an offence under this section to prove that his possession of the article was not for a purpose connected with the commission, preparation or instigation of an act of terrorism.

(3) In proceedings for an offence under this section, if it is proved that an article—
- (a) was on any premises at the same time as the accused, or
- (b) was on premises of which the accused was the occupier or which he habitually used otherwise than as a member of the public,

the court may assume that the accused possessed the article, unless he proves that he did not know of its presence on the premises or that he had no control over it.

## 58. Collection of information

(1) A person commits an offence if—
- (a) he collects or makes a record of information of a kind likely to be useful to a person committing or preparing an act of terrorism,
- (b) he possesses a document or record containing information of that kind, or
- (c) the person views, or otherwise accesses, by means of the internet a document or record containing information of that kind.

(1A) The cases in which a person collects or makes a record for the purposes of subsection (1)(a) include (but are not limited to) those in which the person does so by means of the internet (whether by downloading the record or otherwise).

(2) In this section 'record' includes a photographic or electronic record.

(3) It is a defence for a person charged with an offence under this section to prove that he had a reasonable excuse for his action or possession.

(3A) The cases in which a person has a reasonable excuse for the purposes of subsection (3) include (but are not limited to) those in which—
- (a) at the time of the person's action or possession the person did not know, and had no reason to believe, that the document or record in question contained, or was likely to contain, information of a kind likely to be useful to a person committing or preparing an act of terrorism, or
- (b) the person's action or possession was for the purposes of—
  - (i) carrying out work as a journalist, or
  - (ii) academic research.

## 58A. Eliciting, publishing or communicating information about members of armed forces etc.

(1) A person commits an offence who—
- (a) elicits or attempts to elicit information about an individual who is or has been—
  - (i) a member of Her Majesty's forces,

(ii) a member of any of the intelligence services, or
(iii) a constable,
which is of a kind likely to be useful to a person committing or preparing an act of terrorism, or
(b) publishes or communicates any such information.
(2) It is a defence for a person charged with an offence under this section to prove that they had a reasonable excuse for their action.
(4) In this section 'the intelligence services' means the Security Service, the Secret Intelligence Service and GCHQ (within the meaning of section 3 of the Intelligence Services Act 1994).
(5) Schedule 8A to this Act contains supplementary provisions relating to the offence under this section.

## 59. England and Wales

(1) A person commits an offence if—
(a) he incites another person to commit an act of terrorism wholly or partly outside the United Kingdom, and
(b) the act would, if committed in England and Wales, constitute one of the offences listed in subsection (2).
(2) Those offences are—
(a) murder,
(b) an offence under section 18 of the Offences against the Person Act 1861 (wounding with intent),
(c) an offence under section 23 or 24 of that Act (poison),
(d) an offence under section 28 or 29 of that Act (explosions), and
(e) an offence under section 1 (2) of the Criminal Damage Act 1971 (endangering life by damaging property).
(3) A person guilty of an offence under this section shall be liable to any penalty to which he would be liable on conviction of the offence listed in subsection (2) which corresponds to the act which he incites.
(4) For the purposes of subsection (1) it is immaterial whether or not the person incited is in the United Kingdom at the time of the incitement.
(5) Nothing in this section imposes criminal liability on any person acting on behalf of, or holding office under, the Crown.

## 62. Terrorist bombing: jurisdiction

(1) If—
(a) a person does anything outside the United Kingdom as an act of terrorism or for the purposes of terrorism, and
(b) his action would have constituted the commission of one of the offences listed in subsection (2) if it had been done in the United Kingdom,
he shall be guilty of the offence.
(2) The offences referred to in subsection (1)(b) are—
(a) an offence under section 2, 3 or 5 of the Explosive Substances Act 1883 (causing explosions, &c),
(b) an offence under section 1 of the Biological Weapons Act 1974 (biological weapons), and
(c) an offence under section 2 of the Chemical Weapons Act 1996 (chemical weapons).

PART VIII
GENERAL

## 118. Defences

(1) Subsection (2) applies where in accordance with a provision mentioned in subsection (5) it is a defence for a person charged with an offence to prove a particular matter.
(2) If the person adduces evidence which is sufficient to raise an issue with respect to the matter the court or jury shall assume that the defence is satisfied unless the prosecution proves beyond reasonable doubt that it is not.

(3) Subsection (4) applies where in accordance with a provision mentioned in subsection (5) a court—
  (a) may make an assumption in relation to a person charged with an offence unless a particular matter is proved, or
  (b) may accept a fact as sufficient evidence unless a particular matter is proved.
(4) If evidence is adduced which is sufficient to raise an issue with respect to the matter mentioned in subsection (3)(a) or (b) the court shall treat it as proved unless the prosecution disproves it beyond reasonable doubt.
(5) The provisions in respect of which subsections (2) and (4) apply are—
  (a) sections 12(4), 39(5)(a), 54, 57, 58, 58A, 58B, 77 and 103 of this Act.

## 121. Interpretation

In this Act—
'act' and 'action' include omission,
'article' includes substance and any other thing,
'customs officer' means an officer of Revenue and Customs,
'dwelling' means a building or part of a building used as a dwelling, and a vehicle which is habitually stationary and which is used as a dwelling,
'explosive' means—
(a) an article or substance manufactured for the purpose of producing a practical effect by explosion,
(b) materials for making an article or substance within paragraph (a),
(c) anything used or intended to be used for causing or assisting in causing an explosion, and
(d) a part of anything within paragraph (a) or (c),
'firearm' includes an air gun or air pistol,
'immigration officer' means a person appointed as an immigration officer under paragraph 1 of Schedule 2 to the Immigration Act 1971,
'the Islands' means the Channel Islands and the Isle of Man,
'organisation' includes any association or combination of persons,
'premises', except in section 63D, includes any place and in particular includes—
(a) a vehicle,
(b) an offshore installation within the meaning given in section 44 of the Petroleum Act 1998, and
(c) a tent or moveable structure,
'property' includes property wherever situated and whether real or personal, heritable or moveable, and things in action and other intangible or incorporeal property,
'public place' means a place to which members of the public have or are permitted to have access, whether or not for payment,
'road' has the same meaning as in the Road Traffic Act 1988 (in relation to England and Wales), and includes part of a road, and
'vehicle', except in sections 48 to 52 and Schedule 7, includes an aircraft, hovercraft, train or vessel.

# ANTI-TERRORISM, CRIME AND SECURITY ACT 2001

## 113. Use of noxious substances or things to cause harm and intimidate

(1) A person who takes any action which—
  (a) involves the use of a noxious substance or other noxious thing;
  (b) has or is likely to have an effect falling within subsection (2); and
  (c) is designed to influence the government or an international governmental organisation or to intimidate the public or a section of the public, is guilty of an offence.
(2) Action has an effect falling within this subsection if it—
  (a) causes serious violence against a person anywhere in the world;
  (b) causes serious damage to real or personal property anywhere in the world;

(c) endangers human life or creates a serious risk to the health or safety of the public or a section of the public; or

(d) induces in members of the public the fear that the action is likely to endanger their lives or create a serious risk to their health or safety;

but any effect on the person taking the action is to be disregarded.

(3) A person who—

(a) makes a threat that he or another will take any action which constitutes an offence under subsection (1); and

(b) intends thereby to induce in a person anywhere in the world the fear that the threat is likely to be carried out, is guilty of an offence.

(5) In this section—

'the government' means the government of the United Kingdom, of a part of the United Kingdom or of a country other than the United Kingdom; and

'the public' includes the public of a country other than the United Kingdom.

## 113A. Application of section 113

(1) Section 113 applies to conduct done—

(a) in the United Kingdom; or

(b) outside the United Kingdom which satisfies the following two conditions.

(2) The first condition is that the conduct is done for the purpose of advancing a political, religious, racial or ideological cause.

(3) The second condition is that the conduct is—

(a) by a United Kingdom national or a United Kingdom resident;

(b) by any person done to, or in relation to, a United Kingdom national, a United Kingdom resident or a protected person; or

(c) by any person done in circumstances which fall within section 63D(1)(b) and (c) or (3) (b) and (c) of the Terrorism Act 2000.

(4) The following expressions have the same meaning as they have for the purposes of sections 63C and 63D of that Act—

(a) 'United Kingdom national';

(b) 'United Kingdom resident';

(c) 'protected person'.

(5) For the purposes of this section it is immaterial whether a person knows that another is a United Kingdom national, a United Kingdom resident or a protected person.

## 114. Hoaxes involving noxious substances or things

(1) A person is guilty of an offence if he—

(a) places any substance or other thing in any place; or

(b) sends any substance or other thing from one place to another (by post, rail or any other means whatever);

with the intention of inducing in a person anywhere in the world a belief that it is likely to be (or contain) a noxious substance or other noxious thing and thereby endanger human life or create a serious risk to human health.

(2) A person is guilty of an offence if he communicates any information which he knows or believes to be false with the intention of inducing in a person anywhere in the world a belief that a noxious substance or other noxious thing is likely to be present (whether at the time the information is communicated or later) in any place and thereby endanger human life or create a serious risk to human health.

## 115. Sections 113 and 114: supplementary

(1) For the purposes of sections 113 and 114 'substance' includes any biological agent and any other natural or artificial substance (whatever its form, origin or method of production).

(2) For a person to be guilty of an offence under section 113(3) or 114 it is not necessary for him to have any particular person in mind as the person in whom he intends to induce the belief in question.

# MOBILE TELEPHONES (RE-PROGRAMMING) ACT 2002

## 1. Re-programming mobile telephone etc.

(1) A person commits an offence if—
  (a) he changes a unique device identifier,
  (b) he interferes with the operation of a unique device identifier,
  (c) he offers or agrees to change, or interfere with the operation of, a unique device identifier, or
  (d) he offers or agrees to arrange for another person to change, or interfere with the operation of, a unique device identifier.

(2) A unique device identifier is an electronic equipment identifier which is unique to a mobile wireless communications device.

(3) But a person does not commit an offence under this section if—
  (a) he is the manufacturer of the device, or
  (b) he does the act mentioned in subsection (1) with the written consent of the manufacturer of the device.

## 2. Possession or supply of anything for re-programming purposes

(1) A person commits an offence if—
  (a) he has in his custody or under his control anything which may be used for the purpose of changing or interfering with the operation of a unique device identifier, and
  (b) he intends to use the thing unlawfully for that purpose or to allow it to be used unlawfully for that purpose.

(2) A person commits an offence if—
  (a) he supplies anything which may be used for the purpose of changing or interfering with the operation of a unique device identifier, and
  (b) he knows or believes that the person to whom the thing is supplied intends to use it unlawfully for that purpose or to allow it to be used unlawfully for that purpose.

(3) A person commits an offence if—
  (a) he offers to supply anything which may be used for the purpose of changing or interfering with the operation of a unique device identifier, and
  (b) he knows or believes that the person to whom the thing is offered intends if it is supplied to him to use it unlawfully for that purpose or to allow it to be used unlawfully for that purpose.

(4) A unique device identifier is an electronic equipment identifier which is unique to a mobile wireless communications device.

(5) A thing is used by a person unlawfully for a purpose if in using it for that purpose he commits an offence under section 1.

# DEALING IN CULTURAL OBJECTS (OFFENCES) ACT 2003

## 1. Offence of dealing in tainted cultural objects

(1) A person is guilty of an offence if he dishonestly deals in a cultural object that is tainted, knowing or believing that the object is tainted.

(2) It is immaterial whether he knows or believes that the object is a cultural object.

## 2. Meaning of 'tainted cultural object

(1) 'Cultural object' means an object of historical, architectural or archaeological interest.

(2) A cultural object is tainted if, after the commencement of this Act—
  (a) a person removes the object in a case falling within subsection (4) or he excavates the object, and
  (b) the removal or excavation constitutes an offence.

(3) It is immaterial whether—
  (a) the removal or excavation was done in the United Kingdom or elsewhere,

(b) the offence is committed under the law of a part of the United Kingdom or under the law of any other country or territory.

(4) An object is removed in a case falling within this subsection if—

(a) it is removed from a building or structure of historical, architectural or archaeological interest where the object has at any time formed part of the building or structure, or

(b) it is removed from a monument of such interest.

(5) 'Monument' means—

(a) any work, cave or excavation,

(b) any site comprising the remains of any building or structure or of any work, cave or excavation,

(c) any site comprising, or comprising the remains of, any vehicle, vessel, aircraft or other movable structure, or part of any such thing.

(6) 'Remains' includes any trace or sign of the previous existence of the thing in question.

(7) It is immaterial whether—

(a) a building, structure or work is above or below the surface of the land,

(b) a site is above or below water.

(8) This section has effect for the purposes of section 1.

### 3. Meaning of 'deals in'

(1) A person deals in an object if (and only if) he—

(a) acquires, disposes of, imports or exports it,

(b) agrees with another to do an act mentioned in paragraph (a), or

(c) makes arrangements under which another person does such an act or under which another person agrees with a third person to do such an act.

(2) 'Acquires' means buys, hires, borrows or accepts.

(3) 'Disposes of' means sells, lets on hire, lends or gives.

(4) In relation to agreeing or arranging to do an act, it is immaterial whether the act is agreed or arranged to take place in the United Kingdom or elsewhere.

(5) This section has effect for the purposes of section 1.

### 5. Offences by bodies corporate

(1) If an offence under section 1 committed by a body corporate is proved—

(a) to have been committed with the consent or connivance of an officer, or

(b) to be attributable to any neglect on his part,

he (as well as the body corporate) is guilty of the offence and liable to be proceeded against and punished accordingly.

(2) 'Officer', in relation to a body corporate, means—

(a) a director, manager, secretary or other similar officer of the body,

(b) a person purporting to act in any such capacity.

(3) If the affairs of a body corporate are managed by its members, subsection (1) applies in relation to the acts and defaults of a member in connection with his functions of management as if he were a director of the body.

## FEMALE GENITAL MUTILATION ACT 2003

### 1. Offence of female genital mutilation

(1) A person is guilty of an offence if he excises, infibulates or otherwise mutilates the whole or any part of a girl's labia majora, labia minora or clitoris.

(2) But no offence is committed by an approved person who performs—

(a) a surgical operation on a girl which is necessary for her physical or mental health, or

(b) a surgical operation on a girl who is in any stage of labour, or has just given birth, for purposes connected with the labour or birth.

(3) The following are approved persons—

(a) in relation to an operation falling within subsection (2)(a), a registered medical practitioner,

(b) in relation to an operation falling within subsection (2)(b), a registered medical practitioner, a registered midwife or a person undergoing a course of training with a view to becoming such a practitioner or midwife.

(4) There is also no offence committed by a person who—

(a) performs a surgical operation falling within subsection (2)(a) or (b) outside the United Kingdom, and

(b) in relation to such an operation exercises functions corresponding to those of an approved person.

(5) For the purpose of determining whether an operation is necessary for the mental health of a girl it is immaterial whether she or any other person believes that the operation is required as a matter of custom or ritual.

## 2. Offence of assisting a girl to mutilate her own genitalia

A person is guilty of an offence if he aids, abets, counsels or procures a girl to excise, infibulate or otherwise mutilate the whole or any part of her own labia majora, labia minora or clitoris.

## 3. Offence of assisting a non-UK person to mutilate overseas a girl's genitalia

(1) A person is guilty of an offence if he aids, abets, counsels or procures a person who is not a United Kingdom national or United Kingdom resident to do a relevant act of female genital mutilation outside the United Kingdom.

(2) An act is a relevant act of female genital mutilation if—

(a) it is done in relation to a United Kingdom national or United Kingdom resident, and

(b) it would, if done by such a person, constitute an offence under section 1.

(3) But no offence is committed if the relevant act of female genital mutilation—

(a) is a surgical operation falling within section 1(2)(a) or (b), and

(b) is performed by a person who, in relation to such an operation, is an approved person or exercises functions corresponding to those of an approved person.

## 3A. Offence of failing to protect girl from risk of genital mutilation

(1) If a genital mutilation offence is committed against a girl under the age of 16, each person who is responsible for the girl at the relevant time is guilty of an offence.
This is subject to subsection (5).

(2) For the purposes of this section a person is 'responsible' for a girl in the following two cases.

(3) The first case is where the person—

(a) has parental responsibility for the girl, and

(b) has frequent contact with her.

(4) The second case is where the person—

(a) is aged 18 or over, and

(b) has assumed (and not relinquished) responsibility for caring for the girl in the manner of a parent.

(5) It is a defence for the defendant to show that—

(a) at the relevant time, the defendant did not think that there was a significant risk of a genital mutilation offence being committed against the girl, and could not reasonably have been expected to be aware that there was any such risk, or

(b) the defendant took such steps as he or she could reasonably have been expected to take to protect the girl from being the victim of a genital mutilation offence.

(6) A person is taken to have shown the fact mentioned in subsection (5)(a) or (b) if—

(a) sufficient evidence of the fact is adduced to raise an issue with respect to it, and

(b) the contrary is not proved beyond reasonable doubt.

(7) For the purposes of subsection (3)(b), where a person has frequent contact with a girl which is interrupted by her going to stay somewhere temporarily, that contact is treated as continuing during her stay there.

(8) In this section—

'genital mutilation offence' means an offence under section 1, 2 or 3 (and for the purposes of subsection (1) the prosecution does not have to prove which section it is);
'parental responsibility'—
(a) in England Wales, has the same meaning as in the Children Act 1989;
'the relevant time' means the time when the mutilation takes place.

## 4. Extension of sections 1 to 3A to extra-territorial acts or omissions

(1) Sections 1 to 3 extend to any act done outside the United Kingdom by a United Kingdom national or United Kingdom resident.
(1A) An offence under section 3A can be committed wholly or partly outside the United Kingdom by a person who is a United Kingdom national or a United Kingdom resident.
(2) If an offence under this Act is committed outside the United Kingdom—
(a) proceedings may be taken, and
(b) the offence may for incidental purposes be treated as having been committed, in any place in England and Wales or Northern Ireland.

## 6. Definitions

(1) Girl includes woman.
(2) A United Kingdom national is an individual who is—
(a) a British citizen, a British overseas territories citizen, a British National (Overseas) or a British Overseas citizen,
(b) a person who under the British Nationality Act 1981 is a British subject, or
(c) a British protected person within the meaning of that Act.
(3) A United Kingdom resident is an individual who is habitually resident in the United Kingdom.
(4) This section has effect for the purposes of this Act.

# SEXUAL OFFENCES ACT 2003

## 1. Rape

(1) A person (A) commits an offence if—
(a) he intentionally penetrates the vagina, anus or mouth of another person (B) with his penis,
(b) B does not consent to the penetration, and
(c) A does not reasonably believe that B consents.
(2) Whether a belief is reasonable is to be determined having regard to all the circumstances, including any steps A has taken to ascertain whether B consents.
(3) Sections 75 and 76 apply to an offence under this section.

## 2. Assault by penetration

(1) A person (A) commits an offence if—
(a) he intentionally penetrates the vagina or anus of another person (B) with a part of his body or anything else,
(b) the penetration is sexual,
(c) B does not consent to the penetration, and
(d) A does not reasonably believe that B consents.
(2) Whether a belief is reasonable is to be determined having regard to all the circumstances, including any steps A has taken to ascertain whether B consents.
(3) Sections 75 and 76 apply to an offence under this section.

## 3. Sexual assault

(1) A person (A) commits an offence if—
(a) he intentionally touches another person (B),
(b) the touching is sexual,
(c) B does not consent to the touching, and
(d) A does not reasonably believe that B consents.
(2) Whether a belief is reasonable is to be determined having regard to all the circumstances, including any steps A has taken to ascertain whether B consents.
(3) Sections 75 and 76 apply to an offence under this section.

## 4. Causing a person to engage in sexual activity without consent

(1) A person (A) commits an offence if—
(a) he intentionally causes another person (B) to engage in an activity,
(b) the activity is sexual,
(c) B does not consent to engaging in the activity, and
(d) A does not reasonably believe that B consents.

(2) Whether a belief is reasonable is to be determined having regard to all the circumstances, including any steps A has taken to ascertain whether B consents.

(3) Sections 75 and 76 apply to an offence under this section.

(4) A person guilty of an offence under this section, if the activity caused involved—
(a) penetration of B's anus or vagina,
(b) penetration of B's mouth with a person's penis,
(c) penetration of a person's anus or vagina with a part of B's body or by B with anything else, or
(d) penetration of a person's mouth with B's penis,
is liable, on conviction on indictment, to imprisonment for life.

## 5. Rape of a child under 13

(1) A person commits an offence if—
(a) he intentionally penetrates the vagina, anus or mouth of another person with his penis, and
(b) the other person is under 13.

## 6. Assault of a child under 13 by penetration

(1) A person commits an offence if—
(a) he intentionally penetrates the vagina or anus of another person with a part of his body or anything else,
(b) the penetration is sexual, and
(c) the other person is under 13.

## 7. Sexual assault of a child under 13

(1) A person commits an offence if—
(a) he intentionally touches another person,
(b) the touching is sexual, and
(c) the other person is under 13.

## 8. Causing or inciting a child under 13 to engage in sexual activity

(1) A person commits an offence if—
(a) he intentionally causes or incites another person (B) to engage in an activity,
(b) the activity is sexual, and
(c) B is under 13.

(2) A person guilty of an offence under this section, if the activity caused or incited involved—
(a) penetration of B's anus or vagina,
(b) penetration of B's mouth with a person's penis,
(c) penetration of a person's anus or vagina with a part of B's body or by B with anything else, or
(d) penetration of a person's mouth with B's penis,
is liable, on conviction on indictment, to imprisonment for life.

## 9. Sexual activity with a child

(1) A person aged 18 or over (A) commits an offence if—
(a) he intentionally touches another person (B),
(b) the touching is sexual, and
(c) either—
(i) B is under 16 and A does not reasonably believe that B is 16 or over, or
(ii) B is under 13.

(2) A person guilty of an offence under this section, if the touching involved—
(a) penetration of B's anus or vagina with a part of A's body or anything else,
(b) penetration of B's mouth with A's penis,

(c) penetration of A's anus or vagina with a part of B's body, or
(d) penetration of A's mouth with B's penis,
is liable, on conviction on indictment, to imprisonment for a term not exceeding 14 years.

## 10. Causing or inciting a child to engage in sexual activity

(1) A person aged 18 or over (A) commits an offence if—
(a) he intentionally causes or incites another person (B) to engage in an activity,
(b) the activity is sexual, and
(c) either—
(i) B is under 16 and A does not reasonably believe that B is 16 or over, or
(ii) B is under 13.

(2) A person guilty of an offence under this section, if the activity caused or incited involved—
(a) penetration of B's anus or vagina,
(b) penetration of B's mouth with a person's penis,
(c) penetration of a person's anus or vagina with a part of B's body or by B with anything else, or
(d) penetration of a person's mouth with B's penis,
is liable, on conviction on indictment, to imprisonment for a term not exceeding 14 years.

## 11. Engaging in sexual activity in the presence of a child

(1) A person aged 18 or over (A) commits an offence if—
(a) he intentionally engages in an activity,
(b) the activity is sexual,
(c) for the purpose of obtaining sexual gratification, he engages in it—
(i) when another person (B) is present or is in a place from which A can be observed, and
(ii) knowing or believing that B is aware, or intending that B should be aware, that he is engaging in it, and
(d) either—
(i) B is under 16 and A does not reasonably believe that B is 16 or over, or
(ii) B is under 13.

## 12. Causing a child to watch a sexual act

(1) A person aged 18 or over (A) commits an offence if—
(a) for the purpose of obtaining sexual gratification, he intentionally causes another person (B) to watch a third person engaging in an activity, or to look at an image of any person engaging in an activity,
(b) the activity is sexual, and
(c) either—
(i) B is under 16 and A does not reasonably believe that B is 16 or over, or
(ii) B is under 13.

## 13. Child sex offences committed by children or young persons

(1) A person under 18 commits an offence if he does anything which would be an offence under any of sections 9 to 12 if he were aged 18.

## 14. Arranging or facilitating commission of a child sex offence

(1) A person commits an offence if—
(a) he intentionally arranges or facilitates something that he intends to do, intends another person to do, or believes that another person will do, in any part of the world, and
(b) doing it will involve the commission of an offence under any of sections 9 to 13.

(2) A person does not commit an offence under this section if—
(a) he arranges or facilitates something that he believes another person will do, but that he does not intend to do or intend another person to do, and
(b) any offence within subsection (1)(b) would be an offence against a child for whose protection he acts.

(3) For the purposes of subsection (2), a person acts for the protection of a child if he acts for the purpose of—
(a) protecting the child from sexually transmitted infection,
(b) protecting the physical safety of the child,
(c) preventing the child from becoming pregnant, or
(d) promoting the child's emotional well-being by the giving of advice,
and not for the purpose of obtaining sexual gratification or for the purpose of causing or encouraging the activity constituting the offence within subsection (1)(b) or the child's participation in it.

## 15. Meeting a child following sexual grooming etc.

(1) A person aged 18 or over (A) commits an offence if—
(a) A has met or communicated with another person (B) on one or more occasions and subsequently—
(i) A intentionally meets B, or
(ii) A travels with the intention of meeting B in any part of the world or arranges to meet B in any part of the world, or
(iii) B travels with the intention of meeting A in any part of the world.
(b) A intends to do anything to or in respect of B, during or after the meeting mentioned in paragraph (a)(i) to (iii) and in any part of the world, which if done will involve the commission by A of a relevant offence,
(c) B is under 16, and
(d) A does not reasonably believe that B is 16 or over.
(2) In subsection (1)—
(a) the reference to A having met or communicated with B is a reference to A having met B in any part of the world or having communicated with B by any means from, to or in any part of the world;
(b) 'relevant offence' means—
(i) an offence under this Part,
(ii) an offence within any of paragraphs 61 to 92 of Schedule 3, or
(iii) anything done outside England and Wales and Northern Ireland which is not an offence within sub-paragraph (i) or (ii) but would be an offence within subparagraph (i) if done in England and Wales.

## 15A. Sexual communication with a child

(1) A person aged 18 or over (A) commits an offence if—
(a) for the purpose of obtaining sexual gratification, A intentionally communicates with another person (B),
(b) the communication is sexual or is intended to encourage B to make (whether to A or to another) a communication that is sexual, and
(c) B is under 16 and A does not reasonably believe that B is 16 or over.
(2) For the purposes of this section, a communication is sexual if—
(a) any part of it relates to sexual activity, or
(b) a reasonable person would, in all the circumstances but regardless of any person's purpose, consider any part of the communication to be sexual;
and in paragraph (a) 'sexual activity' means an activity that a reasonable person would, in all the circumstances but regardless of any person's purpose, consider to be sexual.

## 16. Abuse of position of trust: sexual activity with a child

(1) A person aged 18 or over (A) commits an offence if—
(a) he intentionally touches another person (B),
(b) the touching is sexual,
(c) A is in a position of trust in relation to B,
(d) where subsection (2) applies, A knows or could reasonably be expected to know of the circumstances by virtue of which he is in a position of trust in relation to B, and
(e) either—
(i) B is under 18 and A does not reasonably believe that B is 18 or over, or
(ii) B is under 13.

(2) This subsection applies where A—
(a) is in a position of trust in relation to B by virtue of circumstances within section 21 (2), (3), (4) or (5), and
(b) is not in such a position of trust by virtue of other circumstances.

(3) Where in proceedings for an offence under this section it is proved that the other person was under 18, the defendant is to be taken not to have reasonably believed that that person was 18 or over unless sufficient evidence is adduced to raise an issue as to whether he reasonably believed it.

(4) Where in proceedings for an offence under this section—
(a) it is proved that the defendant was in a position of trust in relation to the other person by virtue of circumstances within section 21(2), (3), (4) or (5), and
(b) it is not proved that he was in such a position of trust by virtue of other circumstances,

it is to be taken that the defendant knew or could reasonably have been expected to know of the circumstances by virtue of which he was in such a position of trust unless sufficient evidence is adduced to raise an issue as to whether he knew or could reasonably have been expected to know of those circumstances.

## 17. Abuse of position of trust: causing or inciting a child to engage in sexual activity

(1) A person aged 18 or over (A) commits an offence if—
(a) he intentionally causes or incites another person (B) to engage in an activity,
(b) the activity is sexual,
(c) A is in a position of trust in relation to B,
(d) where subsection (2) applies, A knows or could reasonably be expected to know of the circumstances by virtue of which he is in a position of trust in relation to B, and
(e) either—
(i) B is under 18 and A does not reasonably believe that B is 18 or over, or
(ii) B is under 13.

(2) This subsection applies where A—
(a) is in a position of trust in relation to B by virtue of circumstances within section 21(2), (3), (4) or (5), and
(b) is not in such a position of trust by virtue of other circumstances.

(3) Where in proceedings for an offence under this section it is proved that the other person was under 18, the defendant is to be taken not to have reasonably believed that that person was 18 or over unless sufficient evidence is adduced to raise an issue as to whether he reasonably believed it.

(4) Where in proceedings for an offence under this section—
(a) it is proved that the defendant was in a position of trust in relation to the other person by virtue of circumstances within section 21 (2), (3), (4) or (5), and
(b) it is not proved that he was in such a position of trust by virtue of other circumstances,

it is to be taken that the defendant knew or could reasonably have been expected to know of the circumstances by virtue of which he was in such a position of trust unless sufficient evidence is adduced to raise an issue as to whether he knew or could reasonably have been expected to know of those circumstances.

## 18. Abuse of position of trust: sexual activity in the presence of a child

(1) A person aged 18 or over (A) commits an offence if—
(a) he intentionally engages in an activity,
(b) the activity is sexual,
(c) for the purpose of obtaining sexual gratification, he engages in it—
(i) when another person (B) is present or is in a place from which A can be observed, and
(ii) knowing or believing that B is aware, or intending that B should be aware, that he is engaging in it,
(d) A is in a position of trust in relation to B,

(e) where subsection (2) applies, A knows or could reasonably be expected to know of the circumstances by virtue of which he is in a position of trust in relation to B, and
(f) either—
(i) B is under 18 and A does not reasonably believe that B is 18 or over, or
(ii) B is under 13.
(2) This subsection applies where A—
(a) is in a position of trust in relation to B by virtue of circumstances within section 21(2), (3), (4) or (5), and
(b) is not in such a position of trust by virtue of other circumstances.
(3) Where in proceedings for an offence under this section it is proved that the other person was under 18, the defendant is to be taken not to have reasonably believed that that person was 18 or over unless sufficient evidence is adduced to raise an issue as to whether he reasonably believed it.
(4) Where in proceedings for an offence under this section—
(a) it is proved that the defendant was in a position of trust in relation to the other person by virtue of circumstances within section 21 (2), (3), (4) or (5), and
(b) it is not proved that he was in such a position of trust by virtue of other circumstances,
it is to be taken that the defendant knew or could reasonably have been expected to know of the circumstances by virtue of which he was in such a position of trust unless sufficient evidence is adduced to raise an issue as to whether he knew or could reasonably have been expected to know of those circumstances.

## 19. Abuse of position of trust: causing a child to watch a sexual act

(1) A person aged 18 or over (A) commits an offence if—
(a) for the purpose of obtaining sexual gratification, he intentionally causes another person (B) to watch a third person engaging in an activity, or to look at an image of any person engaging in an activity,
(b) the activity is sexual,
(c) A is in a position of trust in relation to B,
(d) where subsection (2) applies, A knows or could reasonably be expected to know of the circumstances by virtue of which he is in a position of trust in relation to B, and
(e) either—
(i) B is under 18 and A does not reasonably believe that B is 18 or over, or
(ii) B is under 13.
(2) This subsection applies where A—
(a) is in a position of trust in relation to B by virtue of circumstances within section 21(2), (3), (4) or (5), and
(b) is not in such a position of trust by virtue of other circumstances.
(3) Where in proceedings for an offence under this section it is proved that the other person was under 18, the defendant is to be taken not to have reasonably believed that that person was 18 or over unless sufficient evidence is adduced to raise an issue as to whether he reasonably believed it.
(4) Where in proceedings for an offence under this section—
(a) it is proved that the defendant was in a position of trust in relation to the other person by virtue of circumstances within section 21(2), (3), (4) or (5), and
(b) it is not proved that he was in such a position of trust by virtue of other circumstances,
it is to be taken that the defendant knew or could reasonably have been expected to know of the circumstances by virtue of which he was in such a position of trust unless sufficient evidence is adduced to raise an issue as to whether he knew or could reasonably have been expected to know of those circumstances.

## 20. Abuse of position of trust: acts done in Scotland

Anything which, if done in England and Wales or Northern Ireland, would constitute an offence under any of sections 16 to 19 also constitutes that offence if done in Scotland.

## 21. Positions of trust

(1) For the purposes of sections 16 to 19, a person (A) is in a position of trust in relation to another person (B) if—
 (a) any of the following subsections applies, or
 (b) any condition specified in an order made by the Secretary of State is met.

(2) This subsection applies if A looks after persons under 18 who are detained in an institution by virtue of a court order or under an enactment, and B is so detained in that institution.

(3) This subsection applies if A looks after persons under 18 who are resident in a home or other place in which—
 (a) accommodation and maintenance are provided by an authority in accordance with section 22C(6) of the Children Act 1989 or section 81(6) of the Social Services and Well-being (Wales) Act 2014, or
 (b) accommodation is provided by a voluntary organisation under section 59(1) of the Children Act 1989,

and B is resident, and is so provided with accommodation and maintenance or accommodation, in that place.

(4) This subsection applies if A looks after persons under 18 who are accommodated and cared for in one of the following institutions—
 (a) a hospital,
 (b) in Wales, an independent clinic,
 (c) a care home,
 (d) a community home, voluntary home or children's home, or
 (e) a home provided under section 82(5) of the Children Act 1989,
 (g) a place in Wales at which a care home service is provided,
 (h) premises in Wales at which a secure accommodation service is provided,

and B is accommodated and cared for in that institution.

(5) This subsection applies if A looks after persons under 18 who are receiving education at an educational institution and B is receiving, and A is not receiving, education at that institution.

(7) This subsection applies if A is engaged in the provision of services under, or pursuant to anything done under—
 (a) sections 8 to 10 of the Employment and Training Act 1973, or
 (b) section 114 of the Learning and Skills Act 2000, and, in that capacity, looks after B on an individual basis.

(8) This subsection applies if A regularly has unsupervised contact with B (whether face to face or by any other means)—
 (a) in the exercise of functions of a local authority under section 20 or 21 of the Children Act 1989 or section 76 or 77 of the Social Services and Well-being (Wales) Act 2014.

(9) This subsection applies if A, as a person who is to report to the court under section 7 of the Children Act 1989 on matters relating to the welfare of B, regularly has unsupervised contact with B (whether face to face or by any other means).

(10) This subsection applies if A is a personal adviser appointed for B under—
 (a) section 23B(2) of, or paragraph 19C of Schedule 2 to, the Children Act 1989, or
 (aa) section 106(1) of the Social Services and Well-being (Wales) Act 2014 in respect of category 1 or 2 young persons within the meaning of that Act,

and, in that capacity, looks after B on an individual basis.

(11) This subsection applies if—
 (a) B is subject to a care order, a supervision order or an education supervision order, and
 (b) in the exercise of functions conferred by virtue of the order on an authorised person or the authority designated by the order, A looks after B on an individual basis.

(12) This subsection applies if A—
 (a) is an officer of the Service or Welsh family proceedings officer (within the meaning given by section 35 of the Children Act 2004) appointed for B under section 41(1) of the Children Act 1989,
 (b) is appointed a children's guardian of B under rule 6 or rule 18 of the Adoption Rules 1984, or

(c) is appointed to be the guardian ad litem of B under rule 9.5 of the Family Proceedings Rules 1991,

and, in that capacity, regularly has unsupervised contact with B (whether face to face or by any other means).

(13) This subsection applies if—

(a) B is subject to requirements imposed by or under an enactment on his release from detention for a criminal offence, or is subject to requirements imposed by a court order made in criminal proceedings, and

(b) A looks after B on an individual basis in pursuance of the requirements.

## 22. Positions of trust: interpretation

(1) The following provisions apply for the purposes of section 21.

(2) Subject to subsection (3), a person looks after persons under 18 if he is regularly involved in caring for, training, supervising or being in sole charge of such persons.

(3) A person (A) looks after another person (B) on an individual basis if—

(a) A is regularly involved in caring for, training or supervising B, and

(b) in the course of his involvement, A regularly has unsupervised contact with B (whether face to face or by any other means).

(4) A person receives education at an educational institution if—

(a) he is registered or otherwise enrolled as a pupil or student at the institution, or

(b) he receives education at the institution under arrangements with another educational institution at which he is so registered or otherwise enrolled.

(5) In section 21 —

'authority'—

(a) in relation to England and Wales, means a local authority;

'care home' means an establishment in England which is a care home for the purposes of the Care Standards Act 2000;

'care home service' has the meaning given in Part 1 of the Regulation and Inspection of Social Care (Wales) Act 2016;

'care order' has—

(a) in relation to England and Wales, the same meaning as in the Children Act 1989,

'children's home' has—

(a) in relation to England, the meaning given by section 1 of the Care Standards Act 2000,

'community home' has, in relation to England, the meaning given by section 53 of the Children Act 1989;

'education supervision order' has—

(a) in relation to England and Wales, the meaning given by section 36 of the Children Act 1989,

'hospital' means—

(a) a hospital as defined by section 275 of the National Health Service Act 2006, or section 206 of the National Health Service (Wales) Act 2006; or

(b) any other establishment—

(i) in England, in which any of the services listed in subsection (6) are provided; and

(ii) in Wales, which is a hospital within the meaning given by section 2(3) of the Care Standards Act 2000;

'independent clinic' has—

(a) the meaning given by section 2 of the Care Standards Act 2000;

'residential care home' means an establishment which is a residential care home for the purposes of the 2003 Order;

'secure accommodation service' has the meaning given in Part 1 of the Regulation and Inspection of Social Care (Wales) Act 2016;

'supervision order' has—

(a) in relation to England and Wales, the meaning given by section 31(11) of the Children Act 1989,

'voluntary home' has—

(a) in relation to England, the meaning given by section 60(3) of the Children Act 1989,

(6) The services referred to in paragraph (b)(i) of the definition of 'hospital' are as follows—

(a) medical treatment under anaesthesia or intravenously administered sedation;

(b) dental treatment under general anaesthesia;
(c) obstetric services and, in connection with childbirth, medical services;
(d) termination of pregnancies;
(e) cosmetic surgery, other than—
(i) ear and body piercing;
(ii) tattooing;
(iii) the subcutaneous injection of a substance or substances into the skin for cosmetic purposes; or
(iv) the removal of hair roots or small blemishes on the skin by the application of heat using an electric current.

## 23. Sections 16 to 19: exception for spouses or civil partners

(1) Conduct by a person (A) which would otherwise be an offence under any of sections 16 to 19 against another person (B) is not an offence under that section if at the time—
(a) B is 16 or over, and
(b) A and B are lawfully married or civil partners of each other.
(2) In proceedings for such an offence it is for the defendant to prove that A and B were at the time lawfully married or civil partners of each other.

## 24. Sections 16 to 19: sexual relationships which pre-date position of trust

(1) Conduct by a person (A) which would otherwise be an offence under any of sections 16 to 19 against another person (B) is not an offence under that section if, immediately before the position of trust arose, a sexual relationship existed between A and B.
(2) Subsection (1) does not apply if at that time sexual intercourse between A and B would have been unlawful.
(3) In proceedings for an offence under any of sections 16 to 19 it is for the defendant to prove that such a relationship existed at that time.

## 25. Sexual activity with a child family member

(1) A person (A) commits an offence if—
(a) he intentionally touches another person (B),
(b) the touching is sexual,
(c) the relation of A to B is within section 27,
(d) A knows or could reasonably be expected to know that his relation to B is of a description falling within that section, and
(e) either—
(i) B is under 18 and A does not reasonably believe that B is 18 or over, or
(ii) B is under 13.
(2) Where in proceedings for an offence under this section it is proved that the other person was under 18, the defendant is to be taken not to have reasonably believed that that person was 18 or over unless sufficient evidence is adduced to raise an issue as to whether he reasonably believed it.
(3) Where in proceedings for an offence under this section it is proved that the relation of the defendant to the other person was of a description falling within section 27, it is to be taken that the defendant knew or could reasonably have been expected to know that his relation to the other person was of that description unless sufficient evidence is adduced to raise an issue as to whether he knew or could reasonably have been expected to know that it was.
(6) This subsection applies where the touching involved—
(a) penetration of B's anus or vagina with a part of A's body or anything else,
(b) penetration of B's mouth with A's penis,
(c) penetration of A's anus or vagina with a part of B's body, or
(d) penetration of A's mouth with B's penis.

## 26. Inciting a child family member to engage in sexual activity

(1) A person (A) commits an offence if—
(a) he intentionally incites another person (B) to touch, or allow himself to be touched by, A,
(b) the touching is sexual,
(c) the relation of A to B is within section 27,
(d) A knows or could reasonably be expected to know that his relation to B is of a description falling within that section, and

(e) either—
(i) B is under 18 and A does not reasonably believe that B is 18 or over, or
(ii) B is under 13.

(2) Where in proceedings for an offence under this section it is proved that the other person was under 18, the defendant is to be taken not to have reasonably believed that that person was 18 or over unless sufficient evidence is adduced to raise an issue as to whether he reasonably believed it.

(3) Where in proceedings for an offence under this section it is proved that the relation of the defendant to the other person was of a description falling within section 27, it is to be taken that the defendant knew or could reasonably have been expected to know that his relation to the other person was of that description unless sufficient evidence is adduced to raise an issue as to whether he knew or could reasonably have been expected to know that it was.

(4) A person guilty of an offence under this section, if he was aged 18 or over at the time of the offence, is liable—
(a) where subsection (6) applies, on conviction on indictment to imprisonment for a term not exceeding 14 years;
(b) in any other case—
(i) on summary conviction, to imprisonment for a term not exceeding 6 months or a fine not exceeding the statutory maximum or both;
(ii) on conviction on indictment, to imprisonment for a term not exceeding 14 years.

(6) This subsection applies where the touching to which the incitement related involved—
(a) penetration of B's anus or vagina with a part of A's body or anything else,
(b) penetration of B's mouth with A's penis,
(c) penetration of A's anus or vagina with a part of B's body, or
(d) penetration of A's mouth with B's penis.

## 27. Family relationships

(1) The relation of one person (A) to another (B) is within this section if—
(a) it is within any of subsections (2) to (4), or
(b) it would be within one of those subsections but for section 39 of the Adoption Act 1976 or section 67 of the Adoption and Children Act 2002 (status conferred by adoption).

(2) The relation of A to B is within this subsection if—
(a) one of them is the other's parent, grandparent, brother, sister, half-brother, half-sister aunt or uncle, or
(b) A is or has been B's foster parent.

(3) The relation of A to B is within this subsection if A and B live or have lived in the same household, or A is or has been regularly involved in caring for, training, supervising or being in sole charge of B, and—
(a) one of them is or has been the other's step-parent,
(b) A and B are cousins,
(c) one of them is or has been the other's stepbrother or stepsister, or
(d) the parent or present or former foster parent of one of them is or has been the other's foster parent.

(4) The relation of A to B is within this subsection if—
(a) A and B live in the same household, and
(b) A is regularly involved in caring for, training, supervising or being in sole charge of B.

(5) For the purposes of this section—
(a) 'aunt' means the sister or half-sister of a person's parent, and 'uncle' has a corresponding meaning;
(b) 'cousin' means the child of an aunt or uncle;
(c) a person is a child's foster parent if—
(i) he is a person with whom the child has been placed under section 22C of the Children Act 1989 in a placement falling within subsection (6)(a) or (b) of that section (placement with local authority foster parent),
(ia) he is a person with whom the child has been placed under section 59(1)(a) of that Act (placement by voluntary organisation), or
(ii) he fosters the child privately, within the meaning given by section 66(1)(b) of that Act;

(d) a person is another's partner (whether they are of different sexes or the same sex) if they live together as partners in an enduring family relationship;
(e) 'step-parent' includes a parent's partner and 'stepbrother' and 'stepsister' include the child of a parent's partner.

## 28. Sections 25 and 26: exception for spouses and civil partners

(1) Conduct by a person (A) which would otherwise be an offence under section 25 or 26 against another person (B) is not an offence under that section if at the time—
(a) B is 16 or over, and
(b) A and B are lawfully married or civil partners of each other.
(2) In proceedings for such an offence it is for the defendant to prove that A and B were at the time lawfully married or civil partners of each other.

## 29. Sections 25 and 26: sexual relationships which pre-date family relationships

(1) Conduct by a person (A) which would otherwise be an offence under section 25 or 26 against another person (B) is not an offence under that section if—
(a) the relation of A to B is not within subsection (2) of section 27,
(b) it would not be within that subsection if section 39 of the Adoption Act 1976 or section 67 of the Adoption and Children Act 2002 did not apply, and
(c) immediately before the relation of A to B first became such as to fall within section 27, a sexual relationship existed between A and B.
(2) Subsection (1) does not apply if at the time referred to in subsection (1)(c) sexual intercourse between A and B would have been unlawful.
(3) In proceedings for an offence under section 25 or 26 it is for the defendant to prove the matters mentioned in subsection (1)(a) to (c).

## 30. Sexual activity with a person with a mental disorder impeding choice

(1) A person (A) commits an offence if—
(a) he intentionally touches another person (B),
(b) the touching is sexual,
(c) B is unable to refuse because of or for a reason related to a mental disorder, and
(d) A knows or could reasonably be expected to know that B has a mental disorder and that because of it or for a reason related to it B is likely to be unable to refuse.
(2) B is unable to refuse if—
(a) he lacks the capacity to choose whether to agree to the touching (whether because he lacks sufficient understanding of the nature or reasonably foreseeable consequences of what is being done, or for any other reason), or
(b) he is unable to communicate such a choice to A.
(3) A person guilty of an offence under this section, if the touching involved—
(a) penetration of B's anus or vagina with a part of A's body or anything else,
(b) penetration of B's mouth with A's penis,
(c) penetration of A's anus or vagina with a part of B's body, or
(d) penetration of A's mouth with B's penis,
is liable, on conviction on indictment, to imprisonment for life.

## 31. Causing or inciting a person, with a mental disorder impeding choice, to engage in sexual activity

(1) A person (A) commits an offence if—
(a) he intentionally causes or incites another person (B) to engage in an activity,
(b) the activity is sexual,
(c) B is unable to refuse because of or for a reason related to a mental disorder, and
(d) A knows or could reasonably be expected to know that B has a mental disorder and that because of it or for a reason related to it B is likely to be unable to refuse.
(2) B is unable to refuse if—
(a) he lacks the capacity to choose whether to agree to engaging in the activity caused or incited (whether because he lacks sufficient understanding of the nature or reasonably foreseeable consequences of the activity, or for any other reason), or
(b) he is unable to communicate such a choice to A.

(3) A person guilty of an offence under this section, if the activity caused or incited involved—
(a) penetration of B's anus or vagina,
(b) penetration of B's mouth with a person's penis,
(c) penetration of a person's anus or vagina with a part of B's body or by B with anything else, or
(d) penetration of a person's mouth with B's penis,
is liable, on conviction on indictment, to imprisonment for life.

## 32. Engaging in sexual activity in the presence of a person with a mental disorder impeding choice

(1) A person (A) commits an offence if—
(a) he intentionally engages in an activity,
(b) the activity is sexual,
(c) for the purpose of obtaining sexual gratification, he engages in it—
(i) when another person (B) is present or is in a place from which A can be observed, and
(ii) knowing or believing that B is aware, or intending that B should be aware, that he is engaging in it,
(d) B is unable to refuse because of or for a reason related to a mental disorder, and
(e) A knows or could reasonably be expected to know that B has a mental disorder and that because of it or for a reason related to it B is likely to be unable to refuse.
(2) B is unable to refuse if—
(a) he lacks the capacity to choose whether to agree to being present (whether because he lacks sufficient understanding of the nature of the activity, or for any other reason), or
(b) he is unable to communicate such a choice to A.

## 33. Causing a person, with a mental disorder impeding choice, to watch a sexual act

(1) A person (A) commits an offence if—
(a) for the purpose of obtaining sexual gratification, he intentionally causes another person (B) to watch a third person engaging in an activity, or to look at an image of any person engaging in an activity,
(b) the activity is sexual,
(c) B is unable to refuse because of or for a reason related to a mental disorder, and
(d) A knows or could reasonably be expected to know that B has a mental disorder and that because of it or for a reason related to it B is likely to be unable to refuse.
(2) B is unable to refuse if—
(a) he lacks the capacity to choose whether to agree to watching or looking (whether because he lacks sufficient understanding of the nature of the activity, or for any other reason), or
(b) he is unable to communicate such a choice to A.

## 34. Inducement, threat or deception to procure sexual activity with a person with a mental disorder

(1) A person (A) commits an offence if—
(a) with the agreement of another person (B) he intentionally touches that person,
(b) the touching is sexual,
(c) A obtains B's agreement by means of an inducement offered or given, a threat made or a deception practised by A for that purpose,
(d) B has a mental disorder, and
(e) A knows or could reasonably be expected to know that B has a mental disorder.
(2) A person guilty of an offence under this section, if the touching involved—
(a) penetration of B's anus or vagina with a part of A's body or anything else,
(b) penetration of B's mouth with A's penis,
(c) penetration of A's anus or vagina with a part of B's body, or
(d) penetration of A's mouth with B's penis,
is liable, on conviction on indictment, to imprisonment for life.

## 35. Causing a person with a mental disorder to engage in or agree to engage in sexual activity by inducement, threat or deception

(1) A person (A) commits an offence if—
- (a) by means of an inducement offered or given, a threat made or a deception practised by him for this purpose, he intentionally causes another person (B) to engage in, or to agree to engage in, an activity,
- (b) the activity is sexual,
- (c) B has a mental disorder, and
- (d) A knows or could reasonably be expected to know that B has a mental disorder.

(2) A person guilty of an offence under this section, if the activity caused or agreed to involved—
- (a) penetration of B's anus or vagina,
- (b) penetration of B's mouth with a person's penis,
- (c) penetration of a person's anus or vagina with a part of B's body or by B with anything else, or
- (d) penetration of a person's mouth with B's penis,

is liable, on conviction on indictment, to imprisonment for life.

## 36. Engaging in sexual activity in the presence, procured by inducement, threat or deception, of a person with a mental disorder

(1) A person (A) commits an offence if—
- (a) he intentionally engages in an activity,
- (b) the activity is sexual,
- (c) for the purpose of obtaining sexual gratification, he engages in it—
  - (i) when another person (B) is present or is in a place from which A can be observed, and
  - (ii) knowing or believing that B is aware, or intending that B should be aware, that he is engaging in it,
- (d) B agrees to be present or in the place referred to in paragraph (c)(i) because of an inducement offered or given, a threat made or a deception practised by A for the purpose of obtaining that agreement,
- (e) B has a mental disorder, and
- (f) A knows or could reasonably be expected to know that B has a mental disorder.

## 37. Causing a person with a mental disorder to watch a sexual act by inducement, threat or deception

(1) A person (A) commits an offence if—
- (a) for the purpose of obtaining sexual gratification, he intentionally causes another person (B) to watch a third person engaging in an activity, or to look at an image of any person engaging in an activity,
- (b) the activity is sexual,
- (c) B agrees to watch or look because of an inducement offered or given, a threat made or a deception practised by A for the purpose of obtaining that agreement,
- (d) B has a mental disorder, and
- (e) A knows or could reasonably be expected to know that B has a mental disorder.

## 38. Care workers: sexual activity with a person with a mental disorder

(1) A person (A) commits an offence if—
- (a) he intentionally touches another person (B),
- (b) the touching is sexual,
- (c) B has a mental disorder,
- (d) A knows or could reasonably be expected to know that B has a mental disorder, and
- (e) A is involved in B's care in a way that falls within section 42.

(2) Where in proceedings for an offence under this section it is proved that the other person had a mental disorder, it is to be taken that the defendant knew or could reasonably have been expected to know that that person had a mental disorder unless sufficient evidence is adduced to raise an issue as to whether he knew or could reasonably have been expected to know it.

(3) A person guilty of an offence under this section, if the touching involved—
  (a) penetration of B's anus or vagina with a part of A's body or anything else,
  (b) penetration of B's mouth with A's penis,
  (c) penetration of A's anus or vagina with a part of B's body, or
  (d) penetration of A's mouth with B's penis,

is liable, on conviction on indictment, to imprisonment for a term not exceeding 14 years.

## 39. Care workers: causing or inciting sexual activity

(1) A person (A) commits an offence if—
  (a) he intentionally causes or incites another person (B) to engage in an activity,
  (b) the activity is sexual,
  (c) B has a mental disorder,
  (d) A knows or could reasonably be expected to know that B has a mental disorder, and
  (e) A is involved in B's care in a way that falls within section 42.

(2) Where in proceedings for an offence under this section it is proved that the other person had a mental disorder, it is to be taken that the defendant knew or could reasonably have been expected to know that that person had a mental disorder unless sufficient evidence is adduced to raise an issue as to whether he knew or could reasonably have been expected to know it.

(3) A person guilty of an offence under this section, if the activity caused or incited involved—
  (a) penetration of B's anus or vagina,
  (b) penetration of B's mouth with a person's penis,
  (c) penetration of a person's anus or vagina with a part of B's body or by B with anything else, or
  (d) penetration of a person's mouth with B's penis,

is liable, on conviction on indictment, to imprisonment for a term not exceeding 14 years.

## 40. Care workers: sexual activity in the presence of a person with a mental disorder

(1) A person (A) commits an offence if—
  (a) he intentionally engages in an activity,
  (b) the activity is sexual,
  (c) for the purpose of obtaining sexual gratification, he engages in it—
    (i) when another person (B) is present or is in a place from which A can be observed, and
    (ii) knowing or believing that B is aware, or intending that B should be aware, that he is engaging in it,
  (d) B has a mental disorder,
  (e) A knows or could reasonably be expected to know that B has a mental disorder, and
  (f) A is involved in B's care in a way that falls within section 42.

(2) Where in proceedings for an offence under this section it is proved that the other person had a mental disorder, it is to be taken that the defendant knew or could reasonably have been expected to know that that person had a mental disorder unless sufficient evidence is adduced to raise an issue as to whether he knew or could reasonably have been expected to know it.

## 41. Care workers: causing a person with a mental disorder to watch a sexual act

(1) A person (A) commits an offence if—
  (a) for the purpose of obtaining sexual gratification, he intentionally causes another person (B) to watch a third person engaging in an activity, or to look at an image of any person engaging in an activity,
  (b) the activity is sexual,
  (c) B has a mental disorder,

(d) A knows or could reasonably be expected to know that B has a mental disorder, and

(e) A is involved in B's care in a way that falls within section 42.

(2) Where in proceedings for an offence under this section it is proved that the other person had a mental disorder, it is to be taken that the defendant knew or could reasonably have been expected to know that that person had a mental disorder unless sufficient evidence is adduced to raise an issue as to whether he knew or could reasonably have been expected to know it.

## 42. Care workers: interpretation

(1) For the purposes of sections 38 to 41, a person (A) is involved in the care of another person (B) in a way that falls within this section if any of subsections (2) to (4) applies.

(2) This subsection applies if—

(a) B is accommodated and cared for in a care home, community home, voluntary home, children's home or premises in Wales at which a secure accommodation service is provided, and

(b) A has functions to perform in the course of employment in the home or the premises which have brought him or are likely to bring him into regular face to face contact with B.

(3) This subsection applies if B is a patient for whom services are provided—

(a) by a National Health Service body or an independent medical agency, or

(b) in an independent hospital, or

(c) in Wales, in an independent clinic,

and A has functions to perform for the body or agency or in the clinic or hospital in the course of employment which have brought him or are likely to bring him into regular face to face contact with B.

(4) This subsection applies if A—

(a) is, whether or not in the course of employment, a provider of care, assistance or services to B in connection with B's mental disorder, and

(b) as such, has had or is likely to have regular face to face contact with B.

(5) In this section—

'care home' means—

(a) an establishment in England which is a care home for the purposes of the Care Standards Act 2000; and

(b) a place in Wales at which a care home service, within the meaning of Part 1 of the Regulation and Inspection of Social Care (Wales) Act 2016 is provided wholly or mainly to persons aged 18 or over;

'children's home'—

(a) has the meaning given by section 1 of the Care Standards Act 2000 in relation to a children's home in England, and

(b) means a place in Wales at which a care home service within the meaning of Part 1 of the Regulation and Inspection of Social Care (Wales) Act 2016 is provided wholly or mainly to persons under the age of 18;

'community home' has the meaning given by section 53 of the Children Act 1989; 'employment' means any employment, whether paid or unpaid and whether under a contract of service or apprenticeship, under a contract for services, or otherwise than under a contract;

'independent clinic' has the meaning given by section 2 of the Care Standards Act 2000; 'independent hospital'—

(a) in England, means—

(i) a hospital as defined by section 275 of the National Health Service Act 2006 that is not a health service hospital as defined by that section; or

(ii) any other establishment in which any of the services listed in section 22(6) are provided and which is not a health service hospital as so defined; and

(b) in Wales, has the meaning given by section 2 of the Care Standards Act 2000;

'independent medical agency' means an undertaking (not being an independent hospital, or in Wales an independent clinic) which consists of or includes the provision of services by medical practitioners;

'National Health Service body' means—

(a) a Local Health Board,
(b) a National Health Service trust,
(ba) the Secretary of State in relation to the exercise of functions under section 2A or 2B of, or paragraph 7C, 8 or 12 of Schedule 1 to, the National Health Service Act 2006,
(bb) a local authority in relation to the exercise of functions under section 2B or 111 of, or any of paragraphs 1 to 7B, or 13 of Schedule 1 to, the National Health Service Act 2006,
(c) ...
(d) a Special Health Authority;

'secure accommodation service' has the meaning given in Part 1 of the Regulation and Inspection of Social Care (Wales) Act 2016;
'voluntary home' has the meaning given by section 60(3) of the Children Act 1989.

(6) In subsection (5), in the definition of 'independent medical agency', 'undertaking' includes any business or profession and—
(a) in relation to a public or local authority, includes the exercise of any functions of that authority; and
(b) in relation to any other body of persons, whether corporate or unincorporate, includes any of the activities of that body.

## 43. Sections 38 to 41: exception for spouses and civil partners

(1) Conduct by a person (A) which would otherwise be an offence under any of sections 38 to 41 against another person (B) is not an offence under that section if at the time—
(a) B is 16 or over, and
(b) A and B are lawfully married or civil partners of each other.

(2) In proceedings for such an offence it is for the defendant to prove that A and B were at the time lawfully married or civil partners of each other.

## 44. Sections 38 to 41: sexual relationships which pre-date care relationships

(1) Conduct by a person (A) which would otherwise be an offence under any of sections 38 to 41 against another person (B) is not an offence under that section if, immediately before A became involved in B's care in a way that falls within section 42, a sexual relationship existed between A and B.

(2) Subsection (1) does not apply if at that time sexual intercourse between A and B would have been unlawful.

(3) In proceedings for an offence under any of sections 38 to 41 it is for the defendant to prove that such a relationship existed at that time.

## 47. Paying for sexual services of a child

(1) A person (A) commits an offence if—
(a) he intentionally obtains for himself the sexual services of another person (B),
(b) before obtaining those services, he has made or promised payment for those services to B or a third person, or knows that another person has made or promised such a payment, and
(c) either—
(i) B is under 18, and A does not reasonably believe that B is 18 or over, or
(ii) B is under 13.

(2) In this section, 'payment' means any financial advantage, including the discharge of an obligation to pay or the provision of goods or services (including sexual services) gratuitously or at a discount.

## 48. Causing or inciting sexual exploitation of a child

(1) A person (A) commits an offence if—
(a) he intentionally causes or incites another person (B) to be sexually exploited in any part of the world, and
(b) either—
(i) B is under 18, and A does not reasonably believe that B is 18 or over, or
(ii) B is under 13.

## 49. Controlling a child in relation to sexual exploitation

(1) A person (A) commits an offence if—
   (a) he intentionally controls any of the activities of another person (B) relating to B's sexual exploitation in any part of the world, and
   (b) either—
      (i) B is under 18, and A does not reasonably believe that B is 18 or over, or
      (ii) B is under 13.

## 50. Arranging or facilitating sexual exploitation of a child

(1) A person (A) commits an offence if—
   (a) he intentionally arranges or facilitates the sexual exploitation in any part of the world of another person (B), and
   (b) either—
      (i) B is under 18, and A does not reasonably believe that B is 18 or over, or
      (ii) B is under 13.

## 51. Sections 48 to 50: interpretation

(2) For the purposes of sections 48 to 50, a person (B) is sexually exploited if—
   (a) on at least one occasion and whether or not compelled to do so, B offers or provides sexual services to another person in return for payment or a promise of payment to B or a third person, or
   (b) an indecent image of B is recorded;

and 'sexual exploitation' is to be interpreted accordingly.

## 51A. Soliciting

(1) It is an offence for a person in a street or public place to solicit another (B) for the purpose of obtaining B's sexual services as a prostitute.
(2) The reference to a person in a street or public place includes a person in a vehicle in a street or public place.
(3) In this section 'street' has the meaning given by section 1(4) of the Street Offences Act 1959.

## 52. Causing or inciting prostitution for gain

(1) A person commits an offence if—
   (a) he intentionally causes or incites another person to become a prostitute in any part of the world, and
   (b) he does so for or in the expectation of gain for himself or a third person.

## 53. Controlling prostitution for gain

(1) A person commits an offence if—
   (a) he intentionally controls any of the activities of another person relating to that person's prostitution in any part of the world, and
   (b) he does so for or in the expectation of gain for himself or a third person.

## 53A. Paying for sexual services of a prostitute subjected to force etc.

(1) A person (A) commits an offence if—
   (a) A makes or promises payment for the sexual services of a prostitute (B),
   (b) a third person (C) has engaged in exploitative conduct of a kind likely to induce or encourage B to provide the sexual services for which A has made or promised payment, and
   (c) C engaged in that conduct for or in the expectation of gain for C or another person (apart from A or B).
(2) The following are irrelevant—
   (a) where in the world the sexual services are to be provided and whether those services are provided,
   (b) whether A is, or ought to be, aware that C has engaged in exploitative conduct.
(3) C engages in exploitative conduct if—
   (a) C uses force, threats (whether or not relating to violence) or any other form of coercion, or
   (b) C practises any form of deception.

## 54. Sections 51A and 53A: interpretation

(1) In sections 52, 53 and 53A, 'gain' means—
  (a) any financial advantage, including the discharge of an obligation to pay or the provision of goods or services (including sexual services) gratuitously or at a discount; or
  (b) the goodwill of any person which is or appears likely, in time, to bring financial advantage.

(2) In sections 51A, 52, 53 and 53A 'prostitute' and 'prostitution' have the meaning given by section 51(2).

(3) In section 53A 'payment' has the meaning given by section 51 (3).

## 61. Administering a substance with intent

(1) A person commits an offence if he intentionally administers a substance to, or causes a substance to be taken by, another person (B)—
  (a) knowing that B does not consent, and
  (b) with the intention of stupefying or overpowering B, so as to enable any person to engage in a sexual activity that involves B.

## 62. Committing an offence with intent to commit a sexual offence

(1) A person commits an offence under this section if he commits any offence with the intention of committing a relevant sexual offence.

(2) In this section, 'relevant sexual offence' means any offence under this Part (including an offence of aiding, abetting, counselling or procuring such an offence).

(3) A person guilty of an offence under this section is liable on conviction on indictment, where the offence is committed by kidnapping or false imprisonment, to imprisonment for life.

## 63. Trespass with intent to commit a sexual offence

(1) A person commits an offence if—
  (a) he is a trespasser on any premises,
  (b) he intends to commit a relevant sexual offence on the premises, and
  (c) he knows that, or is reckless as to whether, he is a trespasser.

(2) In this section—
'premises' includes a structure or part of a structure;
'relevant sexual offence' has the same meaning as in section 62;
'structure' includes a tent, vehicle or vessel or other temporary or movable structure.

## 64. Sex with an adult relative: penetration

(1) A person aged 16 or over (A) (subject to subsection (3A)) commits an offence if—
  (a) he intentionally penetrates another person's vagina or anus with a part of his body or anything else, or penetrates another person's mouth with his penis,
  (b) the penetration is sexual,
  (c) the other person (B) is aged 18 or over,
  (d) A is related to B in a way mentioned in subsection (2), and
  (e) A knows or could reasonably be expected to know that he is related to B in that way.

(2) The ways that A may be related to B are as parent, grandparent, child, grandchild, brother, sister, half-brother, half-sister, uncle, aunt, nephew or niece.

(3) In subsection (2)—
  (za) 'parent' includes an adoptive parent;
  (zb) 'child' includes an adopted person within the meaning of Chapter 4 of Part 1 of the Adoption and Children Act 2002;
  (a) 'uncle' means the brother of a person's parent, and 'aunt' has a corresponding meaning;
  (b) 'nephew' means the child of a person's brother or sister, and 'niece' has a corresponding meaning.

(3A) Where subsection (1) applies in a case where A is related to B as B's child by virtue of subsection (3)(zb), A does not commit an offence under this section unless A is 18 or over.

(4) Where in proceedings for an offence under this section it is proved that the defendant was related to the other person in any of those ways, it is to be taken that the defendant knew or could reasonably have been expected to know that he was related in that way unless sufficient evidence is adduced to raise an issue as to whether he knew or could reasonably have been expected to know that he was.

## 65. Sex with an adult relative: consenting to penetration

(1) A person aged 16 or over (A) (subject to subsection (3A)) commits an offence if—
  (a) another person (B) penetrates A's vagina or anus with a part of B's body or anything else, or penetrates A's mouth with B's penis,
  (b) A consents to the penetration,
  (c) the penetration is sexual,
  (d) B is aged 18 or over,
  (e) A is related to B in a way mentioned in subsection (2), and
  (f) A knows or could reasonably be expected to know that he is related to B in that way.

(2) The ways that A may be related to B are as parent, grandparent, child, grandchild, brother, sister, half-brother, half-sister, uncle, aunt, nephew or niece.

(3) In subsection (2)—
  (za) 'parent' includes an adoptive parent;
  (zb) 'child' includes an adopted person within the meaning of Chapter 4 of Part 1 of the Adoption and Children Act 2002;
  (a) 'uncle' means the brother of a person's parent, and 'aunt' has a corresponding meaning;
  (b) 'nephew' means the child of a person's brother or sister, and 'niece' has a corresponding meaning.

(3A) Where subsection (1) applies in a case where A is related to B as B's child by virtue of subsection (3)(zb), A does not commit an offence under this section unless A is 18 or over.

(4) Where in proceedings for an offence under this section it is proved that the defendant was related to the other person in any of those ways, it is to be taken that the defendant knew or could reasonably have been expected to know that he was related in that way unless sufficient evidence is adduced to raise an issue as to whether he knew or could reasonably have been expected to know that he was.

## 66. Exposure

(1) A person commits an offence if—
  (a) he intentionally exposes his genitals, and
  (b) he intends that someone will see them and be caused alarm or distress.

## 67. Voyeurism

(1) A person commits an offence if—
  (a) for the purpose of obtaining sexual gratification, he observes another person doing a private act, and
  (b) he knows that the other person does not consent to being observed for his sexual gratification.

(2) A person commits an offence if—
  (a) he operates equipment with the intention of enabling another person to observe, for the purpose of obtaining sexual gratification, a third person (B) doing a private act, and
  (b) he knows that B does not consent to his operating equipment with that intention.

(3) A person commits an offence if—
  (a) he records another person (B) doing a private act,
  (b) he does so with the intention that he or a third person will, for the purpose of obtaining sexual gratification, look at an image of B doing the act, and
  (c) he knows that B does not consent to his recording the act with that intention.

(4) A person commits an offence if he installs equipment, or constructs or adapts a structure or part of a structure, with the intention of enabling himself or another person to commit an offence under subsection (1).

## 67A. Voyeurism: additional offences

(1) A person (A) commits an offence if—
  (a) A operates equipment beneath the clothing of another person (B),
  (b) A does so with the intention of enabling A or another person (C), for a purpose mentioned in subsection (3), to observe—
    (i) B's genitals or buttocks (whether exposed or covered with underwear), or
    (ii) the underwear covering B's genitals or buttocks,
    in circumstances where the genitals, buttocks or underwear would not otherwise be visible, and
  (c) A does so—
    (i) without B's consent, and
    (ii) without reasonably believing that B consents.

(2) A person (A) commits an offence if—
  (a) A records an image beneath the clothing of another person (B),
  (b) the image is of—
    (i) B's genitals or buttocks (whether exposed or covered with underwear), or
    (ii) the underwear covering B's genitals or buttocks,
  in circumstances where the genitals, buttocks or underwear would not otherwise be visible,
  (c) A does so with the intention that A or another person (C) will look at the image for a purpose mentioned in subsection (3), and
  (d) A does so—
    (i) without B's consent, and
    (ii) without reasonably believing that B consents.

(3) The purposes referred to in subsections (1) and (2) are—
  (a) obtaining sexual gratification (whether for A or C);
  (b) humiliating, alarming or distressing B.

(4) A person guilty of an offence under this section is liable—
  (a) on summary conviction, to imprisonment for a term not exceeding 12 months, or to a fine, or to both;
  (b) on conviction on indictment, to imprisonment for a term not exceeding 2 years.

(5) In relation to an offence committed before the coming into force of section 154(1) of the Criminal Justice Act 2003 (increase in maximum term that may be imposed on summary conviction of offence triable either way), the reference in subsection (4)(a) to 12 months is to be read as a reference to 6 months.

## 68. Voyeurism: interpretation

(1) For the purposes of section 67, a person is doing a private act if the person is in a place which, in the circumstances, would reasonably be expected to provide privacy, and—
  (a) the person's genitals, buttocks or breasts are exposed or covered only with underwear,
  (b) the person is using a lavatory, or
  (c) the person is doing a sexual act that is not of a kind ordinarily done in public.

(1A) For the purposes of sections 67 and 67A, operating equipment includes enabling or securing its activation by another person without that person's knowledge.

(2) In section 67, 'structure' includes a tent, vehicle or vessel or other temporary or movable structure.

## 69. Intercourse with an animal

(1) A person commits an offence if—
  (a) he intentionally performs an act of penetration with his penis,
  (b) what is penetrated is the vagina or anus of a living animal, and
  (c) he knows that, or is reckless as to whether, that is what is penetrated.

(2) A person (A) commits an offence if—
  (a) A intentionally causes, or allows, A's vagina or anus to be penetrated,
  (b) the penetration is by the penis of a living animal, and
  (c) A knows that, or is reckless as to whether, that is what A is being penetrated by.

## 70. Sexual penetration of a corpse

(1) A person commits an offence if—
  (a) he intentionally performs an act of penetration with a part of his body or anything else,
  (b) what is penetrated is a part of the body of a dead person,
  (c) he knows that, or is reckless as to whether, that is what is penetrated, and
  (d) the penetration is sexual.

## 71. Sexual activity in a public lavatory

(1) A person commits an offence if—
  (a) he is in a lavatory to which the public or a section of the public has or is permitted to have access, whether on payment or otherwise,
  (b) he intentionally engages in an activity, and,
  (c) the activity is sexual.
(2) For the purposes of this section, an activity is sexual if a reasonable person would, in all the circumstances but regardless of any person's purpose, consider it to be sexual.

## 72. Offences outside the United Kingdom

(1) If—
  (a) a United Kingdom national does an act in a country outside the United Kingdom, and
  (b) the act, if done in England and Wales or Northern Ireland, would constitute a sexual offence to which this section applies,

  the United Kingdom national is guilty in that part of the United Kingdom of that sexual offence.
(2) If—
  (a) a United Kingdom resident does an act in a country outside the United Kingdom,
  (b) the act constitutes an offence under the law in force in that country, and
  (c) the act, if done in England and Wales or Northern Ireland, would constitute a sexual offence to which this section applies,

  the United Kingdom resident is guilty in that part of the United Kingdom of that sexual offence.
(3) If—
  (a) a person does an act in a country outside the United Kingdom at a time when the person was not a United Kingdom national or a United Kingdom resident,
  (b) the act constituted an offence under the law in force in that country,
  (c) the act, if done in England and Wales or Northern Ireland, would have constituted a sexual offence to which this section applies, and
  (d) the person meets the residence or nationality condition at the relevant time, proceedings may be brought against the person in that part of the United Kingdom for that sexual offence as if the person had done the act there.
(4) The person meets the residence or nationality condition at the relevant time if the person is a United Kingdom national or a United Kingdom resident at the time when the proceedings are brought.
(5) An act punishable under the law in force in any country constitutes an offence under that law for the purposes of subsections (2) and (3) however it is described in that law.
(6) The condition in subsection (2)(b) or (3)(b) is to be taken to be met unless, not later than rules of court may provide, the defendant serves on the prosecution a notice—
  (a) stating that, on the facts as alleged with respect to the act in question, the condition is not in the defendant's opinion met,
  (b) showing the grounds for that opinion, and
  (c) requiring the prosecution to prove that it is met.
(7) But the court, if it thinks fit, may permit the defendant to require the prosecution to prove that the condition is met without service of a notice under subsection (6).
(8) In the Crown Court the question whether the condition is met is to be decided by the judge alone.
(9) In this section—

  'country' includes territory;

  'United Kingdom national' means an individual who is—

(a) a British citizen, a British overseas territories citizen, a British National (Overseas) or a British Overseas citizen;
(b) a person who under the British Nationality Act 1981 is a British subject; or
(c) a British protected person within the meaning of that Act;
'United Kingdom resident' means an individual who is resident in the United Kingdom.

(10) Schedule 2 lists the sexual offences to which this section applies.

## 73. Exceptions to aiding, abetting and counselling

(1) A person is not guilty of aiding, abetting or counselling the commission against a child of an offence to which this section applies if he acts for the purpose of—
(a) protecting the child from sexually transmitted infection,
(b) protecting the physical safety of the child,
(c) preventing the child from becoming pregnant, or
(d) promoting the child's emotional well-being by the giving of advice,
and not for the purpose of obtaining sexual gratification or for the purpose of causing or encouraging the activity constituting the offence or the child's participation in it.

(2) This section applies to—
(a) an offence under any of sections 5 to 7 (offences against children under 13);
(b) an offence under section 9 (sexual activity with a child);
(c) an offence under section 13 which would be an offence under section 9 if the offender were aged 18;
(d) an offence under any of sections 16, 25, 30, 34 and 38 (sexual activity) against a person under 16.

(3) This section does not affect any other enactment or any rule of law restricting the circumstances in which a person is guilty of aiding, abetting or counselling an offence under this Part.

## 74. 'Consent'

For the purposes of this Part, a person consents if he agrees by choice, and has the freedom and capacity to make that choice.

## 75. Evidential presumptions about consent

(1) If in proceedings for an offence to which this section applies it is proved—
(a) that the defendant did the relevant act,
(b) that any of the circumstances specified in subsection (2) existed, and
(c) that the defendant knew that those circumstances existed,
the complainant is to be taken not to have consented to the relevant act unless sufficient evidence is adduced to raise an issue as to whether he consented, and the defendant is to be taken not to have reasonably believed that the complainant consented unless sufficient evidence is adduced to raise an issue as to whether he reasonably believed it.

(2) The circumstances are that—
(a) any person was, at the time of the relevant act or immediately before it began, using violence against the complainant or causing the complainant to fear that immediate violence would be used against him;
(b) any person was, at the time of the relevant act or immediately before it began, causing the complainant to fear that violence was being used, or that immediate violence would be used, against another person;
(c) the complainant was, and the defendant was not, unlawfully detained at the time of the relevant act;
(d) the complainant was asleep or otherwise unconscious at the time of the relevant act;
(e) because of the complainant's physical disability, the complainant would not have been able at the time of the relevant act to communicate to the defendant whether the complainant consented;
(f) any person had administered to or caused to be taken by the complainant, without the complainant's consent, a substance which, having regard to when it was administered or taken, was capable of causing or enabling the complainant to be stupefied or overpowered at the time of the relevant act.

(3) In subsection (2)(a) and (b), the reference to the time immediately before the relevant act began is, in the case of an act which is one of a continuous series of sexual activities, a reference to the time immediately before the first sexual activity began.

## 76. Conclusive presumptions about consent

(1) If in proceedings for an offence to which this section applies it is proved that the defendant did the relevant act and that any of the circumstances specified in subsection (2) existed, it is to be conclusively presumed—
   (a) that the complainant did not consent to the relevant act, and
   (b) that the defendant did not believe that the complainant consented to the relevant act.

(2) The circumstances are that—
   (a) the defendant intentionally deceived the complainant as to the nature or purpose of the relevant act;
   (b) the defendant intentionally induced the complainant to consent to the relevant act by impersonating a person known personally to the complainant.

## 77. Sections 75 and 76: relevant acts

In relation to an offence to which sections 75 and 76 apply, references in those sections to the relevant act and to the complainant are to be read as follows—

| *Offence* | *Relevant Act* |
|---|---|
| An offence under section 1 (rape). | The defendant intentionally penetrating, with his penis, the vagina, anus or mouth of another person ('the complainant'). |
| An offence under section 2 (assault by penetration). | The defendant intentionally penetrating, with a part of his body or anything else, the vagina or anus of another person ('the complainant'), where the penetration is sexual. |
| An offence under section 3 (sexual assault). | The defendant intentionally touching another person ('the complainant'), where the touching is sexual. |
| An offence under section 4 (causing a person to engage in sexual activity without consent). | The defendant intentionally causing another person ('the complainant') to engage in an activity, where the activity is sexual. |

## 78. Sexual

For the purposes of this Part (except sections 15A and 71), penetration, touching or any other activity is sexual if a reasonable person would consider that—
   (a) whatever its circumstances or any person's purpose in relation to it, it is because of its nature sexual, or
   (b) because of its nature it may be sexual and because of its circumstances or the purpose of any person in relation to it (or both) it is sexual.

## 79. Part 1: general interpretation

(1) The following apply for the purposes of this Part.
(2) Penetration is a continuing act from entry to withdrawal.
(3) References to a part of the body include references to a part surgically constructed (in particular, through gender reassignment surgery).
(4) 'Image' means a moving or still image and includes an image produced by any means and, where the context permits, a three-dimensional image.
(5) References to an image of a person include references to an image of an imaginary person.
(6) 'Mental disorder' has the meaning given by section 1 of the Mental Health Act 1983.
(7) References to observation (however expressed) are to observation whether direct or by looking at an image.
(8) Touching includes touching—
   (a) with any part of the body,

(b) with anything else,
(c) through anything,
and in particular includes touching amounting to penetration.
(9) 'Vagina' includes vulva.
(10) In relation to an animal, references to the vagina or anus include references to any similar part.

SCHEDULE 2

1. In relation to England and Wales, the following are sexual offences to which section 72 applies—
(a) an offence under any of sections 5 to 19, 25 and 26 and 47 to 50;
(b) an offence under any of sections 1 to 4, 30 to 41 and 61 where the victim of the offence was under 18 at the time of the offence;
(c) an offence under section 62 or 63 where the intended offence was an offence against a person under 18;
(d) an offence under—
(i) section 1 of the Protection of Children Act 1978 (indecent photographs of children), or
(ii) section 160 of the Criminal Justice Act 1988 (possession of indecent photograph of child).

# CHILDREN ACT 2004

## 58. Reasonable punishment

(1) In relation to any offence specified in subsection (2), battery of a child cannot be justified on the ground that it constituted reasonable punishment.
(2) The offences referred to in subsection (1) are—
(a) an offence under section 18 or 20 of the Offences against the Person Act 1861 (wounding and causing grievous bodily harm);
(b) an offence under section 47 of that Act (assault occasioning actual bodily harm);
(c) an offence under section 1 of the Children and Young Persons Act 1933 (cruelty to persons under 16).
(3) Battery of a child causing actual bodily harm to the child cannot be justified in any civil proceedings on the ground that it constituted reasonable punishment.
(4) For the purposes of subsection (3) 'actual bodily harm' has the same meaning as it has for the purposes of section 47 of the Offences against the Person Act 1861.

# DOMESTIC VIOLENCE, CRIME AND VICTIMS ACT 2004

PART 1
DOMESTIC VIOLENCE ETC.

## 5. Causing or allowing the death of a child or vulnerable adult

(1) A person ('D') is guilty of an offence if—
(a) a child or vulnerable adult ('V') dies or suffers serious physical harm as a result of the unlawful act of a person who—
(i) was a member of the same household as V, and
(ii) had frequent contact with him,
(b) D was such a person at the time of that act,
(c) at that time there was a significant risk of serious physical harm being caused to V by the unlawful act of such a person, and
(d) either D was the person whose act caused the death or serious physical harm or—
(i) D was, or ought to have been, aware of the risk mentioned in paragraph (c),
(ii) D failed to take such steps as he could reasonably have been expected to take to protect V from the risk, and

(iii) the act occurred in circumstances of the kind that D foresaw or ought to have foreseen.

(2) The prosecution does not have to prove whether it is the first alternative in subsection (1)(d) or the second (sub-paragraphs (i) to (iii)) that applies.

(3) If D was not the mother or father of V—

(a) D may not be charged with an offence under this section if he was under the age of 16 at the time of the act that caused the death or serious physical harm;

(b) for the purposes of subsection (1)(d)(ii) D could not have been expected to take any such step as is referred to there before attaining that age.

(4) For the purposes of this section—

(a) a person is to be regarded as a 'member' of a particular household, even if he does not live in that household, if he visits it so often and for such periods of time that it is reasonable to regard him as a member of it;

(b) where V lived in different households at different times, 'the same household as V' refers to the household in which V was living at the time of the act that caused the death or serious physical harm.

(5) For the purposes of this section an 'unlawful' act is one that—

(a) constitutes an offence, or

(b) would constitute an offence but for being the act of—

(i) a person under the age of ten, or

(ii) a person entitled to rely on a defence of insanity.

Paragraph (b) does not apply to an act of D.

(6) In this section—

'act' includes a course of conduct and also includes omission;

'child' means a person under the age of 16;

'serious' harm means harm that amounts to grievous bodily harm for the purposes of the Offences against the Person Act 1861;

'vulnerable adult' means a person aged 16 or over whose ability to protect himself from violence, abuse or neglect is significantly impaired through physical or mental disability or illness, through old age or otherwise.

# GENDER RECOGNITION ACT 2004

## 9. General

(1) Where a full gender recognition certificate is issued to a person, the person's gender becomes for all purposes the acquired gender (so that, if the acquired gender is the male gender, the person's sex becomes that of a man and, if it is the female gender, the person's sex becomes that of a woman).

(2) Subsection (1) does not affect things done, or events occurring, before the certificate is issued; but it does operate for the interpretation of enactments passed, and instruments and other documents made, before the certificate is issued (as well as those passed or made afterwards).

## 20. Gender-specific offences

(1) Where (apart from this subsection) a relevant gender-specific offence could be committed or attempted only if the gender of a person to whom a full gender recognition certificate has been issued were not the acquired gender, the fact that the person's gender has become the acquired gender does not prevent the offence being committed or attempted.

(2) An offence is a 'relevant gender-specific offence' if—

(a) either or both of the conditions in subsection (3) are satisfied, and

(b) the commission of the offence involves the accused engaging in sexual activity.

(3) The conditions are—

(a) that the offence may be committed only by a person of a particular gender, and

(b) that the offence may be committed only on, or in relation to, a person of a particular gender,

and the references to a particular gender include a gender identified by reference to the gender of the other person involved.

# GAMBLING ACT 2005

## 42. Cheating

(1) A person commits an offence if he—
- (a) cheats at gambling, or
- (b) does anything for the purpose of enabling or assisting another person to cheat at gambling.

(2) For the purposes of subsection (1) it is immaterial whether a person who cheats—
- (a) improves his chances of winning anything, or
- (b) wins anything.

(3) Without prejudice to the generality of subsection (1) cheating at gambling may, in particular, consist of actual or attempted deception or interference in connection with—
- (a) the process by which gambling is conducted, or
- (b) a real or virtual game, race or other event or process to which gambling relates.

(6) Section 17 of the Gaming Act 1845 (winning by cheating) shall cease to have effect.

## 43. Chain-gift schemes

(1) A person commits an offence if he—
- (a) invites another to join a chain-gift scheme, or
- (b) knowingly participates in the promotion, administration or management of a chain- gift scheme.

(2) An arrangement is a 'chain-gift' scheme if—
- (a) in order to participate in the arrangement a person must make a payment to one or more other participants (a 'joining fee'), and
- (b) each person who participates in the arrangement—
  - (i) is required or invited to invite others to participate, and
  - (ii) is encouraged to believe that he will receive the joining fees, or part of the joining fees, of other participants, to an amount in excess of the joining fee paid by him.

(3) For the purposes of subsection (2)—
- (a) 'payment' means a payment of money or money's worth, but does not include the provision of goods or services, and
- (b) it is immaterial whether a payment is made directly or through a person responsible for managing or administering the scheme.

# SERIOUS ORGANISED CRIME AND POLICE ACT 2005

## 128. Offence of trespassing on designated site

(1) A person commits an offence if he enters, or is on, any protected site in England and Wales or Northern Ireland as a trespasser.

(1A) In this section 'protected site' means—
- (a) a nuclear site; or
- (b) a designated site.

(1B) In this section 'nuclear site' means—
- (a) so much of any premises in respect of which a nuclear site licence (within the meaning of the Nuclear Installations Act 1965) is for the time being in force as lies within the outer perimeter of the protection provided for those premises; and
- (b) so much of any other premises of which premises falling within paragraph (a) form a part as lies within that outer perimeter.

(1C) For this purpose—
- (a) the outer perimeter of the protection provided for any premises is the line of the outermost fences, walls or other obstacles provided or relied on for protecting those premises from intruders; and
- (b) that line shall be determined on the assumption that every gate, door or other barrier across a way through a fence, wall or other obstacle is closed.

(2) A 'designated site' means a site—
  (a) specified or described (in any way) in an order made by the Secretary of State, and
  (b) designated for the purposes of this section by the order.

(3) The Secretary of State may only designate a site for the purposes of this section if—
  (a) it is comprised in Crown land; or
  (b) it is comprised in land belonging to Her Majesty in Her private capacity or to the immediate heir to the Throne in his private capacity; or
  (c) it appears to the Secretary of State that it is appropriate to designate the site in the interests of national security.

(4) It is a defence for a person charged with an offence under this section to prove that he did not know, and had no reasonable cause to suspect, that the site in relation to which the offence is alleged to have been committed was a protected site.

(7) For the purposes of this section a person who is on any protected site as a trespasser does not cease to be a trespasser by virtue of being allowed time to leave the site.

(8) In this section—
  (a) 'site' means the whole or part of any building or buildings, or any land, or both;
  (b) 'Crown land' means land in which there is a Crown interest or a Duchy interest.

(9) For this purpose—
'Crown interest' means an interest belonging to Her Majesty in right of the Crown, and 'Duchy interest' means an interest belonging to Her Majesty in right of the Duchy of Lancaster or belonging to the Duchy of Cornwall.

## 145. Interference with contractual relationships so as to harm animal research organisation

(1) A person (A) commits an offence if, with the intention of harming an animal research organisation, he—
  (a) does a relevant act, or
  (b) threatens that he or somebody else will do a relevant act,

in circumstances in which that act or threat is intended or likely to cause a second person (B) to take any of the steps in subsection (2).

(2) The steps are—
  (a) not to perform any contractual obligation owed by B to a third person (C) (whether or not such non-performance amounts to a breach of contract);
  (b) to terminate any contract B has with C;
  (c) not to enter into a contract with C

(3) For the purposes of this section, a 'relevant act' is—
  (a) an act amounting to a criminal offence, or
  (b) a tortious act causing B to suffer loss or damage of any description;

but paragraph (b) does not include an act which is actionable on the ground only that it induces another person to break a contract with B.

(4) For the purposes of this section, 'contract' includes any other arrangement (and 'contractual' is to be read accordingly).

(5) For the purposes of this section, to 'harm' an animal research organisation means—
  (a) to cause the organisation to suffer loss or damage of any description, or
  (b) to prevent or hinder the carrying out by the organisation of any of its activities.

(6) This section does not apply to any act done wholly or mainly in contemplation or furtherance of a trade dispute.

(7) In subsection (6) 'trade dispute' has the same meaning as in Part 4 of the Trade Union and Labour Relations (Consolidation) Act 1992, except that section 218 of that Act shall be read as if—
  (a) it made provision corresponding to section 244(4) of that Act, and
  (b) in subsection (5), the definition of 'worker' included any person falling within paragraph (b) of the definition of 'worker' in section 244(5).

## 146. Intimidation of persons connected with animal research organisation

(1) A person (A) commits an offence if, with the intention of causing a second person (B) to abstain from doing something which B is entitled to do (or to do something which B is entitled to abstain from doing)—

(a) A threatens B that A or somebody else will do a relevant act, and
(b) A does so wholly or mainly because B is a person falling within subsection (2).

(2) A person falls within this subsection if he is—
(a) an employee or officer of an animal research organisation;
(b) a student at an educational establishment that is an animal research organisation;
(c) a lessor or licensor of any premises occupied by an animal research organisation;
(d) a person with a financial interest in, or who provides financial assistance to, an animal research organisation;
(e) a customer or supplier of an animal research organisation;
(f) a person who is contemplating becoming someone within paragraph (c), (d) or (e);
(g) a person who is, or is contemplating becoming, a customer or supplier of someone within paragraph (c), (d), (e) or (f);
(h) an employee or officer of someone within paragraph (c), (d), (e), (f) or (g);
(i) a person with a financial interest in, or who provides financial assistance to, someone within paragraph (c), (d), (e), (f) or (g);
(j) a spouse, civil partner, friend or relative of, or a person who is known personally to, someone within any of paragraphs (a) to (i);
(k) a person who is, or is contemplating becoming, a customer or supplier of someone within paragraph (a), (b), (h), (i) or (j); or
(l) an employer of someone within paragraph (j).

(3) For the purposes of this section, an 'officer' of an animal research organisation or a person includes—
(a) where the organisation or person is a body corporate, a director, manager or secretary;
(b) where the organisation or person is a charity, a charity trustee (within the meaning of the Charities Act 2011);
(c) where the organisation or person is a partnership, a partner.

(4) For the purposes of this section—
(a) a person is a customer or supplier of another person if he purchases goods, services or facilities from, or (as the case may be) supplies goods, services or facilities to, that other; and
(b) 'supplier' includes a person who supplies services in pursuance of any enactment that requires or authorises such services to be provided.

(5) For the purposes of this section, a 'relevant act' is—
(a) an act amounting to a criminal offence, or
(b) a tortious act causing B or another person to suffer loss or damage of any description.

(6) The Secretary of State may by order amend this section so as to include within subsection (2) any description of persons framed by reference to their connection with—
(a) an animal research organisation, or
(b) any description of persons for the time being mentioned in that subsection.

(7) This section does not apply to any act done wholly or mainly in contemplation or furtherance of a trade dispute.

(8) In subsection (7) 'trade dispute' has the meaning given by section 145(7).

## 148. Animal research organisations

(1) For the purposes of sections 145 and 146 'animal research organisation' means any person or organisation falling within subsection (1A), (2) or (3).

(1A) A person or organisation falls within this subsection if the person or organisation holds a licence granted under section 2C of the 1986 Act (licensing of undertakings involving the use of animals for scientific procedures).

(2) A person or organisation falls within this subsection if he or it is the owner, lessee or licensee of premises constituting or including a place specified in a licence granted under that section or under section 5 of the 1986 Act (licensing of projects involving the use of animals for scientific procedures).

(3) A person or organisation falls within this subsection if he or it employs, or engages under a contract for services, any of the following in his capacity as such—

(za) the holder of a licence granted under section 2C of the 1986 Act,
(zb) a person specified under section 2C(5) of that Act,
(a) the holder of a personal licence granted under section 4 of the 1986 Act, or
(b) the holder of a project licence granted under section 5 of that Act,

(4) The Secretary of State may by order amend this section so as to include a reference to any description of persons whom he considers to be involved in, or to have a direct connection with persons who are involved in, the application of regulated procedures.

(5) In this section—
'the 1986 Act' means the Animals (Scientific Procedures) Act 1986;
'organisation' includes any institution, trust, undertaking or association of persons;
'premises' includes any place within the meaning of the 1986 Act;
'regulated procedures' has the meaning given by section 2 of the 1986 Act.

# ANIMAL WELFARE ACT 2006

## 1. Animals to which the Act applies

(1) In this Act, except subsections (4) and (5), 'animal' means a vertebrate other than man.
(2) Nothing in this Act applies to an animal while it is in its foetal or embryonic form.
(3) The appropriate national authority may by regulations for all or any of the purposes of this Act—
(a) extend the definition of 'animal' so as to include invertebrates of any description;
(b) make provision in lieu of subsection (2) as respects any invertebrates included in the definition of 'animal';
(c) amend subsection (2) to extend the application of this Act to an animal from such earlier stage of its development as may be specified in the regulations.
(4) The power under subsection (3)(a) or (c) may only be exercised if the appropriate national authority is satisfied, on the basis of scientific evidence, that animals of the kind concerned are capable of experiencing pain or suffering.
(5) In this section, 'vertebrate' means any animal of the Sub-phylum Vertebrata of the Phylum Chordata and 'invertebrate' means any animal not of that Sub-phylum.

## 2. 'Protected animal'

An animal is a 'protected animal' for the purposes of this Act if—
(a) it is of a kind which is commonly domesticated in the British Islands,
(b) it is under the control of man whether on a permanent or temporary basis, or
(c) it is not living in a wild state.

## 3. Responsibility for animals

(1) In this Act, references to a person responsible for an animal are to a person responsible for an animal whether on a permanent or temporary basis.
(2) In this Act, references to being responsible for an animal include being in charge of it.
(3) For the purposes of this Act, a person who owns an animal shall always be regarded as being a person who is responsible for it.
(4) For the purposes of this Act, a person shall be treated as responsible for any animal for which a person under the age of 16 years of whom he has actual care and control is responsible.

## 4. Unnecessary suffering

(1) A person commits an offence if—
(a) an act of his, or a failure of his to act, causes an animal to suffer,
(b) he knew, or ought reasonably to have known, that the act, or failure to act, would have that effect or be likely to do so,
(c) the animal is a protected animal, and
(d) the suffering is unnecessary.
(2) A person commits an offence if—
(a) he is responsible for an animal,
(b) an act, or failure to act, of another person causes the animal to suffer,

(c) he permitted that to happen or failed to take such steps (whether by way of supervising the other person or otherwise) as were reasonable in all the circumstances to prevent that happening, and
(d) the suffering is unnecessary.

(3) The considerations to which it is relevant to have regard when determining for the purposes of this section whether suffering is unnecessary include—
(a) whether the suffering could reasonably have been avoided or reduced;
(b) whether the conduct which caused the suffering was in compliance with any relevant enactment or any relevant provisions of a licence or code of practice issued under an enactment;
(c) whether the conduct which caused the suffering was for a legitimate purpose, such as—
(i) the purpose of benefiting the animal, or
(ii) the purpose of protecting a person, property or another animal;
(d) whether the suffering was proportionate to the purpose of the conduct concerned;
(e) whether the conduct concerned was in all the circumstances that of a reasonably competent and humane person.

(4) Nothing in this section applies to the destruction of an animal in an appropriate and humane manner.

## 5. Mutilation

(1) A person commits an offence if—
(a) he carries out a prohibited procedure on a protected animal;
(b) he causes such a procedure to be carried out on such an animal.

(2) A person commits an offence if—
(a) he is responsible for an animal,
(b) another person carries out a prohibited procedure on the animal, and
(c) he permitted that to happen or failed to take such steps (whether by way of supervising the other person or otherwise) as were reasonable in all the circumstances to prevent that happening.

(3) References in this section to the carrying out of a prohibited procedure on an animal are to the carrying out of a procedure which involves interference with the sensitive tissues or bone structure of the animal, otherwise than for the purpose of its medical treatment.

(6) Nothing in this section applies to the removal of the whole or any part of a dog's tail.

## 6. Docking of dogs' tails

(1) A person commits an offence if—
(a) he removes the whole or any part of a dog's tail, otherwise than for the purpose of its medical treatment;
(b) he causes the whole or any part of a dog's tail to be removed by another person, otherwise than for the purpose of its medical treatment.

(2) A person commits an offence if—
(a) he is responsible for a dog,
(b) another person removes the whole or any part of the dog's tail, otherwise than for the purpose of its medical treatment, and
(c) he permitted that to happen or failed to take such steps (whether by way of supervising the other person or otherwise) as were reasonable in all the circumstances to prevent that happening.

(3) Subsections (1) and (2) do not apply if the dog is a certified working dog that is not more than 5 days old.

(4) For the purposes of subsection (3), a dog is a certified working dog if a veterinary surgeon has certified, in accordance with regulations made by the appropriate national authority, that the first and second conditions mentioned below are met.

(5) The first condition referred to in subsection (4) is that there has been produced to the veterinary surgeon such evidence as the appropriate national authority may by regulations require for the purpose of showing that the dog is likely to be used for work in connection with—
(a) law enforcement,
(b) activities of Her Majesty's armed forces,
(c) emergency rescue,

(d) lawful pest control, or
(e) the lawful shooting of animals.

(6) The second condition referred to in subsection (4) is that the dog is of a type specified for the purposes of this subsection by regulations made by the appropriate national authority.

(7) It is a defence for a person accused of an offence under subsection (1) or (2) to show that he reasonably believed that the dog was one in relation to which subsection (3) applies.

(8) A person commits an offence if—
(a) he owns a subsection (3) dog, and
(b) fails to take reasonable steps to secure that, before the dog is 3 months old, it is identified as a subsection (3) dog in accordance with regulations made by the appropriate national authority.

(9) A person commits an offence if—
(a) he shows a dog at an event to which members of the public are admitted on payment of a fee,
(b) the dog's tail has been wholly or partly removed (in England and Wales or elsewhere), and
(c) removal took place on or after the commencement day.

(10) Where a dog is shown only for the purpose of demonstrating its working ability, subsection (9) does not apply if the dog is a subsection (3) dog.

(11) It is a defence for a person accused of an offence under subsection (9) to show that he reasonably believed—
(a) that the event was not one to which members of the public were admitted on payment of an entrance fee,
(b) that the removal took place before the commencement day, or
(c) that the dog was one in relation to which subsection (10) applies.

(12) A person commits an offence if he knowingly gives false information to a veterinary surgeon in connection with the giving of a certificate for the purposes of this section.

## 7. Administration of poisons etc.

(1) A person commits an offence if, without lawful authority or reasonable excuse, he—
(a) administers any poisonous or injurious drug or substance to a protected animal, knowing it to be poisonous or injurious, or
(b) causes any poisonous or injurious drug or substance to be taken by a protected animal, knowing it to be poisonous or injurious.

(2) A person commits an offence if—
(a) he is responsible for an animal,
(b) without lawful authority or reasonable excuse, another person administers a poisonous or injurious drug or substance to the animal or causes the animal to take such a drug or substance, and
(c) he permitted that to happen or, knowing the drug or substance to be poisonous or injurious, he failed to take such steps (whether by way of supervising the other person or otherwise) as were reasonable in all the circumstances to prevent that happening.

(3) In this section, references to a poisonous or injurious drug or substance include a drug or substance which, by virtue of the quantity or manner in which it is administered or taken, has the effect of a poisonous or injurious drug or substance.

## 8. Fighting etc.

(1) A person commits an offence if he—
(a) causes an animal fight to take place, or attempts to do so;
(b) knowingly receives money for admission to an animal fight;
(c) knowingly publicises a proposed animal fight;
(d) provides information about an animal fight to another with the intention of enabling or encouraging attendance at the fight;
(e) makes or accepts a bet on the outcome of an animal fight or on the likelihood of anything occurring or not occurring in the course of an animal fight;
(f) takes part in an animal fight;
(g) has in his possession anything designed or adapted for use in connection with an animal fight with the intention of its being so used;
(h) keeps or trains an animal for use for in connection with an animal fight;
(i) keeps any premises for use for an animal fight.

(2) A person commits an offence if, without lawful authority or reasonable excuse, he is present at an animal fight.
(3) A person commits an offence if, without lawful authority or reasonable excuse, he—
(a) knowingly supplies a video recording of an animal fight,
(b) knowingly publishes a video recording of an animal fight,
(c) knowingly shows a video recording of an animal fight to another, or
(d) possesses a video recording of an animal fight, knowing it to be such a recording, with the intention of supplying it.
(7) In this section—
'animal fight' means an occasion on which a protected animal is placed with an animal, or with a human, for the purpose of fighting, wrestling or baiting;
'video recording' means a recording, in any form, from which a moving image may by any means be reproduced and includes data stored on a computer disc or by other electronic means which is capable of conversion into a moving image.
(8) In this section—
(a) references to supplying or publishing a video recording are to supplying or publishing a video recording in any manner, including, in relation to a video recording in the form of data stored electronically, by means of transmitting such data;
(b) references to showing a video recording are to showing a moving image reproduced from a video recording by any means.

### 9. Duty of person responsible for animal to ensure welfare

(1) A person commits an offence if he does not take such steps as are reasonable in all the circumstances to ensure that the needs of an animal for which he is responsible are met to the extent required by good practice.
(2) For the purposes of this Act, an animal's needs shall be taken to include—
(a) its need for a suitable environment,
(b) its need for a suitable diet,
(c) its need to be able to exhibit normal behaviour patterns,
(d) any need it has to be housed with, or apart from, other animals, and
(e) its need to be protected from pain, suffering, injury and disease.
(3) The circumstances to which it is relevant to have regard when applying subsection (1) include, in particular—
(a) any lawful purpose for which the animal is kept, and
(b) any lawful activity undertaken in relation to the animal.
(4) Nothing in this section applies to the destruction of an animal in an appropriate and humane manner.

## FRAUD ACT 2006

### 1. Fraud

(1) A person is guilty of fraud if he is in breach of any of the sections listed in subsection (2) (which provide for different ways of committing the offence).
(2) The sections are—
(a) section 2 (fraud by false representation),
(b) section 3 (fraud by failing to disclose information), and
(c) section 4 (fraud by abuse of position).
(3) A person who is guilty of fraud is liable—
(a) on summary conviction, to imprisonment for a term not exceeding 12 months or to a fine not exceeding the statutory maximum (or to both);
(b) on conviction on indictment, to imprisonment for a term not exceeding 10 years or to a fine (or to both).
(4) Subsection (3)(a) applies in relation to Northern Ireland as if the reference to 12 months were a reference to 6 months.

### 2. Fraud by false representation

(1) A person is in breach of this section if he—
(a) dishonestly makes a false representation, and
(b) intends, by making the representation—

(i) to make a gain for himself or another, or
(ii) to cause loss to another or to expose another to a risk of loss.

(2) A representation is false if—
(a) it is untrue or misleading, and
(b) the person making it knows that it is, or might be, untrue or misleading.

(3) 'Representation' means any representation as to fact or law, including a representation as to the state of mind of—
(a) the person making the representation, or
(b) any other person.

(4) A representation may be express or implied.

(5) For the purposes of this section a representation may be regarded as made if it (or anything implying it) is submitted in any form to any system or device designed to receive, convey or respond to communications (with or without human intervention).

## 3. Fraud by failing to disclose information

A person is in breach of this section if he—
(a) dishonestly fails to disclose to another person information which he is under a legal duty to disclose, and
(b) intends, by failing to disclose the information—
(i) to make a gain for himself or another, or
(ii) to cause loss to another or to expose another to a risk of loss.

## 4. Fraud by abuse of position

(1) A person is in breach of this section if he—
(a) occupies a position in which he is expected to safeguard, or not to act against, the financial interests of another person,
(b) dishonestly abuses that position, and
(c) intends, by means of the abuse of that position—
(i) to make a gain for himself or another, or
(ii) to cause loss to another or to expose another to a risk of loss.

(2) A person may be regarded as having abused his position even though his conduct consisted of an omission rather than an act.

## 5. 'Gain' and 'loss'

(1) The references to gain and loss in sections 2 to 4 are to be read in accordance with this section.

(2) 'Gain' and 'loss—
(a) extend only to gain or loss in money or other property;
(b) include any such gain or loss whether temporary or permanent;
and 'property' means any property whether real or personal (including things in action and other intangible property).

(3) 'Gain' includes a gain by keeping what one has, as well as a gain by getting what one does not have.

(4) 'Loss' includes a loss by not getting what one might get, as well as a loss by parting with what one has.

## 6. Possession etc. of articles for use in frauds

(1) A person is guilty of an offence if he has in his possession or under his control any article for use in the course of or in connection with any fraud.

## 7. Making or supplying articles for use in frauds

(1) A person is guilty of an offence if he makes, adapts, supplies or offers to supply any article—
(a) knowing that it is designed or adapted for use in the course of or in connection with fraud, or
(b) intending it to be used to commit, or assist in the commission of, fraud.

## 8. 'Article'

(1) For the purposes of—
(a) sections 6 and 7, and

(b) the provisions listed in subsection (2), so far as they relate to articles for use in the course of or in connection with fraud,

'article' includes any program or data held in electronic form.

(2) The provisions are—

(a) section 1(7)(b) of the Police and Criminal Evidence Act 1984,

(b) section 2(8)(b) of the Armed Forces Act 2001, and

(c) Article 3(7)(b) of the Police and Criminal Evidence (Northern Ireland) Order 1989; (meaning of 'prohibited articles' for the purposes of stop and search powers).

### 11. Obtaining services dishonestly

(1) A person is guilty of an offence under this section if he obtains services for himself or another—

(a) by a dishonest act, and

(b) in breach of subsection (2).

(2) A person obtains services in breach of this subsection if—

(a) they are made available on the basis that payment has been, is being or will be made for or in respect of them,

(b) he obtains them without any payment having been made for or in respect of them or without payment having been made in full, and

(c) when he obtains them, he knows—

(i) that they are being made available on the basis described in paragraph (a), or

(ii) that they might be,

but intends that payment will not be made, or will not be made in full.

## HEALTH ACT 2006

### 2. Smoke-free premises

(1) Premises are smoke-free if they are open to the public.

But unless the premises also fall within subsection (2), they are smoke-free only when open to the public.

(2) Premises are smoke-free if they are used as a place of work—

(a) by more than one person (even if the persons who work there do so at different times, or only intermittently), or

(b) where members of the public might attend for the purpose of seeking or receiving goods or services from the person or persons working there (even if members of the public are not always present).

They are smoke-free all the time.

(3) If only part of the premises is open to the public or (as the case may be) used as a place of work mentioned in subsection (2), the premises are smoke-free only to that extent.

(4) In any case, premises are smoke-free only in those areas which are enclosed or substantially enclosed.

(5) The appropriate national authority may specify in regulations what 'enclosed' and 'substantially enclosed' mean.

(6) Section 3 provides for some premises, or areas of premises, not to be smoke-free despite this section.

(7) Premises are 'open to the public' if the public or a section of the public has access to them, whether by invitation or not, and whether on payment or not.

(8) 'Work', in subsection (2), includes voluntary work.

### 3. Smoke-free premises: exemptions

(1) The appropriate national authority may make regulations providing for specified descriptions of premises, or specified areas within specified descriptions of premises, not to be smoke-free despite section 2.

(2) Descriptions of premises which may be specified under subsection (1) include, in particular, any premises where a person has his home, or is living whether permanently or temporarily (including hotels, care homes, and prisons and other places where a person may be detained).

(3) The power to make regulations under subsection (1) is not exercisable so as to specify any description of—
  (a) premises in respect of which a premises licence under the Licensing Act 2003 authorising the sale by retail of alcohol for consumption on the premises has effect,
  (b) premises in respect of which a club premises certificate (within the meaning of section 60 of that Act) has effect.

(4) But subsection (3) does not prevent the exercise of that power so as to specify any area, within a specified description of premises mentioned in subsection (3), where a person has his home, or is living whether permanently or temporarily.

(5) For the purpose of making provision for those participating as performers in a performance, or in a performance of a specified description, not to be prevented from smoking if the artistic integrity of the performance makes it appropriate for them to smoke—
  (a) the power in subsection (1) also includes power to provide for specified descriptions of premises or specified areas within such premises not to be smoke-free in relation only to such performers, and
  (b) subsection (3) does not prevent the exercise of that power as so extended.

(6) The regulations may provide, in relation to any description of premises or areas of premises specified in the regulations, that the premises or areas are not smoke-free—
  (a) in specified circumstances,
  (b) if specified conditions are satisfied, or
  (c) at specified times,

  or any combination of those.

(7) The conditions may include conditions requiring the designation in accordance with the regulations, by the person in charge of the premises, of any rooms in which smoking is to be permitted.

(8) For the purposes of subsection (5), the references to a performance—
  (a) include, for example, the performance of a play, or a performance given in connection with the making of a film or television programme, and
  (b) if the regulations so provide, include a rehearsal.

## 6. No-smoking signs

(1) It is the duty of any person who occupies or is concerned in the management of smoke-free premises to make sure that no-smoking signs complying with the requirements of this section are displayed in those premises in accordance with the requirements of this section.

(3) The signs must be displayed in accordance with any requirements contained in regulations made by the appropriate national authority.

(4) The signs must conform to any requirements specified in regulations made by the appropriate national authority (for example, requirements as to content, size, design, colour, or wording).

(5) A person who fails to comply with the duty in subsection (1), or any corresponding duty in regulations under subsection (2), commits an offence.

(6) It is a defence for a person charged with an offence under subsection (5) to show—
  (a) that he did not know, and could not reasonably have been expected to know, that the premises were smoke-free ..., or
  (b) that he did not know, and could not reasonably have been expected to know, that no-smoking signs complying with the requirements of this section were not being displayed in accordance with the requirements of this section, or
  (c) that on other grounds it was reasonable for him not to comply with the duty.

## 7. Offence of smoking in smoke-free place

(1) In this section, a 'smoke-free place' means any of the following—
  (a) premises, so far as they are smoke-free under or by virtue of sections 2 and 3 (including premises which by virtue of regulations under section 3(5) are smoke-free except in relation to performers).

(2) A person who smokes in a smoke-free place commits an offence.

(3) But a person who smokes in premises which are not smoke-free in relation to performers by virtue of regulations under section 3(5) does not commit an offence if he is such a performer.

(4) It is a defence for a person charged with an offence under subsection (2) to show that he did not know, and could not reasonably have been expected to know, that it was a smoke- free place.

## 8. Offence of failing to prevent smoking in smoke-free place

(1) It is the duty of any person who controls or is concerned in the management of smoke-free premises to cause a person smoking there to stop smoking.
(2) The reference in subsection (1) to a person smoking does not include a performer in relation to whom the premises are not smoke-free by virtue of regulations under section 3(5).
(4) A person who fails to comply with the duty in subsection (1), or any corresponding duty in regulations under subsection (3), commits an offence.
(5) It is a defence for a person charged with an offence under subsection (4) to show—
  (a) that he took reasonable steps to cause the person in question to stop smoking, or
  (b) that he did not know, and could not reasonably have been expected to know, that the person in question was smoking, or
  (c) that on other grounds it was reasonable for him not to comply with the duty.

# TERRORISM ACT 2006

## 1. Encouragement of terrorism

(1) This section applies to a statement that is likely to be understood by a reasonable person as a direct or indirect encouragement or other inducement, to some or all of the members of the public to whom it is published, to the commission, preparation or instigation of acts of terrorism or Convention offences.
(2) A person commits an offence if—
  (a) he publishes a statement to which this section applies or causes another to publish such a statement; and
  (b) at the time he publishes it or causes it to be published, he—
    (i) intends members of the public to be directly or indirectly encouraged or otherwise induced by the statement to commit, prepare or instigate acts of terrorism or Convention offences; or
    (ii) is reckless as to whether members of the public will be directly or indirectly encouraged or otherwise induced by the statement to commit, prepare or instigate such acts or offences.
(3) For the purposes of this section, the statements that are likely to be understood by a reasonable person as indirectly encouraging the commission or preparation of acts of terrorism or Convention offences include every statement which—
  (a) glorifies the commission or preparation (whether in the past, in the future or generally) of such acts or offences; and
  (b) is a statement from which members of the public could reasonably be expected to infer that what is being glorified is being glorified as conduct that should be emulated by them in existing circumstances.
(4) For the purposes of this section the questions how a statement is likely to be understood and what members of the public could reasonably be expected to infer from it must be determined having regard both—
  (a) to the contents of the statement as a whole; and
  (b) to the circumstances and manner of its publication.
(5) It is irrelevant for the purposes of subsections (1) to (3)—
  (a) whether anything mentioned in those subsections relates to the commission, preparation or instigation of one or more particular acts of terrorism or Convention offences, of acts of terrorism or Convention offences of a particular description or of acts of terrorism or Convention offences generally; and,
  (b) whether any person is in fact encouraged or induced by the statement to commit, prepare or instigate any such act or offence.
(6) In proceedings for an offence under this section against a person in whose case it is not proved that he intended the statement directly or indirectly to encourage or otherwise induce the commission, preparation or instigation of acts of terrorism or Convention offences, it is a defence for him to show—

(a) that the statement neither expressed his views nor had his endorsement (whether by virtue of section 3 or otherwise); and

(b) that it was clear, in all the circumstances of the statement's publication, that it did not express his views and (apart from the possibility of his having been given and failed to comply with a notice under subsection (3) of that section) did not have his endorsement.

## 2. Dissemination of terrorist publications

(1) A person commits an offence if he engages in conduct falling within subsection (2) and, at the time he does so—

(a) he intends an effect of his conduct to be a direct or indirect encouragement or other inducement to the commission, preparation or instigation of acts of terrorism;

(b) he intends an effect of his conduct to be the provision of assistance in the commission or preparation of such acts; or

(c) he is reckless as to whether his conduct has an effect mentioned in paragraph (a) or (b).

(2) For the purposes of this section a person engages in conduct falling within this subsection if he—

(a) distributes or circulates a terrorist publication;

(b) gives, sells or lends such a publication;

(c) offers such a publication for sale or loan;

(d) provides a service to others that enables them to obtain, read, listen to or look at such a publication, or to acquire it by means of a gift, sale or loan;

(e) transmits the contents of such a publication electronically; or

(f) has such a publication in his possession with a view to its becoming the subject of conduct falling within any of paragraphs (a) to (e).

(3) For the purposes of this section a publication is a terrorist publication, in relation to conduct falling within subsection (2), if matter contained in it is likely—

(a) to be understood by a reasonable person as a direct or indirect encouragement or other inducement, to some or all of the persons to whom it is or may become available as a result of that conduct, to the commission, preparation or instigation of acts of terrorism; or

(b) to be useful in the commission or preparation of such acts and to be understood, by some or all of those persons, as contained in the publication, or made available to them, wholly or mainly for the purpose of being so useful to them.

(4) For the purposes of this section matter that is likely to be understood by a reasonable person as indirectly encouraging the commission or preparation of acts of terrorism includes any matter which—

(a) glorifies the commission or preparation (whether in the past, in the future or generally) of such acts; and

(b) is matter from which a person could reasonably be expected to infer that what is being glorified is being glorified as conduct that should be emulated by him in existing circumstances.

(5) For the purposes of this section the question whether a publication is a terrorist publication in relation to particular conduct must be determined—

(a) as at the time of that conduct; and

(b) having regard both to the contents of the publication as a whole and to the circumstances in which that conduct occurs.

(6) In subsection (1) references to the effect of a person's conduct in relation to a terrorist publication include references to an effect of the publication on one or more persons to whom it is or may become available as a consequence of that conduct.

(7) It is irrelevant for the purposes of this section whether anything mentioned in subsections to (4) is in relation to the commission, preparation or instigation of one or more particular acts of terrorism, of acts of terrorism of a particular description or of acts of terrorism generally.

(8) For the purposes of this section it is also irrelevant, in relation to matter contained in any article whether any person—

(a) is in fact encouraged or induced by that matter to commit, prepare or instigate acts of terrorism; or
(b) in fact makes use of it in the commission or preparation of such acts.

(9) In proceedings for an offence under this section against a person in respect of conduct to which subsection (10) applies, it is a defence for him to show—
(a) that the matter by reference to which the publication in question was a terrorist publication neither expressed his views nor had his endorsement (whether by virtue of section 3 or otherwise); and
(b) that it was clear, in all the circumstances of the conduct, that that matter did not express his views and (apart from the possibility of his having been given and failed to comply with a notice under subsection (3) of that section) did not have his endorsement.

(10) This subsection applies to the conduct of a person to the extent that—
(a) the publication to which his conduct related contained matter by reference to which it was a terrorist publication by virtue of subsection (3)(a); and
(b) that person is not proved to have engaged in that conduct with the intention specified in subsection (1)(a).

(13) In this section—
'lend' includes let on hire, and 'loan' is to be construed accordingly;
'publication' means an article or record of any description that contains any of the following, or any combination of them—
(a) matter to be read;
(b) matter to be listened to;
(c) matter to be looked at or watched.

## 3. Application of ss. 1 and 2 to internet activity etc.

(1) This section applies for the purposes of sections 1 and 2 in relation to cases where—
(a) a statement is published or caused to be published in the course of, or in connection with, the provision or use of a service provided electronically; or
(b) conduct falling within section 2(2) was in the course of, or in connection with, the provision or use of such a service.

(2) The cases in which the statement, or the article or record to which the conduct relates, is to be regarded as having the endorsement of a person ('the relevant person') at any time include a case in which—
(a) a constable has given him a notice under subsection (3);
(b) that time falls more than 2 working days after the day on which the notice was given; and
(c) the relevant person has failed, without reasonable excuse, to comply with the notice.

(3) A notice under this subsection is a notice which—
(a) declares that, in the opinion of the constable giving it, the statement or the article or record is unlawfully terrorism-related;
(b) requires the relevant person to secure that the statement or the article or record, so far as it is so related, is not available to the public or is modified so as no longer to be so related;
(c) warns the relevant person that a failure to comply with the notice within 2 working days will result in the statement, or the article or record, being regarded as having his endorsement; and
(d) explains how, under subsection (4), he may become liable by virtue of the notice if the statement, or the article or record, becomes available to the public after he has complied with the notice.

(4) Where—
(a) a notice under subsection (3) has been given to the relevant person in respect of a statement, or an article or record, and he has complied with it, but
(b) he subsequently publishes or causes to be published a statement which is, or is for all practical purposes, the same or to the same effect as the statement to which the notice related, or to matter contained in the article or record to which it related, (a 'repeat statement');

the requirements of subsection (2)(a) to (c) shall be regarded as satisfied in the case of the repeat statement in relation to the times of its subsequent publication by the relevant person.

(5) In proceedings against a person for an offence under section 1 or 2 the requirements of subsection (2)(a) to (c) are not, in his case, to be regarded as satisfied in relation to any time by virtue of subsection (4) if he shows that he—
  (a) has, before that time, taken every step he reasonably could to prevent a repeat statement from becoming available to the public and to ascertain whether it does; and
  (b) was, at that time, a person to whom subsection (6) applied.

(6) This subsection applies to a person at any time when he—
  (a) is not aware of the publication of the repeat statement; or
  (b) having become aware of its publication, has taken every step that he reasonably could to secure that it either ceased to be available to the public or was modified as mentioned in subsection (3)(b).

(7) For the purposes of this section a statement or an article or record is unlawfully terrorism-related if it constitutes, or if matter contained in the article or record constitutes—
  (a) something that is likely to be understood, by any one or more of the persons to whom it has or may become available, as a direct or indirect encouragement or other inducement to the commission, preparation or instigation of acts of terrorism or Convention offences; or
  (b) information which—
    (i) is likely to be useful to any one or more of those persons in the commission or preparation of such acts; and
    (ii) is in a form or context in which it is likely to be understood by any one or more of those persons as being wholly or mainly for the purpose of being so useful.

(8) The reference in subsection (7) to something that is likely to be understood as an indirect encouragement to the commission or preparation of acts of terrorism or Convention offences includes anything which is likely to be understood as—
  (a) the glorification of the commission or preparation (whether in the past, in the future or generally) of such acts or such offences; and
  (b) a suggestion that what is being glorified is being glorified as conduct that should be emulated in existing circumstances.

(9) In this section 'working day' means any day other than—
  (a) a Saturday or a Sunday;
  (b) Christmas Day or Good Friday; or
  (c) a day which is a bank holiday under the Banking and Financial Dealings Act 1971 in any part of the United Kingdom.

## 4. Giving of notices under s. 3

(1) Except in a case to which any of subsections (2) to (4) applies, a notice under section 3(3) may be given to a person only—
  (a) by delivering it to him in person; or
  (b) by sending it to him, by means of a postal service providing for delivery to be recorded, at his last known address.

(2) Such a notice may be given to a body corporate only—
  (a) by delivering it to the secretary of that body in person; or
  (b) by sending it to the appropriate person, by means of a postal service providing for delivery to be recorded, at the address of the registered or principal office of the body.

(3) Such a notice may be given to a firm only—
  (a) by delivering it to a partner of the firm in person;
  (b) by so delivering it to a person having the control or management of the partnership business; or
  (c) by sending it to the appropriate person, by means of a postal service providing for delivery to be recorded, at the address of the principal office of the partnership.

(4) Such a notice may be given to an unincorporated body or association only—
  (a) by delivering it to a member of its governing body in person; or
  (b) by sending it to the appropriate person, by means of a postal service providing for delivery to be recorded, at the address of the principal office of the body or association.

(5) In the case of—
  (a) a company registered outside the United Kingdom,
  (b) a firm carrying on business outside the United Kingdom, or
  (c) an unincorporated body or association with offices outside the United Kingdom, the references in this section to its principal office include references to its principal office within the United Kingdom (if any).

(6) In this section 'the appropriate person' means—
  (a) in the case of a body corporate, the body itself or its secretary;
  (b) in the case of a firm, the firm itself or a partner of the firm or a person having the control or management of the partnership business; and
  (c) in the case of an unincorporated body or association, the body or association itself or a member of its governing body.

(7) For the purposes of section 3 the time at which a notice under subsection (3) of that section is to be regarded as given is—
  (a) where it is delivered to a person, the time at which it is so delivered; and
  (b) where it is sent by a postal service providing for delivery to be recorded, the time recorded as the time of its delivery.

(8) In this section 'secretary', in relation to a body corporate, means the secretary or other equivalent officer of the body.

## 5. Preparation of terrorist acts

(1) A person commits an offence if, with the intention of—
  (a) committing acts of terrorism, or
  (b) assisting another to commit such acts,

he engages in any conduct in preparation for giving effect to his intention.

(2) It is irrelevant for the purposes of subsection (1) whether the intention and preparations relate to one or more particular acts of terrorism, acts of terrorism of a particular description or acts of terrorism generally.

## 6. Training for terrorism

(1) A person commits an offence if—
  (a) he provides instruction or training in any of the skills mentioned in subsection (3); and
  (b) at the time he provides the instruction or training, he knows that a person receiving it intends to use the skills in which he is being instructed or trained—
    (i) for or in connection with the commission or preparation of acts of terrorism or Convention offences; or
    (ii) for assisting the commission or preparation by others of such acts or offences.

(2) A person commits an offence if—
  (a) he receives instruction or training in any of the skills mentioned in subsection (3); and
  (b) at the time of the instruction or training, he intends to use the skills in which he is being instructed or trained—
    (i) for or in connection with the commission or preparation of acts of terrorism or Convention offences; or
    (ii) for assisting the commission or preparation by others of such acts or offences.

(3) The skills are—
  (a) the making, handling or use of a noxious substance, or of substances of a description of such substances;
  (b) the use of any method or technique for doing anything else that is capable of being done for the purposes of terrorism, in connection with the commission or preparation of an act of terrorism or Convention offence or in connection

with assisting the commission or preparation by another of such an act or offence; and

(c) the design or adaptation for the purposes of terrorism, or in connection with the commission or preparation of an act of terrorism or Convention offence, of any method or technique for doing anything.

(4) It is irrelevant for the purposes of subsection s (1) and (2)—

(a) whether any instruction or training that is provided is provided to one or more particular persons or generally;

(b) whether the acts or offences in relation to which a person intends to use skills in which he is instructed or trained consist of one or more particular acts of terrorism or Convention offences, acts of terrorism or Convention offences of a particular description or acts of terrorism or Convention offences generally; and

(c) whether assistance that a person intends to provide to others is intended to be provided to one or more particular persons or to one or more persons whose identities are not yet known.

(7) In this section—

'noxious substance' means—

(a) a dangerous substance within the meaning of Part 7 of the Anti-terrorism, Crime and Security Act 2001; or

(b) any other substance which is hazardous or noxious or which may be or become hazardous or noxious only in certain circumstances;

'substance' includes any natural or artificial substance (whatever its origin or method of production and whether in solid or liquid form or in the form of a gas or vapour) and any mixture of substances.

## 8. Attendance at a place used for terrorist training

(1) A person commits an offence if—

(a) he attends at any place, whether in the United Kingdom or elsewhere;

(b) while he is at that place, instruction or training of the type mentioned in section 6(1) of this Act or section 54(1) of the Terrorism Act 2000 (weapons training) is provided there;

(c) that instruction or training is provided there wholly or partly for purposes connected with the commission or preparation of acts of terrorism or Convention offences; and

(d) the requirements of subsection (2) are satisfied in relation to that person.

(2) The requirements of this subsection are satisfied in relation to a person if—

(a) he knows or believes that instruction or training is being provided there wholly or partly for purposes connected with the commission or preparation of acts of terrorism or Convention offences; or

(b) a person attending at that place throughout the period of that person's attendance could not reasonably have failed to understand that instruction or training was being provided there wholly or partly for such purposes.

(3) It is immaterial for the purposes of this section—

(a) whether the person concerned receives the instruction or training himself; and

(b) whether the instruction or training is provided for purposes connected with one or more particular acts of terrorism or Convention offences, acts of terrorism or Convention offences of a particular description or acts of terrorism or Convention offences generally.

(6) References in this section to instruction or training being provided include references to its being made available.

## 9. Making and possession of devices or materials

(1) A person commits an offence if—

(a) he makes or has in his possession a radioactive device, or

(b) he has in his possession radioactive material,

with the intention of using the device or material in the course of or in connection with the commission or preparation of an act of terrorism or for the purposes of terrorism, or of making it available to be so used.

(2) It is irrelevant for the purposes of subsection (1) whether the act of terrorism to which an intention relates is a particular act of terrorism, an act of terrorism of a particular description or an act of terrorism generally.

(4) In this section—
'radioactive device' means—
(a) a nuclear weapon or other nuclear explosive device;
(b) a radioactive material dispersal device;
(c) a radiation-emitting device;
'radioactive material' means nuclear material or any other radioactive substance which—
(a) contains nuclides that undergo spontaneous disintegration in a process accompanied by the emission of one or more types of ionising radiation, such as alpha radiation, beta radiation, neutron particles or gamma rays; and
(b) is capable, owing to its radiological or fissile properties, of—
(i) causing serious bodily injury to a person;
(ii) causing serious damage to property;
(iii) endangering a person's life; or
(iv) creating a serious risk to the health or safety of the public.

(5) In subsection (4)—
'device' includes any of the following, whether or not fixed to land, namely, machinery, equipment, appliances, tanks, containers, pipes and conduits;
'nuclear material' has the same meaning as in the Nuclear Material (Offences) Act 1983 (see section 6 of that Act).

## 10. Misuse of devices or material and misuse and damage of facilities

(1) A person commits an offence if he uses—
(a) a radioactive device, or
(b) radioactive material,
in the course of or in connection with the commission of an act of terrorism or for the purposes of terrorism.

(2) A person commits an offence if, in the course of or in connection with the commission of an act of terrorism or for the purposes of terrorism, he uses or damages a nuclear facility in a manner which—
(a) causes a release of radioactive material; or
(b) creates or increases a risk that such material will be released.

(4) In this section—
'nuclear facility' means—
(a) a nuclear reactor, including a reactor installed in or on any transportation device for use as an energy source in order to propel it or for any other purpose; or
(b) a plant or conveyance being used for the production, storage, processing or transport of radioactive material;
'radioactive device' and 'radioactive material' have the same meanings as in section 9.

(5) In subsection (4)—
'nuclear reactor' has the same meaning as in the Nuclear Installations Act 1965 (see section 26 of that Act);
'transportation device' means any vehicle or any space object (within the meaning of the Outer Space Act 1986).

## 11. Terrorist threats relating to devices, materials or facilities

(1) A person commits an offence if, in the course of or in connection with the commission of an act of terrorism or for the purposes of terrorism—
(a) he makes a demand—
(i) for the supply to himself or to another of a radioactive device or of radioactive material;
(ii) for a nuclear facility to be made available to himself or to another; or
(iii) for access to such a facility to be given to himself or to another;
(b) he supports the demand with a threat that he or another will take action if the demand is not met; and

(c) the circumstances and manner of the threat are such that it is reasonable for the person to whom it is made to assume that there is real risk that the threat will be carried out if the demand is not met.

(2) A person also commits an offence if—

(a) he makes a threat falling within subsection (3) in the course of or in connection with the commission of an act of terrorism or for the purposes of terrorism; and

(b) the circumstances and manner of the threat are such that it is reasonable for the person to whom it is made to assume that there is real risk that the threat will be carried out, or would be carried out if demands made in association with the threat are not met.

(3) A threat falls within this subsection if it is—

(a) a threat to use radioactive material;

(b) a threat to use a radioactive device; or

(c) a threat to use or damage a nuclear facility in a manner that releases radioactive material or creates or increases a risk that such material will be released.

(5) In this section—

'nuclear facility' has the same meaning as in section 10;

'radioactive device' and 'radioactive material' have the same meanings as in section 9.

# VIOLENT CRIME REDUCTION ACT 2006

## 28. Using someone to mind a weapon

(1) A person is guilty of an offence if—

(a) he uses another to look after, hide or transport a dangerous weapon for him; and

(b) he does so under arrangements or in circumstances that facilitate, or are intended to facilitate, the weapon's being available to him for an unlawful purpose.

(2) For the purposes of this section the cases in which a dangerous weapon is to be regarded as available to a person for an unlawful purpose include any case where—

(a) the weapon is available for him to take possession of it at a time and place; and

(b) his possession of the weapon at that time and place would constitute, or be likely to involve or to lead to, the commission by him of an offence.

(3) In this section 'dangerous weapon' means—

(a) a firearm other than an air weapon or a component part of, or accessory to, an air weapon; or

(b) a weapon to which section 141 or 141A of the Criminal Justice Act 1988 (c 33) applies (specified offensive weapons, knives and bladed weapons).

## 36. Manufacture, import and sale of realistic imitation firearms

(1) A person is guilty of an offence if—

(a) he manufactures a realistic imitation firearm;

(b) he modifies an imitation firearm so that it becomes a realistic imitation firearm;

(c) he sells a realistic imitation firearm; or

(d) he brings a realistic imitation firearm into Great Britain or causes one to be brought into Great Britain.

(2) Subsection (1) has effect subject to the defences in section 37.

(3) The Secretary of State may by regulations—

(a) provide for exceptions and exemptions from the offence under subsection (1); and

(b) provide for it to be a defence in proceedings for such an offence to show the matters specified or described in the regulations.

(4) Regulations under subsection (3) may—

(a) frame any exception, exemption or defence by reference to an approval or consent given in accordance with the regulations;

(b) provide for approvals and consents to be given in relation to particular cases or in relation to such descriptions of case as may be specified or described in the regulations; and

(c) confer the function of giving approvals or consents on such persons specified or described in the regulations as the Secretary of State thinks fit.

(5) The power of the Secretary of State to make regulations under subsection (3) shall be exercisable by statutory instrument subject to annulment in pursuance of a resolution of either House of Parliament.

(6) That power includes power—

(a) to make different provision for different cases;

(b) to make provision subject to such exemptions and exceptions as the Secretary of State thinks fit; and

(c) to make such incidental, supplemental, consequential and transitional provision as he thinks fit.

(11) In this section 'realistic imitation firearm' has the meaning given by section 38.

## 37. Specific defences applying to the offence under s. 36

(1) It shall be a defence for a person charged with an offence under section 36 in respect of any conduct to show that the conduct was for the purpose only of making the imitation firearm in question available for one or more of the purposes specified in subsection (2).

(2) Those purposes are—

(a) the purposes of a museum or gallery;

(b) the purposes of theatrical performances and of rehearsals for such performances;

(c) the production of films (within the meaning of Part 1 of the Copyright, Designs and Patents Act 1988 – see section 5B of that Act);

(d) the production of television programmes (within the meaning of the Communications Act 2003 – see section 405(1) of that Act);

(e) the organisation and holding of historical re-enactments organised and held by persons specified or described for the purposes of this section by regulations made by the Secretary of State;

(f) the purposes of functions that a person has in his capacity as a person in the service of Her Majesty.

(3) It shall also be a defence for a person charged with an offence under section 36 in respect of conduct falling within subsection (1)(d) of that section to show that the conduct—

(a) was in the course of carrying on any trade or business; and

(b) was for the purpose of making the imitation firearm in question available to be modified in a way which would result in its ceasing to be a realistic imitation firearm.

(4) For the purposes of this section a person shall be taken to have shown a matter specified in subsection (1) or (3) if—

(a) sufficient evidence of that matter is adduced to raise an issue with respect to it; and

(b) the contrary is not proved beyond a reasonable doubt.

(5) The power of the Secretary of State to make regulations under this section shall be exercisable by statutory instrument subject to annulment in pursuance of a resolution of either House of Parliament.

(6) That power includes power—

(a) to make different provision for different cases;

(b) to make provision subject to such exemptions and exceptions as the Secretary of State thinks fit; and

(c) to make such incidental, supplemental, consequential and transitional provision as he thinks fit.

(7) In this section—

'historical re-enactment' means any presentation or other event held for the purpose of re-enacting an event from the past or of illustrating conduct from a particular time or period in the past;

'museum or gallery' includes any institution which—

(a) has as its purpose, or one of its purposes, the preservation, display and interpretation of material of historical, artistic or scientific interest; and

(b) gives the public access to it.

### 38. Meaning of 'realistic imitation firearm'

(1) In sections 36 and 37 'realistic imitation firearm' means an imitation firearm which—
 (a) has an appearance that is so realistic as to make it indistinguishable, for all practical purposes, from a real firearm; and
 (b) is neither a de-activated firearm nor itself an antique.

(2) For the purposes of this section, an imitation firearm is not (except by virtue of subsection (b)) to be regarded as distinguishable from a real firearm for any practical purpose if it could be so distinguished only—
 (a) by an expert;
 (b) on a close examination; or
 (c) as a result of an attempt to load or to fire it.

(3) In determining for the purposes of this section whether an imitation firearm is distinguishable from a real firearm—
 (a) the matters that must be taken into account include any differences between the size, shape and principal colour of the imitation firearm and the size, shape and colour in which the real firearm is manufactured; and
 (b) the imitation is to be regarded as distinguishable if its size, shape or principal colour is unrealistic for a real firearm.

(4) The Secretary of State may by regulations provide that, for the purposes of subsection (3)(b)—
 (a) the size of an imitation firearm is to be regarded as unrealistic for a real firearm only if the imitation firearm has dimensions that are less than the dimensions specified in the regulations; and
 (b) a colour is to be regarded as unrealistic for a real firearm only if it is a colour specified in the regulations.

(7) In this section—
 'colour' is to be construed in accordance with subsection (9);
 'de-activated firearm' means an imitation firearm that consists in something which—
 (a) was a firearm; but
 (b) has been so rendered incapable of discharging a shot, bullet or other missile as no longer to be a firearm;
 'real firearm' means—
 (a) a firearm of an actual make or model of modern firearm (whether existing or discontinued); or
 (b) something falling within a description which could be used for identifying, by reference to their appearance, the firearms falling within a category of actual modern firearms which, even though they include firearms of different makes or models (whether existing or discontinued) or both, all have the same or a similar appearance.

(8) In subsection (7) 'modern firearm' means any firearm other than one the appearance of which would tend to identify it as having a design and mechanism of a sort first dating from before the year 1870.

(9) References in this section, in relation to an imitation firearm or a real firearm, to its colour include references to its being made of transparent material.

## CORPORATE MANSLAUGHTER AND CORPORATE HOMICIDE ACT 2007

### 1. The offence

(1) An organisation to which this section applies is guilty of an offence if the way in which its activities are managed or organised—
 (a) causes a person's death, and
 (b) amounts to a gross breach of a relevant duty of care owed by the organisation to the deceased.

(2) The organisations to which this section applies are—
 (a) a corporation;
 (b) a department or other body listed in Schedule 1;

(c) a police force;
(d) a partnership, or a trade union or employers' association, that is an employer.

(3) An organisation is guilty of an offence under this section only if the way in which its activities are managed or organised by its senior management is a substantial element in the breach referred to in subsection (1).

(4) For the purposes of this Act—
(a) 'relevant duty of care' has the meaning given by section 2, read with sections 3 to 7;
(b) a breach of a duty of care by an organisation is a 'gross' breach if the conduct alleged to amount to a breach of that duty falls far below what can reasonably be expected of the organisation in the circumstances;
(c) 'senior management', in relation to an organisation, means the persons who play significant roles in—
(i) the making of decisions about how the whole or a substantial part of its activities are to be managed or organised, or
(ii) the actual managing or organising of the whole or a substantial part of those activities.

(5) The offence under this section is called—
(a) corporate manslaughter, in so far as it is an offence under the law of England and Wales or Northern Ireland;
(b) corporate homicide, in so far as it is an offence under the law of Scotland.

## 2. Meaning of 'relevant duty of care'

(1) A 'relevant duty of care', in relation to an organisation, means any of the following duties owed by it under the law of negligence—
(a) a duty owed to its employees or to other persons working for the organisation or performing services for it;
(b) a duty owed as occupier of premises;
(c) a duty owed in connection with—
(i) the supply by the organisation of goods or services (whether for consideration or not),
(ii) the carrying on by the organisation of any construction or maintenance operations,
(iii) the carrying on by the organisation of any other activity on a commercial basis, or
(iv) the use or keeping by the organisation of any plant, vehicle or other thing;
(d) a duty owed to a person who, by reason of being a person within subsection (2), is someone for whose safety the organisation is responsible.

(2) A person is within this subsection if—
(a) he is detained at a custodial institution or in a custody area at a court, a police station or customs premises;
(aa) he is detained in service custody premises;
(b) he is detained at a removal centre, a short-term holding facility or in pre-departure accommodation;
(c) he is being transported in a vehicle, or being held in any premises, in pursuance of prison escort arrangements or immigration escort arrangements;
(d) he is living in secure accommodation in which he has been placed;
(e) he is a detained patient.

(3) Subsection (1) is subject to sections 3 to 7.

(4) A reference in subsection (1) to a duty owed under the law of negligence includes a reference to a duty that would be owed under the law of negligence but for any statutory provision under which liability is imposed in place of liability under that law.

(5) For the purposes of this Act, whether a particular organisation owes a duty of care to a particular individual is a question of law.
The judge must make any findings of fact necessary to decide that question.

(6) For the purposes of this Act there is to be disregarded—
(a) any rule of the common law that has the effect of preventing a duty of care from being owed by one person to another by reason of the fact that they are jointly engaged in unlawful conduct;

(b) any such rule that has the effect of preventing a duty of care from being owed to a person by reason of his acceptance of a risk of harm.

(7) In this section—

'construction or maintenance operations' means operations of any of the following descriptions—

(a) construction, installation, alteration, extension, improvement, repair, maintenance, decoration, cleaning, demolition or dismantling of—
    (i) any building or structure,
    (ii) anything else that forms, or is to form, part of the land, or
    (iii) any plant, vehicle or other thing;

(b) operations that form an integral part of, or are preparatory to, or are for rendering complete, any operations within paragraph (a);

'custodial institution' means a prison, a young offender institution, a secure training centre, a secure college, a young offenders institution, a young offenders centre, a juvenile justice centre or a remand centre;

'customs premises' means premises wholly or partly occupied by persons designated under section 3 (general customs officials) or 11 (customs revenue officials) of the Borders, Citizenship and Immigration Act 2009;

'detained patient' means—

(a) a person who is detained in any premises under—
    (i) Part 2 or 3 of the Mental Health Act 1983 ('the 1983 Act'), ...

(b) a person who (otherwise than by reason of being detained as mentioned in paragraph (a)) is deemed to be in legal custody by—
    (i) section 137 of the 1983 Act,
    (ii) Article 131 of the 1986 Order, ...

'immigration escort arrangements' means arrangements made under section 156 of the Immigration and Asylum Act 1999;

'the law of negligence' includes—

(a) in relation to England and Wales, the Occupiers' Liability Act 1957, the Defective Premises Act 1972 and the Occupiers' Liability Act 1984;

'prison escort arrangements' means arrangements made under section 80 of the Criminal Justice Act 1991 or under section 102 or 118 of the Criminal Justice and Public Order Act 1994;

'removal centre', 'short-term holding facility' and 'pre-departure accommodation' have the meaning given by section 147 of the Immigration and Asylum Act 1999;

'secure accommodation' means accommodation, not consisting of or forming part of a custodial institution, provided for the purpose of restricting the liberty of persons under the age of 18;

'service custody premises' has the meaning given by section 300(7) of the Armed Forces Act 2006.

## 3. Public policy decisions, exclusively public functions and statutory inspections

(1) Any duty of care owed by a public authority in respect of a decision as to matters of public policy (including in particular the allocation of public resources or the weighing of competing public interests) is not a 'relevant duty of care'.

(2) Any duty of care owed in respect of things done in the exercise of an exclusively public function is not a 'relevant duty of care' unless it falls within section 2(1)(a), (b) ...

(3) Any duty of care owed by a public authority in respect of inspections carried out in the exercise of a statutory function is not a 'relevant duty of care' unless it falls within section 2(1)(a) or (b).

(4) In this section—

'exclusively public function' means a function that falls within the prerogative of the Crown or is, by its nature, exercisable only with authority conferred—

(a) by the exercise of that prerogative, or

(b) by or under a statutory provision;

'statutory function' means a function conferred by or under a statutory provision.

## 4. Military activities

(1) Any duty of care owed by the Ministry of Defence in respect of—
   (a) operations within subsection (2),
   (b) activities carried on in preparation for, or directly in support of, such operations, or
   (c) training of a hazardous nature, or training carried out in a hazardous way, which it is considered needs to be carried out, or carried out in that way, in order to improve or maintain the effectiveness of the armed forces with respect to such operations, is not a 'relevant duty of care'.

(2) The operations within this subsection are operations, including peacekeeping operations and operations for dealing with terrorism, civil unrest or serious public disorder, in the course of which members of the armed forces come under attack or face the threat of attack or violent resistance.

(3) Any duty of care owed by the Ministry of Defence in respect of activities carried on by members of the special forces is not a 'relevant duty of care'.

(4) In this section 'the special forces' means those units of the armed forces the maintenance of whose capabilities is the responsibility of the Director of Special Forces or which are for the time being subject to the operational command of that Director.

## 5. Policing and law enforcement

(1) Any duty of care owed by a public authority in respect of—
   (a) operations within subsection (2),
   (b) activities carried on in preparation for, or directly in support of, such operations, or
   (c) training of a hazardous nature, or training carried out in a hazardous way, which it is considered needs to be carried out, or carried out in that way, in order to improve or maintain the effectiveness of officers or employees of the public authority with respect to such operations,

   is not a 'relevant duty of care'.

(2) Operations are within this subsection if—
   (a) they are operations for dealing with terrorism, civil unrest or serious disorder,
   (b) they involve the carrying on of policing or law-enforcement activities, and
   (c) officers or employees of the public authority in question come under attack, or face the threat of attack or violent resistance, in the course of the operations.

(3) Any duty of care owed by a public authority in respect of other policing or law-enforcement activities is not a 'relevant duty of care' unless it falls within section 2(1)(a), (b) ...

(4) In this section 'policing or law-enforcement activities' includes—
   (a) activities carried on in the exercise of functions that are—
      (i) functions of police forces, or
      (ii) functions of the same or a similar nature exercisable by public authorities other than police forces;
   (b) activities carried on in the exercise of functions of constables employed by a public authority;
   (c) activities carried on in the exercise of functions exercisable under Chapter 4 of Part 2 of the Serious Organised Crime and Police Act 2005 (protection of witnesses and other persons);
   (d) activities carried on to enforce any provision contained in or made under the Immigration Acts.

## 6. Emergencies

(1) Any duty of care owed by an organisation within subsection (2) in respect of the way in which it responds to emergency circumstances is not a 'relevant duty of care' unless it falls within section 2(1)(a) or (b).

(2) The organisations within this subsection are—
   (a) a fire and rescue authority in England and Wales;
   (b) the Scottish Fire and Rescue Service;
   (c) the Northern Ireland Fire and Rescue Service Board;

(d) any other organisation providing a service of responding to emergency circumstances either—
(i) in pursuance of arrangements made with an organisation within paragraph (a), (b) or (c), or
(ii) (if not in pursuance of such arrangements) otherwise than on a commercial basis;
(e) a relevant NHS body;
(f) an organisation providing ambulance services in pursuance of arrangements—
(i) made by, or at the request of, a relevant NHS body, or
(ii) made with the Secretary of State or with the Welsh Ministers;
(g) an organisation providing services for the transport of organs, blood, equipment or personnel in pursuance of arrangements of the kind mentioned in paragraph (f);
(h) an organisation providing a rescue service;
(i) the armed forces.

(3) For the purposes of subsection (1), the way in which an organisation responds to emergency circumstances does not include the way in which—
(a) medical treatment is carried out, or
(b) decisions within subsection (4) are made.

(4) The decisions within this subsection are decisions as to the carrying out of medical treatment, other than decisions as to the order in which persons are to be given such treatment.

(5) Any duty of care owed in respect of the carrying out, or attempted carrying out, of a rescue operation at sea in emergency circumstances is not a 'relevant duty of care' unless it falls within section 2(1)(a) or (b).

(6) Any duty of care owed in respect of action taken—
(a) in order to comply with a direction under Schedule 3A to the Merchant Shipping Act 1995 (safety directions), or
(b) by virtue of paragraph 4 of that Schedule (action in lieu of direction), is not a 'relevant duty of care' unless it falls within section 2(1)(a) or (b).

(7) In this section—
'emergency circumstances' means circumstances that are present or imminent and—
(a) are causing, or are likely to cause, serious harm or a worsening of such harm, or
(b) are likely to cause the death of a person;
'medical treatment' includes any treatment or procedure of a medical or similar nature;
'relevant NHS body' means—
(za) the National Health Service Commissioning Board;
(a) a clinical commissioning group, NHS trust, Special Health Authority or NHS foundation trust in England;
(b) a Local Health Board, NHS trust or Special Health Authority in Wales;
'serious harm' means—
(a) serious injury to or the serious illness (including mental illness) of a person;
(b) serious harm to the environment (including the life and health of plants and animals);
(c) serious harm to any building or other property.

(8) A reference in this section to emergency circumstances includes a reference to circumstances that are believed to be emergency circumstances.

## 7. Child-protection and probation functions

(1) A duty of care to which this section applies is not a 'relevant duty of care' unless it falls within section 2(1)(a), (b) or (d).

(2) This section applies to any duty of care that a local authority or other public authority owes in respect of the exercise by it of functions conferred by or under—
(a) Parts 4 and 5 of the Children Act 1989,

(3) This section also applies to any duty of care that a local probation board, a provider of probation services or other public authority owes in respect of the exercise by it of functions conferred by or under—
(a) Chapter 1 of Part 1 of the Criminal Justice and Court Services Act 2000,
(aa) section 13 of the Offender Management Act 2007,

(4) This section also applies to any duty of care that a provider of probation services owes in respect of the carrying out by it of activities in pursuance of arrangements under section 3 of the Offender Management Act 2007.

## 8. Factors for jury

(1) This section applies where—
  (a) it is established that an organisation owed a relevant duty of care to a person, and
  (b) it falls to the jury to decide whether there was a gross breach of that duty.

(2) The jury must consider whether the evidence shows that the organisation failed to comply with any health and safety legislation that relates to the alleged breach, and if so—
  (a) how serious that failure was;
  (b) how much of a risk of death it posed.

(3) The jury may also—
  (a) consider the extent to which the evidence shows that there were attitudes, policies, systems or accepted practices within the organisation that were likely to have encouraged any such failure as is mentioned in subsection (2), or to have produced tolerance of it;
  (b) have regard to any health and safety guidance that relates to the alleged breach.

(4) This section does not prevent the jury from having regard to any other matters they consider relevant.

(5) In this section 'health and safety guidance' means any code, guidance, manual or similar publication that is concerned with health and safety matters and is made or issued (under a statutory provision or otherwise) by an authority responsible for the enforcement of any health and safety legislation.

## 9. Power to order breach etc., to be remedied

(1) A court before which an organisation is convicted of corporate manslaughter or corporate homicide may make an order (a 'remedial order') requiring the organisation to take specified steps to remedy—
  (a) the breach mentioned in section 1(1) ('the relevant breach');
  (b) any matter that appears to the court to have resulted from the relevant breach and to have been a cause of the death;
  (c) any deficiency, as regards health and safety matters, in the organisation's policies, systems or practices of which the relevant breach appears to the court to be an indication.

(2) A remedial order may be made only on an application by the prosecution specifying the terms of the proposed order.
Any such order must be on such terms (whether those proposed or others) as the court considers appropriate having regard to any representations made, and any evidence adduced, in relation to that matter by the prosecution or on behalf of the organisation.

(3) Before making an application for a remedial order the prosecution must consult such enforcement authority or authorities as it considers appropriate having regard to the nature of the relevant breach.

(4) A remedial order—
  (a) must specify a period within which the steps referred to in subsection (1) are to be taken;
  (b) may require the organisation to supply to an enforcement authority consulted under subsection (3), within a specified period, evidence that those steps have been taken.

A period specified under this subsection may be extended or further extended by order of the court on an application made before the end of that period or extended period.

(5) An organisation that fails to comply with a remedial order is guilty of an offence, and liable on conviction on indictment to a fine.

## 11. Application to Crown bodies

(1) An organisation that is a servant or agent of the Crown is not immune from prosecution under this Act for that reason.

(2) For the purposes of this Act—
   (a) a department or other body listed in Schedule 1, or
   (b) a corporation that is a servant or agent of the Crown,
   is to be treated as owing whatever duties of care it would owe if it were a corporation that was not a servant or agent of the Crown.

(3) For the purposes of section 2—
   (a) a person who is—
      (i) employed by or under the Crown for the purposes of a department or other body listed in Schedule 1, or
      (ii) employed by a person whose staff constitute a body listed in that Schedule,
      is to be treated as employed by that department or body;
   (b) any premises occupied for the purposes of—
      (i) a department or other body listed in Schedule 1, or
      (ii) a person whose staff constitute a body listed in that Schedule,
   are to be treated as occupied by that department or body.

(4) For the purposes of sections 2 to 7 anything done purportedly by a department or other body listed in Schedule 1, although in law by the Crown or by the holder of a particular office, is to be treated as done by the department or other body itself.

## 12. Application to armed forces

(1) In this Act 'the armed forces' means any of the naval, military or air forces of the Crown raised under the law of the United Kingdom.

(2) For the purposes of section 2 a person who is a member of the armed forces is to be treated as employed by the Ministry of Defence.

(3) A reference in this Act to members of the armed forces includes a reference to—
   (a) members of the reserve forces (within the meaning given by section 1(2) of the Reserve Forces Act 1996) when in service or undertaking training or duties;
   (b) persons serving on Her Majesty's vessels (within the meaning given by section 132(1) of the Naval Discipline Act 1957).

## 13. Application to police forces

(1) In this Act 'police force' means—
   (a) a police force within the meaning of—
      (i) the Police Act 1996, or
      ...
   ...
   (d) the British Transport Police Force;
   (e) the Civil Nuclear Constabulary;
   (f) the Ministry of Defence Police.

(2) For the purposes of this Act a police force is to be treated as owing whatever duties of care it would owe if it were a body corporate.

(3) For the purposes of section 2—
   (a) a member of a police force is to be treated as employed by that force;
   (b) a special constable appointed for a police area in England and Wales is to be treated as employed by the police force maintained by the local policing body for that area;
   (c) a special constable appointed for a police force mentioned in paragraph (d) or (f) of subsection (1) is to be treated as employed by that force;
   (d) a police cadet undergoing training with a view to becoming a member of a police force mentioned in paragraph (a) or (d) of subsection (1) is to be treated as employed by that force;
   ...
   (g) a member of a police force seconded to the National Crime Agency to serve as a National Crime Agency officer is to be treated as employed by that Agency.

...

(5) For the purposes of section 2 any premises occupied for the purposes of a police force are to be treated as occupied by that force.

(6) For the purposes of sections 2 to 7 anything that would be regarded as done by a police force if the force were a body corporate is to be so regarded.

(7) Where—

(a) by virtue of subsection (3) a person is treated for the purposes of section 2 as employed by a police force, and

(b) by virtue of any other statutory provision (whenever made) he is, or is treated as, employed by another organisation,

the person is to be treated for those purposes as employed by both the force and the other organisation.

## 14. Application to partnerships

(1) For the purposes of this Act a partnership is to be treated as owing whatever duties of care it would owe if it were a body corporate.

(2) Proceedings for an offence under this Act alleged to have been committed by a partnership are to be brought in the name of the partnership (and not in that of any of its members).

(3) A fine imposed on a partnership on its conviction of an offence under this Act is to be paid out of the funds of the partnership.

(4) This section does not apply to a partnership that is a legal person under the law by which it is governed.

## 18. No individual liability

(1) An individual cannot be guilty of aiding, abetting, counselling or procuring the commission of an offence of corporate manslaughter.

(1A) An individual cannot be guilty of an offence under Part 2 of the Serious Crime Act 2007 (encouraging or assisting crime) by reference to an offence of corporate manslaughter.

(2) An individual cannot be guilty of aiding, abetting, counselling or procuring, or being art and part in, the commission of an offence of corporate homicide.

## 20. Abolition of liability of corporations for manslaughter at common law

The common law offence of manslaughter by gross negligence is abolished in its application to corporations, and in any application it has to other organisations to which section 1 applies.

SCHEDULE 1
LIST OF GOVERNMENT DEPARTMENTS ETC.

Attorney General's Office
Cabinet Office
Central Office of Information
Crown Office and Procurator Fiscal Service
Crown Prosecution Service
Department for Business, Energy and Industrial Strategy
Department for Culture, Media and Sport
Department for Education
Department for Environment, Food and Rural Affairs
Department for International Development
Department for Transport
Department for Work and Pensions
Department of Health and Social Care
Export Credits Guarantee Department
Foreign and Commonwealth Office
Forestry Commission
Government Actuary's Department
Her Majesty's Land Registry
Her Majesty's Revenue and Customs
Her Majesty's Treasury

Home Office
Ministry of Defence
Ministry of Housing, Communities and Local Government
Ministry of Justice (including the Scotland Office and the Wales Office)
National Archives
National Crime Agency
National Savings and Investments
National School of Government
Office for National Statistics
Office of Her Majesty's Chief Inspector of Education and Training in Wales
Ordnance Survey
Royal Mint
Serious Fraud Office
Treasury Solicitor's Department
UK Trade and Investment
Welsh Government

# SERIOUS CRIME ACT 2007

## PART 2
## ENCOURAGING OR ASSISTING CRIME

### 44. Intentionally encouraging or assisting an offence

(1) A person commits an offence if—
  (a) he does an act capable of encouraging or assisting the commission of an offence; and
  (b) he intends to encourage or assist its commission.

(2) But he is not to be taken to have intended to encourage or assist the commission of an offence merely because such encouragement or assistance was a foreseeable consequence of his act.

### 45. Encouraging or assisting an offence believing it will be committed

A person commits an offence if—
(a) he does an act capable of encouraging or assisting the commission of an offence; and
(b) he believes—
  (i) that the offence will be committed; and
  (ii) that his act will encourage or assist its commission.

### 46. Encouraging or assisting offences believing one or more will be committed

(1) A person commits an offence if—
  (a) he does an act capable of encouraging or assisting the commission of one or more of a number of offences; and
  (b) he believes—
    (i) that one or more of those offences will be committed (but has no belief as to which); and
    (ii) that his act will encourage or assist the commission of one or more of them.

(2) It is immaterial for the purposes of subsection (1)(b)(ii) whether the person has any belief as to which offence will be encouraged or assisted.

(3) If a person is charged with an offence under subsection (1)—
  (a) the indictment must specify the offences alleged to be the 'number of offences' mentioned in paragraph (a) of that subsection; but
  (b) nothing in paragraph (a) requires all the offences potentially comprised in that number to be specified.

(4) In relation to an offence under this section, reference in this Part to the offences specified in the indictment is to the offences specified by virtue of subsection (3)(a).

## 47. Proving an offence under this Part

(1) Sections 44, 45 and 46 are to be read in accordance with this section.

(2) If it is alleged under section 44(1)(b) that a person (D) intended to encourage or assist the commission of an offence, it is sufficient to prove that he intended to encourage or assist the doing of an act which would amount to the commission of that offence.

(3) If it is alleged under section 45(b) that a person (D) believed that an offence would be committed and that his act would encourage or assist its commission, it is sufficient to prove that he believed—

(a) that an act would be done which would amount to the commission of that offence; and

(b) that his act would encourage or assist the doing of that act.

(4) If it is alleged under section 46(1)(b) that a person (D) believed that one or more of a number of offences would be committed and that his act would encourage or assist the commission of one or more of them, it is sufficient to prove that he believed—

(a) that one or more of a number of acts would be done which would amount to the commission of one or more of those offences; and

(b) that his act would encourage or assist the doing of one or more of those acts.

(5) In proving for the purposes of this section whether an act is one which, if done, would amount to the commission of an offence—

(a) if the offence is one requiring proof of fault, it must be proved that—

(i) D believed that, were the act to be done, it would be done with that fault;

(ii) D was reckless as to whether or not it would be done with that fault; or

(iii) D's state of mind was such that, were he to do it, it would be done with that fault; and

(b) if the offence is one requiring proof of particular circumstances or consequences (or both), it must be proved that—

(i) D believed that, were the act to be done, it would be done in those circumstances or with those consequences; or

(ii) D was reckless as to whether or not it would be done in those circumstances or with those consequences.

(6) For the purposes of subsection (5)(a)(iii), D is to be assumed to be able to do the act in question.

(7) In the case of an offence under section 44—

(a) subsection (5)(b)(i) is to be read as if the reference to 'D believed' were a reference to 'D intended or believed'; but

(b) D is not to be taken to have intended that an act would be done in particular circumstances or with particular consequences merely because its being done in those circumstances or with those consequences was a foreseeable consequence of his act of encouragement or assistance.

(8) Reference in this section to the doing of an act includes reference to—

(a) a failure to act;

(b) the continuation of an act that has already begun;

(c) an attempt to do an act (except an act amounting to the commission of the offence of attempting to commit another offence).

(9) In the remaining provisions of this Part (unless otherwise provided) a reference to the anticipated offence is—

(a) in relation to an offence under section 44, a reference to the offence mentioned in subsection (2); and

(b) in relation to an offence under section 45, a reference to the offence mentioned in subsection (3).

## 48. Proving an offence under section 46

(1) This section makes further provision about the application of section 47 to an offence under section 46.

(2) It is sufficient to prove the matters mentioned in section 47(5) by reference to one offence only.

(3) The offence or offences by reference to which those matters are proved must be one of the offences specified in the indictment.

(4) Subsection (3) does not affect any enactment or rule of law under which a person charged with one offence may be convicted of another and is subject to section 57.

## 49. Supplemental provisions

(1) A person may commit an offence under this Part whether or not any offence capable of being encouraged or assisted by his act is committed.

(2) If a person's act is capable of encouraging or assisting the commission of a number of offences—

(a) section 44 applies separately in relation to each offence that he intends to encourage or assist to be committed; and

(b) section 45 applies separately in relation to each offence that he believes will be encouraged or assisted to be committed.

(3) A person may, in relation to the same act, commit an offence under more than one provision of this Part.

(4) In reckoning whether—

(a) for the purposes of section 45, an act is capable of encouraging or assisting the commission of an offence; or

(b) for the purposes of section 46, an act is capable of encouraging or assisting the commission of one or more of a number of offences;

offences under this Part and listed offences are to be disregarded.

(5) 'Listed offence' means—

(a) in England and Wales, an offence listed in Part 1, 2 or 3 of Schedule 3; and

...

(6) The Secretary of State may by order amend Schedule 3.

(7) For the purposes of sections 45(b)(i) and 46(1)(b)(i) it is sufficient for the person concerned to believe that the offence (or one or more of the offences) will be committed if certain conditions are met.

*Reasonableness defence*

## 50. Defence of acting reasonably

(1) A person is not guilty of an offence under this Part if he proves—

(a) that he knew certain circumstances existed; and

(b) that it was reasonable for him to act as he did in those circumstances.

(2) A person is not guilty of an offence under this Part if he proves—

(a) that he believed certain circumstances to exist;

(b) that his belief was reasonable; and

(c) that it was reasonable for him to act as he did in the circumstances as he believed them to be.

(3) Factors to be considered in determining whether it was reasonable for a person to act as he did include—

(a) the seriousness of the anticipated offence (or, in the case of an offence under section 46, the offences specified in the indictment);

(b) any purpose for which he claims to have been acting;

(c) any authority by which he claims to have been acting.

*Limitation on liability*

## 51. Protective offences: victims not liable

(1) In the case of protective offences, a person does not commit an offence under this Part by reference to such an offence if—

(a) he falls within the protected category; and

(b) he is the person in respect of whom the protective offence was committed or would have been if it had been committed.

(2) 'Protective offence' means an offence that exists (wholly or in part) for the protection of a particular category of persons ('the protected category').

## 51A. Exceptions to section 44 for encouraging or assisting suicide

Section 44 does not apply to an offence under section 2(1) of the Suicide Act 1961.

*Jurisdiction and procedure*

## 52. Jurisdiction

(1) If a person (D) knows or believes that what he anticipates might take place wholly or partly in England or Wales, he may be guilty of an offence under section 44, 45 or 46 no matter where he was at any relevant time.

(2) If it is not proved that D knows or believes that what he anticipates might take place wholly or partly in England or Wales, he is not guilty of an offence under section 44, 45 or 46 unless paragraph 1, 2 or 3 of Schedule 4 applies.

(3) A reference in this section (and in any of those paragraphs) to what D anticipates is to be read as follows—

(a) in relation to an offence under section 44 or 45, it refers to the act which would amount to the commission of the anticipated offence;

(b) in relation to an offence under section 46, it refers to an act which would amount to the commission of any of the offences specified in the indictment.

(5) Nothing in this section or Schedule 4 restricts the operation of any enactment by virtue of which an act constituting an offence under this Part is triable under the law of England and Wales or Northern Ireland.

## 56. Persons who may be perpetrators or encouragers etc.

(1) In proceedings for an offence under this Part ('the inchoate offence') the defendant may be convicted if—

(a) it is proved that he must have committed the inchoate offence or the anticipated offence; but

(b) it is not proved which of those offences he committed.

(b) For the purposes of this section, a person is not to be treated as having committed the anticipated offence merely because he aided, abetted, counselled or procured its commission.

(c) In relation to an offence under section 46, a reference in this section to the anticipated offence is to be read as a reference to an offence specified in the indictment.

## 57. Alternative verdicts and guilty pleas

(1) If in proceedings on indictment for an offence under section 44 or 45 a person is not found guilty of that offence by reference to the specified offence, he may be found guilty of that offence by reference to an alternative offence.

(2) If in proceedings for an offence under section 46 a person is not found guilty of that offence by reference to any specified offence, he may be found guilty of that offence by reference to one or more alternative offences.

(3) If in proceedings for an offence under section 46 a person is found guilty of the offence by reference to one or more specified offences, he may also be found guilty of it by reference to one or more other alternative offences.

(4) For the purposes of this section, an offence is an alternative offence if—

(a) it is an offence of which, on a trial on indictment for the specified offence, an accused may be found guilty; or

(b) it is an indictable offence, or one to which section 40 of the Criminal Justice Act 1988 applies (power to include count for common assault etc. in indictment), and the condition in subsection (5) is satisfied.

(5) The condition is that the allegations in the indictment charging the person with the offence under this Part amount to or include (expressly or by implication) an allegation of that offence by reference to it.

(6) Subsection (4)(b) does not apply if the specified offence, or any of the specified offences, is murder or treason.

(7) In the application of subsection (5) to proceedings for an offence under section 44, the allegations in the indictment are to be taken to include an allegation of that offence by reference to the offence of attempting to commit the specified offence.

(8) Section 49(4) applies to an offence which is an alternative offence in relation to a specified offence as it applies to that specified offence.

(9) In this section—

(a) in relation to a person charged with an offence under section 44 or 45, 'the specified offence' means the offence specified in the indictment as the one alleged to be the anticipated offence;

(b) in relation to a person charged with an offence under section 46, 'specified offence' means an offence specified in the indictment (within the meaning of subsection (4) of that section), and related expressions are to be read accordingly.

(10) A person arraigned on an indictment for an offence under this Part may plead guilty to an offence of which he could be found guilty under this section on that indictment.

(11) This section applies to an indictment containing more than one count as if each count were a separate indictment.

(12) This section is without prejudice to—

(a) section 6(1)(b) and (3) of the Criminal Law Act 1967;

...

## SCHEDULE 3
## LISTED OFFENCES

**Section 49(5)**

### PART 1
### OFFENCES COMMON TO ENGLAND AND WALES AND NORTHERN IRELAND

*Offences against the Person Act 1861*

1. An offence under section 4 of the Offences against the Person Act 1861 (solicitation etc. of murder).
2. An offence under section 21 of that Act (attempting to choke etc. in order to commit or assist in the committing of any indictable offence) so far as it may be committed with the intention of enabling any other person to commit, or assisting any other person in the commission of, an indictable offence.
3. An offence under section 22 of that Act (using chloroform etc. to commit or assist in the committing of any indictable offence) so far as it may be committed with the intention of enabling any other person to commit, or assisting any other person in the commission of, an indictable offence.
4. But references in paragraphs 2 and 3 to any other person do not include reference to the person whose act is capable of encouraging or assisting the commission of the offence under section 21 or, as the case may be, section 22 of that Act.

*Aliens Restriction (Amendment) Act 1919*

5. An offence under section 3(1) of the Aliens Restriction (Amendment) Act 1919 (acts calculated or likely to cause sedition or disaffection amongst HM forces etc.) consisting in attempting an act calculated or likely to cause sedition or disaffection in contravention of that subsection.
6. An offence under section 3(2) of that Act (promoting or attempting to promote industrial unrest) consisting in attempting to promote industrial unrest in contravention of that subsection.

*Official Secrets Act 1920*

7. An offence under section 7 of the Official Secrets Act 1920 (soliciting etc. commission of an offence under that Act or the Official Secrets Act 1911.

*Incitement to Disaffection Act 1934*

8. An offence under section 1 of the Incitement to Disaffection Act 1934 (endeavouring to seduce members of HM forces from their duty or allegiance).

*Misuse of Drugs Act 1971*

9. An offence under section 19 of the Misuse of Drugs Act 1971 (inciting any other offence under that Act).

10. An offence under section 20 of that Act (assisting or inducing commission outside United Kingdom of offence punishable under corresponding law).

*Immigration Act 1971*

11. An offence under section 25 of the Immigration Act 1971 (assisting unlawful immigration to a member State).
12. An offence under section 25B of that Act (assisting entry to the United Kingdom in breach of deportation or exclusion order).

*Representation of the People Act 1983*

13. An offence under section 97(1) of the Representation of the People Act 1983 (public meetings) consisting in the incitement of others to act in a disorderly manner for the purpose of preventing at a lawful public meeting to which that section applies the transaction of the business for which the meeting was called.

*Computer Misuse Act 1990*

14. An offence under section 3A(1) of the Computer Misuse Act 1990 (making etc. article intending it to be used to commit, or to assist in the commission of, an offence under section 1 or 3 of that Act).
15. An offence under section 3A(2) of that Act (supply or offer to supply article believing it is likely to be used to commit, or to assist in the commission of, an offence under section 1 or 3 of that Act).
16. An offence under section 3A(3) of that Act (obtaining an article with a view to its being supplied for use to commit, or to assist in the commission of, an offence under section 1 or 3 of that Act).

*Criminal Justice Act 1993*

17. An offence under section 52(2)(a) of the Criminal Justice Act 1993 (encouraging insider dealing).

*Reserve Forces Act 1996*

18. An offence under section 101 of the Reserve Forces Act 1996 (inducing a person to desert or absent himself).

*Landmines Act 1998*

19. An offence under section 2(2) of the Landmines Act 1998 (encouraging, assisting or inducing an offence under section 2(1) of that Act).

*Terrorism Act 2006*

20. An offence under section 1(2) of the Terrorism Act 2006 (encouraging terrorism).
21. An offence under section 2(1) of that Act (disseminating terrorist publications).
22. An offence under section 5 of that Act (engaging in conduct in preparation for giving effect to intention to commit or assisting another to commit acts of terrorism).
23. An offence under section 6(1) of that Act (provision of instruction or training knowing that a person trained or instructed intends to use the skills obtained for or in connection with the commission of acts of terrorism or for assisting the commission or preparation of such acts by others).
24. An offence under section 6(2) of that Act as a result of paragraph (b)(ii) of that subsection (receipt of instruction or training intending to use the skills obtained for assisting the commission or preparation of acts of terrorism by others).

*Cluster Munitions (Prohibitions) Act 2010*

24A. An offence under section 2(2) of the Cluster Munitions (Prohibitions) Act 2010 (assisting, encouraging or inducing another to engage in conduct mentioned in section 2(1) of that Act).

PART 2
OFFENCES UNDER PARTICULAR ENACTMENTS:
ENGLAND AND WALES

*Perjury Act 1911*

26. An offence under section 7(2) of the Perjury Act 1911 (inciting a person to commit an offence under that Act).

*Suicide Act 1961*

27A. An offence under section 2(1) of the Suicide Act 1961 (encouraging or assisting suicide).

*Criminal Law Act 1967*

28. An offence under section 4(1) of the Criminal Law Act 1967 (assisting persons who have committed an offence).
29. An offence under section 5(1) of that Act (accepting or agreeing to accept consideration for not disclosing information about an offence).

*Criminal Law Act 1977*

32. An offence under section 1(1) of the Criminal Law Act 1977 (conspiracy).

*Criminal Attempts Act 1981*

32. An offence under section 1(1) of the Criminal Attempts Act 1981 (attempting to commit an offence).

*Terrorism Act 2000*

38. An offence under section 59 of the Terrorism Act 2000 (inciting in England and Wales the commission of acts of terrorism outside the United Kingdom).

*Serious Crime Act 2015*

38A. An offence under section 45 of the Serious Crime Act 2015 (participating in activities of organised crime group).

PART 3
OTHER OFFENCES: ENGLAND AND WALES

39. An offence of conspiracy falling within section 5(2) or (3) of the Criminal Law Act 1977 (forms of conspiracy not affected by abolition of offence of conspiracy at common law).
40. (1) An attempt under a special statutory provision.
 (2) Sub-paragraph (1) is to be read with section 3 of the Criminal Attempts Act 1981.

## CRIMINAL JUSTICE AND IMMIGRATION ACT 2008

PART 5
CRIMINAL LAW

*Pornography etc.*

### 63. Possession of extreme pornographic images

(1) It is an offence for a person to be in possession of an extreme pornographic image.
(2) An 'extreme pornographic image' is an image which is both—
 (a) pornographic, and
 (b) an extreme image.

(3) An image is 'pornographic' if it is of such a nature that it must reasonably be assumed to have been produced solely or principally for the purpose of sexual arousal.

(4) Where (as found in the person's possession) an image forms part of a series of images, the question whether the image is of such a nature as is mentioned in subsection (3) is to be determined by reference to—

(a) the image itself, and

(b) (if the series of images is such as to be capable of providing a context for the image) the context in which it occurs in the series of images.

(5) So, for example, where—

(a) an image forms an integral part of a narrative constituted by a series of images, and

(b) having regard to those images as a whole, they are not of such a nature that they must reasonably be assumed to have been produced solely or principally for the purpose of sexual arousal,

the image may, by virtue of being part of that narrative, be found not to be pornographic, even though it might have been found to be pornographic if taken by itself.

(5A) In relation to possession of an image in England and Wales, an 'extreme image' is an image which—

(a) falls within subsection (7) or (7A), and

(b) is grossly offensive, disgusting or otherwise of an obscene character.

(7) An image falls within this subsection if it portrays, in an explicit and realistic way, any of the following—

(a) an act which threatens a person's life,

(b) an act which results, or is likely to result, in serious injury to a person's anus, breasts or genitals,

(c) an act which involves sexual interference with a human corpse, or

(d) a person performing an act of intercourse or oral sex with an animal (whether dead or alive),

and a reasonable person looking at the image would think that any such person or animal was real.

(7A) An image falls within this subsection if it portrays, in an explicit and realistic way, either of the following—

(a) an act which involves the non-consensual penetration of a person's vagina, anus or mouth by another with the other person's penis, or

(b) an act which involves the non-consensual sexual penetration of a person's vagina or anus by another with a part of the other person's body or anything else,

and a reasonable person looking at the image would think that the persons were real.

(7B) For the purposes of subsection (7A)—

(a) penetration is a continuing act from entry to withdrawal;

(b) 'vagina' includes vulva.

(8) In this section 'image' means—

(a) a moving or still image (produced by any means); or

(b) data (stored by any means) which is capable of conversion into an image within paragraph (a).

(9) In this section references to a part of the body include references to a part surgically constructed (in particular through gender reassignment surgery).

(10) Proceedings for an offence under this section may not be instituted—

(a) in England and Wales, except by or with the consent of the Director of Public Prosecutions.

## 64. Exclusion of classified films etc.

(1) Section 63 does not apply to excluded images.

(2) An 'excluded image' is an image which forms part of a series of images contained in a recording of the whole or part of a classified work.

(3) But such an image is not an 'excluded image' if—

(a) it is contained in a recording of an extract from a classified work, and

(b) it is of such a nature that it must reasonably be assumed to have been extracted (whether with or without other images) solely or principally for the purpose of sexual arousal.

(4) Where an extracted image is one of a series of images contained in the recording, the question whether the image is of such a nature as is mentioned in subsection (3)(b) is to be determined by reference to—
(a) the image itself, and
(b) (if the series of images is such as to be capable of providing a context for the image) the context in which it occurs in the series of images;
and section 63(5) applies in connection with determining that question as it applies in connection with determining whether an image is pornographic.

(5) In determining for the purposes of this section whether a recording is a recording of the whole or part of a classified work, any alteration attributable to—
(a) a defect caused for technical reasons or by inadvertence on the part of any person, or
(b) the inclusion in the recording of any extraneous material (such as advertisements),
is to be disregarded.

(6) Nothing in this section is to be taken as affecting any duty of a designated authority to have regard to section 63 (along with other enactments creating criminal offences) in determining whether a video work is suitable for a classification certificate to be issued in respect of it.

(7) In this section—
'classified work' means (subject to subsection (8)) a video work in respect of which a classification certificate has been issued by a designated authority (whether before or after the commencement of this section);
'classification certificate' and 'video work' have the same meanings as in the Video Recordings Act 1984;
'designated authority' means an authority which has been designated by the Secretary of State under section 4 of that Act;
'extract' includes an extract consisting of a single image;
'image' and 'pornographic' have the same meanings as in section 63;
'recording' means any disc, tape or other device capable of storing data electronically and from which images may be produced (by any means).

(8) Section 22(3) of the Video Recordings Act 1984 (effect of alterations) applies for the purposes of this section as it applies for the purposes of that Act.

## 65. Defences: general

(1) Where a person is charged with an offence under section 63, it is a defence for the person to prove any of the matters mentioned in subsection (2).

(2) The matters are—
(a) that the person had a legitimate reason for being in possession of the image concerned;
(b) that the person had not seen the image concerned and did not know, nor had any cause to suspect, it to be an extreme pornographic image;
(c) that the person—
(i) was sent the image concerned without any prior request having been made by or on behalf of the person, and
(ii) did not keep it for an unreasonable time.

(3) In this section 'extreme pornographic image' and 'image' have the same meanings as in section 63.

## 66. Defence: participation in consensual acts

(A1) Subsection (A2) applies where in England and Wales—
(a) a person ('D') is charged with an offence under section 63, and
(b) the offence relates to an image that portrays an act or acts within subsection (7) (a) to (c) or (7A) of that section (but does not portray an act within subsection (7) (d) of that section).

(A2) It is a defence for D to prove—
(a) that D directly participated in the act or any of the acts portrayed, and
(b) that the act or acts did not involve the infliction of any non-consensual harm on any person, and

(c) if the image portrays an act within section 63(7)(c), that what is portrayed as a human corpse was not in fact a corpse, and
(d) if the image portrays an act within section 63(7A), that what is portrayed as non-consensual penetration was in fact consensual.

(3) For the purposes of this section harm inflicted on a person is 'non-consensual' harm if—
(a) the harm is of such a nature that the person cannot, in law, consent to it being inflicted on himself or herself; or
(b) where the person can, in law, consent to it being so inflicted, the person does not in fact consent to it being so inflicted.

*Self-defence etc.*

## 76. Reasonable force for purposes of self-defence etc.

(1) This section applies where in proceedings for an offence—
(a) an issue arises as to whether a person charged with the offence ('D') is entitled to rely on a defence within subsection (2), and
(b) the question arises whether the degree of force used by D against a person ('V') was reasonable in the circumstances.

(2) The defences are—
(a) the common law defence of self-defence;
(aa) the common law defence of defence of property; and
(b) the defences provided by section 3(1) of the Criminal Law Act 1967 (use of force in prevention of crime or making arrest).

(3) The question whether the degree of force used by D was reasonable in the circumstances is to be decided by reference to the circumstances as D believed them to be, and subsections (4) to (8) also apply in connection with deciding that question.

(4) If D claims to have held a particular belief as regards the existence of any circumstances—
(a) the reasonableness or otherwise of that belief is relevant to the question whether D genuinely held it; but
(b) if it is determined that D did genuinely hold it, D is entitled to rely on it for the purposes of subsection (3), whether or not—
(i) it was mistaken, or
(ii) (if it was mistaken) the mistake was a reasonable one to have made.

(5) But subsection (4)(b) does not enable D to rely on any mistaken belief attributable to intoxication that was voluntarily induced.

(5A) In a householder case, the degree of force used by D is not to be regarded as having been reasonable in the circumstances as D believed them to be if it was grossly disproportionate in those circumstances.

(6) In a case other than a householder case, the degree of force used by D is not to be regarded as having been reasonable in the circumstances as D believed them to be if it was disproportionate in those circumstances.

(6A) In deciding the question mentioned in subsection (3), a possibility that D could have retreated is to be considered (so far as relevant) as a factor to be taken into account, rather than giving rise to a duty to retreat.

(7) In deciding the question mentioned in subsection (3) the following considerations are to be taken into account (so far as relevant in the circumstances of the case)—
(a) that a person acting for a legitimate purpose may not be able to weigh to a nicety the exact measure of any necessary action; and
(b) that evidence of a person's having only done what the person honestly and instinctively thought was necessary for a legitimate purpose constitutes strong evidence that only reasonable action was taken by that person for that purpose.

(8) Subsection (7) is not to be read as preventing other matters from being taken into account where they are relevant to deciding the question mentioned in subsection (3).

(8A) For the purposes of this section 'a householder case' is a case where—
(a) the defence concerned is the common law defence of self-defence,
(b) the force concerned is force used by D while in or partly in a building, or part of a building, that is a dwelling or is forces accommodation (or is both),

(c) D is not a trespasser at the time the force is used, and
(d) at that time D believed V to be in, or entering, the building or part as a trespasser.

(8B) Where—
(a) a part of a building is a dwelling where D dwells,
(b) another part of the building is a place of work for D or another person who dwells in the first part, and
(c) that other part is internally accessible from the first part,
that other part, and any internal means of access between the two parts, are each treated for the purposes of subsection (8A) as a part of a building that is a dwelling.

(8C) Where—
(a) a part of a building is forces accommodation that is living or sleeping accommodation for D,
(b) another part of the building is a place of work for D or another person for whom the first part is living or sleeping accommodation, and
(c) that other part is internally accessible from the first part,
that other part, and any internal means of access between the two parts, are each treated for the purposes of subsection (8A) as a part of a building that is forces accommodation.

(8D) Subsections (4) and (5) apply for the purposes of subsection (8A)(d) as they apply for the purposes of subsection (3).

(8E) The fact that a person derives title from a trespasser, or has the permission of a trespasser, does not prevent the person from being a trespasser for the purposes of subsection (8A).

(8F) In subsections (8A) to (8C)—
'building' includes a vehicle or vessel, and
'forces accommodation' means service living accommodation for the purposes of Part 3 of the Armed Forces Act 2006 by virtue of section 96(1)(a) or (b) of that Act.

(9) This section, except so far as making separate provision for householder cases, is intended to clarify the operation of the existing defences mentioned in subsection (2).

(10) In this section—
(a) 'legitimate purpose' means—
(i) the purpose of self-defence under the common law, or
(ii) the prevention of crime or effecting or assisting in the lawful arrest of persons mentioned in the provisions referred to in subsection (2)(b);
(b) references to self-defence include acting in defence of another person; and
(c) references to the degree of force used are to the type and amount of force used.

# CORONERS AND JUSTICE ACT 2009

## 54. Partial defence to murder: loss of control

(1) Where a person ('D') kills or is a party to the killing of another ('V'), D is not to be convicted of murder if—
(a) D's acts and omissions in doing or being a party to the killing resulted from D's loss of self-control,
(b) the loss of self-control had a qualifying trigger, and
(c) a person of D's sex and age, with a normal degree of tolerance and self-restraint and in the circumstances of D, might have reacted in the same or in a similar way to D.

(2) For the purposes of subsection (1)(a), it does not matter whether or not the loss of control was sudden.

(3) In subsection (1)(c) the reference to 'the circumstances of D' is a reference to all of D's circumstances other than those whose only relevance to D's conduct is that they bear on D's general capacity for tolerance or self-restraint.

(4) Subsection (1) does not apply if, in doing or being a party to the killing, D acted in a considered desire for revenge.

(5) On a charge of murder, if sufficient evidence is adduced to raise an issue with respect to the defence under subsection (1), the jury must assume that the defence is satisfied unless the prosecution proves beyond reasonable doubt that it is not.

(6) For the purposes of subsection (5), sufficient evidence is adduced to raise an issue with respect to the defence if evidence is adduced on which, in the opinion of the trial judge, a jury, properly directed, could reasonably conclude that the defence might apply.
(7) A person who, but for this section, would be liable to be convicted of murder is liable instead to be convicted of manslaughter.
(8) The fact that one party to a killing is by virtue of this section not liable to be convicted of murder does not affect the question whether the killing amounted to murder in the case of any other party to it.

## 55. Meaning of 'qualifying trigger'

(1) This section applies for the purposes of section 54.
(2) A loss of self-control had a qualifying trigger if subsection (3), (4) or (5) applies.
(3) This subsection applies if D's loss of self-control was attributable to D's fear of serious violence from V against D or another identified person.
(4) This subsection applies if D's loss of self-control was attributable to a thing or things done or said (or both) which—
  (a) constituted circumstances of an extremely grave character, and
  (b) caused D to have a justifiable sense of being seriously wronged.
(5) This subsection applies if D's loss of self-control was attributable to a combination of the matters mentioned in subsections (3) and (4).
(6) In determining whether a loss of self-control had a qualifying trigger—
  (a) D's fear of serious violence is to be disregarded to the extent that it was caused by a thing which D incited to be done or said for the purpose of providing an excuse to use violence;
  (b) a sense of being seriously wronged by a thing done or said is not justifiable if D incited the thing to be done or said for the purpose of providing an excuse to use violence;
  (c) the fact that a thing done or said constituted sexual infidelity is to be disregarded.
(7) In this section references to 'D' and 'V' are to be construed in accordance with section 54.

## 56. Abolition of common law defence of provocation

(1) The common law defence of provocation is abolished and replaced by sections 54 and 55.
(2) Accordingly, the following provisions cease to have effect—
  (a) section 3 of the Homicide Act 1957 (questions of provocation to be left to the jury);
  ...

## 62. Possession of prohibited images of children

(1) It is an offence for a person to be in possession of a prohibited image of a child.
(2) A prohibited image is an image which—
  (a) is pornographic,
  (b) falls within subsection (6), and
  (c) is grossly offensive, disgusting or otherwise of an obscene character.
(3) An image is 'pornographic' if it is of such a nature that it must reasonably be assumed to have been produced solely or principally for the purpose of sexual arousal.
(4) Where (as found in the person's possession) an image forms part of a series of images, the question whether the image is of such a nature as is mentioned in subsection (3) is to be determined by reference to—
  (a) the image itself, and
  (b) (if the series of images is such as to be capable of providing a context for the image) the context in which it occurs in the series of images.
(5) So, for example, where—
  (a) an image forms an integral part of a narrative constituted by a series of images, and
  (b) having regard to those images as a whole, they are not of such a nature that they must reasonably be assumed to have been produced solely or principally for the purpose of sexual arousal,

the image may, by virtue of being part of that narrative, be found not to be pornographic, even though it might have been found to be pornographic if taken by itself.

(6) An image falls within this subsection if it—
(a) is an image which focuses solely or principally on a child's genitals or anal region, or
(b) portrays any of the acts mentioned in subsection (7).
(7) Those acts are—
(a) the performance by a person of an act of intercourse or oral sex with or in the presence of a child;
(b) an act of masturbation by, of, involving or in the presence of a child;
(c) an act which involves penetration of the vagina or anus of a child with a part of a person's body or with anything else;
(d) an act of penetration, in the presence of a child, of the vagina or anus of a person with a part of a person's body or with anything else;
(e) the performance by a child of an act of intercourse or oral sex with an animal (whether dead or alive or imaginary);
(f) the performance by a person of an act of intercourse or oral sex with an animal (whether dead or alive or imaginary) in the presence of a child.
(8) For the purposes of subsection (7), penetration is a continuing act from entry to withdrawal.
(9) Proceedings for an offence under subsection (1) may not be instituted—
(a) in England and Wales, except by or with the consent of the Director of Public Prosecutions;

## 63. Exclusion of classified film etc.

(1) Section 62(1) does not apply to excluded images.
(2) An 'excluded image' is an image which forms part of a series of images contained in a recording of the whole or part of a classified work.
(3) But such an image is not an 'excluded image' if—
(a) it is contained in a recording of an extract from a classified work, and
(b) it is of such a nature that it must reasonably be assumed to have been extracted (whether with or without other images) solely or principally for the purpose of sexual arousal.
(4) Where an extracted image is one of a series of images contained in the recording, the question whether the image is of such a nature as is mentioned in subsection (3)(b) is to be determined by reference to—
(a) the image itself, and
(b) (if the series of images is such as to be capable of providing a context for the image) the context in which it occurs in the series of images;
and section 62(5) applies in connection with determining that question as it applies in connection with determining whether an image is pornographic.
(5) In determining for the purposes of this section whether a recording is a recording of the whole or part of a classified work, any alteration attributable to—
(a) a defect caused for technical reasons or by inadvertence on the part of any person, or
(b) the inclusion in the recording of any extraneous material (such as advertisements),
is to be disregarded.
(6) Nothing in this section is to be taken as affecting any duty of a designated authority to have regard to section 62 (along with other enactments creating criminal offences) in determining whether a video work is suitable for a classification certificate to be issued in respect of it.
(7) In this section—
'classified work' means (subject to subsection (8)) a video work in respect of which a classification certificate has been issued by a designated authority (whether before or after the commencement of this section);
'classification certificate' and 'video work' have the same meaning as in the Video Recordings Act 1984;
'designated authority' means an authority which has been designated by the Secretary of State under section 4 of that Act;
'extract' includes an extract consisting of a single image;
'pornographic' has the same meaning as in section 62;

'recording' means any disc, tape or other device capable of storing data electronically and from which images may be produced (by any means).

(8) Section 22(3) of the Video Recordings Act 1984 (effect of alterations) applies for the purposes of this section as it applies for the purposes of that Act.

### 64. Defences

(1) Where a person is charged with an offence under section 62(1), it is a defence for the person to prove any of the following matters—
  (a) that the person had a legitimate reason for being in possession of the image concerned;
  (b) that the person had not seen the image concerned and did not know, nor had any cause to suspect, it to be a prohibited image of a child;
  (c) that the person—
    (i) was sent the image concerned without any prior request having been made by or on behalf of the person, and
    (ii) did not keep it for an unreasonable time.

(2) In this section 'prohibited image' has the same meaning as in section 62.

### 65. Meaning of 'image' and 'child'

(1) The following apply for the purposes of sections 62 to 64.

(2) 'Image' includes—
  (a) a moving or still image (produced by any means), or
  (b) data (stored by any means) which is capable of conversion into an image within paragraph (a).

(3) 'Image' does not include an indecent photograph, or indecent pseudo-photograph, of a child.

(4) In subsection (3) 'indecent photograph' and 'indecent pseudo-photograph' are to be construed—
  (a) in relation to England and Wales, in accordance with the Protection of Children Act 1978,

(5) 'Child', subject to subsection (6), means a person under the age of 18.

(6) Where an image shows a person the image is to be treated as an image of a child if—
  (a) the impression conveyed by the image is that the person shown is a child, or
  (b) the predominant impression conveyed is that the person shown is a child despite the fact that some of the physical characteristics shown are not those of a child.

(7) References to an image of a person include references to an image of an imaginary person.

(8) References to an image of a child include references to an image of an imaginary child.

## BRIBERY ACT 2010

### 1. Offences of bribing another person

(1) A person ('P') is guilty of an offence if either of the following cases applies.

(2) Case 1 is where—
  (a) P offers, promises or gives a financial or other advantage to another person, and
  (b) P intends the advantage—
    (i) to induce a person to perform improperly a relevant function or activity, or
    (ii) to reward a person for the improper performance of such a function or activity.

(3) Case 2 is where—
  (a) P offers, promises or gives a financial or other advantage to another person, and
  (b) P knows or believes that the acceptance of the advantage would itself constitute the improper performance of a relevant function or activity.

(4) In case 1 it does not matter whether the person to whom the advantage is offered, promised or given is the same person as the person who is to perform, or has performed, the function or activity concerned.

(5) In cases 1 and 2 it does not matter whether the advantage is offered, promised or given by P directly or through a third party.

## 2. Offences relating to being bribed

(1) A person ('R') is guilty of an offence if any of the following cases applies.

(2) Case 3 is where R requests, agrees to receive or accepts a financial or other advantage intending that, in consequence, a relevant function or activity should be performed improperly (whether by R or another person).

(3) Case 4 is where—
- (a) R requests, agrees to receive or accepts a financial or other advantage, and
- (b) the request, agreement or acceptance itself constitutes the improper performance by R of a relevant function or activity.

(4) Case 5 is where R requests, agrees to receive or accepts a financial or other advantage as a reward for the improper performance (whether by R or another person) of a relevant function or activity.

(5) Case 6 is where, in anticipation of or in consequence of R requesting, agreeing to receive or accepting a financial or other advantage, a relevant function or activity is performed improperly—
- (a) by R, or
- (b) by another person at R's request or with R's assent or acquiescence.

(6) In cases 3 to 6 it does not matter—
- (a) whether R requests, agrees to receive or accepts (or is to request, agree to receive or accept) the advantage directly or through a third party,
- (b) whether the advantage is (or is to be) for the benefit of R or another person.

(7) In cases 4 to 6 it does not matter whether R knows or believes that the performance of the function or activity is improper.

(8) In case 6, where a person other than R is performing the function or activity, it also does not matter whether that person knows or believes that the performance of the function or activity is improper.

## 3. Function or activity to which bribe relates

(1) For the purposes of this Act a function or activity is a relevant function or activity if—
- (a) it falls within subsection (2), and
- (b) meets one or more of conditions A to C.

(2) The following functions and activities fall within this subsection—
- (a) any function of a public nature,
- (b) any activity connected with a business,
- (c) any activity performed in the course of a person's employment,
- (d) any activity performed by or on behalf of a body of persons (whether corporate or unincorporate).

(3) Condition A is that a person performing the function or activity is expected to perform it in good faith.

(4) Condition B is that a person performing the function or activity is expected to perform it impartially.

(5) Condition C is that a person performing the function or activity is in a position of trust by virtue of performing it.

(6) A function or activity is a relevant function or activity even if it—
- (a) has no connection with the United Kingdom, and
- (b) is performed in a country or territory outside the United Kingdom.

(7) In this section 'business' includes trade or profession.

## 4. Improper performance to which bribe relates

(1) For the purposes of this Act a relevant function or activity—
- (a) is performed improperly if it is performed in breach of a relevant expectation, and
- (b) is to be treated as being performed improperly if there is a failure to perform the function or activity and that failure is itself a breach of a relevant expectation.

(2) In subsection (1) 'relevant expectation'—
- (a) in relation to a function or activity which meets condition A or B, means the expectation mentioned in the condition concerned, and
- (b) in relation to a function or activity which meets condition C, means any expectation as to the manner in which, or the reasons for which, the function or activity will be performed that arises from the position of trust mentioned in that condition.

(3) Anything that a person does (or omits to do) arising from or in connection with that person's past performance of a relevant function or activity is to be treated for the purposes of this Act as being done (or omitted) by that person in the performance of that function or activity.

## 5. Expectation test

(1) For the purposes of sections 3 and 4, the test of what is expected is a test of what a reasonable person in the United Kingdom would expect in relation to the performance of the type of function or activity concerned.

(2) In deciding what such a person would expect in relation to the performance of a function or activity where the performance is not subject to the law of any part of the United Kingdom, any local custom or practice is to be disregarded unless it is permitted or required by the written law applicable to the country or territory concerned.

(3) In subsection (2) 'written law' means law contained in—
- (a) any written constitution, or provision made by or under legislation, applicable to the country or territory concerned, or
- (b) any judicial decision which is so applicable and is evidenced in published written sources.

## 6. Bribery of foreign public officials

(1) A person ('P') who bribes a foreign public official ('F') is guilty of an offence if P's intention is to influence F in F's capacity as a foreign public official.

(2) P must also intend to obtain or retain—
- (a) business, or
- (b) an advantage in the conduct of business.

(3) P bribes F if, and only if—
- (a) directly or through a third party, P offers, promises or gives any financial or other advantage—
  - (i) to F, or
  - (ii) to another person at F's request or with F's assent or acquiescence, and
- (b) F is neither permitted nor required by the written law applicable to F to be influenced in F's capacity as a foreign public official by the offer, promise or gift.

(4) References in this section to influencing F in F's capacity as a foreign public official mean influencing F in the performance of F's functions as such an official, which includes—
- (a) any omission to exercise those functions, and
- (b) any use of F's position as such an official, even if not within F's authority.

(5) 'Foreign public official' means an individual who—
- (a) holds a legislative, administrative or judicial position of any kind, whether appointed or elected, of a country or territory outside the United Kingdom (or any subdivision of such a country or territory),
- (b) exercises a public function—
  - (i) for or on behalf of a country or territory outside the United Kingdom (or any subdivision of such a country or territory), or
  - (ii) for any public agency or public enterprise of that country or territory (or subdivision), or
- (c) is an official or agent of a public international organisation.

(6) 'Public international organisation' means an organisation whose members are any of the following—
- (a) countries or territories,
- (b) governments of countries or territories,
- (c) other public international organisations,
- (d) a mixture of any of the above.

(7) For the purposes of subsection (3)(b), the written law applicable to F is—
- (a) where the performance of the functions of F which P intends to influence would be subject to the law of any part of the United Kingdom, the law of that part of the United Kingdom,
- (b) where paragraph (a) does not apply and F is an official or agent of a public international organisation, the applicable written rules of that organisation,

(c) where paragraphs (a) and (b) do not apply, the law of the country or territory in relation to which F is a foreign public official so far as that law is contained in—
  (i) any written constitution, or provision made by or under legislation, applicable to the country or territory concerned, or
  (ii) any judicial decision which is so applicable and is evidenced in published written sources.

(8) For the purposes of this section, a trade or profession is a business.

## 7. Failure of commercial organisations to prevent bribery

(1) A relevant commercial organisation ('C') is guilty of an offence under this section if a person ('A') associated with C bribes another person intending—
  (a) to obtain or retain business for C, or
  (b) to obtain or retain an advantage in the conduct of business for C.

(2) But it is a defence for C to prove that C had in place adequate procedures designed to prevent persons associated with C from undertaking such conduct.

(3) For the purposes of this section, A bribes another person if, and only if, A—
  (a) is, or would be, guilty of an offence under section 1 or 6 (whether or not A has been prosecuted for such an offence), or
  (b) would be guilty of such an offence if section 12(2)(c) and (4) were omitted.

(4) See section 8 for the meaning of a person associated with C and see section 9 for a duty on the Secretary of State to publish guidance.

(5) In this section—

'partnership' means—
  (a) a partnership within the Partnership Act 1890, or
  (b) a limited partnership registered under the Limited Partnerships Act 1907,

or a firm or entity of a similar character formed under the law of a country or territory outside the United Kingdom,

'relevant commercial organisation' means—
  (a) a body which is incorporated under the law of any part of the United Kingdom and which carries on a business (whether there or elsewhere),
  (b) any other body corporate (wherever incorporated) which carries on a business, or part of a business, in any part of the United Kingdom,
  (c) a partnership which is formed under the law of any part of the United Kingdom and which carries on a business (whether there or elsewhere), or
  (d) any other partnership (wherever formed) which carries on a business, or part of a business, in any part of the United Kingdom,

and, for the purposes of this section, a trade or profession is a business.

## 8. Meaning of associated person

(1) For the purposes of section 7, a person ('A') is associated with C if (disregarding any bribe under consideration) A is a person who performs services for or on behalf of C.

(2) The capacity in which A performs services for or on behalf of C does not matter.

(3) Accordingly A may (for example) be C's employee, agent or subsidiary.

(4) Whether or not A is a person who performs services for or on behalf of C is to be determined by reference to all the relevant circumstances and not merely by reference to the nature of the relationship between A and C.

(5) But if A is an employee of C, it is to be presumed unless the contrary is shown that A is a person who performs services for or on behalf of C.

## 9. Guidance about commercial organisations preventing bribery

(1) The Secretary of State must publish guidance about procedures that relevant commercial organisations can put in place to prevent persons associated with them from bribing as mentioned in section 7(1).

(2) The Secretary of State may, from time to time, publish revisions to guidance under this section or revised guidance.

...

(4) Publication under this section is to be in such manner as the Secretary of State considers appropriate.

(5) Expressions used in this section have the same meaning as in section 7.

## 10. Consent to prosecution

(1) No proceedings for an offence under this Act may be instituted in England and Wales except by or with the consent of—
  (a) the Director of Public Prosecutions, or
  (b) the Director of the Serious Fraud Office.

...

(3) No proceedings for an offence under this Act may be instituted in England and Wales or Northern Ireland by a person—
  (a) who is acting—
    (i) under the direction or instruction of the Director of Public Prosecutions or the Director of the Serious Fraud Office, or
    (ii) on behalf of such a Director, or
  (b) to whom such a function has been assigned by such a Director,

except with the consent of the Director concerned to the institution of the proceedings.

(4) The Director of Public Prosecutions and the Director of the Serious Fraud Office must exercise personally any function under subsection (1), (2) or (3) of giving consent.

(5) The only exception is if—
  (a) the Director concerned is unavailable, and
  (b) there is another person who is designated in writing by the Director acting personally as the person who is authorised to exercise any such function when the Director is unavailable.

(6) In that case, the other person may exercise the function but must do so personally.

(7) Subsections (4) to (6) apply instead of any other provisions which would otherwise have enabled any function of the Director of Public Prosecutions or the Director of the Serious Fraud Office under subsection (1), (2) or (3) of giving consent to be exercised by a person other than the Director concerned.

## 13. Defence for certain bribery offences etc.

(1) It is a defence for a person charged with a relevant bribery offence to prove that the person's conduct was necessary for—
  (a) the proper exercise of any function of an intelligence service, or
  (b) the proper exercise of any function of the armed forces when engaged on active service.

(2) The head of each intelligence service must ensure that the service has in place arrangements designed to ensure that any conduct of a member of the service which would otherwise be a relevant bribery offence is necessary for a purpose falling within subsection (1)(a).

(3) The Defence Council must ensure that the armed forces have in place arrangements designed to ensure that any conduct of—
  (a) a member of the armed forces who is engaged on active service, or
  (b) a civilian subject to service discipline when working in support of any person falling within paragraph (a),

which would otherwise be a relevant bribery offence is necessary for a purpose falling within subsection (1)(b).

(4) The arrangements which are in place by virtue of subsection (2) or (3) must be arrangements which the Secretary of State considers to be satisfactory.

(5) For the purposes of this section, the circumstances in which a person's conduct is necessary for a purpose falling within subsection (1)(a) or (b) are to be treated as including any circumstances in which the person's conduct—
  (a) would otherwise be an offence under section 2, and
  (b) involves conduct by another person which, but for subsection (1)(a) or (b), would be an offence under section 1.

(6) In this section—

'active service' means service in—
  (a) an action or operation against an enemy,
  (b) an operation outside the British Islands for the protection of life or property, or
  (c) the military occupation of a foreign country or territory,

'armed forces' means Her Majesty's forces (within the meaning of the Armed Forces Act 2006),
'civilian subject to service discipline' and 'enemy' have the same meaning as in the Act of 2006,
'GCHQ' has the meaning given by section 3(3) of the Intelligence Services Act 1994,
'head' means—
(a) in relation to the Security Service, the Director General of the Security Service,
(b) in relation to the Secret Intelligence Service, the Chief of the Secret Intelligence Service, and
(c) in relation to GCHQ, the Director of GCHQ,
'intelligence service' means the Security Service, the Secret Intelligence Service or GCHQ,
'relevant bribery offence' means—
(a) an offence under section 1 which would not also be an offence under section 6,
(b) an offence under section 2,
(c) an offence committed by aiding, abetting, counselling or procuring the commission of an offence falling within paragraph (a) or (b),
(d) an offence of attempting or conspiring to commit, or of inciting the commission of, an offence falling within paragraph (a) or (b), or
(e) an offence under Part 2 of the Serious Crime Act 2007 (encouraging or assisting crime) in relation to an offence falling within paragraph (a) or (b).

## 14. Offences under sections 1, 2 and 6 by bodies corporate etc.

(1) This section applies if an offence under section 1,2 or 6 is committed by a body corporate or a Scottish partnership.
(2) If the offence is proved to have been committed with the consent or connivance of—
(a) a senior officer of the body corporate or Scottish partnership, or
(b) a person purporting to act in such a capacity,
the senior officer or person (as well as the body corporate or partnership) is guilty of the offence and liable to be proceeded against and punished accordingly.
(3) But subsection (2) does not apply, in the case of an offence which is committed under section 1,2 or 6 by virtue of section 12(2) to (4), to a senior officer or person purporting to act in such a capacity unless the senior officer or person has a close connection with the United Kingdom (within the meaning given by section 12(4)).
(4) In this section—
'director', in relation to a body corporate whose affairs are managed by its members, means a member of the body corporate,
'senior officer' means—
(a) in relation to a body corporate, a director, manager, secretary or other similar officer of the body corporate
...

## 15. Offences under section 7 by partnerships

(1) Proceedings for an offence under section 7 alleged to have been committed by a partnership must be brought in the name of the partnership (and not in that of any of the partners).
(2) For the purposes of such proceedings—
(a) rules of court relating to the service of documents have effect as if the partnership were a body corporate, and
(b) the following provisions apply as they apply in relation to a body corporate—
(i) section 33 of the Criminal Justice Act 1925 and Schedule 3 to the Magistrates' Courts Act 1980, ...
(4) In this section 'partnership' has the same meaning as in section 7.

## 16. Application to Crown

This Act applies to individuals in the public service of the Crown as it applies to other individuals.

# LEGAL AID, SENTENCING AND PUNISHMENT OF OFFENDERS ACT 2012

## 144. Offence of squatting in a residential building

(1) A person commits an offence if—
   (a) the person is in a residential building as a trespasser having entered it as a trespasser,
   (b) the person knows or ought to know that he or she is a trespasser, and
   (c) the person is living in the building or intends to live there for any period.

(2) The offence is not committed by a person holding over after the end of a lease or licence (even if the person leaves and re-enters the building).

(3) For the purposes of this section—
   (a) 'building' includes any structure or part of a structure (including a temporary or moveable structure), and
   (b) a building is 'residential' if it is designed or adapted, before the time of entry, for use as a place to live.

(4) For the purposes of this section the fact that a person derives title from a trespasser, or has the permission of a trespasser, does not prevent the person from being a trespasser.

(6) In relation to an offence committed before the commencement of section 281(5) of the Criminal Justice Act 2003, the reference in subsection (5) to 51 weeks is to be read as a reference to 6 months.

(7) For the purposes of subsection (1)(a) it is irrelevant whether the person entered the building as a trespasser before or after the commencement of this section.

# ANTI-SOCIAL BEHAVIOUR, CRIME AND POLICING ACT 2014

## 121. Offence of forced marriage: England and Wales

(1) A person commits an offence under the law of England and Wales if he or she—
   (a) uses violence, threats or any other form of coercion for the purpose of causing another person to enter into a marriage, and
   (b) believes, or ought reasonably to believe, that the conduct may cause the other person to enter into the marriage without free and full consent.

(2) In relation to a victim who lacks capacity to consent to marriage, the offence under subsection (1) is capable of being committed by any conduct carried out for the purpose of causing the victim to enter into a marriage (whether or not the conduct amounts to violence, threats or any other form coercion).

(3) A person commits an offence under the law of England and Wales if he or she—
   (a) practises any form of deception with the intention of causing another person to leave the United Kingdom, and
   (b) intends the other person to be subjected to conduct outside the United Kingdom that is an offence under subsection (1) or would be an offence under that subsection if the victim were in England or Wales.

(4) 'Marriage' means any religious or civil ceremony of marriage (whether or not legally binding).

(5) 'Lacks capacity' means lacks capacity within the meaning of the Mental Capacity Act 2005.

(6) It is irrelevant whether the conduct mentioned in paragraph (a) of subsection (1) is directed at the victim of the offence under that subsection or another person.

(7) A person commits an offence under subsection (1) or (3) only if, at the time of the conduct or deception—
   (a) the person or the victim or both of them are in England or Wales,
   (b) neither the person nor the victim is in England or Wales but at least one of them is habitually resident in England and Wales, or
   (c) neither the person nor the victim is in the United Kingdom but at least one of them is a UK national.

(8) 'UK national' means an individual who is—
(a) a British citizen, a British overseas territories citizen, a British National (Overseas) or a British Overseas citizen;
(b) a person who under the British Nationality Act 1981 is a British subject; or
(c) a British protected person within the meaning of that Act.

# CRIMINAL JUSTICE AND COURTS ACT 2015

## OFFENCES INVOLVING POLICE OR PRISON OFFICERS

### 26. Corrupt or other improper exercise of police powers and privileges

(1) A police constable listed in subsection (3) commits an offence if he or she—
(a) exercises the powers and privileges of a constable improperly, and
(b) knows or ought to know that the exercise is improper.

(2) A police constable guilty of an offence under this section is liable, on conviction on indictment, to imprisonment for a term not exceeding 14 years or a fine (or both).

(3) The police constables referred to in subsection (1) are—
(a) a constable of a police force in England and Wales;
(b) a special constable for a police area in England and Wales;
(c) a constable or special constable of the British Transport Police Force;
(d) a constable of the Civil Nuclear Constabulary;
(e) a constable of the Ministry of Defence Police;
(f) a National Crime Agency officer designated under section 9 or 10 of the Crime and Courts Act 2013 as having the powers and privileges of a constable.

(4) For the purposes of this section, a police constable exercises the powers and privileges of a constable improperly if—
(a) he or she exercises a power or privilege of a constable for the purpose of achieving—
(i) a benefit for himself or herself, or
(ii) a benefit or a detriment for another person, and
(b) a reasonable person would not expect the power or privilege to be exercised for the purpose of achieving that benefit or detriment.

(5) For the purposes of this section, a police constable is to be treated as exercising the powers and privileges of a constable improperly in the cases described in subsections (6) and (7).

(6) The first case is where—
(a) the police constable fails to exercise a power or privilege of a constable,
(b) the purpose of the failure is to achieve a benefit or detriment described in subsection (4)(a), and
(c) a reasonable person would not expect a constable to fail to exercise the power or privilege for the purpose of achieving that benefit or detriment.

(7) The second case is where—
(a) the police constable threatens to exercise, or not to exercise, a power or privilege of a constable,
(b) the threat is made for the purpose of achieving a benefit or detriment described in subsection (4)(a), and
(c) a reasonable person would not expect a constable to threaten to exercise, or not to exercise, the power or privilege for the purpose of achieving that benefit or detriment.

(8) An offence is committed under this section if the act or omission in question takes place in the United Kingdom or in United Kingdom waters.

(9) In this section—
'benefit' and 'detriment' mean any benefit or detriment, whether or not in money or other property and whether temporary or permanent;
'United Kingdom waters' means the sea and other waters within the seaward limits of the United Kingdom's territorial sea.

(10) References in this section to exercising, or not exercising, the powers and privileges of a constable include performing, or not performing, the duties of a constable.

(11) Nothing in this section affects what constitutes the offence of misconduct in public office at common law in England and Wales or Northern Ireland.

## 33. Disclosing private sexual photographs and films with intent to cause distress

(1) It is an offence for a person to disclose a private sexual photograph or film if the disclosure is made—
   (a) without the consent of an individual who appears in the photograph or film, and
   (b) with the intention of causing that individual distress.

(2) But it is not an offence under this section for the person to disclose the photograph or film to the individual mentioned in subsection (1)(a) and (b).

(3) It is a defence for a person charged with an offence under this section to prove that he or she reasonably believed that the disclosure was necessary for the purposes of preventing, detecting or investigating crime.

(4) It is a defence for a person charged with an offence under this section to show that—
   (a) the disclosure was made in the course of, or with a view to, the publication of journalistic material, and
   (b) he or she reasonably believed that, in the particular circumstances, the publication of the journalistic material was, or would be, in the public interest.

(5) It is a defence for a person charged with an offence under this section to show that—
   (a) he or she reasonably believed that the photograph or film had previously been disclosed for reward, whether by the individual mentioned in subsection (1)(a) and (b) or another person, and
   (b) he or she had no reason to believe that the previous disclosure for reward was made without the consent of the individual mentioned in subsection (1)(a) and (b).

(6) A person is taken to have shown the matters mentioned in subsection (4) or (5) if—
   (a) sufficient evidence of the matters is adduced to raise an issue with respect to it, and
   (b) the contrary is not proved beyond reasonable doubt.

(7) For the purposes of subsections (1) to (5)—
   (a) 'consent' to a disclosure includes general consent covering the disclosure, as well as consent to the particular disclosure, and
   (b) 'publication' of journalistic material means disclosure to the public at large or to a section of the public.

(8) A person charged with an offence under this section is not to be taken to have disclosed a photograph or film with the intention of causing distress merely because that was a natural and probable consequence of the disclosure.

## 34. Meaning of 'disclose' and 'photograph or film'

(1) The following apply for the purposes of section 33, this section and section 35.

(2) A person 'discloses' something to a person if, by any means, he or she gives or shows it to the person or makes it available to the person.

(3) Something that is given, shown or made available to a person is disclosed—
   (a) whether or not it is given, shown or made available for reward, and
   (b) whether or not it has previously been given, shown or made available to the person.

(4) 'Photograph or film' means a still or moving image in any form that—
   (a) appears to consist of or include one or more photographed or filmed images, and
   (b) in fact consists of or includes one or more photographed or filmed images.

(5) The reference in subsection (4)(b) to photographed or filmed images includes photographed or filmed images that have been altered in any way.

(6) 'Photographed or filmed image' means a still or moving image that—
   (a) was originally captured by photography or filming, or
   (b) is part of an image originally captured by photography or filming.

(7) 'Filming' means making a recording, on any medium, from which a moving image may be produced by any means.

(8) References to a photograph or film include—
  (a) a negative version of an image described in subsection (4), and
  (b) data stored by any means which is capable of conversion into an image described in subsection (4).

### 35. Meaning of 'private' and 'sexual'

(1) The following apply for the purposes of section 33.

(2) A photograph or film is 'private' if it shows something that is not of a kind ordinarily seen in public.

(3) A photograph or film is 'sexual' if—
  (a) it shows all or part of an individual's exposed genitals or pubic area,
  (b) it shows something that a reasonable person would consider to be sexual because of its nature, or
  (c) its content, taken as a whole, is such that a reasonable person would consider it to be sexual.

(4) Subsection (5) applies in the case of—
  (a) a photograph or film that consists of or includes a photographed or filmed image that has been altered in any way,
  (b) a photograph or film that combines two or more photographed or filmed images, and
  (c) a photograph or film that combines a photographed or filmed image with something else.

(5) The photograph or film is not private and sexual if—
  (a) it does not consist of or include a photographed or filmed image that is itself private and sexual,
  (b) it is only private or sexual by virtue of the alteration or combination mentioned in subsection (4), or
  (c) it is only by virtue of the alteration or combination mentioned in subsection (4) that the person mentioned in section 33(1)(a) and (b) is shown as part of, or with, whatever makes the photograph or film private and sexual.

# MODERN SLAVERY ACT 2015

## PART 1
## OFFENCES

### 1. Slavery, servitude and forced or compulsory labour

(1) A person commits an offence if—
  (a) the person holds another person in slavery or servitude and the circumstances are such that the person knows or ought to know that the other person is held in slavery or servitude, or
  (b) the person requires another person to perform forced or compulsory labour and the circumstances are such that the person knows or ought to know that the other person is being required to perform forced or compulsory labour.

(2) In subsection (1) the references to holding a person in slavery or servitude or requiring a person to perform forced or compulsory labour are to be construed in accordance with Article 4 of the Human Rights Convention.

(3) In determining whether a person is being held in slavery or servitude or required to perform forced or compulsory labour, regard may be had to all the circumstances.

(4) For example, regard may be had—
  (a) to any of the person's personal circumstances (such as the person being a child, the person's family relationships, and any mental or physical illness) which may make the person more vulnerable than other persons;
  (b) to any work or services provided by the person, including work or services provided in circumstances which constitute exploitation within section 3(3) to (6).

(5) The consent of a person (whether an adult or a child) to any of the acts alleged to constitute holding the person in slavery or servitude, or requiring the person to perform forced or compulsory labour, does not preclude a determination that the person is being held in slavery or servitude, or required to perform forced or compulsory labour.

## 2. Human trafficking

(1) A person commits an offence if the person arranges or facilitates the travel of another person ('V') with a view to V being exploited.
(2) It is irrelevant whether V consents to the travel (whether V is an adult or a child).
(3) A person may in particular arrange or facilitate V's travel by recruiting V, transporting or transferring V, harbouring or receiving V, or transferring or exchanging control over V.
(4) A person arranges or facilitates V's travel with a view to V being exploited only if—
  (a) the person intends to exploit V (in any part of the world) during or after the travel, or
  (b) the person knows or ought to know that another person is likely to exploit V (in any part of the world) during or after the travel.
(5) 'Travel' means—
  (a) arriving in, or entering, any country,
  (b) departing from any country,
  (c) travelling within any country.
(6) A person who is a UK national commits an offence under this section regardless of—
  (a) where the arranging or facilitating takes place, or
  (b) where the travel takes place.
(7) A person who is not a UK national commits an offence under this section if—
  (a) any part of the arranging or facilitating takes place in the United Kingdom, or
  (b) the travel consists of arrival in or entry into, departure from, or travel within, the United Kingdom.

## 3. Meaning of exploitation

(1) For the purposes of section 2 a person is exploited only if one or more of the following subsections apply in relation to the person.

*Slavery, servitude and forced or compulsory labour*

(2) The person is the victim of behaviour—
  (a) which involves the commission of an offence under section 1, or
  (b) which would involve the commission of an offence under that section if it took place in England and Wales.

*Sexual exploitation*

(3) Something is done to or in respect of the person—
  (a) which involves the commission of an offence under—
    (i) section 1(1)(a) of the Protection of Children Act 1978 (indecent photographs of children), or
    (ii) Part 1 of the Sexual Offences Act 2003 (sexual offences), as it has effect in England and Wales, or
  (b) which would involve the commission of such an offence if it were done in England and Wales.

*Removal of organs etc.*

(4) The person is encouraged, required or expected to do anything—
  (a) which involves the commission, by him or her or another person, of an offence under section 32 or 33 of the Human Tissue Act 2004 (prohibition of commercial dealings in organs and restrictions on use of live donors) as it has effect in England and Wales, or
  (b) which would involve the commission of such an offence, by him or her or another person, if it were done in England and Wales.

*Securing services etc. by force, threats or deception*

(5) The person is subjected to force, threats or deception designed to induce him or her—
   (a) to provide services of any kind,
   (b) to provide another person with benefits of any kind, or
   (c) to enable another person to acquire benefits of any kind.

*Securing services etc. from children and vulnerable persons*

(6) Another person uses or attempts to use the person for a purpose within paragraph (a), (b) or (c) of subsection (5), having chosen him or her for that purpose on the grounds that—
   (a) he or she is a child, is mentally or physically ill or disabled, or has a family relationship with a particular person, and
   (b) an adult, or a person without the illness, disability, or family relationship, would be likely to refuse to be used for that purpose.

### 4. Committing offence with intent to commit offence under section 2

A person commits an offence under this section if the person commits any offence with the intention of committing an offence under section 2 (including an offence committed by aiding, abetting, counselling or procuring an offence under that section).

## SERIOUS CRIME ACT 2015

### 45. Offence of participating in activities of organised crime group

(1) A person who participates in the criminal activities of an organised crime group commits an offence.

(2) For this purpose, a person participates in the criminal activities of an organised crime group if the person takes part in any activities that the person knows or reasonably suspects—
   (a) are criminal activities of an organised crime group, or
   (b) will help an organised crime group to carry on criminal activities.

(3) 'Criminal activities' are activities within subsection (4) or (5) that are carried on with a view to obtaining (directly or indirectly) any gain or benefit.

(4) Activities are within this subsection if—
   (a) they are carried on in England or Wales, and
   (b) they constitute an offence in England and Wales punishable on conviction on indictment with imprisonment for a term of 7 years or more.

(5) Activities are within this subsection if—
   (a) they are carried on outside England and Wales,
   (b) they constitute an offence under the law in force of the country where they are carried on, and
   (c) they would constitute an offence in England and Wales of the kind mentioned in subsection (4)(b) if the activities were carried on in England and Wales.

(6) 'Organised crime group' means a group that—
   (a) has as its purpose, or as one of its purposes, the carrying on of criminal activities, and
   (b) consists of three or more persons who act, or agree to act, together to further that purpose.

(7) For a person to be guilty of an offence under this section it is not necessary—
   (a) for the person to know any of the persons who are members of the organised crime group,
   (b) for all of the acts or omissions comprising participation in the group's criminal activities to take place in England and Wales (so long as at least one of them does), or
   (c) for the gain or benefit referred to in subsection (3) to be financial in nature.

(8) It is a defence for a person charged with an offence under this section to prove that the person's participation was necessary for a purpose related to the prevention or detection of crime.

## 69. Possession of paedophile manual

(1) It is an offence to be in possession of any item that contains advice or guidance about abusing children sexually.
(2) It is a defence for a person (D) charged with an offence under this section—
  (a) to prove that D had a legitimate reason for being in possession of the item;
  (b) to prove that—
    (i) D had not read, viewed or (as appropriate) listened to the item, and
    (ii) D did not know, and had no reason to suspect, that it contained advice or guidance about abusing children sexually; or
  (c) to prove that—
    (i) the item was sent to D without any request made by D or on D's behalf, and
    (ii) D did not keep it for an unreasonable time.

...

(8) In this section—
'abusing children sexually' means doing anything that constitutes—
  (a) an offence under Part 1 of the Sexual Offences Act 2003 ... against a person under 16, ...
  (b) an offence under section 1 of the Protection of Children Act 1978 ... involving indecent photographs (but not pseudo-photographs), or
  (c) an offence under section 2 of the Modern Slavery Act 2015 (human trafficking) committed with a view to exploitation that consists of or includes behaviour within section 3(3) of that Act (sexual exploitation),

or doing anything outside England and Wales or Northern Ireland that would constitute such an offence if done in England and Wales or Northern Ireland;
'item' includes anything in which information of any description is recorded;
'prohibited item' means an item within subsection (1).

*Domestic abuse*

## 76. Controlling or coercive behaviour in an intimate or family relationship

(1) A person (A) commits an offence if—
  (a) A repeatedly or continuously engages in behaviour towards another person (B) that is controlling or coercive,
  (b) at the time of the behaviour, A and B are personally connected,
  (c) the behaviour has a serious effect on B, and
  (d) A knows or ought to know that the behaviour will have a serious effect on B.
(2) A and B are 'personally connected' if—
  (a) A is in an intimate personal relationship with B, or
  (b) A and B live together and—
    (i) they are members of the same family, or
    (ii) they have previously been in an intimate personal relationship with each other.
(3) But A does not commit an offence under this section if at the time of the behaviour in question—
  (a) A has responsibility for B, for the purposes of Part 1 of the Children and Young Persons Act 1933 (see section 17 of that Act), and
  (b) B is under 16.
(4) A's behaviour has a 'serious effect' on B if—
  (a) it causes B to fear, on at least two occasions, that violence will be used against B, or
  (b) it causes B serious alarm or distress which has a substantial adverse effect on B's usual day-to-day activities.
(5) For the purposes of subsection (1)(d) A 'ought to know' that which a reasonable person in possession of the same information would know.
(6) For the purposes of subsection (2)(b)(i) A and B are members of the same family if—
  (a) they are, or have been, married to each other;
  (b) they are, or have been, civil partners of each other;

(c) they are relatives;
(d) they have agreed to marry one another (whether or not the agreement has been terminated);
(e) they have entered into a civil partnership agreement (whether or not the agreement has been terminated);
(f) they are both parents of the same child;
(g) they have, or have had, parental responsibility for the same child.

(7) In subsection (6)—
'civil partnership agreement' has the meaning given by section 73 of the Civil Partnership Act 2004;
'child' means a person under the age of 18 years;
'parental responsibility' has the same meaning as in the Children Act 1989;
'relative' has the meaning given by section 63(1) of the Family Law Act 1996.

(8) In proceedings for an offence under this section it is a defence for A to show that—
(a) in engaging in the behaviour in question, A believed that he or she was acting in B's best interests, and
(b) the behaviour was in all the circumstances reasonable.

(9) A is to be taken to have shown the facts mentioned in subsection (8) if—
(a) sufficient evidence of the facts is adduced to raise an issue with respect to them, and
(b) the contrary is not proved beyond reasonable doubt.

(10) The defence in subsection (8) is not available to A in relation to behaviour that causes B to fear that violence will be used against B.

# PSYCHOACTIVE SUBSTANCES ACT 2016

## 2. Meaning of 'psychoactive substance' etc.

(1) In this Act 'psychoactive substance' means any substance which—
(a) is capable of producing a psychoactive effect in a person who consumes it, and
(b) is not an exempted substance (see section 3).

(2) For the purposes of this Act a substance produces a psychoactive effect in a person if, by stimulating or depressing the person's central nervous system, it affects the person's mental functioning or emotional state; and references to a substance's psychoactive effects are to be read accordingly.

(3) For the purposes of this Act a person consumes a substance if the person causes or allows the substance, or fumes given off by the substance, to enter the person's body in any way.

## 3. Exempted substances

(1) In this Act 'exempted substance' means a substance listed in Schedule 1.

(2) The Secretary of State may by regulations amend Schedule 1 in order to—
(a) add or vary any description of substance;
(b) remove any description of substance added under paragraph (a).

(3) Before making any regulations under this section the Secretary of State must consult—
(a) the Advisory Council on the Misuse of Drugs, and
(b) such other persons as the Secretary of State considers appropriate.

(4) The power to make regulations under this section is exercisable by statutory instrument.

(5) A statutory instrument containing regulations under this section may not be made unless a draft of the instrument has been laid before, and approved by a resolution of, each House of Parliament.

*Offences*

## 4. Producing a psychoactive substance

(1) A person commits an offence if—
(a) the person intentionally produces a psychoactive substance,
(b) the person knows or suspects that the substance is a psychoactive substance, and

(c) the person—
(i) intends to consume the psychoactive substance for its psychoactive effects, or
(ii) knows, or is reckless as to whether, the psychoactive substance is likely to be consumed by some other person for its psychoactive effects.
(2) This section is subject to section 11 (exceptions to offences).

## 5. Supplying, or offering to supply, a psychoactive substance

(1) A person commits an offence if—
(a) the person intentionally supplies a substance to another person,
(b) the substance is a psychoactive substance,
(c) the person knows or suspects, or ought to know or suspect, that the substance is a psychoactive substance, and
(d) the person knows, or is reckless as to whether, the psychoactive substance is likely to be consumed by the person to whom it is supplied, or by some other person, for its psychoactive effects.
(2) A person ('P') commits an offence if—
(a) P offers to supply a psychoactive substance to another person ('R'), and
(b) P knows or is reckless as to whether R, or some other person, would, if P supplied a substance to R in accordance with the offer, be likely to consume the substance for its psychoactive effects.
(3) For the purposes of subsection (2)(b), the reference to a substance's psychoactive effects includes a reference to the psychoactive effects which the substance would have if it were the substance which P had offered to supply to R.
(4) This section is subject to section 11 (exceptions to offences).

## 6. Aggravation of offence under section 5

(1) This section applies if—
(a) a court is considering the seriousness of an offence under section 5, and
(b) at the time the offence was committed the offender was aged 18 or over.
(2) If condition A, B or C is met the court—
(a) must treat the fact that the condition is met as an aggravating factor (that is to say, a factor that increases the seriousness of the offence), and
(b) must state in open court that the offence is so aggravated.
(3) Condition A is that the offence was committed on or in the vicinity of school premises at a relevant time.
(4) For the purposes of subsection (3) a 'relevant time' is—
(a) any time when the school premises are in use by persons under the age of 18;
(b) one hour before the start and one hour after the end of any such time.
(5) In this section—
'school premises' means land used for the purposes of a school, other than any land occupied solely as a dwelling by a person employed at the school;
'school' has the same meaning—
(a) in England and Wales, as in section 4 of the Education Act 1996;
(b) in Scotland, as in section 135(1) of the Education (Scotland) Act 1980;
...
(6) Condition B is that in connection with the commission of the offence the offender used a courier who, at the time the offence was committed, was under the age of 18.
(7) For the purposes of subsection (6) a person ('P') uses a courier in connection with an offence under section 5 if P causes or permits another person (the courier)—
(a) to deliver a substance to a third person, or
(b) to deliver a drug-related consideration to P or a third person.
(8) A drug-related consideration is a consideration of any description which—
(a) is obtained in connection with the supply of a psychoactive substance, or
(b) is intended to be used in connection with obtaining a psychoactive substance.
(9) Condition C is that the offence was committed in a custodial institution.
(10) In this section—
'custodial institution' means any of the following—
(a) a prison;

(b) a young offender institution, secure training centre, secure college, young offenders institution, young offenders centre, juvenile justice centre or remand centre;
(c) a removal centre, a short-term holding facility or pre-departure accommodation;
(d) service custody premises;

'removal centre', 'short-term holding facility' and 'pre-departure accommodation' have the meaning given by section 147 of the Immigration and Asylum Act 1999;
'service custody premises' has the meaning given by section 300(7) of the Armed Forces Act 2006.

## 7. Possession of psychoactive substance with intent to supply

(1) A person commits an offence if—
(a) the person is in possession of a psychoactive substance,
(b) the person knows or suspects that the substance is a psychoactive substance, and
(c) the person intends to supply the psychoactive substance to another person for its consumption, whether by any person to whom it is supplied or by some other person, for its psychoactive effects.

(2) This section is subject to section 11 (exceptions to offences).

## 8. Importing or exporting a psychoactive substance

(1) A person commits an offence if—
(a) the person intentionally imports a substance,
(b) the substance is a psychoactive substance,
(c) the person knows or suspects, or ought to know or suspect, that the substance is a psychoactive substance, and
(d) the person—
(i) intends to consume the psychoactive substance for its psychoactive effects, or
(ii) knows, or is reckless as to whether, the psychoactive substance is likely to be consumed by some other person for its psychoactive effects.

(2) A person commits an offence if—
(a) the person intentionally exports a substance,
(b) the substance is a psychoactive substance,
(c) the person knows or suspects, or ought to know or suspect, that the substance is a psychoactive substance, and
(d) the person—
(i) intends to consume the psychoactive substance for its psychoactive effects, or
(ii) knows, or is reckless as to whether, the psychoactive substance is likely to be consumed by some other person for its psychoactive effects.

(3) In a case where a person imports or exports a controlled drug suspecting it to be a psychoactive substance, the person is to be treated for the purposes of this section as if the person had imported or exported a psychoactive substance suspecting it to be such a substance.
In this subsection 'controlled drug' has the same meaning as in the Misuse of Drugs Act 1971.

(4) Section 5 of the Customs and Excise Management Act 1979 (time of importation, exportation, etc.) applies for the purposes of this section as it applies for the purposes of that Act.

(5) This section is subject to section 11 (exceptions to offences).

## 9. Possession of a psychoactive substance in a custodial institution

(1) A person commits an offence if—
(a) the person is in possession of a psychoactive substance in a custodial institution,
(b) the person knows or suspects that the substance is a psychoactive substance, and
(c) the person intends to consume the psychoactive substance for its psychoactive effects.

(2) In this section 'custodial institution' has the same meaning as in section 6.

(3) This section is subject to section 11 (exceptions to offences).

## 11. Exceptions to offences

(1) It is not an offence under this Act for a person to carry on any activity listed in subsection (3) if, in the circumstances in which it is carried on by that person, the activity is an exempted activity.

(2) In this section 'exempted activity' means an activity listed in Schedule 2.

(3) The activities referred to in subsection (1) are—

(a) producing a psychoactive substance;
(b) supplying such a substance;
(c) offering to supply such a substance;
(d) possessing such a substance with intent to supply it;
(e) importing or exporting such a substance;
(f) possessing such a substance in a custodial institution (within the meaning of section 9).

(4) The Secretary of State may by regulations amend Schedule 2 in order to—

(a) add or vary any description of activity;
(b) remove any description of activity added under paragraph (a).

(5) Before making any regulations under this section the Secretary of State must consult—

(a) the Advisory Council on the Misuse of Drugs, and
(b) such other persons as the Secretary of State considers appropriate.

(6) The power to make regulations under this section is exercisable by statutory instrument.

(7) A statutory instrument containing regulations under this section may not be made unless a draft of the instrument has been laid before, and approved by a resolution of, each House of Parliament.

## 56. Offences by directors, partners, etc.

(1) Where an offence under this Act has been committed by a body corporate and it is proved that the offence—

(a) has been committed with the consent or connivance of a person falling within subsection (2), or
(b) is attributable to any neglect on the part of such a person,

that person (as well as the body corporate) is guilty of that offence and liable to be proceeded against and punished accordingly.

(2) The persons are—

(a) a director, manager, secretary or similar officer of the body corporate;
(b) any person who was purporting to act in such a capacity.

(3) Where the affairs of a body corporate are managed by its members, subsection (1) applies in relation to the acts and defaults of a member, in connection with that management, as if the member were a director of the body corporate.

(4) Where an offence under this Act has been committed by a Scottish firm and it is proved that the offence—

(a) has been committed with the consent or connivance of a partner in the firm or a person purporting to act as such a partner, or
(b) is attributable to any neglect on the part of such a person,

that person (as well as the firm) is guilty of that offence and liable to be proceeded against and punished accordingly.

### SCHEDULE 1
### EXEMPTED SUBSTANCES

*Controlled drugs*

1. Controlled drugs (within the meaning of the Misuse of Drugs Act 1971).

*Medicinal products*

2. Medicinal products.
In this paragraph 'medicinal product' has the same meaning as in the Human Medicines Regulations 2012 (see regulation 2 of those Regulations).

*Alcohol*

3. Alcohol or alcoholic products.
In this paragraph—
'alcohol' means ethyl alcohol, and
'alcoholic product' means any product which—
(a) contains alcohol, and
(b) does not contain any psychoactive substance.

*Nicotine and tobacco products*

4. Nicotine.
5. Tobacco products.
In this paragraph 'tobacco product' means—
(a) anything which is a tobacco product within the meaning of the Tobacco Products Duty Act 1979 (see section 1 of that Act), and
(b) any other product which—
  (i) contains nicotine, and
  (ii) does not contain any psychoactive substance.

*Caffeine*

6. Caffeine or caffeine products.
In this paragraph 'caffeine product' means any product which—
(a) contains caffeine, and
(b) does not contain any psychoactive substance.

*Food*

7. Any substance which—
(a) is ordinarily consumed as food, and
(b) does not contain a prohibited ingredient.
In this paragraph—
'food' includes drink;
'prohibited ingredient', in relation to a substance, means any psychoactive substance—
(a) which is not naturally occurring in the substance, and
(b) the use of which in or on food is not authorised by an EU instrument.

## SCHEDULE 2
## EXEMPTED ACTIVITIES

*Healthcare-related activities*

1. Any activity carried on by a person who is a health care professional and is acting in the course of his or her profession.
In this paragraph 'health care professional' has the same meaning as in the Human Medicines Regulations 2012 (see regulation 8 of those Regulations).
2. Any activity carried on for the purpose of, or in connection with—
(a) the supply to, or the consumption by, any person of a substance prescribed for that person by a health care professional acting in the course of his or her profession, or
(b) the supply to, or the consumption by, any person of a substance in accordance with the directions of a health care professional acting in the course of his or her profession.
In this paragraph 'health care professional' has the same meaning as in the Human Medicines Regulations 2012 (see regulation 8 of those Regulations).
3. Any activity carried on in respect of an active substance by a person who—
(a) is registered in accordance with regulation 45N of the Human Medicines Regulations 2012, or
(b) is exempt from any requirement to be so registered by virtue of regulation 45M(2) or (3) of those Regulations.
In this paragraph 'active substance' has the same meaning as in the Human Medicines Regulations 2012 (see regulation 8 of those Regulations).

*Research*

4. Any activity carried on in the course of, or in connection with, approved scientific research. In this paragraph—
'approved scientific research' means scientific research carried out by a person who has approval from a relevant ethics review body to carry out that research;
'relevant ethics review body' means—
(a) a research ethics committee recognised or established by the Health Research Authority under Chapter 2 of Part 3 of the Care Act 2014, or
(b) a body appointed by any of the following for the purpose of assessing the ethics of research involving individuals—
(i) the Secretary of State, the Scottish Ministers, the Welsh Ministers, or a Northern Ireland department;
(ii) a relevant NHS body;
(iii) United Kingdom Research and Innovation or a body that is a Research Council for the purposes of the Science and Technology Act 1965;
(iv) an institution that is a research institution for the purposes of Chapter 4A of Part 7 of the Income Tax (Earnings and Pensions) Act 2003 (see section 457 of that Act);
(v) a charity which has as its charitable purpose (or one of its charitable purposes) the advancement of health or the saving of lives;
'charity' means—
(a) a charity as defined by section 1(1) of the Charities Act 2011,
(b) a body entered in the Scottish Charity Register, or
(c) a charity as defined by section 1(1) of the Charities Act (Northern Ireland) 2008;
'relevant NHS body' means—
(a) an NHS trust or NHS foundation trust in England,
(b) an NHS trust or Local Health Board in Wales,
(c) a Health Board or Special Health Board constituted under section 2 of the National Health Service (Scotland) Act 1978,
(d) the Common Services Agency for the Scottish Health Service, or
(e) any of the health and social care bodies in Northern Ireland falling within paragraphs (a) to (d) of section 1(5) of the Health and Social Care (Reform) Act (Northern Ireland) 2009.

# CULTURAL PROPERTY (ARMED CONFLICTS) ACT 2017

## 1. 'The Convention' and related expressions

(1) In this Act—
'the Convention' means the Convention for the Protection of Cultural Property in the Event of Armed Conflict, done at the Hague on 14 May 1954;
'the Regulations for the execution of the Convention' means the Regulations for the execution of the Convention for the Protection of Cultural Property in the Event of Armed Conflict;
'the First Protocol' means the Protocol to the Convention, done at the Hague on 14 May 1954;
'the Second Protocol' means the Second Protocol to the Convention, done at the Hague on 26 March 1999.

## 2. 'Cultural property'

In this Act 'cultural property' has the meaning given in Article 1 of the Convention.

## 3. Offence of serious violation of Second Protocol

(1) A person commits an offence if—
(a) the person does an intentional act of a kind described in any of sub-paragraphs (a) to (e) of paragraph 1 of Article 15 of the Second Protocol,
(b) the act is a violation of the Convention or the Second Protocol, and

(c) the person knows that the property to which the act relates is cultural property.

(2) It does not matter whether the act is done in the United Kingdom or elsewhere.

(3) If the act is of a kind described in paragraph 1(a), (b) or (c) of Article 15 of the Second Protocol it does not matter whether the person is a UK national.

(4) If the act is of a kind described in paragraph 1(d) or (e) of that Article and is done outside the United Kingdom an offence is committed only if the person is—

(a) a UK national, or

(b) a person subject to UK service jurisdiction.

(5) In this Part 'UK national' means—

(a) a British citizen, a British overseas territories citizen, a British National (Overseas) or a British Overseas Citizen,

(b) a person who under the British Nationality Act 1981 is a British subject,

(c) a British protected person within the meaning of that Act, or

(d) a body incorporated under the law of any part of the United Kingdom.

(6) In this Part 'person subject to UK service jurisdiction' means—

(a) a person subject to service law within the meaning of the Armed Forces Act 2006, or

(b) a civilian subject to service discipline within the meaning of that Act.

## 4. Ancillary offences

(1) An offence ancillary to an offence under section 3 is capable of being committed in the United Kingdom or elsewhere.

(2) An offence ancillary to an offence under section 3 in respect of an act of a kind described in paragraph 1(a), (b) or (c) of Article 15 of the Second Protocol is capable of being committed by any person, whether a UK national or not.

(3) An offence ancillary to an offence under section 3 in respect of an act done outside the United Kingdom of a kind described in paragraph 1(d) or (e) of Article 15 of the Second Protocol is capable of being committed by a person outside the United Kingdom only if the person is—

(a) a UK national, or

(b) a person subject to UK service jurisdiction.

(4) In the application of this Part to England and Wales, references to an offence that is ancillary to an offence under section 3 are to—

(a) attempting or conspiring to commit that offence, or

(b) an offence under section 4(1) or 5(1) of the Criminal Law Act 1967 (assisting an offender or concealing the commission of an offence) where the relevant offence mentioned there is an offence under section 3 of this Act.

...

(7) A reference in this Part to an offence that is ancillary to an offence under section 3 includes a reference to an offence that is ancillary to such an ancillary offence, and so on.

(8) Subsections (4) to (6) apply for the purposes of subsection (7) as if any reference to an offence under section 3 included a reference to an offence that is ancillary to an offence under section 3, and so on.

## 5. Responsibility of commanders and other superiors

(1) A person described in this section as responsible for a section 3 offence is to be treated as—

(a) aiding, abetting, counselling or procuring the commission of the offence under the laws of England and Wales ..., and

...

(2) A military commander is responsible for a section 3 offence committed by forces under the commander's effective command and control if—

(a) the offence is committed as a result of the commander's failure to exercise control properly over those forces,

(b) the commander either knew or, owing to the circumstances at the time, should have known that the forces were committing or about to commit the offence, and

(c) the commander failed to take all necessary and reasonable measures within the commander's power to prevent or repress the commission of the offence or to submit the matter to the competent authorities for investigation and prosecution.

(3) In subsection (2)—
(a) references to a military commander include a reference to a person effectively acting as a military commander, and
(b) in relation to such a person, the reference to effective command and control is to effective authority and control.

# LASER MISUSE (VEHICLES) ACT 2018

## 1. Offence of shining or directing a laser beam towards a vehicle

(1) A person commits an offence if—
(a) the person shines or directs a laser beam towards a vehicle which is moving or ready to move, and
(b) the laser beam dazzles or distracts, or is likely to dazzle or distract, a person with control of the vehicle.

(2) It is a defence to show—
(a) that the person had a reasonable excuse for shining or directing the laser beam towards the vehicle, or
(b) that the person—
(i) did not intend to shine or direct the laser beam towards the vehicle, and
(ii) exercised all due diligence and took all reasonable precautions to avoid doing so.

(3) A person is taken to have shown a fact mentioned in subsection (2) if—
(a) sufficient evidence is adduced to raise an issue with respect to it, and
(b) the contrary is not proved beyond reasonable doubt.

...

(6) A mechanically propelled vehicle which is not moving or ready to move but whose engine or motor is running is to be treated for the purposes of subsection (1)(a) as ready to move.

(7) In relation to an aircraft, the reference in subsection (1)(b) to 'a person with control of the vehicle' is a reference to any person on the aircraft who is engaged in controlling it, or in monitoring the controlling of it.

(8) In relation to a vessel, hovercraft or submarine, the reference in subsection (1)(b) to 'a person with control of the vehicle' is a reference to the master, the pilot or any person engaged in navigating the vessel, hovercraft or submarine.

## 2. Offences relating to air traffic services

(1) A person commits an offence if—
(a) the person shines or directs a laser beam—
(i) towards an air traffic facility, or
(ii) towards a person providing air traffic services, and
(b) the laser beam dazzles or distracts, or is likely to dazzle or distract, a person providing air traffic services.

(2) It is a defence to show—
(a) that the person had a reasonable excuse for shining or directing the laser beam towards the facility or person, or
(b) that the person—
(i) did not intend to shine or direct the laser beam towards the facility or person, and
(ii) exercised all due diligence and took all reasonable precautions to avoid doing so.

(3) A person is taken to have shown a fact mentioned in subsection (2) if—
(a) sufficient evidence is adduced to raise an issue with respect to it, and
(b) the contrary is not proved beyond reasonable doubt.

...

(6) In this section—
'air traffic facility' means any building, structure, vehicle or other place from which air traffic services are provided;
'air traffic services' has the meaning given by section 98(1) of the Transport Act 2000.

## 3. Interpretation

In this Act—
'aircraft' means any vehicle used for travel by air;
'laser beam' means a beam of coherent light produced by a device of any kind;
'vehicle' means any vehicle used for travel by land, water or air;
'vessel' has the meaning given by section 255(1) of the Merchant Shipping Act 1995.

# INDEX

Printed by Printforce, United Kingdom